The Encyclopedia of
BLACK
COLLECTIBLES

The Encyclopedia of

BLACK COLLECTIBLES

A Value and Identification Guide

Dawn E. Reno

Wallace-Homestead Book Company
Radnor, Pennsylvania

Dedicated to my friends
Steve Lewis and Malinda Saunders
and to all the contributors
who have helped me through the years.

Copyright © 1996 by Dawn E. Reno

All Rights Reserved

Published in Radnor, Pennsylvania 19089, by Wallace-Homestead,
a division of Chilton Book Company

Designed by Jerry O'Brien

Manufactured in the United States of America

Library of Congress Cataloging-in-Publication Data
Reno, Dawn E.
    The encyclopedia of black collectibles / by Dawn E. Reno.
       p.   cm.
    Includes bibliographical references and index.
    ISBN 0-87069-703-X (pb)
       1. Afro-Americans—Collectibles.   I. Title.
NK839.3.A35R47   1995
973'.0496073'0075—dc20   95-11637
                                            CIP

1 2 3 4 5 6 7 8 9 0   5 4 3 2 1 0 9 8 7 6

On the front cover (*left to right, from top*): **Wooden doll,** found in upstate New York, nineteenth century, near mint condition, photo courtesy of Connie Covent, Sign of the Windsor Chair; **Banjo Tobacco box label,** manufactured by David Dunlop in Petersburg, Va., courtesy of Jim Bollman, The Music Emporium, photo by Donald Vogt; **Blue-eyed mammy kitchen set,** made in Japan, rare, unmarked, 1930s–1940s, 10½″ cookie jar, 8″ biscuit jar, 3″ creamer, 3½″ sugar, collection of Leonard Davis, photo by Bob Reno; **Three wax figures,** the man on right was originally holding bags, excellent detail, clothing all original nineteenth century, courtesy of Rose Fontanella, photo by Donald Vogt; **Band of black musicians,** intricately carved and painted, from an anonymous private collection, courtesy of Ken and Ida Monko; **Victorian carte de visite,** or photographic calling card, of girl with building blocks, photo by Donald Vogt.

CONTENTS

Foreword by Steven Lewis of the Lewis-Blalock Collection ix

Introduction. xi

PART ONE   ART AND LITERATURE. 2
  Chapter 1   Art 3
    African-American Art History: An Overview. 3
    Introduction to Collecting Prints 14
    Price Guidelines for the Work of Major Artists 16
    Prices for Art. 18
  Chapter 2   Folk Art 23
    Defining African-American Folk Art. 23
    Some Types of Folk Art 26
    Prices for Folk Art 40
  Chapter 3   Photographica. 46
    Types of Photographs to Collect 47
    Prices for Photographica. 53
  Chapter 4   Books 56
    Children's Books 56
    Slave Writings 58
    The Twentieth Century 59
    Prices for Books. 68

PART TWO   EVERYDAY ARTIFACTS. 73
  Chapter 5   Advertising 75
    Types of Collectible Advertising 78
    Prices for Advertising 87
  Chapter 6   Dolls. 101
    A Short History of Black Dolls in America 102
    Types of Collectible Black Dolls 106
    Prices for Black Dolls. 113

Chapter 7   Kitchen Collectibles **121**
    Types of Kitchen Collectibles 121
    Prices for Kitchen Collectibles 128
Chapter 8   Paper Ephemera **141**
    How to Collect Ephemera 141
    Types of Ephemera. 142
    Prices for Paper Ephemera 151
Chapter 9   Pottery, Porcelain, and Glass **163**
    Types of Items Collected 163
    Prices for Pottery, Porcelain, and Glass 167
Chapter 10   Toys **174**
    Types of Collectible Toys 176
    Prices for Toys 184
Chapter 11   Miscellaneous Everyday Artifacts **193**
    Avon Collectibles. 193
    Clocks. 193
    Commemorative Items. 194
    Golliwogs 194
    Iron Collectibles. 195
    Jewelry 197
    Johnny Griffin Collectibles. 197
    Lawn Items 198
    Masonic Collectibles 198
    Textiles and Sewing Collectibles 199
    Tourist Trade Items 204
    Prices for Miscellaneous Everyday Artifacts 205

PART THREE   HISTORICAL ARTIFACTS **213**
    Chapter 12   Militaria and Related Collectibles **215**
        A Short History of African-Americans in the Military 216
        African-American Cowboys 221
        African-Americans Considered to be American Indians 223
        Prices for Militaria and Related Collectibles. 224
    Chapter 13   Political Memorabilia **228**
        A History of African-Americans in Public Life. 228
        Prices for Political Memorabilia 237

PART FOUR   ENTERTAINMENT MEMORABILIA **241**
    Chapter 14   Music and Dance Memorabilia **243**
        The Collectibles. 243
        Types of African-American Music. 244
        A History of African-Americans in Dance 251
        Prices for Music and Dance Memorabilia 252
    Chapter 15   Movie, Television, and Theater Memorabilia **257**
        The Collectibles. 257

A History of African-Americans in the Movie Industry 258
A History of African-Americans in Television 263
A Brief History of African-Americans in Theater 264
Prices for Movie, Theater, and Television Memorabilia 267
Chapter 16 Sports Memorabilia **269**
Sports in Which Black Athletes Have Participated 270
Prices for Sports Memorabilia 281
Appendix Reproductions **289**
Reproduction Versus New Items 289
Some Items that Have Been Reproduced 290
Prices for Reproductions 292

Bibliography 295

List of Contributors 301

Index 302

FOREWORD

When I think of dates important to black memorabilia collectors, the first ones that come to mind are October 26–28, 1984, the weekend of the first Black Memorabilia Show and Sale in Silver Spring, Maryland. The show was produced by M & J Productions and embodied a dream of the founder, Malinda F. Saunders, and her partner, Jeannette B. Carson. How well I remember all the excitement and energy the show created in its particular world of collecting. Little did I know what role I was to play in the phenomenon.

In the years prior to the show, I collected whatever caught my attention—a black doll, a cookie jar, majolica porcelain. I was a mere "infant" in the presence of some of the most experienced collectors in the country. They graciously took me under their wing, remarking that "it was nice" someone my age was even interested in collecting.

I remember vividly my position at the show: a porter unloading the merchandise of these collectors, the unofficial curators of black memorabilia. I eagerly witnessed firsthand the unveiling of precious artifacts as they were unwrapped and placed into position for public viewing and purchase. Often I felt in awe of and amazed by these rare icons of history, each with its own story about the pride and pain of a people—*my* people.

At first as speechless as a child on Christmas morning, and then eager enough to push aside my shyness and ask questions, I quickly became a sponge, absorbing the wealth of knowledge made available to my receptive mind. Like a griot in training, I quickly became a storehouse of precious information. As a result of this wonderful experience, I wedded myself forever to the world of collecting black memorabilia.

One can imagine my frustration when attempting to research my newfound interest: documentation of black memorabilia was scarce to nonexistent! And this brings me to my second-most important "collecting" date: October 4, 1986.

October 4, 1986, is the date *Collecting Black Americana,* by Dawn E. Reno, was premiered at the Third Annual Black Memorabilia Show and Sale in Silver Spring, Maryland. *Here* was the missing link I needed to research and collect black memorabilia. Reno had written a comprehensive book on collecting black memorabilia that included historical details, a moderate price guide, and photographs documenting many different types of black artifacts. This was the first book to fully validate the subject of black Americana. It's no surprise to me that *Collecting Black Americana* sold as fast as Nancy Green's hotcakes at the Chicago World's Fair in 1893 (Nancy Green portrayed the Aunt Jemima trademark character for the first thirty years of the company's existence).

Reno's *Collecting Black Americana* became a standard reference guide for dealers, advanced collectors, and novices. It also became, and still is, one of the books that I reference in my lectures, seminars, and workshops. Unfortunately, *Collecting Black Americana* has grown to be somewhat of a collector's item itself. Although I'm sure the demand was there, the publisher never did a second printing, and the book quickly disappeared onto the shelves of collectors and libraries. Often people ask me, "Where do I get this book?" and I have to tell them it can only be found on the secondary market. For those of us who are collectors, we know what the lack of a trusted guide to quality and prices means: risky bargaining and hard trading.

Since that first show in 1984 and the debut of *Collecting Black Americana* in 1986, there have been several black memorabilia books published, and numerous articles on the subject have appeared in magazines and newspapers. Black artifacts have been listed in major price guides, and black memorabilia has been the subject of television and radio shows. However, even with all of this coverage, a lot of vital information regarding black history and black memorabilia never reaches the public.

I have often spent many hours in the library wading through tons of books and papers to find only one photograph or a small bit of information. My efforts are always intended to further the education of the black memorabilia collector and thereby empower that collector to make more informed choices for his or her individual collection or in buying and selling. Thus, I was ecstatic to receive the news of Dawn E. Reno's new book for which I am writing this foreword. With updated prices, additional information in each chapter, and new sections on militaria; political memorabilia; pottery, porcelain, and glass; reproductions; and sports memorabilia, this new version is proof positive that black memorabilia is *real,* that it is here to stay, and that there is a hungry market for it!

Steven Lewis
Collector, Dealer, Lecturer, and Curator
of the Lewis-Blalock Collection
November, 1995

INTRODUCTION

It's been almost a decade since I wrote the first book on black memorabilia, and it's truly amazing how much has changed during that period. The information I needed to research this new book was easier to find. Magazines and books about the subject area have been published and organizations formed. There are more ready sources (collectors, dealers, auctioneers) who are willing to share their knowledge. But the items that I once found so easily are now disappearing into private or museum collections and probably will not be in front of the public again for another decade or more. Yet, the most astounding change of all has been in the prices paid by collectors for black items. In most cases, the prices have doubled, and in some cases tripled. Although this is expected to happen over a period of time in the antiques and collectibles world, no one could have predicted how quickly the value of black memorabilia escalated.

Over and over in my years in this business, I have heard dealers patiently educating collectors about a piece that was changing hands. Dealers often are responsible for knowing not only the value of a piece, but its history, including tales about the people or company that produced an article. That's a huge responsibility and mistakes are sometimes made—sometimes because the dealer simply forgot information about the item being sold and sometimes because the dealer received wrong information from a previous seller or a research source. It is for these reasons—as well as my own thirst for knowledge—that this book is different from others on the market.

This new volume will give you a chance to explore the history behind the items you collect. Though I believe photographs and price listings are paramount in identifying

certain items, I also believe that ninety percent of the dealing and collecting public is interested in more than what a piece is worth.

The field of collecting black memorabilia is a huge one, and my first suggestion to new collectors is to specialize, specialize, specialize! One can be overwhelmed quickly. If you concentrate on one particular type of item (kitchen collectibles or folk art, for example), then your expertise in that area will be more solid. You'll learn how to tell a reproduction from an old item, how to identify an artist by his or her style or the medium he or she uses, and you'll come to know when a piece is worthy of being added to your collection.

The second piece of advice is one that most collectors hear over and over, but it is important enough to bear repeating: *Buy the best you can possibly afford.* Try not to buy a damaged piece unless you are certain you may never find another one. Should the time come when you want to upgrade your collection, you will find it extremely difficult to get rid of the damaged piece—unless it's a rare one.

Finally, education. I still consider myself a neophyte when I speak to collectors whose accumulation of items overwhelms me. These people have been able to touch and own the artifacts and collectibles I've only seen through research. Most times, day-to-day exposure to the field will teach you more than any book possibly could. Even so, when was the last time you met a collector who didn't own any books written specifically about the objects he or she collects?

So, let me introduce you to this volume. It includes additional information about everything I included almost a decade ago, and, thanks to a wise editor, new chapters about some "hot" areas of collecting: sports memorabilia; militaria; political memorabilia; reproductions; and pottery, porcelain, and glass. Certain chapters have grown impressively (i.e. entertainment), others have been combined with like chapters to make it easier for the reader to find information, and one (furniture) has been completely deleted because there simply wasn't enough on the market to warrant a chapter.

In almost every chapter, you'll find short biographies of people (and sometimes of companies) whose actions or creations have resulted in collectible items. Artists, athletes, authors, and politicians are covered in the appropriate chapters, as are companies that manufactured toys or that used black characters in their advertising. Each of these biography lists is necessarily incomplete and should be used only as a starting point for your research. Look in the Bibliography for books and articles that will help you further investigate items of interest. Also, don't neglect other collectors and your local libraries and museums as sources of information. I have only exposed the tip of the iceberg here. There is much more to be uncovered.

Each chapter includes a price guide that gives a price *range* for each item described. The range may go up or down, depending on the area of the country where you buy an item, the expertise of the person from whom you buy, the availability of an item, and the state of the antiques and collectibles market at the time. I have also included the condition of each item listed. The condition ranges from fair to near mint. If an item is currently available in retail stores or through another retail outlet, I've listed the condition as "new." It is important to remember that the price listed is based on the condition of that particular item. An item in better condition is likely to fetch a higher price.

I have no crystal ball. I cannot predict what will be hot in 1996 (if I could, I'd be rich); therefore, I cannot predict what price changes you will see in the next five or ten years. I can, however, promise that you'll have a wonderful time collecting these items, you'll learn a lot about the history of an oppressed people, and you'll often be stunned by the derogatory items you come across. Collecting black memorabilia will arouse your emotions one way or the other. It is a rollercoaster ride through the antiques and collectibles world that no other field can offer.

Enjoy, but remember that education is of utmost importance, for it is the one thing that will finally erase the lines of discrimination and prejudice.

PART ONE

Art and Literature

CHAPTER ONE

Art

No matter how little money you have, you can collect art. Connoisseurs as well as collectors with smaller checkbooks can fill their walls with original art that gives them visual pleasure and, as a bonus, is likely to rise in value as time goes by. With few exceptions, we can count on art to increase in value.

If you decide to collect black American art, you will have many avenues from which to choose. You can accumulate works by African-American artists, or you can decide to collect paintings and other art that depict black people (both are covered in this chapter). You can limit your collecting to a particular medium—only sculpture, only paintings, or even only acrylic paintings, for example—or to a particular artist (see "Some Biographies of African-American Artists," later in this chapter).

This chapter provides a brief history of black American art and then gives short biographies of some of the prominent artists whose work is often collected by those interested in black artifacts. Collecting prints is covered in its own section in the chapter, partly because the art world considers prints separately from original single works and partly because prints are usually more readily available to collectors. Folk art is covered in Chapter 2, and photography is covered in Chapter 3.

African-American Art History: An Overview

If we attempt to study the routes black American art has taken, we can also follow the political history of Blacks, because the art and the history of black Americans are so closely connected. The influences on black American artists before the Civil War were basically religious. Few, if any, black artists made any other kind of social statement in their paintings. In fact, black artists before, during, and immediately after the Civil War were more concerned with style, color, and making a living than with angering any white people "kind" enough to pay the prices the artists put on their work. If the artist was bold enough to include a feeling for the black heritage in his or her work, the reception was usually negative.

Artistic works created by black Americans often reflected the political ideas of the times. For instance, some drawings and paintings done post-Emancipation included the phrase "We's Free" or something similar.

Edmonia Lewis, a female sculptor of the mid- to late 1800s, used her African- and Native-American heritages as models for her work. One sculpture in particular (*Forever Free*) depicts slaves breaking free of the chains of bondage. The influence of political and social events continued to be mirrored by art from post–Civil War days through the civil rights movement of the 1950s and 1960s to the tumultuous violence of the present-day city neighborhoods and gang wars.

BEFORE THE CIVIL WAR: THE ALMOST INVISIBLE BLACK ARTIST

Although there are some eighteenth-century paintings and drawings of a style that is usually attributed to Blacks, there is no way to tell who these artists were because most pieces from that time were not signed. Early African-American artists experienced many hardships in their careers. First and foremost was the difficulty of being accepted in the art world; second was the challenge of trying to preserve their African heritage in such a way that their artistic statements were not overt enough to jeopardize the artists' acceptance.

Before the Civil War and for some time after, Blacks concentrated their artistic skills in areas such as silverwork, sign painting, and even ornamental gravestones (see also Chapter 2). Excellent examples of art by slaves can be seen in much of the ironwork and metalwork found on mansions throughout the South.

One early black artist who was able to surmount the stringent laws of those days was Robert Scott Duncanson. He joined the ranks of portrait painters in Cincinnati in 1841, determined to become the greatest landscape painter in America. Because of his early education in Canada, Duncanson had had opportunities that most American Blacks did not. The fact that he grew up in Wilberforce (near Toronto), a town devoted to abolition, meant that the young Duncanson emerged well edu-

Nate Johnson, *The Cotton Picker*, oil on canvas, signed; excellent condition, **$300–500.**

cated and basically untouched by the effects of American slavery.

During the 1840s and 1850s, Duncanson was commissioned by wealthy Cincinnati art patrons, traveled widely painting landscapes, and proved himself a noteworthy portraitist. In the early 1850s, the Anti-Slavery League sponsored Duncanson and artist William Sonntag on a trip to Europe to study the masters. Like many other black American artists, Duncanson felt more at home in Europe, where the pressure of prejudice was less noticeable.

When he returned to America, Duncanson once more was faced with slavery and race conflicts. He dealt with such volatile issues by sequestering himself in isolated areas where he could paint in peace. He chose to divorce himself from racial problems and could never quite accept his role in these social issues.

O. Man Rathall (?); oil on artist board; of a black man picking cotton, very bright colors; signed in lower right corner; excellent condition, **$200–250.** Courtesy of Rose Fontanella; photo by Donald Vogt.

Duncanson's ambition, intelligence, strength, and talent could not be ignored by the white world. Because of work like his, many of the myths that the American public believed began to dissipate and art patrons were forced to start to take note of black American art.

THE LATE NINETEENTH CENTURY: FIGHTING TO BE RECOGNIZED

Because the work and lives of artists who worked in the nineteenth century have been better documented than those working in the eighteenth century, the collector has a better sense of the obstacles these black artists had to overcome. Henry Ossawa Tanner, Robert Duncanson, Meta Warwick Fuller, Edmonia Lewis, Edward Mitchell Bannister, William Harper, and others who achieved prominence during the nineteenth century found the road to recognition a rough and rocky one.

The "Black Laws" that were enacted shortly after the Civil War—and that continued to be enforced, added to, and strengthened for the better part of the century—prohibited black people from settling in certain areas of the country. In some places, Blacks had to post a bond to assure the white community that they were going to behave in a "proper" way. Few people of color could raise the price of the bonds, which was as high as $500 in some areas. Thus a number of black American artists went to Europe to seek acceptance. Some, like Edmonia Lewis and Meta Warwick Fuller, never returned to America.

Black artists of the late nineteenth century certainly worked in the fashion of the time. But most of these artists also tried to

Unknown artist, oil on board, of a young black girl; $85–125. Courtesy of Rose Fontanella; photo by Donald Vogt.

as they strum the strings. The characters are lifelike and warm; the feeling is familiar. It seems a shame that Tanner could not, or would not, do more paintings of this type, but perhaps it was easier for him to turn to biblical scenes—a subject more easily understood and accepted by the American public.

Although Tanner eventually gained recognition in America as the first black to be elected to the National Academy of Design, he refused to come back to start a school of black art. He made it known that he resented his being used as a role model for young black artists, because he never forgot the prejudice he suffered. Tanner clung to his acceptance as an *artist,* rejecting, as many who came after him, the label *black* American painter. His pain went so deep that he chose to ignore his homeland. However, he did help young black artists who were able to come to Europe.

weave their heritage and culture into the style of their art.

One black American artist of the nineteenth century deeply affected by the politics of his day was Henry Ossawa Tanner (1859–1937). Influenced by his religious upbringing—his father was a minister—Tanner was torn by his country's strife and agonized over his need to become an artist. He found it nearly impossible to maintain a career as a black artist in America and thus spent a good part of his life in Europe, where he was strongly influenced by European styles and artists.

Tanner's early painting *The Banjo Lesson,* done in 1863, depicts a grandfatherly black man holding a young black boy against his leg. The boy holds a banjo that seems too large for him, and both figures are concentrating on the movement of the boy's hands

THE TWENTIETH CENTURY: BLACK ART COMES OF AGE

Much of black art tended to be stilted and imitative until after World War I, when paintings produced by black Americans broke the mold. Painters working during this period included Archibald Motley, Palmer Hayden, Malvin Gray Johnson, Laura Wheeler Waring, and W. E. Scott.

In 1915, a center for cultural activities called Karamu House, in Cleveland, produced such talents as Hughie Lee-Smith, Bell Ingrams, Charles Salki, Elmer Brown, William E. Smith, and George Hulsinger. Other artists from this era included a group of "realist" painters and sculptors, among them Lenwood Morris, W. O. Thompson, Laura Wheeler Waring, T. E. Hunster, John Henry Adams Jr., and Alan Freelon.

Painters such as William Scott and Edwin A. Harleston began assertively selling their art and promoting themselves, entering the art world by painting scenes using black subjects in ways that projected positive images. Black American art now leaned toward specifically black themes. It was time for black artists to "tell the story," to show intimate, daily views of African-Americans on the farm, in the city, and at home.

The 1920s were years of unrest, yet it was an era when black people saw that something positive might be coming their way. Black writers, artists, musicians, and actors emerged on the popular scene, and people began to pay attention to the advice and feelings of black leaders. It seemed that black people had given a new definition to *community*, and the new community was Harlem. Black art suddenly became modern, colorful, social, and political. Black artists began discovering their roots and proudly displayed these "new" evidences of their African background.

This was a time when the white art world was also taking a closer look at black American life. White photographers, artists, and musicians sought the secret to portraying black Americans, while writers were producing pieces like *Porgy and Bess* and *Emperor Jones*.

In 1928, Archibald Motley became the second black artist (the first was Henry O. Tanner) to have a one-man show in New York City. The two artists' styles are totally opposite. While Tanner's style follows the classic lines of European painters of his day, Motley's paintings are brightly colored, realistic views of a gritty side of "modern black life." Motley, active during the 1930s, paint-

Agnes M. Richmond, *Rose,* oil on canvas, signed and dated, 1925; near mint condition, **$300–500.** Courtesy of Jeffrey Alan Gallery.

ed humorous night scenes such as *The Barbecue* and *The Chicken Snack*.

Unfortunately, The Depression caused an upheaval in American life that made black artists' achievements of the 1920s seem like an illusion. Black and white artists were as hard hit as the rest of the U.S. population. In 1933, the Public Works of Art Project and the Federal Art Project of the WPA were organized. Artists were then hired at craftsmen's wages to paint, sculpt, or fix public buildings. By 1934, old government office buildings had murals and drawings, and parks had sculptures. WPA work was a profitable way for all artists, not just black artists, to support themselves while using and developing their skills.

The art of this era is full of social criticism

Rose Kohler, oil on canvas, of a young black girl, signed and dated, July 1935; excellent condition, **$150–250**. Courtesy of Rose Fontanella; photo by Donald Vogt.

and tends graphically to reflect the artists' poverty. The period is not one in which artists reached great heights, but painters who had done well in the 1920s—Motley, Hayden, Barthe—continued to be productive.

Artists such as Horace Pippin, Leslie Bolling, and William H. Johnson painted in the primitive and neoprimitive style. The style is almost abstract in its lines, and the portraits are stiff and unrealistic. The black artist continued to paint black life, but the style of putting colors to canvas had changed. It was a sign of growth, a good sign because they were creating a style of their own.

In 1939, the first all-black artists' exhibition was held at and sponsored by the Baltimore Museum. Richard Barthe, Malvin Gray Johnson, Henry Bannarn, Florence Purviance, Hale Woodruff, Dox Thrash, Robert Blackburn, and Archibald Motley were all represented and the show was well received.

In the 1940s, the United States was concerned with World War II. Though the artists of the 1930s still worked, art was pushed into the background during the war years.

During the 1950s and 1960s, black museums and art centers started appearing in major cities across the United States. In 1953, a group of southern artists formed the National Conference of Artists (NCA), which first met at Florida A&M. Less than six years later, the NCA had developed into a strong organization that supported, stimulated, and promoted black American artists. The 1960s, a period of civil rights activism, prompted many established museums to respond to the demand that black artists be represented and exhibited. Social realist artists, such as David Hammons, Leslie Price, and John Outerbridge, began establishing their own artistic style by the mid-1960s.

Artists of the 1960s itched for more support and demanded political, as well as social, recognition. Looking for alternate

Elizabeth Catlett (a WPA artist), *Negro Woman,* **lithograph, 1945; near mint condition, $250–350. Courtesy of Rose Fontanella; photo by Donald Vogt.**

methods of exposure, the artists formed a number of groups and programs and founded new galleries and museums. The Acts of Art Gallery of New York was established by Nigel Jackson in 1969, and exhibits included such artists as Faith Ringgold, Lois Mailou Jones, Robert Threadgill, and James Denmark. Also established in 1969, the Studio Museum in Harlem originally offered artists studio space. It then branched out to exhibit those artists' work. Later galleries, such as the Just above Midtown Gallery, the Cinque Gallery, the Weusi Ya Nambe Yasana Gallery, and many others opened to showcase African-American art.

In 1985, the Smithsonian Institution's National Museum of American Art put together an exhibition called "Sharing Tradition: Five Black Artists in 19th Century America." The artists included Henry O. Tanner, Edward Mitchell Bannister, Robert Scott Duncanson, Edmonia Lewis, and Joshua Johnson. It was a major museum showing and an impressive one.

Although the ranks of African-American artists continue to grow, there have been few major changes in the American art world in general. Some galleries still won't show black artists' work, but as a group, black artists are determined to inform the public about the scope and quality of art produced by African-Americans.

Current significant black American artists include printmaker/sculptor Elizabeth Catlett; multimedia artists Faith Ringgold (who recently wrote and illustrated a children's book titled *Dinner at Aunt Connie's House*), Betye Saar, David Hammons, and Howardena Pindell; sculptors Melvin Edwards and Richard Hunt; and painters Jacob Lawrence, Al Loving, Ed Clark, Benny Andrews, Frederick Brown, and Robert Colescott. And there are many other black artists, working in a variety of areas, who have yet to get the attention of the American public.

Black curators, museum representatives, and gallery owners are trying to further this trend. The ice is being broken by exhibits like "Art as a Verb," first shown at the Maryland Institute and then at the Metropolitan Life Gallery and the Studio Museum in Harlem in 1989. The show featured thirteen "first-generation" African-American artists who explore performance art, video art, and installation. Included in the exhibit were Kaylynn Sullivan, Joyce Scott, Martha Jackson-Jarvas, Candace Hill, Charles Abramson, Senga Nengudi, Maren Hassinger, Adrian Piper, and Lorraine O'Grady.

Albert Wagner, *Shark's Dinner,* **oil painting, 1970s; near mint condition, $350–500.** This painting was done for a Cleveland seafood restaurant, but the owner refused to accept it when the artist presented the final version. It is said that Wagner meant the painting to be humorous. Perhaps the owner of the restaurant saw nothing funny about the subject matter. From the collection of Gene and Linda Kangas; photo by Gene Kangas.

Some Biographies of African-American Artists

Edward Mitchell Bannister was born in St. Andrews, New Brunswick, Canada, in 1828 and moved to Boston in 1848 to begin his artistic career. He studied with artist and physician William Rimmer at Lowell Institute in the mid-1860s. After graduating, he painted portraits, biblical subjects, seascapes, and landscapes. When he moved to Providence, Rhode Island, in 1870, he started the Providence Art Club. His painting *Under the Oaks* won a first-place bronze medal at the 1876 Centennial Exposition in Philadelphia, but officials tried to revoke the award when they found out he was black. He died in Providence in 1901.

Bannister's works include *Under the Oaks, Sad Memories, Pleasant Pastures, Driving Home the Cows, The Old Ferry, Lady with Bouquet, Sunrise, At Pawtucket, Fort off Jamestown, Sabin Point, Narragansett Bay,* and *After the Storm.* His work has been exhibited at the Rhode Island

School of Design, Howard University, the National Center of Afro-American Artists (Boston, 1972), and the Museum of Fine Arts (Boston). Collections of Bannister's work are located at the Frederick Douglass Institute of Negro Arts and History in Washington, D.C.; the Rhode Island School of Design Museum of Art; and the Schomburg Art Collection at the New York Public Library.

Richard Barthe, the first African-American sculptor to become a member of the National Headquarters of Arts and Sciences, was born in Bay St. Louis, Mississippi, in 1901 and began his training as a painter at the Chicago Art Institute. His works were bought by the Whitney Museum in New York, and his sculpture of Booker T. Washington was placed in New York University's Hall of Fame.

Robert Scott Duncanson, born in 1821, spent most of his childhood in the tolerant atmosphere of Canada, and little is known of his artistic career until he emerged in the art world of

Cincinnati in 1841. He traveled to Europe several times, and his landscapes often reflect his knowledge of English, Irish, and Scottish literature. He was more accepted in Europe than in America, especially during the Civil War years. The London press called him the equal of English artists. He died in 1872.

His works are included in the National Museum of American Art exhibit "Sharing Tradition: Five Black Artists in 19th Century America." (For more about Duncanson, see the history section of this chapter.)

Meta Vaux Warrick Fuller, a sculptor, illustrator, and writer, was born in Philadelphia in 1877 and studied at the Pennsylvania School of Industrial Art from 1899 to 1904, at the Pennsylvania Academy of Fine Arts in 1907, and at the Academie Colarossi and the École des Beaux Arts in Paris in later years. While in Europe, she studied with a number of well-known sculptors, including Rodin, Gauguin, and Raphael Collin. She was one of the first black American sculptors to turn away from antislavery pieces. She died in 1967.

Fuller's works include *Water Boy, Procession of Arts and Crafts, Oedipus, Three Gray Women, Swing Along Chillun, Exodus, Mother and Child, The Dancing Girl, Man Carrying a Dead Comrade, The Madonna of Consolation,* and *The Good Samaritan.* She was also known for her busts of famous people. In 1910, a fire in Philadelphia destroyed most of her early works. Her work has been exhibited at the Paris Salon (1898, 1899, 1903); the Boston Art Club (1930s); Howard University (1961); the American Negro Exposition; the Boston Public Library (1922); the New York Public Library (1921); and the City College of New York (1967). She was awarded an honorary degree of doctor of letters from Livingston College in 1962, a silver medal for the "New Vistas in American Art" exhibition at Howard University in 1961, and a fellowship at the Academy of Fine Arts. Her works appear in the collections of the Cleveland Art Museum, the Schomburg Collection at the New York Public Library, the Framingham (Massachusetts) Center Library, the San Francisco Museum of Fine Arts, Howard University, and the Business and Professional Women's Club of Washington, D.C.

William A. Harper painted landscapes at the same time that Henry Ossawa Tanner was working in Europe. Born in 1873 in Canada, Harper was a student of Tanner's and was an important black painter of the nineteenth century. His landscapes have an impressionist touch that Harper acquired while traveling in France, Mexico, and the American West. He died in 1910, at age thirty-seven, in Mexico City.

William Henry Johnson, born in 1901 in Florence, South Carolina, was a painter and graphic artist who studied at the National Academy of Design in New York, at the Cape Cod School of Art under Charles Hawthorne, and later in Paris. From 1930 to 1940, he taught at the Federal Project of the Harlem Art Center.

Some of his works include *Looking from My Balcony; Flowers to the Teacher; Mother and Child; Study of a Man of Letters; Norway Landscape; Flowering Trees; Three Great Abolitionists, A. Lincoln, F. Douglass and J. Brown;* and *Jitter Bugs VI.* His work was exhibited in Europe during the 1930s and at the Harlem Art Center of New York, Howard University, and the American Negro Exposition in Chicago in 1940. He was awarded the Harmon Foundation's gold medal (1930), the Cannon Prize, and the National Academy of Design's Hallgarten Prize.

Leon Lank Leonard Sr., a prolific painter and sculptor, was born in Waco, Texas, in 1922. He studied at Texas College and the University of Denver School of Art. His paintings include *African Laborer, Negro Statesman, Black Nun, Dr. George Washington Carver, Black Christ, Three Wise Men,* and *Africa's Black Pilgrimage.* An example of his sculpture is the marble *Black Prophet.* His work has been exhibited at Atlanta University (1956–1970), the All-City Outdoor Show in Los Angeles (1969), the California State Exposition in Sacramento (1972), Whittier College, and Dominguez College. Collections of his work are owned by Atlanta University, the Reverend Harold Perry, Bill Cosby, and "Sugar" Ray Robinson.

Edmonia Lewis, the first known black woman sculptor in the United States, was born in Albany, New York, in 1845. Her father, a free Black, and her mother, a Chippewa Indian, died when she was young, and after that she and her brother traveled with their mother's tribe until Lewis was accepted to Oberlin College in Ohio (at the age of twelve). After leaving Ohio, Lewis traveled east and eventually worked with Boston sculptor Edmund Brackett. Her bust of Robert Gould Shave, a Civil War colonel, brought her work to the eyes of Boston's Story family, and the family encouraged her to study in Rome. While in Rome, she perfected her work with marble and was commissioned by various Europeans and Americans to do work in the neoclassical style. When the neoclassical vogue faded in the 1880s, so did interest in Lewis's work. She died in Rome around 1890.

Lewis's marble works include *Unknown Woman* (1867); *Old Indian Arrow Maker and Daughter* (1872); busts of Abraham Lincoln, Henry Wadsworth Longfellow, William Lloyd Garrison, Wendell Phillips, Harriet Hosmer,

Unknown artist, plaster bust, of a girl's face; near mint condition, **$150–250.** Courtesy of Rose Fontanella; photo by Donald Vogt.

John Brown, and Charles Sumner; *Morning of Liberty (Forever Free);* and *Death of Cleopatra.* Her sculptures have been exhibited at the Soldiers Aid Fair in Boston (1864), the San Francisco Art Association (1873), the Philadelphia Centennial (1876), the American Negro Exposition (1940), Vassar College (1972), and at many other places throughout the United States and Europe. Collections of her work are owned by the Frederick Douglass Institute of Negro Arts and History in Washington, D.C.; the Harvard College Library; and the Kennedy Gallery in New York City.

Scipio Morehead is the only eighteenth-century black American artist to have received enough recognition for his work to be recorded. He was aided by two prominent Bostonian women, one a white patron of the arts and the other the black poet Phyllis Wheatley.

Henry Ossawa Tanner was born in 1859 in Pittsburgh, the son of Benjamin Tucker Tanner, an African Methodist Episcopal Church bishop, and Sarah Miller Tanner. Henry was expected to follow in his father's footsteps, but he preferred art. Despite his family's protests, he entered the Pennsylvania Academy of Fine Arts, where he studied under Thomas Eakins and William Chase. When he wanted to study in Europe after graduation, his family instead sent him to Atlanta to visit his brother, who was a pastor there. While in Atlanta, Tanner became a photographer and made his living teaching art at Clark University and selling his paintings and photographs.

In 1892, Tanner became a student at the Academie Julian in Paris, studying under Benjamin Constant and Paul Laurens. Four years later, his paintings *Music Lesson* and *Young Sabot-Maker* were noticed by European critics, and his career began to take off.

Tanner was a prolific painter, producing more than a hundred works during his career. The majority of his paintings deal with religious subjects, such as *Destruction of Sodom and Gomorrah, Flight from Egypt, Moses and the Burning Bush, Christ at the Home of Mary and Martha, Study for Christ,* and *Nicodemus on a Rooftop.* His work hangs in major museums of the world and has been exhibited in France and the United States. Pieces or collections of his work can be seen in the Louvre (Paris), the Carnegie Institute (Pittsburgh), the Frederick Douglass Institute (Washington, D.C.), the Houston Museum of Fine Arts, the Howard University Gallery of Art, the Metropolitan Museum of Art, and the New York Public Library's Schomburg Collection. Tanner was awarded many honors in Paris around the turn of the century and won the National Arts Club bronze medal at the Exhibition of Arts Club Galleries in New York in 1927. He was a member of many organizations, including the Legion of Honor, Paris Society of American Painters, and the American Artists Professional League as well as being an associate at the National Academy. Most significant, however, Tanner was the first African-American artist known to live solely from his art.

In 1991, a collection of Tanner's paintings and other works was exhibited throughout the United States. Permanent collections of his works are held by the National Museum of American Art in Washington, D.C., and the Hampton University Museum in Virginia. (For more about Tanner, see the history section of this chapter.)

Some Biographies of Other Artists Who Depicted Black Subjects

Theresa Bernstein was born in Philadelphia and received her art training at the Philadelphia School of Design and the Pennsylvania Academy. In 1910, she moved to New York City, where she established her reputation as an independent-minded "modern realist." Choosing her subject matter from the New York streets, she painted in the ashcan tradition while developing and maintaining her own style.

In 1983, Bernstein and her husband, artist William Meyerowitz, exhibited their work at the New York Historical Society. It was the first time that institution had shown a living artist's work. Bernstein's work is in many museum collections, including those of the Corcoran Gallery, the Metropolitan Museum, the Brooklyn Museum, and the Chicago Art Institute.

Eleazer Hutchinson Miller, born in Shepherdstown, West Virginia, in 1831, lived most of his life in Washington, D.C. He worked as painter, illustrator, and etcher, producing both work for periodicals and illustrations for books such as *Tam O'Shanter* and Mrs. Springer's *Songs of the Sea.* Miller was a member of the prestigious New York Etchers' Club and also a founding member of the Washington Art Club and the Society of Washington Artists. While living in Washington, Miller worked for the *National Intelligencer.* In 1875, he moved to Europe, where he studied the Old Masters. He died in Washington in 1921.

William Sidney Mount, a nineteenth-century American artist, painted barn scenes, one of the most familiar of which is *Power of Music,* which was added to the Cleveland Museum of Art's collection in 1992; it went on display in January 1993. The museum paid approximately $4 million for the painting, which shows a young black man leaning against a barn door. Inside the barn sit three rural musicians playing what is apparently a lively tune, because the onlookers are dancing.

Edward H. Potthast, born in Cincinnati in 1857, studied there as well as in Munich and Paris. In 1906, he was elected a member of the National Academy. He was well known both as a fine art painter and as an illustrator for *Scribner's* and *Century* magazines. His work is represented in major collections such as those of the Cincinnati Art Museum, the Brooklyn Museum, and the Buffalo Museum.

Frederic Remington, best known for his illustrations of the Old West, drew black cavalry troopers while working for *Harper's Weekly* in 1888.

Agnes M. Richmond was born about 1870 in Alton, Illinois, and was educated at the St. Louis School of Fine Arts. In 1888, she studied at the Art Students League in New York and later with John Henry Twachtmann, Walter Appleton Clark, and Kenyon Cox. She taught at the League from 1910 to 1914. She died in Brooklyn in 1964.

Richmond won many prizes, including the Watrous Figure Prize. She was a member of many art organizations and had her work exhib-

Agnes M. Richmond, oil on canvas, signed and dated upper right corner, 1925; near mint condition, **$300–500**. Courtesy Jeffrey Alan Gallery.

ited at the Smithsonian, the Carnegie Institute, the Art Association at Newport, Rhode Island, the Brooklyn Museum, the San Diego Fine Arts Society, and the Hickory North Carolina Museum of Art, among others.

Harry Roseland, born in Brooklyn in 1867, studied in New York with Beckwith and was a member of the Brooklyn Art Club. Roseland painted scenes of late-nineteenth-century well-heeled white women with black women. He often shows the women involved in a card or tea reading, or the two women seem to be sharing some kind of knowledge. Roseland won the 1898 Hallgarten prize for *An Interesting Letter* and the 1887 gold medal from the Brooklyn Art Club for *Pea Pickers of Long Island.*

William Aiken Walker, born in 1838, lived in Charleston, North Carolina; Baltimore; New Orleans; and other cities throughout the South. He was largely self-taught, although he spent time during the 1860s studying in Dusseldorf, Germany. In 1888, Currier and Ives published two of his lithographs. Walker preferred to paint rural Blacks at work, on the docks, in the fields, and at home. His style had a folk art feel to it.

Introduction to Collecting Prints

Many prints have been made of black subjects. Some were originally made as prints, and others were reprints of works created in another medium, such as Harry Roseland's paintings.

Prints can be divided into many categories, such as chromolithographs, lithographs, first-edition prints, numbered prints, and so on. First-edition and numbered prints are valuable to the collector because they are first off the press and are made in limited quantities. Later prints, while still collectible, are not as highly valued because they are not as rare. Chromolithographs are colored prints produced by lithography. Lithographs are produced by making a "picture" on a stone or metal plate and transferring it to a material that will accept ink.

During the 1870s and 1880s, quite a few black artists made their living as lithographers and engravers. Grafton T. Brown is one of the more notable. White printmakers also depicted Blacks and are included here because of their great impact on the antiques world—for example, Currier and Ives.

Some Biographies of Printmakers

John J. Audubon's parents were Pierre Audubon, a wealthy, society Frenchman, and Jeanne Rabine, Audubon's mulatto servant. John Audubon was born on April 26, 1785, in Haiti. He traveled throughout the United States and Europe, studying nature, animals, and birds for most of his life, until his health and age prevented him from spending long periods of time in the woods. Many of his specimens of plants and animals were obtained along the Mississippi River. Audubon's nature prints are widely collected and quite valuable in today's antiques market. His bird drawings were first published in England in the book *The Birds of America*. Few people realize that Audubon's ancestry was partly black.

Grafton T. Brown made his living as a draftsman, painter, and lithographer. He spent most of his career in San Francisco, where, even though he was black, he opened his own lithographic business in 1867. He worked in a seminaturalistic style, picturing geographic locations in a way that made them recognizable. During the last fifty years of his life, Brown changed his focus, becoming involved in engineering and geological science. He died in 1918 in St. Paul, Minnesota.

Currier and Ives, well-known nineteenth-century printmakers, painted quite a few black subjects. Nathaniel Currier, who perfected the art of hand-coloring black-and-white stone lithographs, began his print business in 1834 and was joined by James Merritt Ives in 1852. Currier and Ives, both white, created political and humorous prints and prints depicting major events in American history. At times they were inaccurate, but they printed what they believed to be true. They published more than seven thousand individual prints, but they kept no records on how many copies of each print were made. Currier and Ives used artists such as Fanny F. Palmer, Charles Parsons, James E. Butterworth, Louis Maurer, George Catlin, A. F. Tait, George Henry Durrier, and Thomas Worth.

During the Civil War, Currier and Ives began to get away from depicting the black American as a bumbling "darky." Instead they depicted Blacks as valiant soldiers—part of the all black 54th Regiment, a courageous unit that fought under the white Colonel Robert Shaw, for example.

Although Currier and Ives's scenes of the Mississippi are interesting and uplifting, the prints are generally inaccurate images of the way life was lived on that river highway. An example of such a print shows Blacks poling a ferry boat across the river. In their defense, however, Currier and Ives were probably working to supply a demand. Also, they showed a way of life that was foreign to the many Americans who had not seen the rich river life of the Mississippi.

Louis Prang owned a chromolithograph factory in Boston that produced prints over several decades in the latter part of the nineteenth century. They were so popular that *The American Women's Home,* written by Catherine E. Beecher and Harriet Beecher Stowe, recommended that people decorate their homes with Prang's prints. One Prang chromo, *The Old Kentucky Home*

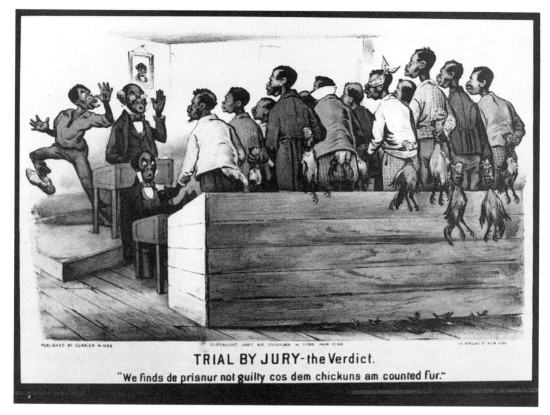

Currier and Ives, *Trial by Jury—the Verdict,* **Darktown series print; excellent condition, $350–500. Courtesy of Rose Fontanella; photo by Donald Vogt.**

(after E. Johnson), shows the back of a house where various members of a black family are relaxing and talking. Other Prang prints depict black American life in a romantic fashion. In 1890, Prang began producing greeting cards and postcards (see Chapter 8).

Patrick H. Reason was a free mulatto whose engravings and lithographs in support of abolition were widely distributed. He actively applied his art in support of the antislavery cause in the early nineteenth century, using his works to speak out against slavery whenever possible. He devoted much of his time to illustrating abolitionist literature.

Price Guidelines for the Work of Major Artists

Prices for works of art change much more rapidly than prices for antiques and collectibles. Especially when buying art, you should be prepared to pay whatever is comfortable for you for a piece you will enjoy rather than buying solely for monetary gain. But to make good investments, you should be aware of popularity trends and of what an artist's paintings have brought in the past—paintings by Edward Mitchell Bannister, for example, usually fetch a four-figure sum. In other words, educate thyself! Don't be afraid to hesitate before buying an expensive painting, sculpture, bronze, or print. Back off from the painting, think about your purchase, and if necessary, wait a day or two so that you can do the proper research before emptying out your bank account. If you buy what you love, you'll never be sorry.

You cannot expect to get a bargain when a painting with a black subject is offered for sale. Most dealers and collectors are now

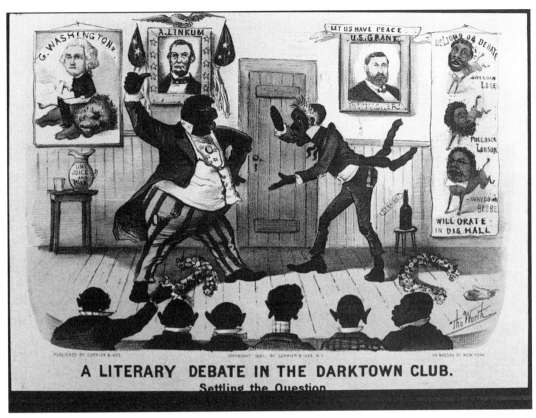

Currier and Ives, *A Literary Debate in the Darktown Club,* Darktown series print, copyright 1884; excellent condition, **$350–500.** Courtesy of Rose Fontanella; photo by Donald Vogt.

pretty savvy about black items, and the price asked for a work of art is often far beyond what the piece is really worth. However, when buying the work of a black artist, you may be able to pick up valuable paintings for a song.

For those who like some kind of guide, I have researched some of the major artists, and below are my estimates of what their works are likely to be worth. New price records are being set every day, so these prices should not be taken as stable and permanent.

Edward M. Bannister—Recent prices for paintings by this artist, who painted in the Renaissance style, range from the low thousands to the mid and upper teens. His best pieces would bring quite a bit more, but most are held by museums or in private collections.

Harry Roseland—Roseland's prints often garner between $250 and $400, while his paint-

ings have ranged from $2,000 to $25,000. His subjects often contribute to the high prices of his paintings. His romanticized characters are attractive, and the subjects are well illustrated and often touching. His well-known scenes of black fortune-tellers are often populated by obviously well-to-do white women and the stereotypical caricature of a black mammy. Yet it appears that the higher-class white women envy the black woman's knowledge in such things as predicting the future. Roseland prints are usually found in general collections of black Americana.

Henry Ossawa Tanner—Tanner's works hang in major museums throughout the world. He is one of the best known early black artists, and his work is highly acclaimed and expensive, with average prices around $250,000. His works are not for the beginning collector, but many well-known collectors have a Tanner.

William Aiken Walker—Walker's works are well known for the Southern scenes they depict. His paintings of cotton pickers and slave life have been reproduced in a series of bisque dolls. His paintings run from approximately $4,000 to somewhere around $15,000. His rich colors and poignant renditions of life on the plantation have attracted many collectors, and I expect you will see this painter's worth climb even higher. Walker's paintings often sell through Morton Goldberg's Auction Galleries in New Orleans.

If you want to find out the value of the works of a particular artist, your local library should have a number of volumes to help you. The one most art dealers and antiques dealers use is *Jacobsen's Price Guide. Fielding's* gives a concise and accurate history for many artists. Other, more specialized books are also available to help you in your research (see also the "Bibliography").

PRICES FOR ART

Charcoal sketch, Curtis Woody, young black child getting hair cut by older person (all you see of other person are hands), marked "17/200", excellent condition, **$175–200.**

Drawing, John Wright, caption says, "Lawyer: My client did not assault this man. He thought he swallowed a fish bone and merely patted him on the back to get it back up," May 15, 1848; excellent condition, **$50–100.**

Etching, *The Gleaners (Field Slaves),* sepia, framed, late 19th century; 17″ × 13″; near mint condition, **$125–200.**

Painting

    Gibson, J., group of three oil paintings showing Florida scenery; artist is black and from the Fort Pierce, Florida–area; this work was displayed in the White House during the Johnson administration; excellent condition, **$150–200 for the set.**

    Jones, Lois, *Two Youths with Kites,* oil on canvas; two boys, one daydreaming, one intent and leaning against a tree; hills and trees in the background have Cubist slant; 1959; framed size, 34″ × 25″; artist is a well-known black female painter born in Boston, Massachusetts, in 1905; she has an extensive exhibition record; excellent condition, **$16,000–18,000.**

    Madison, Reginald, *Family Portrait,* expressionistic, conveys the joys and brooding intensities of family life; Chicago-born Madison is mostly self-taught and painted in Paris, Venice, and Copenhagen; mint condition, **$1,000–7,000.**

Unknown black artist; pen and watercolor illustration drawn for the *Atlanta Constitution,* of a black woman making dough and her kids playing all over the house, colorful, framed; 1960s; 14″ × 11″; excellent condition, **$150–200. Courtesy of American Eye; photo by Bob Reno.**

Unknown artist, painting on leather or possibly oil crayon, of a minstrel man; very good condition, $200–250. Courtesy of Rose Fontanella; photo by Donald Vogt.

Portrait (from shoulders up) of Augustus Jones, Philadelphia, Pennsylvania, opaque watercolor on paperboard, inscribed on verso: "Augustus Jones at age 49, July 1 1852. Born Dec. 16, 1803 in Philadelphia, married Lucy Gillette on April 18, 1825 in New Brunswick, N.J., was an active member of African Methodist Episcopal Church. Father, Charles Lee Jones, born 1776, died 1861. Grandfather, Absalom Jones, born a slave in 1746 in Sussex, Delaware, bought his freedom, was married in 1770, died 1818, was active and responsible for the establishment of the African Episcopal Church in Philadelphia," elegant, sensitive, and sophisticated, original frame, very rare; 7½″ × 5½″; mint condition, **$27,000–29,000.**

Walker, William Aiken (1838–1921)

Cabin Scene, oil on academy board, black family outside, clothes on the line drying, signed; 6¼″ × 12¼″; mint condition, **$7,000–10,000.**

Sharecroppers Cabin, oil on academy board, chickens and tree stumps in foreground and black man standing surveying a field of cotton in background, signed; 6″ × 12¼″; mint condition, **$7,000–10,000.**

Print

Audubon, John J.

Black Tailed Deer, in frame; excellent condition, **$1,500–1,750.**

Buntings and Finches; excellent condition, **$1,500–1,750.**

Hare Indian Dog, in frame; excellent condition, **$1,500–1,750.**

Brown, J. G., *Card Shark,* early steel engraving, sepia and black and white, black boy doing card tricks for three white boys, copyrighted and signed, framed; 15″ × 13″; mint condition, **$50–100.**

Children eating watermelon, chromolithograph in watermelon frame, ca. 1880; 24″ × 17″; excellent condition, **$800–1,000.**

Currier and Ives

American Jockey Club Races, Jerome Park, lithograph; excellent condition, **$900–1,100.**

Darktown Fire Brigade—Under Full Steam and *Darktown Fire Brigade—Hook and Ladder Gymnastics;* 18½″ × 15″ each (excluding mat and frame); good condition, **$450–700 for the pair.**

A Line Shot, The Champion in Danger, and *The Champion in Luck,* satires, 1882; 14″ × 11″ each (excluding mat and frame); very good condition, **$375–500 for set of three.**

O Dat Watermillon, lithograph; excellent condition, **$350–500.**

Forbes, Edwin, *The Supply Train,* hard card print, copper-plate etching, fairly rare edition; dated 1876, 13″ × 18″; excellent condition, **$20–30.**

Gomillion, T. H., limited edition of 100–500, each signed and numbered; 17″ × 21¾″; new, **$25.**

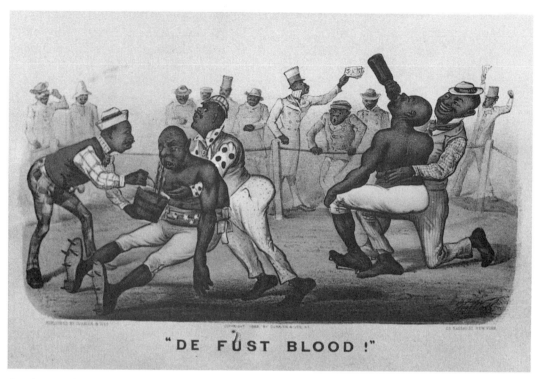

"DE FUST BLOOD!"

Currier and Ives, *De Fust Blood!,* Darktown series print; excellent condition, **$350–500.** Courtesy of Rose Fontanella; photo by Donald Vogt.

Hutty, Alfred H., *Young Blacks,* city scene framed in gold leaf; 9″ × 9″ image, 17″ × 17″ with matting; very good condition, **$200–500.**

Martin and Johnson of Wisconsin, *Emancipation Proclamation by Abraham Lincoln,* lithograph, features 12 vignettes of black slaves surrounding a copy of the handwritten document, wood-backed frame, 1864; very good condition, **$450–700.**

Mosley, C., copper-plate engraving showing Ms. Britainnia seated and at her feet and side are nations plying their goods: a naked slave girl with ivory from Africa, a naked American Indian with tobacco leaf, with large sailing vessels in the background illustrating the port of England, ca. 1760; 9″ × 16″ with text beneath; very good condition, **$65–100.**

Roseland, Harry, *Fortunes,* black woman with cards spread on an overturned bucket doing a psychic reading for a fashionable white lady with parasol and fancy hat; 16″ × 20″; new, **$20.**

Statue

Ayers, *Rock of All Nations,* head on loosely, unusual piece, near mint condition, **$750–1,000.**

Naked African native man with shield, unsigned, 3½′ high; excellent condition, **$195–225.**

Smiling black boy sitting in a chair with bare feet crossed, terra-cotta, attributed to Arthur Strasser who was employed by the Frederick Goldscheider Co. in Vienna, Austria; at one time used to advertise stove blacking at Napoleon, Ohio, general store, ca 1890; 42″ high; excellent condition, **$8,000–9,000.**

Woodblock print

A Slave Auction in Virginia, slave family on the block with bidding plantation owners and slaves waiting their turn on the block, from *Illustrated London News,* February 1861; 11″ × 15″; excellent condition, **$20–30.**

Currier and Ives, *Darktown Opera—The Serenade,* Darktown series print; near mint condition, **$350–500.** Courtesy of Rose Fontanella; photo by Donald Vogt.

William Nash, full color print, of a black woman washing her little girl in tub beside old woodburning stove, framed, dated 1984; excellent condition, **$75–100.** Collection of Dawn and Bob Reno; photo by Bob Reno.

Harper's Weekly

Early morning scene of happy slaves in rags being welcomed by a large column of Federal soldiers, dated 1864; 11″ × 15″; very good condition, **$12–20.**

Emancipated Slaves, young white and black children liberated from the schools in New Orleans, black adults in background, one slave branded on forehead, dated 1864; 11″ × 15″; very good condition, **$12–20.**

Freed men leading slaves out of bondage at night, black and grays, dated 1864; 11″ × 15″; very good condition, **$12–20.**

Gen. Sherman's Rear Guard, General Sherman's huge army in Georgia with the wounded and sick being cared for, with wagon trains coming and black contrabands clogging up the roads, many blacks helping the soldiers, dated 1864; 11″ × 15″; very good condition, **$12–20.**

The Hoe Down or the Break Down, scenes of the home, the quilting bee, the dance, the apple cut, slaves, the breakdown, raffling, corn husking, 1861, nice print; 16″ × 22″; excellent condition, **$10–20.**

Massacre at Fort Pillow, hand-to-hand battle with unarmed black soldiers being bayoneted by white Confederate soldiers with white officers standing by watching, dated 1864; 11″ × 15″; very good condition, **$12–20.**

Nast, Thomas, *Emancipation,* slave auction, slaves being beaten and run down by dogs, reverse side depicts scenes of freedom and home in the center, may be the most important print of its time, dated 1863; 16″ × 22″; very good condition, **$15–25.**

The Stampede of Slaves to Fort Monroe, moonlit night with slaves racing for the bridge into the Union lines, 1861; 11½″ × 16″; very good condition, **$8–18.**

Uncle Tom and slaves working on the fortification, dancing contrabands when the day is over, from cover, 1861; 11½″ × 16″; very good condition, **$10–20.**

The state of Georgia with the slaves in each county and a second woodblock of an overall map of the southern states, along with a print of a dark night scene showing slaves taking in Union soldiers for hiding, all dated 1861; each 11½″ × 16″; very good condition, **$13–23 each.**

CHAPTER TWO

Folk Art

Although black folk artists make up more than half of the known folk art community, they are not as well known or as fully recognized as they should be. Some have been shown in various galleries and museums or have been interviewed by national newspapers and magazines, yet their names are not recognized by people outside the folk art field.

The art of African-Americans, like their music, is undeniably their own. Yet black folk arts and crafts have not been given the same attention as black music, even though arts and crafts are just as important a part of American culture.

Defining African-American Folk Art

Folk art is the expression of the common people and usually has nothing to do with the fashionable (or formal) art of the times. The folk artist follows his or her own emotions and applies them directly to the craft. Thus the difference between the folk artist and the fine artist is only a matter of training. The folk artist is rarely schooled, uses readily available tools and supplies, and creates naive forms of art, art that has only recently, in the long history of antiques, become appreciated as true works of art.

American folk art differs from European folk art in that European folk art was rooted in distinct racial or class traditions. American folk artists' patterns of design appear to be

Man's head, by Edgar Tolson, polychromed wood, red painted lips and wide white eyes, ca. 1965; 7" × 8½"; very good condition, **$3,500–5,000. Courtesy of American Eye; photo by Bob Reno.**

old, inherited ones created by skilled crafts-people who specialized in that art. It is difficult to tell the age of a piece of European folk art, because patterns were copied and the art has remained timeless; for example, the paintings on the sides of goat carts and horse-drawn wagons in the Mediterranean area.

American folk artists' styles partially came from their inherited traditions; however, through time, knowledge of some of the specifics of those traditions was lost. Thus the artists "reinvented" their styles, combining aspects of their ethnic backgrounds with what they had learned in their adopted or new country. All early Americans had both an Old World history and a new, distinctly American life. This is especially true of black Americans, since they were not only torn from their homes in Africa but were often separated from family and friends once they arrived in America. It was difficult, sometimes impossible, for Blacks to keep their African heritage alive and to build an artistic tradition based on their native culture. Over time, the Africanness of the early slaves faded, and black Americans began to become assimilated with the world around them.

Black American folk art is largely the work of men, women, and children who had little or no artistic training and no regard for what was artistically acceptable at the time. For the most part, they did not copy the work of their ancestors, although there was undoubtedly some influence. They worked from the heart and designed items that were useful or fanciful, and usually created objects for their own use and enjoyment. Early black folk artists did not follow trends or traditions, just their own beliefs.

Some of the work now considered folk art was done by professional artisans who were creating products for a specific use. Shop signs, ship figureheads, house decorations, canes, and pottery pieces were made primarily to suit a purpose. Other types of folk art were made by Blacks who were con-cerned with pleasing themselves or others. This category encompasses embroidered pieces, quilts, and young women's samplers (see Chapter 11); dolls (see Chapter 6); and decorative painting, which was applied to furniture or to the walls of homes.

Slaves learned European traditions at the hands of their masters. Very few Blacks were allowed (or had the time) to create artistic objects. Many black folk painters and crafts-people were unable to develop their natural abilities to create a style that was recognizable or distinguishable from others; it wasn't

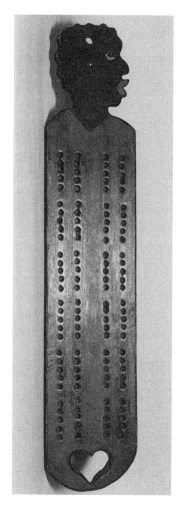

Cribbage board, woman's head carved at top, heart carved in bottom, possibly contemporary (or reproduction); 5½" wide × 28½" tall; excellent condition, **$300–400.**

acceptable for Blacks to have a trade. Most were forced to be satisfied with a small amount of public or familial attention.

The folk artists who concentrated on portraits often did other work as well; few nineteenth-century communities could support a full-time resident portrait painter. Often the artist's other jobs included sign painting and lettering, coach and carriage painting, clock face decoration, and architectural and ironwork renderings.

Itinerant folk artists, called "travelers" by their compatriots, went from town to town offering their services. They would stay in an area, sometimes in a client's home, painting portraits until their work was done. The artist often painted the portraits in return for room and board. One of the better known black portraitists was Joshua Johnson. Traveling painters would often barter their services for something other than room and board; one painter worked for "three months' worth of shaves." During the mid-1800s, it became the fashion for young white women to be schooled in art at a seminary. This trend made it more difficult for the black traveling painter to find work, because he was now in competition with these women, who wanted to nurture their own artistic leanings.

Although African influence was still somewhat strong during the years before the Civil War, after Emancipation some of those ties were broken. The black American folk artist began to display his or her own values, styles, and forms, which were distinctive and truly unique. American folk art, like American people, is diversified and reflects a broad range of expressions, talents, and emotions. It has a straightforward simplicity, which reveals only a basic understanding of design and color. It also shows a disarming naïveté, indicative of what we call the primitive arts. Whatever the painter felt, whatever societal influences were the greatest during his or her growth years, and whatever traditions he or she had been exposed to were all part of what came out on the canvas, wood carving, or sculpture. Thus each piece is a special work of art in its own right and in its own category.

The work of black folk artists is distinctive in that their portrayal of African-Americans is more realistic than that of their white counterparts. The features of the figures done by African-Americans are less pronounced, the expressions on the faces are more believable, sometimes even painful. Gone are the flared nostrils, bulging eyes, and exaggerated lips so often seen on figures painted or sculpted by nonblack folk artists. Black folk artists reveal their deep-rooted Africanism and the belief in witchcraft and non-Western religions. The dignity with which the characterized figures hold their heads, the subdued emotional looks on their faces, and the lack of grotesque overtones, makes the folk art done by Blacks an extremely valuable part of black Americana, highly prized by today's collectors.

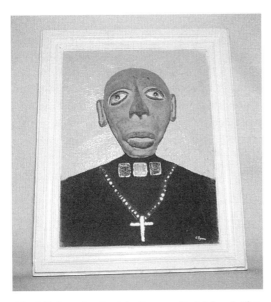

The Minister, by Archie Byron, Outsider Artist, sawdust and glue composition, 1989, 19" × 23½"; excellent condition, **$800–1,200.** Courtesy of American Eye; photo by Bob Reno.

Man's head, carved from southern hard pine, by a prisoner in Winston-Salem, "James" carved on back and "Amock S3" on top, illegible signature, 1940–1960, 14¼" × 5½"; excellent condition, **$300–500.** Courtesy of American Eye; photo by Bob Reno.

Today's collectors are discovering a new field in folk art, dubbed "Outsider Art." There is an argument about whether Outsider Art is fine art or folk art. Because the definition of Outsider Art is "art created by unschooled people, often those with psychological, criminal, or poor backgrounds," I am including objects of this type here. Someday, Outsider Art may have a chapter of its own, but since I consider "fine art" to be produced by someone who has had some kind of formal training—an apprenticeship or college degree—I feel more comfortable

including Outsider Art with folk art. The major difference between the two is that the Outsider Artist often works *outside* society's normal boundaries (e.g., they might be emotionally or physically impaired or in prison), whereas the folk artist *reflects* the society around him or her.

Outsider Artists are Archie Burnside (born 1944; living in Pendleton, South Carolina); Archie Bryon (a former Atlanta, Georgia, city councilman); Sam Doyle (1906–1985; from St. Helena Island, South Carolina), who sometimes used house paint on old tin roofing panels; Lonnie Holly (born 1950; living in Birmingham, Alabama); Katherine (Kate) Lange (born 1910, living in northern Virginia); Charles Lucas (born 1951; living in Prattville, Alabama); Bernise Sims (born 1919); Marcus Staples (born 1938; living in Reading, Pennsylvania); Jimmy Lee Sudduth (born 1910; living in Fayette, Alabama); and Inez Nathaniel Walker (1911–1990; from Willard, New York). Other Outsider Artists are profiled later in this chapter.

Beginning with slavery, many influences contributed to art forms that we now classify as black folk art. Carpentry, carving, pottery (see Chapter 9), grave decorations, quilting (Chapter 11), basket weaving, and ironwork are all areas in which black artisans practiced. From these beginnings, artists created a new field of energy—one that has often been undervalued.

Some Types of Folk Art

BASKETS

Baskets have been woven by African-Americans for use at home and in the fields. Though functional, baskets have become folk art because the makers wove their own styles into the baskets they produced. Usually, basketmaking was a necessity, made

Painting and sign, by Lonnie Holly, Outsider Artist, painting on lid of industrial drum using house paint, pine board sign, mid-1980s, 24″ diameter painting, 29½″ × 6″ sign; excellent condition, **painting: $600–800; sign: $100–150.** Courtesy of American Eye; photo by Bob Reno.

enjoyable by those folk artists with a talent for turning their work into art.

One of the first crops produced by slaves was rice, and baskets were created to thresh the grain, or "fan" the rice. These baskets, made by black hands, reflected African designs. Made during the eighteenth century, work baskets such as these can broadly be split into two categories: the baskets made by men from reeds and split palmetto butt, and those made by women and children from light grasses and strips of palmetto leaves.

By the nineteenth century, new forms and shapes of baskets began being used, for example, large round baskets with shallow sides, tall storage baskets, oblong baskets, and baskets with strap handles. Materials used by basket makers who sold their work to tourists included pine needles and white

oak strips. The materials used in the basket and the style of weaving indicate where a basket was made. For example, in Sharon, Missis-sippi, baskets were made of laced strips of white oak, but in Charleston, South Carolina, pine needles were coiled into baskets.

In some areas of the United States, basketmaking was considered a cottage industry, providing basket makers with the means to keep their families clothed and sheltered. In the 1920s and 1930s, roadside basket stands were common in the South. The main basketmaking communities were located on the eastern seaboard, stretching south from Maryland to Georgia, then inland to Mississippi. Early basket makers, however, seemed to be centered along the South Carolina and Georgia coasts. (Today's

Beaver, alligator, and bird, by Willie Massey (1910–1990s), wood and aluminum foil, painted red and green, bird 12″ tall × 6½″ at widest point, beaver 7½″ × 4″, alligator 15½″ × 4″; all in excellent condition, $100–300 each. Courtesy of American Eye; photo by Bob Reno.

basket makers are centralized at the northern end of the Sea Islands chain, particularly around Mount Pleasant, South Carolina.) Although most of the early baskets were coiled, each area seemed to have its own particular style. Two stands just seven or eight miles apart could sell completely different styles of baskets.

Basket makers generally used local materials. Tough, long brown grasses were used in the South Carolina low country, sweet grass was used north of Charleston; pine needles and palmetto fronds were also turned into baskets.

BOATS

A skill that slaves brought with them from Africa was the ability to make dugout canoes and shallow boats. Most of the boats that traveled the South's many rivers and lakes were manned by slaves, and it was often noted how well the Blacks maneu-

vered the boats. Accounts from Virginia and South Carolina state that some slaves had served as canoe men in their homelands and learned how to make boats from logs in Africa or the West Indies.

Some of the canoes were quite large and could be fitted with a mast and sail. Few canoes survived; they were built for immediate use and most have disintegrated with time.

CARVINGS

The world of antiques knew very little about carving until a 1937 survey (now part of the "Index of American Design" of the National Gallery of Art) uncovered an enormous amount of slave carvings. One of the pieces attributed to a slave carver is a large figure of a man, which is thought to have once been attached to a post. The figure was carved from one solid piece of walnut and was originally painted gray-green. A slave of pirate Jean Lafitte was thought to have

are now classified as folk art. One of the earliest examples of this craft is said to have been carved by Henry Gudgell, a slave blacksmith who lived in Livington County, Missouri, during the 1860s. This type of carving is said to be the most common sculptural form and black carvers have made canes from the time they were brought to this country up to the present.

Canes were thought to have been a craft taught in same African cultures. Indeed, if one compares an African cane with an African-American one, the similarities are amazing. Both usually depict a reptile winding its way up the stick; the head of the stick is often in the shape of a human or animal. Alligators, snakes, lizards and turtles are common subjects.

Boundary marker from eastern Pennsylvania, face with black features carved in tree, 1860–1890, about 4′ tall; excellent condition, **$750–1,000**. Courtesy of American Eye; photo by Bob Reno.

carved a pair of chickens sometime between 1810 and 1815. A seated preacher with an open book in his lap, now in the Art Institute of Chicago, was carved in Kentucky during the mid-1850s. Because the preacher's features are extremely realistic, the work is attributed to a black American. Though only 29 inches high, the piece exudes a quiet dignity, a thoughtfulness and pride, that can be felt even when looking at a photograph of the carving.

Walking sticks or canes, carved by hand and often decorated with animals or reptiles,

Man's head, realistic features, 1880–1900, 12″ high × 6″; excellent condition, **$800–1,200**. Courtesy of American Eye; photo by Bob Reno.

Many African cultures believed that witches traveled as animals—bats, reptiles, black cats—bringing death and disease to their enemies. This superstition is reflected in black American folk art. Although early black Americans had a strong belief in witchcraft, slaves also embraced Christianity. Christian themes were often chosen by the black artisan. In fact, sometimes one work will illustrate both the good and the evil that the early black American saw in everyday life.

Howard Miller of Dixie, Georgia, carved canes of figures in full relief, while another Georgian, William Rogers, used beads to make the eyes of both the animal and human figures he carved into his canes. Leon Rucker, a Mississippi carver, created canes decorated with snakes and lizards whose eyes are delineated with brass studs. Lester Willis, another Mississippi carver, made plain canes that he decorated only with the owner's name. Willis also made canes with Scriptures carved into them and some with figures of men in top hats. His repertoire was wide and varied.

Henry Gudgell, a Kentucky slave, is credited with the most spectacular of early American canes. He made this cane in 1867 for John Bryan. Its top portion boasted a 5-inch section of serpentine fluting carved above a "smaller section of the same curvilinear decoration bracketed by plain bands. This portion of the cane is followed by two raised rings, a band of raised diamond forms, and two final encircling rings" (Vlach, 1991). The geometric pattern covered about a fourth of the cane and was followed by carvings of a lizard; a tortoise; and a man dressed in shirt, trousers, and shoes (encircling the cane as if giving it a hug).

A group of more than 180 canes were highlighted in 1992 at the Museum of American Folk Art's Feld Gallery at Lincoln Square in New York City. The owner of the collection, George Meyer, notes that if you find a cane with heads or figures that are inlaid with rhinestones or mirrors, the cane is probably African-American, since that type of decoration is an African tradition. He also states that he "wouldn't expect to spend less than $900 to $2400 for a good cane" and that fifteen years ago the prices were "$100 to $400."

Other types of carving that are attributed to black folk artists include a wooden throne, which supposedly belonged to a black Presbyterian church in Victoria, Texas. Another throne and altar were made by James Hampton of Washington, D.C. Both of these pieces can be compared with thrones and altars made by the Tikar of Cameroon or the Chokwe of Zaire.

Carving often led to carpentry, and some slave narratives report that men would make furniture or spinning wheels out of leftover lumber their masters would give them. One particular furniture maker, Thomas Day, ended up becoming a master at his craft; he was quite well known and respected within his community and sold to politicians, educators, and society members. Pieces made by him seldom come on the market, but when they do, they are extremely expensive.

Contemporary artisan Asanti Owusu creates carved figures and scenes on a flat wooden surface. His work reflects his southern African-American background as well as what life is like in African villages. The blend is representative of his own heritage. Born in Ghana, Owusu lived there with his parents until they moved to Charleston, South Carolina, his father's hometown, in 1956. Owusu traveled back to Ghana in the early 1970s, studied there for four years, and then returned to the United States where he began carving. He sold his first piece three days later and continues to follow wherever his spirit leads him.

African natives (man and woman), carved wood, 1960s; excellent condition, **$250–300.** Courtesy of and photo by Bold Soul, Black Memorabilia Museum.

GRAVESTONES

Gravestones were embellished with animal figures and objects to drive away evil spirits. According to a plantation journal, slaves decorated the graves of the dead with the most recent possession used by the departed. Sometimes a crudely carved wooden figure (idol) was added to the grave and often a quilt would be thrown over the grave as if to warm the body buried there.

Archaeologists who have studied early slave graves report that pieces of glass, shards of dishes, and other objects of little or no value were buried with the bodies. The scientists noted that some African graves also contain crockery, bottles, and old cooking pots. This funeral practice is common in Zaire and Gabon as well as throughout the Caribbean. The objects are meant to keep the deceased happy so that his or her spirit rests and doesn't come back to haunt the living.

Grave markers were often concrete and made to imitate professionally-cut stones. Sometimes these markers have a piece of glass or pottery within the concrete. A piece of white paper is often included, following the Bakongo belief that dead people were white and that white is the color of death. Wooden markers were also used; sometimes one marker was put at the head and another at the foot of the grave. The head marker is sometimes cut in the vague shape of a person.

Some grave marker creators eventually began to sculpt. One such person was William Edmondson, who sculpted Adam and Eve, Jack Johnson (the boxer), and Eleanor Roosevelt. He began carving gravestones in the 1930s, long after the roots of African-American grave decorating were established. His grave markers served to continue the funerary rituals and to cement those customs. At first, Edmondson used simple geometric patterns to decorate his stones, but he was then influenced by the work done on other American gravestones (e.g., cherubs, portraits, and animals). Though he occasionally did portraits on stones, he usually decorated his pieces with

Man on donkey, possibly watercolor, unsigned. Courtesy of Rose Fontella; very good condition, $250–300. Photo by Donald Vogt.

doves and lambs. He continued to make gravestones until approximately 1947, generally working in Tennessee, particularly around the Nashville area.

Another gravestone sculptor was Eugene Warbourg of New Orleans. He was a sculptor who left his home to study ornamental gravestones in Europe and returned to share his knowledge with others in the business.

IRONWORK

Early southern blacksmiths were quite often African-American. They worked as gunsmiths, ornamental ironmakers, farriers, wheelwrights, and ax makers. In 1769, Bernard Moore of Todd's Warehouse, Virginia, had seventeen slaves working in his ironworks. Other southern cities had ironworks where African-Americans turned out most of their wares. Records state that

between 1710 and 1769 at least one-seventh of the African slaves working in Virginia came from the Senegambian area of Africa, thus the slave blacksmiths from that area would have been influenced by the wrought-iron sculpture created in the western Sudan. These blacksmiths still had strong memories of their homeland. In 1792, one group armed themselves with spears that had been made by a slave blacksmith. They were rebelling against their white Virginian owner.

It has often been argued by craftsmen and connoisseurs alike that the lacy grilles, lunettes, and balconies of New Orleans were not made by slaves. Or, the arguers admit, they *were* made by slaves, but those slaves had European supervisors because the work is too intricate and the wrought-iron is beautifully and sensitively created in the European fashion. Yet the argument for the black craftsman is handily won, because all skilled trades and crafts were monopolized by blacks slaves until after 1830, when new white immigrants pushed into areas that had been, for years, areas of black craftsmanship.

New Orleans was founded in 1718 by French settlers. Ceded to Spain in 1763, Louisiana was under Spanish rule until 1801. Records from 1802 indicate that forges employed Blacks to make the ironwork on most of the buildings there. The buildings that remain standing from that period reflect a Latin architectural influence that has a beauty and grace all its own. It takes little common sense to realize that the Spanish people who inhabited this area wanted to have their homes look like the ones they left behind.

All Louisiana plantations had blacksmiths who made tools, horseshoes, and other iron necessities, and the smiths were indeed black. Often a talented blacksmith would be sent to New Orleans to work, and his wages would be sent back to the plantation owner. Thus the argument that slaves did not do the ironwork in the South is lost.

They were the ironworkers and were more than likely taught by the homeowners to make the decorative accents in a Spanish style. Being sent to work in New Orleans often was to the slave's advantage. If the wrought-iron worker chose to buy his freedom, he need only put in some overtime to save toward the fee he would be charged for his freedom—usually $500.

The ironworker/blacksmith of that time was blessed with the luck that gave him unlimited opportunities to show off his talent. Everyone needed ironwork in some shape or form. The mansions of New Orleans with their marvelously intricate balconies, railings, courtyards, and architectural additives were a consequence of the fire of 1788, which burned the city down. Forced to start anew, the French and Spanish entrepreneurs of the city hired black artists to provide the

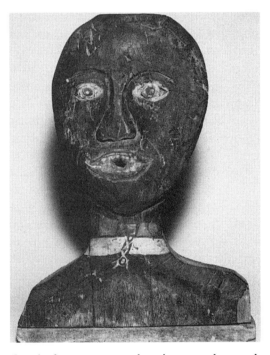

Carnival toss game head, carved wood, white incised eyes, round hole in mouth, early 1900s; 16½" tall × 11½" at widest point; excellent condition, **$800–1,000.** Courtesy of American Eye; photo by Bob Reno.

work needed to build grandiose houses to compete with the ones they had left behind in Europe.

The gentleman or his architect would show the slave blacksmith an engraving of a European house and ask the slave to produce something similar. The black artisan then went about the task of interpreting the curves of rococo styling or the clean, strong lines of the classic revival style into iron. Thus the designs found in the Vieux Carre section of New Orleans combine the grace and modeling of the Old World while ever so subtly giving us a glimpse of the black artisan's style.

Lacy grillework on southern houses was liberally used, and seemed to suit the area's warm climate. Though most buildings were privately owned, they housed businesses on the raised pavement beside the street, called a banquette. The living quarters were entered through a paved passageway, more than likely framed by wrought-iron gates. Once in the living quarters, the ironwork became even more ornamental. Galleries, sometimes running continuously from one building to the next down the entire street, were made to offer protection from the sun and showers. The lacy ironwork done by slaves in the South can also be found in older, well-established cities such as New York, Boston, Philadelphia, Baltimore, Georgetown, and Charlestown. A letter written by Mrs. Basil Hall in 1828 showed her delight with New Orleans's "old Continental aspect . . . [a] lively, French tone heard in the streets . . . houses with queerly-shaped high roofs and iron balconies" looking "deliciously cool for summer use."

The Ursuline convent, erected in 1727, houses the oldest examples of wrought-iron work in New Orleans. All the ironwork at the convent was wrought by black slaves.

One "top rank artist in iron" was owned by Christopher Werner, a Charleston metal worker. "Uncle Toby" Richardson's work was

"G.I. Moe," carved wood, painted black and brown, "Captain Charles Reilly, Jr., Room 1008, ASN 0-36-2462, Headquarters Service Command" signed on bottom in ink, 1940s, 8½" × 6"; excellent condition, **$2,000–3,000.** Courtesy of American Eye; photo by Bob Reno.

In 1857, it was noted that iron production in the United States was second only to that of England. The rapid growth of the iron industry was largely due to the popularity of the metal. It could be made into every conceivable design and shape—and at a relatively small cost.

Cast iron was used as columns on buildings, as porches, lawn furniture, doorstops, radiator covers, stoves, and match safes. It was used for so many things in the 1860s and 1870s that enthusiasm for cast iron was soon dubbed "ferromania" (see also Chapter 11).

Ironwork has been considered the first African-American art. It was a craft that ran a forty-year course, allowing the first unmistakable talents of the black artist to show through. And the talent *did* speak out, clearly and boldly. If the period of cast iron had lasted longer, we might have been rewarded with another century of wonders made by black blacksmiths. But progress persists, and the black ironworker ceased to provide decorative accents to graceful southern mansions years before the Civil War awarded slaves their freedom.

The trade is still being carried on today by people such as Philip Simmons, a blacksmith who learned his trade from an ex-slave. His teacher, Peter Simmons (no relation to Philip), died in 1954, passing on his knowledge to Philip. Simmons began to learn how to smith at the age of twelve, and after four years of training, he knew how to do just about everything involved with blacksmithing. His talents included repairing buggies, wagon wheels, and plows; making tools; doing farrier work; and repairing wrought-iron items. However, once Simmons began to use an electric arc welder and oxygen-acetylene torch, he also started working on cars and trucks and then began working on repairing ironwork on houses. He learned how to do decorative ironwork and soon built a reputation in Charleston. He is pass-

recognized by most as some of the finest created in the South. His famous "Sword Gate" is still swinging in Charleston, South Carolina.

Each blacksmith had his own favorite design. The names of the patterns—widow's mite, shell, diamond, tulip—are reminiscent of quilt patterns. Sometimes the delicately turned iron had to be heated as many as eight times in order to bend it into the required pattern. But, contrary to popular belief, most of a smithy's work was done on cold iron by file and saw. The typical image of the early ironworker has him standing in front of a roaring fire, with his sleeves rolled up, sweat oozing from every pore in his body, and muscles bulging with exertion. Yet in all actuality, heat was applied only in the preliminary stages of shaping the iron.

ing on his knowledge to two apprentices, as are other well-known blacksmiths in the South.

MUSICAL INSTRUMENTS

Slaves created musical instruments to help them to get through their monotonous workday. For example, women kept rhythm for rice-husking songs with the help of their thumping pestles. Some of these finely carved mortars may have also been used as drums, a common means for initiating a beat in African music. Some experts suggest that these early slave drums were also used as a means of communication, as were drums in their native African countries.

The earliest known slave drum was given to the British Museum in 1753 and might have been collected in Virginia in 1690. The drum is Akan in shape, size, and decoration, but it is made of American cedar and deerskin. It is obvious that the slave who made the drum had remembered his or her African culture.

Many times black collectibles depict a black person with a banjo. This instrument was originally derived from an African instrument that had a wooden frame, fretless neck, animal-skin head, and sinew strings. Slaves changed the wooden frame to a calabash, or gourd, and used their banjo to play music during dances on special occasions. According to John Michael Vlach's *By the Work of Their Hands,* even Thomas Jefferson admitted that the "banjar" was "brought hither from Africa."

Some Biographies of Black Folk and Outsider Artists

Steve Ashby was born in Fauquier County, Virginia, in 1907. After his wife died in 1962, he began making wood constructions, many of which had moving parts. He worked with a variety of materials and portrayed life as he knew it. He died in 1980.

Romare Bearden was born in 1932 and spent his childhood in the South and his adolescence in Pittsburgh and Harlem. This folk artist, who died in 1988, used his paintings to tell stories of African-American lives. As he got older, his paintings became smaller and more delicate. They investigated the everyday events of small town life, like taking baths or dressing. His works are often collages, mixed-media pieces that catch one's eye. Some reflected what he'd learned from studying Pompeiian frescoes, while others intimated what he thought of life.

As is often the case, Bearden's work became much more valuable upon his death and museums became much more interested in acquiring it. In 1992, the Toledo Museum of Art acquired his 1968 collage *Family Dinner.*

David Butler, born in 1898, works in metal and tin, making whirligigs, trains, biblical scenes, and animals. He did not begin his work until he was hurt in a work-related accident late in life. He then began devoting all his time to "snipped tin" or cut, folded, and painted metal sculptures.

Originally from Louisiana, he was one of eight children. His father, Edward, was a carpenter and his mother was a missionary. His work has been shown at the New Orleans Museum of Art (1976) and was included in the exhibit and book *Black Folk Art in America 1930–1980.*

Ulysses Davis was born in 1914. This woodcarver extraordinaire, one of eleven children, was born and raised in Georgia. Davis's finest accomplishment is thought to be his carved busts of forty presidents. Each bust is carved from mahogany to show the likeness of the man and is signed with the president's name and dates of office. Davis is also known for his freestanding carved figures. One of the Crucifixion, titled *Jesus on the Cross,* stands 40 inches high and is held by the Kiah Museum. His work was included in the exhibit Missing Pieces: Georgia Folk Art 1770–1976, which toured major U.S. museums in 1976. He was also included in the exhibit and book *Black Folk Art in America 1930–1980.* He is also the proprietor of Ulysses' Barber Shop.

William Dawson, born in 1901, is a sculptor who has shown his work at Chicago's Public Library, Phyllis Kind Gallery, Hyde Park Art

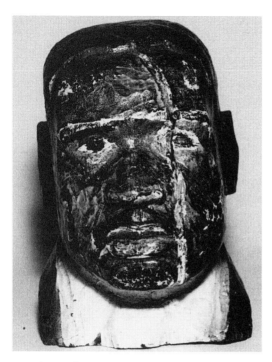

Martin Luther King Jr.'s head, carved wood, painted, done in Texas, crack of wood comes through right side of face, unsigned, 11½″ × 8″ × 7″; excellent condition, $400–600. Courtesy of American Eye; photo by Bob Reno.

Center, School of the Art Institute, and Museum of Contemporary Art. He was included in the exhibit and book *Black Folk Art in America 1930–1980.*

What makes his success so amazing is the fact that he did not begin sculpting until after his retirement in the mid-1960s. His subjects include religious stories (*Joseph in His Blue Robe*), current events (*Idi Amin Walking His Pet Pig*), and characters from folk tales. He has done totem poles and wood relief works. His figures have been carved and painted, and at times he adds varnish and glitter.

William Edmondson was born in 1870. Although it is known that Edmondson's parents were slaves, the precise circumstances of his birth are not known. He is one of the best known black American folk artists and was recognized as an American artist as early as 1937 when he exhibited at the Museum of Modern Art. He worked exclusively in limestone, sculpting fig-

ures and animals with chisels he fashioned himself. One of these figures, *Little Lady,* was sold by Sotheby's in New York in 1982 for $14,950.

His works have been shown at the Nashville Art Gallery (1941); Nashville Artist Guild (1951); Willard Gallery in New York (1964 and 1971); Tennessee Fine Arts Center at Cheekwood, Nashville (1964); Montclair, New Jersey, Art Museum (1975); and Tennessee State Museum in Nashville (1981). He was also included in the exhibit and book titled *Black Folk Art in America 1930–1980.*

James Hertle Sr., a ship's carver who worked in Dartmouth, Nova Scotia, was the subject of an important story in November 1993. It appears Hertle carved a 50-inch-high wooden black figure in a dancing pose. The piece emerged at a New York auction and several museum personnel quickly ascertained the carving to be of Canadian origin and done by Hertle. The sculpture was one of a group of three dancing figures done by the carver and identified in a Nova Scotia Museum publication, *The Woodcarvers of Nova Scotia* by George MacLaren.

By recognizing the piece as having Canadian heritage—especially because it had been a work of folk art that many had attributed to America (since jigs, such as the one in which the sculpture is posed, were common in the colonies)—we also are lucky to learn a little about the black population in the northeast portion of Canada. Black loyalists were welcome in Nova Scotia from the Revolution period forward. If they entered that province, they automatically became free persons. That promise of freedom continued to attract black Americans who fled there; in 1851, their population totaled approximately 28,000 in Nova Scotia alone.

Joshua Johnson, born in about 1765, was a self-taught ex-slave who was an active portrait painter from 1789 to 1825. He lived in Baltimore and in West Virginia and Virginia.

Some scholars have indicated that Johnson was a slave who was trained as a blacksmith. He advertised his services as a "self-taught painter" during the eighteenth century. We know him as the first black portraitist to win recognition in America. He was believed to have served his painting apprenticeship under the Peale family,

Untitled, by Inez Nathaniel Walker, Outsider Artist, colored pencil and crayon on paper, signed and dated 1977, 22″ × 28″; excellent condition, **$1,000–1,200.** Courtesy of American Eye; photo by Bob Reno.

or their contemporaries, and did most of his work between 1796 and 1824. His portraits were commissioned by Maryland's leading families when that occupation was inaccessible to most black Americans. He died in about 1830.

His works include portraits of Mrs. John Moale and her granddaughter, the McCormick family, the Westwood children, Edward and Sarah Rutter, Mary McCurdy and daughters, and Mrs. West and Mary Ann West. A limited number of black portraits have been attributed to Johnson. Because of the times during which he lived, he had to rely on white patronage. Blacks did not have the money or the social position to warrant portraits. Johnson's subjects often hold objects that identify their business or hobby. His style is evident in his brushwork as well as his treatment of clothing, hair, and accessories.

Johnson's work was first exhibited in 1948 at Baltimore's Peale Museum. His paintings were then given a long rest before being shown at the Metropolitan Museum in New York in 1961. Since that time, his works have been exhibited in most of the major museums of the United States.

Auction prices for Johnson's paintings have reached six figures and higher during the last

couple of years, causing a resurgence of interest in the artist. There are collections of his works in the Museum of Early Southern Decorative Arts in Winston-Salem, North Carolina, as well as the Frick Gallery and Metropolitan Museum of Art in New York. The Abby Aldrich Rockefeller Folk Art Center in Williamsburg, Virginia, was awarded a $28,000 grant several years ago to research Johnson's life—and the meaning of that life. Perhaps through their research we will come to know Johnson and his works more intimately than we do now.

Reginald Madison is a self-taught artist who started painting after finding a box of paints on the way to the beach when he was a boy. In 1992, his exhibit Twenty Years of Painting was shown at Spazi Fine Art in Housatonic, Massachusetts. He paints roughly textured, expressionist pieces, which he describes as "painting(s) first, then as narrative." Madison has painted throughout Europe and is inspired by Pollock, Dove, Hartley, and Roualt.

Sister Gertrude Morgan was born in 1900. Driven by a powerful belief in God and a determination to fulfill his purpose for her, Morgan

37

produced a number of drawings that depict biblical prophecies or her understanding of them. She was a painter, talented singer, and preacher who believed she was to become the bride of Christ. Her work reveals her exuberance through the use of bright and vibrant colors, and her writings and gospel lyrics are often repeated in her art.

Morgan's work was exhibited widely during her lifetime, at such places as the Borenstein Gallery, New Orleans (1970); Louisiana Arts and Science Center, Baton Rouge (1972); and New Orleans Jazz and Heritage Fair (1974). She has also been included in such exhibits as Dimensions in Black at the La Jolla, California, Museum of Contemporary Art (1970); Louisiana Folk Paintings at the Museum of American Folk Art, New York (1973); and Black Folk Art in America 1930–1980. She died in 1980.

Elijah Pierce, a prolific woodcarver born in 1892, began his life as the son of an ex-slave in northeastern Mississippi. Pierce did not follow in the footsteps of his father, a farmer; instead, he preferred the life of wanderer, barber, and preacher. He was married three times. His third wife joined him during the period of his life when he traveled throughout the Midwest giving sermons—he was awarded a preacher's license by the Mt. Zion Baptist Church—and used his carvings to illustrate those sermons. His work includes pieces that tell of his culture: folk and popular carved scenes with religious images, Masonic themes, sports figures, and cultural heroes. His work also reflects what Pierce read in newspapers and magazines and his takeoffs on songs and hymns.

During the early 1970s, his works were shown in solo exhibitions throughout the Midwest as well as in New York. In 1973, he was awarded first prize at the International Meeting of Naïve Art in Zagreb, Yugoslavia. He was included in the exhibit and book *Black Folk Art in America 1930–1980* and has been the subject of films and magazine articles. In 1993, to celebrate the 100th anniversary of Pierce's birth, a special exhibit—Elijah Pierce, Woodcarver—was held at the Columbus (Ohio) Museum of Art. The exhibit spotlighted 173 pieces of Pierce's work, including *Slavery Time* (1973), a carved and painted wood relief with glitter; *Monday Morning Gossip* (1934), mounted on a painted panel; *Obey God and Live* (1956), showing a family Bible reading at home; and many others.

William Matthew Prior was born in Bath, Maine, in 1806, the son of Sarah Bryant and Matthew Prior. He took up painting in 1816 after his father was lost at sea. Prior also supported himself by doing ornamental painting and japanning. He married Rosamund Clark Hamblen in Bath in 1828. Her brothers were also artists. In 1840, the Priors and Hamblens moved to Boston and began working as a team producing portraits. Between 1842 and 1844, they lived in East Boston. Prior was a Millerite and painted the Reverand Lawson and his wife, and Jess and Lucy Hartshorn of Maine in 1825. These portraits were on exhibit recently at the Old Sturbridge Village in Massachusetts. Hartshorn was a joiner and carpenter whose portrait focuses on his large, capable hands. It is said that Prior charged his customers a price in proportion with how difficult the paintings would be for him to create, with his most expensive being $10–25. He died in 1873.

James Henry "Son Ford" Thomas was born in 1926. He was one of the last Delta blues musicians and also sculpted in clay. He lived in Eden, Mississippi (Yazoo County), where he died in 1993. His work was part of the Corcoran exhibit of 1982.

Bill Traylor was born in 1854 as a slave in Alabama. Traylor remained on the farm where he was born until he was eighty-four, when he moved to Montgomery, where he held a job until rheumatism forced him to quit. A photograph of Traylor shows an elderly, bearded man whose eyes are forceful and piercing. He sits at a table with a pencil held in each hand, a drawing on the table in front of him. The hands are large, working hands. His figure and countenance do not appear to be that of a man close to ninety years old, yet Traylor did not begin to draw until 1939 at the age of eighty-five.

His drawings are geometric stick figures, usually showing people in action or at work. His work, like that of many folk artists, was taken from life. Traylor seemed surprised when people

Carnival toss game head, carved wood, red eyes and red exaggerated lips outlined in white, painted ears, from eastern United States, 1890s–nearly 1900s, 18½″ tall × 4½″ at widest part of head; **$800–1,000.** Courtesy of American Eye; photo by Bob Reno.

bought his drawings. He must have been even more shocked when his art was shown in Montgomery in 1940 at the New South art center and in 1941 at the Fieldston School in New York City. His work was also shown after his death in a New York gallery as well as in an exhibition circulated by the Southern Arts Federation in 1981–1982 titled Southern Works on Paper. Traylor's works and biography were included in the exhibit and book *Black Folk Art in America 1930–1980*. He died in 1947.

George White, born in 1903, was a man of many professions: an adventurer, lawman, and artist. His work *Emancipation House* is included in the pieces displayed at the National Museum of American Art of the Smithsonian Institution in Washington, D.C. His carved wood reliefs are detailed glimpses into American life. He painted his figures in oil and sometimes used a mixed-media construction, but whatever the formula, his sculptured scenes of his life in the South and as an outdoorsman in Texas were realistic down to the smallest detail.

Other carvings of his are housed in New York galleries, the Waco Creative Art Center in Texas—where he received a solo exhibition in 1975—as well as the Smithsonian. White was included in the exhibition and book *Black Folk Art in America 1930–1980*. He died in 1970.

39

PRICES FOR FOLK ART

Paintings

Brannan, Lou E., *The Scheme, The Trick,* and *The Escape,* all watercolor, sequential scenes showing girl eating watermelon, then boys come in and drench her, then Mama comes out and chases boys away, probably done in Southern Georgia/Florida area, 1900–1920; excellent condition, **$1,200–1,800 for the set.**

Burnside, Richard, *The Drunkard at the Party,* enamel paints and pieces of pine cones, Outsider Artist (born November 29, 1944, Baltimore, Maryland, lives in Pendleton, South Carolina, untrained artist represented in galleries); late 1989, 2′ × 4′; **$1,200–1,800.**

DeHaven, Gladys, oil, black family dancing and playing banjo in front of their log cabin, late 1800s; excellent condition, **$1,500–3,000.**

Doyle, Sam, *Le Bit,* Outsider Artist (born March 23, 1906, died September 24, 1985, lived on St. Helena Island, South Carolina, all his life, used house paint to create art on used tin roofing panels); 27″ × 35½″; excellent condition, **$8,000–12,000.**

Gilham, Sigsbee L., watercolor on board, cotton fields and black family in log cabin at side of road, original frame, Washington, D.C., 1948; excellent condition, **$1,500–2,000.**

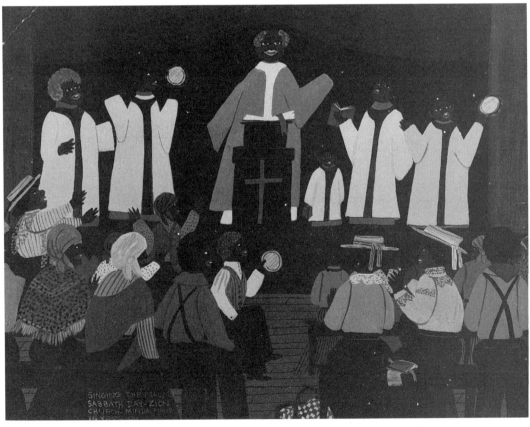

Oil painting, singed: "Singing the Psalms, Sabbath Day Zion Church, Minda Pires, 14 years, 1911," on academy board, 16″ × 19½″ framed, academy board is embossed: "Champlain Studios, Boston, New York"; excellent condition; $7,700–8,000. Courtesy of Frank and Barbara Pollack.

Hunter, Clementine, *Wash Day at Melrose Plantation,* large home across center, three black children in right foreground and a cooking pot and black woman holding container on head in left foreground, a "self-taught" work; excellent condition, **$1,900–2,200.**

Lange, Katherine (Kate) Louise Barboura, Outsider Artist, signed "Kate"

Aunt Emma Cooking Clothes; 18″ × 24″; excellent condition, **$400–600.**

Jackie Robinson, painted in March 1991; 24″ × 30″; excellent condition, **$500–700.**

Old Storyteller—Uncle Elmer, oil enamel on canvas, 1990; 24″ × 20″; excellent condition, **$400–500.**

Lucas, Charlie, Outsider Artist

Dinosaur, plywood board with acrylic paints, 1987; 12¼″ × 23¾″; excellent condition, **$800–1,000.**

Walking Away, acrylic on board, framed with green garden hose, 1988; 13″ × 19½″; excellent condition, **$800–1,000.**

Morgan, Sister Gertrude, *The Falling Stars of 1883—He Will Come for His Own,* ballpoint and acrylic, handwritten verse and small figures in upper right-hand corner, 1970s; excellent condition, **$3,000–4,000.**

Sims, Bernice, *Old Bradley Street,* oil, street shown is in Brewton, Alabama, Outsider Artist, 24″ × 48″; excellent condition, **$600–800.**

Staples, Marcus, Outsider Artist

Abe Lincoln as a Lawyer, oil on artist's board, handmade wooden cross-cornered frame, 1982; 12″ × 15″ (board); very good condition, **$300–400.**

Seminole Man, watercolor on paper, portrait of Seminole Indian, very colorful, mid-1980s; 12″ × 18″; very good condition, **$400–600.**

Sudduth, Jimmy Lee, Outsider Artist

Bith Al, house paint, mud, and white chalk, signed, fall 1990; 24″ × 24″; very good condition, **$400–600.**

Eagle, paint and pencil on plywood, white eagle painted on black background, white house, signed "Jim," fall 1989; 29″ × 24″; very good condition, **$800–1,200.**

Tolliver, Mose, Outside Artist

Snow Bus, 1982; 17¼″ × 20¾″; excellent condition, **$400–600.**

Texas Watermelon, 1982; 13″ × 20½″; excellent condition, **$300–400.**

The Wildest Man in the World—Pear Toe Charlie, 1981–1982; 20″ × 15″; excellent condition, **$500–700.**

Unknown artist

Black man trying to kiss white man, watercolor, primitive, signed "H.S.S.," ca. 1830; 2½″ × 3″; excellent condition, **$595–700.**

Children on Christmas Eve in front of fireplace, on wood, multicolored, primitive, ca. 1900; 12″ × 12″; excellent condition, **$200–300.**

Primitive, unsigned, young girl, ribbon in hair, ca. 1890; excellent condition, **$295–400.**

Woman with large plaid skirt, watercolor, original frame, 1840–1860; 3½″ × 4½″; excellent condition, **$675–850.**

Sculpture and Carvings

Fritzke, Fred J. (known only from signature), scene, relief carving on pine board, checker game with one player, an old man with hat, and a dog in foreground, signed on reverse side, early 20th century; 11″ × 14″; very good condition, **$400–450.**

Lyde, Bridget Ann (ninth grade student), man's head, composition, clay and wood, painted brown face, red neck, green eyes; 1937, 5″ × 4½″; excellent condition, **$50–75.**

Thomas, James Henry "Son Ford"

Bullfrog, unfired clay, painted green, white and brown, 6″ × 3¾″ high; excellent condition, **$300–500.**

Man's head (two), clay, foil, paint, and wax, real hair, teeth are corn kernels, painted clay eyes; large head is 8″ × 5″, small head is 6″ × 4″; excellent condition, **small: $600–800; large: $750–1,000.**

George Washington bust, unfired clay, painted white and pink; 6½″ × 7″; excellent condition, **$1,000–1,200.**

Chicken, paper and cardboard, painted red, black, yellow, and white, primitive, free-standing, 1931; 12″ × 12″; near mint condition, **$100–150.**

Crows, carved wood, one is marked "Amos," the other "Andy"; 14½″ × 16½″ high; excellent condition, **$150–250 for the pair.**

Dancing figure, pine, contemporary stand, articulated legs and feet, moving arms, legs painted yellow, features painted white, body painted green and soft yellow; 22″ × 5″ × 4½″; excellent condition, **$300–500.**

Man's head, carved burl wood, painted eyes and lips, piece of French-Canadian newspaper inside, early 1900s, 9½″ × 5″; excellent condition, $1,200–1,500. Courtesy of American Eye; photo by Bob Reno.

Unknown artist

African native boy with drum, mahogany or cherry, carved and chiseled, contemporary; approximately 3′ tall; **$65–80.**

African native man, polychrome pottery, 21¼″; excellent condition, **$600–750.**

Articulated figure, pine, painted body (originally had clothes where pine is unpainted), red shoes, 21½″ × 4″; excellent condition, $300–500. Courtesy of American Eye; photo by Bob Reno.

42

Figure, boy holding watermelon, carved wood, painted; 5½″; excellent condition, $75–125.

Mammy, redware, buxom mammy, southern "offhand" piece, extremely heavy, last quarter 19th century; 1″ thick, excellent condition, **$1,200–1,800.**

Man's head, pottery, possibly made from cinders or black clay, old black man with beard, partly bald, 5″; excellent condition, **$150–300.**

Woman, carved pine, shown standing, black painted body with necklace, felt hat with feathers, gold lamé belt, painted facial features, 1930s–1950s; excellent condition, **$200–250.**

Woman's head, mahogany, with head scarf, possibly from the Caribbean (when purchased, it was said the piece was from North

Carolina); 8″ high × 5½″; excellent condition, **$200–300.**

Woman wearing apron, pressed wood, hands on hips, ca. 1935; 6″; excellent condition, **$75–100.**

Woman with basket on head, carved wood, painted, done by homeless black woman in Atlanta, Georgia, 1980s; 7¾″; excellent condition, **$25–40.**

Useful Items (see also Chapter 11)

Butler smoking stand (black man in butler's uniform, sometimes holding ashtray)

Wood

Hand carved, dressed as a porter, upper torso with working music box, outstretched arms hold removable copper ashtray, 20th century; 35″; excellent condition, **$2,500–3,500.**

Hand carved, wavy hair and painted suit, not the usual type; 3½′ tall; excellent condition, **$395–500.**

Handmade, very exaggerated features, alligatored orange/red over gray jacket, hat, stripe down pants and shoes, 1925–1935; 36″; excellent condition, **$300–400.**

Long skinny legs, holds ashtray, blue suit with black shoes, 1920s; 40″; excellent condition, **$350–450.**

Metal, painted, holding ashtray, excellent condition, **$210–260.**

Carnival toss game head

Head only, used to be attached to a barrel and would pop up, painted face, red lips, probably from Baltimore; 17½″ × 8¾″; nose is broken off but otherwise in excellent condition, **$1,000–1,200.**

Wood, painted yellow, red, black, blue, and white; hole in mouth where penny was tossed, rare; 26″ diameter; excellent condition, **$500–600.**

Cigar store figure, wood, black man, original pants, blue jacket, red vest, Maine, purchased from Frank Witson of Baltimore, Maryland; early 20th century, 30″ high × 12″ wide; excellent condition, **$4,000–7,000.**

Mask, cotton, hand sewn, sewn-on ears, red-and-white painted mouth, rim of eyes painted red with some white, yellow above eye, 1920s–1930s; excellent condition, $200–300. Courtesy of American Eye; photo by Bob Reno.

Man and woman (mammy and butler), carved pine, painted red, yellow, black, and white, 1940s–1960s, 10″ man, 9½″ woman; excellent condition, $75–125 for the pair. Courtesy of American Eye; photo by Bob Reno.

Cribbage board, wood, woman's head carved at top, heart carved in bottom, possibly contemporary (or reproduction); 5½″ wide × 28½″; excellent condition, **$300–400.**

Jar, earthenware, alkaline glaze, signed "Dave the Slave," deep green, artisan was a slave on a South Carolina plantation in 1865; excellent condition, **$25,000–29,000.**

Measuring stick, hickory, bar slides up and down pole with carved measuring lines, found in a tunnel beneath the Lankford House in Somerset, Maryland, reportedly used by the abolitionist Patty Cannon, who smuggled slaves; 81½″ × 15″ × 11″ base; excellent condition, **$675–975.**

Pitcher, redware, black man's head, hand formed, decorated with red-brown, manganese and green glazes, partial inscription "Jeffrey" on base (middle initial and last name beneath glaze), discovered in the southeastern United States, very rare, mid-19th century; 12¾″ high; some stress cracking but no restoration, good glaze and color, very good condition, **$2,800–3,800.**

Sign

Advertises January 14th minstrel show, watercolor on paper, colorful, 1920s–1930s; approximately 36″ tall × 20″ wide; excellent condition, **$1,500–2,500.**

Advertises Minstrel Medicine Show, large two-sided figure of man dancing and strumming banjo, colorfully painted, peppermint striped pants and shirt, green jacket and socks, outdoor sign, found in western South Dakota barn, 1900–1910; 55″ to top of head, 60½″ to neck of banjo; excellent condition, **$3,000–5,000.**

"Colored," wood, black hand at right end, carved fingers, hand painted, found on Eastern shore of Maryland/Virginia/Delaware (Chesapeake Bay area), early 19th century,

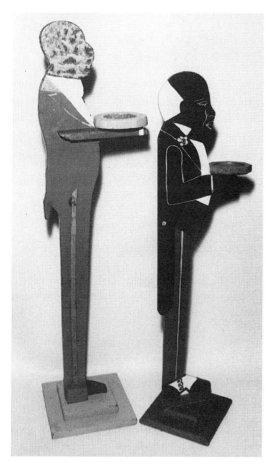

Butler stands, painted wood; *left:* mustard yellow, 41", *right:* brown face, black jacket, red cummerbund, blue pants, and white and black spatted shoes, 36"; excellent condition, **$150–200 each.** Courtesy of American Eye; photo by Bob Reno.

Man's head, carved wood, wearing bandage, possibly used as apothecary "sign" because there appears to be a pill on the man's tongue; very good condition, **$500–750.**

37½" long (to fingers) × 5" high; excellent condition, **$1,000–1,500.**

Tray, inscribed by a black servant in memory of her slave parents, Tiffany; 18" × 12¾"; fair to good condition, **$3,250–3,750.**

Ventriloquist's dummy, moveable lower lip, paper label inside body box, wearing old clothing which appears original along with two left shoes, 1860–1870, used on showboat on Cumberland River, later used in Skeets Mayo's Blackface Minstrel Show in Nashville, purchased by James H. Young in 1943 from Mayo's sister; excellent condition, **$7,500–10,000.**

Violin, mahogany, head of black woman carved on neck; very good condition, **$1,800–3,000.**

Whirligig, includes windmill and mammy, scrubbing clothes; 10¾"; excellent condition, **$450–600.**

Miscellaneous

Video cassette, *Made in Mississippi,* portraits of Black folk artists and their works, James "Son Ford" Thomas (clay sculpture), Amanda and Mary Gordon (quilts), Othar Turner (cane fifes), Luster Willis (painting and sculpted canes), and Leon Clark (white oak baskets), color; 20 minutes; new, **$40.**

45

CHAPTER THREE

Photographica

Photography was developed over a period of centuries, beginning with Leonardo da Vinci's description of the *camera obscura.* In 1822, Nicephore Niepce, a Frenchman, developed the first fixing agent, which allowed permanent photographs to be produced. The daguerreotype process was fully developed by 1839, but roll film, developed by George Eastman, was not used until 1884, and the first Kodak camera did not come on the market until 1888.

By the 1850s, photography in the United States became a widely practiced craft that rivaled painting. Portraits of famous people were done as daguerreotypes instead of as oil paintings. Photographs were dubbed "portraits for the poor."

Collecting old photographs of black Americans—or photographs taken by black American photographers—can be a fascinating and time-consuming hobby. Although photographs were once discarded from old frames so that the frames would be more salable, there are now enough collectors to make the photographs themselves valuable.

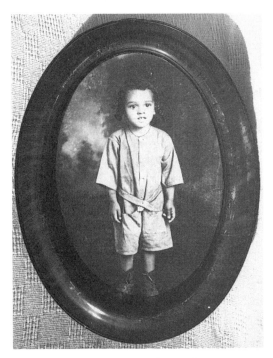

Photograph, young girl, under concave glass, framed, about 1920s; excellent condition, **$150–200.** Courtesy of and photo by Bold Soul, Black Memorabilia Museum.

Types of Photographs to Collect

DAGUERREOTYPES

Invented by Frenchman L. J. M. Daguerre, daguerreotypes were the first practical photographs. Used from 1839 to 1855, daguerreotypes usually fit into specially made cases. The most commonly found size is 2½ by 3¼ inches.

The first step in making a daguerreotype consisted of polishing a copper- and silver-plated sheet. Then the sheet was made light sensitive by exposing it to iodine vapors in an iodizing box. After the sheet was exposed in a camera, the image would be formed by the effect of light, then developed by vapor of mercury heated over a spirit lamp. The mercury would attach itself to certain parts of silver iodide and form a visible image. The image was then fixed with a strong salt solution, which dissolved away the remaining light-sensitive silver salts. The silver coating of the daguerrotype base created a mirrorlike surface.

AMBROTYPES

Used between 1852 and 1870, ambrotypes were often called collodion positives. First, a sheet of glass was coated with nitrocellulose dissolved in ether, and then alcohol would be sensitized with potassium iodide and silver nitrate. Then the plate was exposed and developed before the emulsion dried. These glass plates could be made in several different sizes and the cases for plates were similar to those used for daguerreotypes.

TINTYPES

Made from 1854 to 1900, tintypes are also called ferrotypes or melainotypes. They were used by American traveling photographers, who took portraits of civilians, Civil War soldiers, and landscapes. This process was cheap, sturdy, and easily produced. A sheet of black japanned iron was coated with an emulsion to produce a direct positive image. The prints were then mounted under glass in decorative leather cases. Tintypes varied in size from 2½ by 3½ inches to ½ inch square.

Stereo card, man with banjo; very good condition, **$50–75.** Courtesy of Jim Bollman, The Music Emporium; photo by Donald Vogt.

OTHER TYPES OF PRINTS

Salt print or salted paper print was used between 1839 and 1860 and was often toned in sepia, gold, platinum, or brown. The *albumen print* was invented by Louis-Desire Blanguart-Evrard in 1850. It was used until the end of the century (most albumen prints are thin and thus mounted on board or in albums). The *carte de visite,* patented in 1854 in France and introduced in 1859 to America, was used as a calling card extensively throughout the Civil War.

Cabinet cards were used after 1866; they measure 4½ by 6½ inches and often have the photographer's name and address imprinted on them. *Stereograph* was used between 1859 and 1890 in the United States; the prints were mounted on 3 by 7-inch cards. *Aristotype* was used between 1818 and approximately 1910. *Platinum print,* also called platinotype, was patented in England in 1873 and used until approximately 1937. *Postcards* have been made since 1880 (see Chapter 8 for more information).

Sepia tone photograph, four well-dressed men wearing bowlers; very good condition, **$10–25.** Courtesy of American Eye; photo by Bob Reno.

Some Biographies of Photographers

The first *Black Photographers' Annual* appeared in 1973. Information about black photographers working before that time is scanty and difficult to find, making the list that follows necessarily incomplete.

James Latimer Allen, born in 1907, began taking photographs while still in grade school. He worked throughout the Harlem Renaissance and photographed such celebrities as Countee Cullen, Langston Hughes, and Arthur Schomburg.

Allen's commercial photography was published regularly and he also exhibited at the Carnegie Institute, the National Gallery of Art, and the Texas Centennial Exposition, among others. His work is held by the Library of Congress, Moorland-Spingarn Research Center (Washington, D.C.), and Yale University. He died in 1977.

James Presley Ball, born in 1825, worked in Ohio, Montana, and Washington. He was taught photography by another black photographer, John B. Bailey of Boston. Ball owned a daguerrean gallery in Cincinnati in 1845, then left the gallery to become an itinerant photographer. He traveled throughout Pennsylvania and Virginia before heading back to Cincinnati to open another gallery to show the photographs he had taken on his travels. He called the exhibit Negro Life on the Ohio, Susquehanna and Mississippi Rivers.

Ball's subjects included prominent people of Cincinnati and Helena, street scenes, lynchings, crowds, and funerals. He earned quite a remarkable reputation during his lifetime and has been included in many books of photography. Collections of his work are owned by the Schomburg Center for Research in Black Culture in New York City, the Cincinnati Public Library, and the Montana Historical Society in Helena. He died in 1905.

Cornelius M. Battey, born in Augusta, Georgia, in 1873, spent most of his life in the North and owned studios in Cleveland and New York City. By 1916, Battey had moved to Tuskegee, Alabama, where he eventually became head of the photograph division of the Tuskegee Institute. He specialized in portraits, taking shots of famous black leaders and entertainers. He also did pictorial photographs and photojournalist studies at the Tuskegee Institute. Collections of his work are held by the Library of Congress and the Schomburg Center for Research in Black Culture in New York City.

Mathew B. Brady, born in 1823, was America's foremost nineteenth-century white photographer. His portraits of politicians and views of the Civil War are represented in textbooks all over the world. Brady also photographed every president from John Quincy Adams to William McKinley. In 1861, when the Civil War broke out, Brady decided to make a complete pictorial record of the war. He hired a staff of twenty photographers and dispatched them throughout the war zones. Brady personally photographed the battles at Bull Run, Antietam, and Gettysburg as well as Robert E. Lee's surrender at Appomattox. He and his (white) staff are responsible for the majority of photographs taken of black Americans during the Civil War period. In 1873, Brady was forced into bankruptcy, and the War Department later bought his plates for $2,840 at public auction. He died alone, in 1896, in a hospital charity ward.

Bruce Davidson, born in 1933, studied at the Rochester Institute of Technology and at Yale. His work is candid; as he described it, "I look at people with my camera, but as much to find out what's inside me—to reflect my own emotional state, the struggles, the states of consciousness, and to discover who the person was who took the picture."

Davidson, a member of the Magnum photo agency since 1958, did photos for such magazines as *Life, Vogue,* and *Esquire.* During the 1970s, he ventured into filmmaking and later wrote the screenplay for Isaac Bashevis Singer's *Enemies: A Love Story.* His photo essay *Black Americans* was done during the years 1962–1965. Collections of Davidson's work are held by the Chicago Museum of Art, Harvard University, Metropolitan Museum of Art, Smithsonian Institution, and Yale University, among other museums.

" Uncle Gabriel,"
52 years old.

" Aunt " Hennie,
90 years old.

" Uncle " Lev,
77 years old.

" Uncle " Fielding,
50 years old.

" Uncle " Willis,
63 years old.

" Uncle " Edmond,
80 years old.

Former slaves of Major Willis Menefee, who attended remarkable reunion
held at old Menefee Homestead in Palmetto.

Black-and-white photograph, from a magazine, ex-slaves who attended a reunion at Menefee Homestead in Palmetto; very good condition, $25–50. Courtesy of Rose Fontanella; photo by Donald Vogt.

Roy DeCarava was the first black photographer to be awarded a Guggenheim scholarship. He used the money to pay for supplies so he could photograph residents of Harlem. Born in New York in 1919, DeCarava studied art at Cooper Union in New York City, the Work Progress Administration's Harlem Art Center, and the George Washington Carver Art School. He began photographing Harlem, its people, and its musicians in the 1940s. He also worked as a *Sports Illustrated* photographer and taught at Hunter College in New York. Examples of his work are held in collections throughout the United States, including Andover Art Gallery/Phillips Academy (in Massachusetts), Belafonte Enter-

prises, Inc. (in California), the Corcoran Gallery of Art (in Washington, D.C.), and the Museum of Modern Art (in New York).

Robert Scott Duncanson was active during the middle to late 1800s and was listed as a daguerreotype artist in the 1851–1852 Cincinnati Art Directory. He often used his camera to capture landscapes, which he would later paint. His daguerreotype *View of Cincinnati, Ohio, from Covington, Kentucky* remains one of the few city scenes of life in early nineteenth-century America. (See also Chapter 1.)

James Conway Farley, born the son of slaves in 1854, began working as a phototechnician in

Black-and-white photograph, boy in Cub Scout uniform; excellent condition, $25–50. Courtesy of Rose Fontanella; photo by Donald Vogt.

Richmond, Virginia, in 1872. He began taking photos in 1875 and became the sole photographer for the G. W. Davis Photographic Gallery. His first exhibit was held in 1884 at the Colored Industrial Fair in Richmond. A decade later, he opened his own studio and specialized in portraits of individuals and groups which he then printed on playing cards. Collections of his work are owned by the Valentine Museum in Richmond, Virginia, and the Virginia Historical Society.

Roland Freeman, considered the only black photographer to commit his life to chronicling life in the South through his photographs, started working in the 1960s. He grew up on a Maryland tobacco farm and attended school in Baltimore. The 1960s social movements and the work of Gordon Parks influenced him. Freeman became a freelance photographer, working for

publications all over the world, including *Time, Newsweek, Essence,* and *National Geographic.* He worked for the Smithsonian Institution, becoming a field research photographer in folklore. His work has been exhibited throughout the world, and he has also written articles and books. His finest venture is the research project While There Is Still Time, in conjunction with the Center for the Study of Southern Culture and Diogenes Editions, Inc. The forty-five sets of twelve signed and numbered prints are priced at $5,000 per portfolio plus shipping (as of winter, 1993).

King Daniel Ganaway worked in Chicago from 1914 through the 1930s, shooting the Chicago River, family life, and agricultural workers. Born in 1883, Ganaway did not start his work in photography until late in his life. He won first prize in the John Wanamaker Annual Exhibition of photographs in 1918 and eventually became a photographer at the Chicago newspaper *The Bee.* Collections of his work are held by the Library of Congress and the National Archive and Records Service at the Harmon Foundation Collection in Washington, D.C.

The Goodridge Brothers (Glenalvin, Wallace, and William) were successful photographers and ambrotypists who worked in Pennsylvania and Michigan throughout the 1850s and 1880s. Glenalvin won a prize for his ambrotypes at the York County Fair in 1863, and the brothers opened their first studio in East Saginaw, Michigan, in 1867. After fire destroyed that studio, Wallace and William built another in 1872 (Glenalvin seems to have dropped out of sight). They began taking photographs at night as well as portraits and landscape views of the Saginaw Valley. The brothers used the carte de visite, cabinet cards, and stereograph processes. Collections of their work are held by the New York Public Library; the Clarke Historical Library in Mt. Pleasant, Michigan; the Saginaw County Historical Society Museum; and the *Saginaw News.*

Danny Lyon was born in 1942 and received his bachelor's degree from the University of Chicago in 1963. He joined the Student Non-Violent Coordinating Committee (SNCC) in 1963 and began to document the civil rights movement through photography. The photographs of that era were used in his *The Movement.* Lyon is a controversial photographer, with a number of unusual credits, including photographs he took while a motorcycle club member. He has been active in cinema since 1960 and has directed at least four films. Collections of his work are held by museums such as the Houston International Photography Museum and the Modern Art Museum in New York.

Jules Lyon, from Louisiana, introduced the daguerreotype to the people of New Orleans. He took photographs of the St. Louis Hotel, the cathedral, the levee, and other public buildings and places. His daguerreotypes were appreciated as being precise artistic reproductions of the original objects. Born in 1913 in Paris, Lyon was only twenty-six when he made his debut in New Orleans; but by then he had already exhibited in the Paris Salon (in 1831). Following his desire to make the daguerreotype a new form of art, Lyon studied with Louis Jacques Mande Daguerre in Paris for about a year. When he returned to New Orleans, in 1843, he moved to a larger studio. Once again, the New Orleans residents praised him as an artist, lithographer, and photographer. In 1846, he began a series of political portraits for the *New Orleans Bee,* but was unable to complete the project because the owner of the paper died. Lyon's best work is said to be his *Portrait of John J. Audubon,* the well-known naturalist and illustrator. Lyon spent the balance of his career between Paris and New Orleans. He died in 1866.

Gordon Parks, one of the best known contemporary black photographers, was born in Kansas City in 1912. He started learning about photography in 1937 and was hired by the Farm Security Administration. He worked as a correspondent during World War II and for the Standard Oil Company after the war. *Life* hired him as a staff photographer in 1949, during which time he covered stories of the Black Muslims as well as life in black neighborhoods until 1972. His other talents include filmmaking, writing, painting, and composing. Parks's works are held at the Library of Congress, *Life* magazine offices, and the Schomburg Center for Research in Black Culture (in New York City).

Black-and-white photograph, two men (one is black) with prize catfish, marked "on the beach of Gulf of Mexico 60 miles from Tallohasse, Florida—weight 85 pounds"; 5" × 7"; excellent condition, $50–75. Courtesy of American Eye; photo by Bob Reno.

Harry (Henry) Shepherd worked in St. Paul, Minnesota, during the 1880s, opening his first portrait gallery in 1887. He was very successful and popular. He won a gold medal for his work at the 1891 Minnesota State Fair and was one of the few black members of the National Photographers Association of America at the turn of the century. Shepherd primarily photographed portraits and scenes of the Tuskegee Institute. Collections of his work are held by the Library of Congress and the Minnesota Historical Society.

Addison N. Scurlock, born in Fayetteville, North Carolina, in 1883, became a photographer early in the 1900s. He apprenticed at the Rice Studios in Washington, D.C., and opened his first studio in that city in 1911. He operated the studio until he died in 1964, and was assisted by his wife and two sons. Scurlock photographed businessmen, artists, writers, politicians, and celebrities, acting as official photographer for Howard University. He was published by the *Messenger, Opportunity,* and *Crisis* magazines. In 1907, he won the Gold Medal for Excellence at the Jamestown Exposition. His work is held by the Corcoran Gallery of Art (in Washington, D.C.), the Library of Congress, the Moorland-Spingarn Research Center at Howard University, and the Schomburg Center for Research in Black Culture (in New York City).

James Van Der Zee was born in 1886 in New York City, where his mother and father worked as Ulysses S. Grant's maid and butler. James was raised in Lenox, Massachusetts. In 1900, he won a camera outfit and embarked on a career in photography. He opened his first studio in Harlem in 1916 and photographed weddings, funerals, and other social occasions in that area for more than fifty years. Van Der Zee was the largest contributor to a photography exhibit called Harlem on My Mind, held at the Metropolitan Museum of Art in New York in 1969. He died in 1983.

Van Der Zee prints are expensive when they can be bought at auction and are currently enjoying a surge in interest. Collections of his work can be seen at the Metropolitan Museum in New York and in museums in New Orleans and San Francisco.

Augustus Washington, born in Trenton, New Jersey, in 1820, was well educated and became an activist against slavery and for educating Blacks. He opened a daguerrean studio in 1843 in Hartford, Connecticut, so that he could finance his education. In 1847, he opened another daguerrean studio in the same city, but left it the next year so that he could travel—in 1850, he returned to his studio. He migrated to Liberia in 1854 to teach. While there, he took photos, farmed, and bought a store. Collections of his work are owned by the Schomburg Center for Research in Black Culture in New York City and the Connecticut Historical Society. It is not known when he died.

PRICES FOR PHOTOGRAPHICA

Most of the photographs in this price list are not by well-known photographers because such prints are rare and often found only in museum collections. (People depicted are black unless otherwise noted.)

Ambrotype, black child with white doll, case, sixth plate; excellent condition, **$325–375.**

Cabinet photograph, Victorian black ladies, pair, 1800s; very good condition, **$85–100 for the pair.**

Carte de visite

Boy with Civil War cap, ca. 1875; excellent condition, **$40–50.**

Children, three mulatto slave children of New Orleans named Rebecca, Rosa, and Charley, liberated by General Banks, revenue stamp on back, dated 1863; very good condition, **$18–28.**

Man dressed in rags, patch over left eye, umbrella in left hand, fan in right hand; excellent condition, **$40–50.**

Daguerreotype, baby; excellent condition, **$150–200.**

Daguerreotype case, gutta-percha

Man, oval; excellent condition, **$55–75.**

Victorian girl; excellent condition, **$85–100.**

Glass plate, picking cotton on Mississippi plantation; excellent condition, **$30–45.**

Glass slides, African natives, three views, about 1920; excellent condition, **$30–35.**

Imperial carte, New Year's greeting, mammy with black baby on lap, 1891; excellent condition, **$150–175.**

Magic lantern slide

"The Little Nigger Boys," portion of illustrated story on each one, color, complete; excellent condition, **$275–375 for the set.**

Two boxers in dress clothes and top hats; excellent condition, **$45–55.**

Photo card, "Better Known as the Six Babb Brothers," original radio promotion, black and white, 1930s; 9″ × 11″; excellent condition, **$35–50.**

Photograph

Black-and-white print

The African and His Natural Protector, white man giving money to a black man in a Civil War uniform, matted, ca. 1874; 5″ × 7″; near mint condition, **$50–75.**

Boy and what appears to be his prize cow, matted; excellent condition, **$12–15.**

Citizens in Embryo, men reclining on grain bags, signed "Winnam Arnold S.C.," matted, ca. 1875; 5″ × 7″; near mint condition, **$50–75.**

Colgate baseball team, one black player in last row, written on back "from Oriskany Falls, New York," framed, 1918; 11½″ × 13½″; excellent condition, **$100–125.**

Group of people and horse-drawn wagon in front of store, marked "L.W. Haupt's Store, Matson, N.C."; 8″ × 10″; excellent condition, **$5–8.**

Man driving horse-drawn wagon; excellent condition, **$4–6.**

Man in white suit and hat holding horse in front of plow; **$2–5.**

Mug shots of prisoners, on back each man and his crime are described; late 1800s–early 1900s, group of four; excellent condition, **$50–75 each.**

NAACP Wartime Conference, July 12–14, 1944; excellent condition, **$200–275.**

Now I'se got some money I'se comin round, black cakewalk, art supplement, November 19, 1899; 14″ × 10″; near mint condition, **$75–125.**

The Rising Generation, children behind a fence, matte, ca. 1875; 5″ × 7″; near mint condition, **$50–75.**

Three white men surrounding old black man holding slice of watermelon to his mouth, 1940s–1950s; 5″ × 7″; excellent condition, **$50–75.**

Two children eating watermelon, matted, framed, 1940s; 4″ × 6″ photo; excellent condition, **$20–40.**

Two young girls in 1940s; 2¾″ × 3¾″; good condition, **$1–5.**

Women making baskets, signed "Margaret Bourne"; excellent condition, **$425–500.**

Sepia tone

Bellvue All-Stars baseball team, gloves and catcher's mask seem to be from 1920s, framed; 18½″ × 16½″; excellent condition, **$600–800.**

Large group of white men and one white child sitting on stairs to large porch, all holding watermelon slices, three black servants standing at top of stairs, Charleston, South Carolina, early 1900s; excellent condition, **$150–200.**

Man holding dog with crowd in background, possibly the beginning of a dog fight, 11-10-27, No. 8005, 1930s–1940s; excellent condition, **$30–40.**

Minstrel troupe on elaborate stage, framed without glass, 1890s; 20″ × 10″; near mint condition, **$100–150.**

Statesville (North Carolina) Flour Mill workers, some of the workers are black, early 1900s, 9½″ × 7½″; excellent condition, **$100–125.**

World War I soldier, in oval, framed by flag and U.S. memorabilia, convex glass frame; approximately 24″; excellent condition, **$350–400.**

Stereo card

Boy eating watermelon, set of four; excellent condition, **$35–50 for the set.**

"Cotton is King," shows children sitting on pile of cotton, color; **$5–12.**

"15th Amendment bringing his crop to town;" excellent condition, **$20–30.**

"Golly! Dis am cheaper dan twofers"; excellent condition, **$20–30.**

"Happy Hours," girl picking boy's head; excellent condition, **$20–30.**

"Loading a Mississippi Steamer in New Orleans, La.," dated 1925; excellent condition, **$5–12.**

"Ma Own Honey," man and woman on a swing; excellent condition, **$6–10.**

"Native Cane Grinders in Sunny Florida," full color; excellent condition, **$20–25.**

"The New South," by Underwood, pale cream mount frames family that includes older man, man with wife and infant, two young boys, and four other youths in the room, musket hangs on wall; **$45–85.**

Old man in cart pulled by oxen; excellent condition, **$25–35.**

"Six pickers in cotton field," by James M. Davis, 1892; excellent condition, **$25–30.**

Tintype

Baby in crib, full plate; excellent condition, **$125–140.**

Black nurse with two white children; excellent condition, **$65–70.**

Couple, sepia; excellent condition, **$35–50.**

Girl, very young, plaid dress; $3'' \times 3\frac{1}{2}''$; excellent condition, **$75–95.**

Mammy with white child, identified as Jenny Jolly and John Carhart; excellent condition, **$75–90.**

Man; $6\frac{1}{2}'' \times 8\frac{1}{2}''$; excellent condition, **$45–55.**

Man, well-dressed, in a jaunty pose, looks to be in early 20s, wearing suit with watch chain; very good condition, **$100–130.**

CHAPTER FOUR

Books

There are many categories of books by and about black Americans, so if you decide to collect books, you'll probably want to specialize. You can limit your collection to published works by black authors or extend your area of interest to include works written about black Americans or black people in general. The latter category includes both black writers and writers of other ethnic backgrounds. You can narrow your scope by collecting, for example, only children's books or only first editions. You can confine your search to only books written by contemporary black authors or to those authors who wrote autobiographies or slave narratives. Whatever you intend to collect, your first and most important step is to familiarize yourself with the biographies of the authors you are interested in and to get a listing of their works.

When you collect books by or about black Americans, you can expect to become frustrated by the lack of information about the author and/or the subject. Research departments in libraries can be of great assistance (university libraries, I've found, are usually better than public libraries).

You can also expect prices on books by and about black Americans to shoot up in value by more than double. Book collectors have long been aware of the value of books by black writers. These books are often more valuable because they were not published in quantity; many books by black Americans were published in only one edition.

Children's Books

Children's illustrated books, such as *Little Black Sambo,* and adaptations of books for children, such as *Uncle Tom's Cabin,* when found in mint condition can be quite expensive. For some time now, collectors of childhood items have known the value of illustrated children's books that feature Blacks as their main characters. If you find a book that was printed in the mid-1800s to early 1900s, you can count on having a treasure. After that time, books were printed on lower-quality paper, and the illustrations were often not quite as bright or as intricately drawn.

Characters in black children's books sometimes underwent many changes during

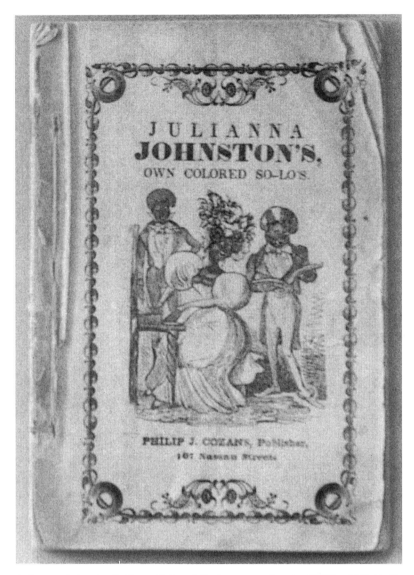

Julianna Johnston's Own Colored So-Los, songbook, 1860s; 2½" × 4"; good condition (no cover) **$25–45. Collection of Dawn and Bob Reno; photo by Bob Reno.**

their literary lives. For example, *Little Black Sambo* was published many times by many different companies, and the quality of each edition is unique. The story depicted a small black boy in a derogatory way. Originally, Sambo was East Indian, but he was at some point changed into a black boy who wore ragged clothes. The story used defaming ter-

minology. If you think of the underlying messages of such stories, you won't be surprised that many children who grew up reading such bedtime tales became prejudiced adults.

Early children's books that focused on black subjects or characters often presented a bigoted point of view. Today's books present

"Mose let out a yell which woke up de woods till de hills hollered it back." *Page 126.*

Boy Holidays in the Louisiana Wilds, illustration by Harold Coe; very good condition, **$15–25.** Courtesy of Valerie Bertrand Collection; photo by Donald Vogt.

a more positive portrait of African-American children while showing a truthful picture of their heritage. Books about slave life on the plantation, about famous African-Americans, and about African holidays are readily available. Contemporary publishers actively seek out black stories, writers, and illustrators.

Collectors would be wise to put away new copies of just-published black books as a "bank account" for their children.

Slave Writings

Poignant and provocative, slave narratives are a popular starting point for studying black American prose. They make up the foundation of the tradition of black American writing. Writers such as Marion Wilson Starling, Charles H. Nichols, Richard Wright, Ralph Ellison, and James Baldwin have written effectively on the subject of the slave narrative.

The first known slave narrative appeared in Boston in 1760 and was titled *A Narrative of the Uncommon Sufferings and Surprising Deliverance of Briton Hammon, a Negro Man.* Some slave narratives, such as *Scenes in the Life of Harriet Tubman* (1869) and *Memoirs of Eleanor Eldridge* (1838), were presented as autobiographies. Some were "told-to" accounts, such as *The Confessions of Nat Turner* (1831), the basis of William Styron's 1967 Pulitzer Prize–winning novel, and *The Narrative of James*

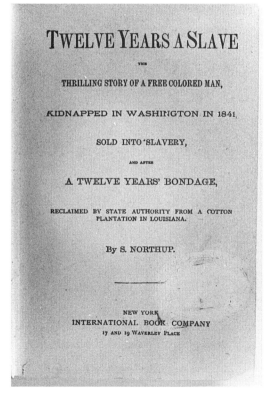

Solomon Northup, *Twelve Years a Slave,* autobiography; very good condition, **$25–45.** Courtesy of Valerie Bertrand Collection; photo by Donald Vogt.

Williams (1938), as dictated to John Greenleaf Whittier. One of the best known and most influential of all slave narratives is *Narrative of the Life of Frederick Douglass, an American Slave, Written by Himself.* Douglass wrote his book in 1844, less than five years after he ran away from slavery; it was published the following year. By the late 1850s, the slave narrative was in vogue with the literary public, and hundreds of narratives were published during that time.

Jupiter Hammon wrote both prose and poetry in the eighteenth century. *An Address to the Negroes in the State of New York* reflected his favored position as the literate slave of a Long Island master. His poetry suggests that he thought slavery a step up or a liberation from barbarism. Hammon, who was a preacher, admonished African-Americans that they should accept their God-given fate.

After the appearance of the works of Hammon and of poet Phyllis Wheatley, the first black American to publish a book in the United States, legal restrictions were placed on the education of slaves in the American colonies. The government wanted to control the slaves, to keep them from spreading slave news and propaganda that would incite a lust for freedom. Thus slave narratives and poetry went underground, to be disseminated orally and through songs.

William Wells Brown, America's first black novelist, assisted the Reverend Elijah Lovejoy of Illinois. Lovejoy, a black man, was killed by a mob that also destroyed the press on which he printed his antislavery editorials. Brown became a novelist and playwright in the 1850s.

Even after the Civil War ended, slave writings did not disappear. Versions of narratives like Douglass's continued to be reissued, and over the years new ones appeared. Booker T. Washington's *Up from Slavery, An Autobiography,* written in 1900, is considered to be a classic example of the American success story.

The Twentieth Century

The Harlem Renaissance began in the 1920s and was born of a need for black writers and artists to have pride in their work. The "Harlem School" of writing encouraged Blacks to express themselves freely and to put an end to the prejudice so evident in the English departments of major universities. Writers such as Willard Motley, Frank Yerby, and Alain Locke emerged triumphantly. The Harlem period is notable because its writers and artists appeared in strong and cohesive groups.

The economic hardships of the Great Depression left most black writers with little money and no support. This resulted in a decline in the sense of a shared community among black writers. It wasn't until the 1940s that luminaries such as Richard Wright and Ralph Ellison drew the public's attention back to black writing. A new era was ushered in on the shirttails of Wright's and Ellison's fame.

During the 1940s, poets such as Margaret Walker ("For My People," 1942), Gwendolyn Brooks (*A Street in Bronzeville,* 1945), and Owen Dodson (*Powerful Long Ladder,* 1946) became well known. They were followed by a procession of poets, experimental and traditional, who garnered attention in the 1950s and '60s.

In the 1960s, several prose writers brought "street" and prison experiences to the written page. Eldridge Cleaver, Malcolm X, and George Jackson all had brushes with the law and wrote about how they'd been treated.

Today's African-American literature has gone through another metamorphosis. Now the strongest voices are female—and they battle for recognition. Alice Walker, Toni Morrison, Rita Dove, Maya Angelou, and Terry McMillan are well-respected members of the literary community—not because of the color of their skin but because of the brillance of their writing.

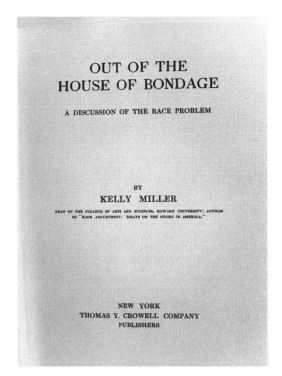

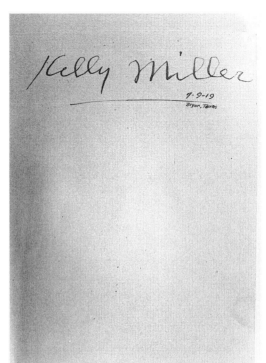

OUT OF THE
HOUSE OF BONDAGE

A DISCUSSION OF THE RACE PROBLEM

BY
KELLY MILLER

DEAN OF THE COLLEGE OF ARTS AND SCIENCES, HOWARD UNIVERSITY; AUTHOR
OF "RACE ADJUSTMENT: ESSAYS ON THE NEGRO IN AMERICA."

NEW YORK
THOMAS Y. CROWELL COMPANY
PUBLISHERS

Kelly Miller, *Out of the House of Bondage,* a discussion of the race problem; **$25–30;** autographed by the author July 19, 1919, in Bryan, Texas; very good condition, **$100–150.** Courtesy of the Valerie Bertrand Collection; photo by Donald Vogt.

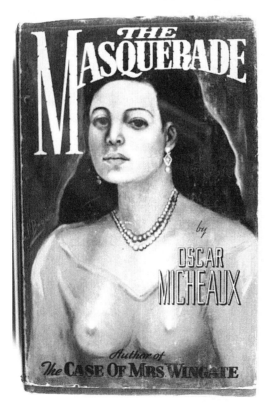

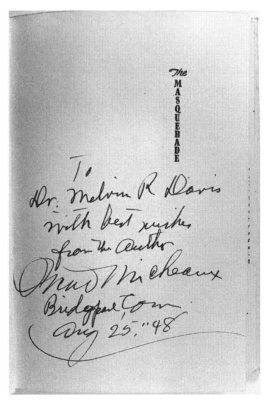

Oscar Micheaux; *The Masquerade;* autographed by the author, a Hollywood screenwriter; 1947; very good condition, **$150–200.** Courtesy of the Valerie Bertrand Collection; photo by Donald Vogt.

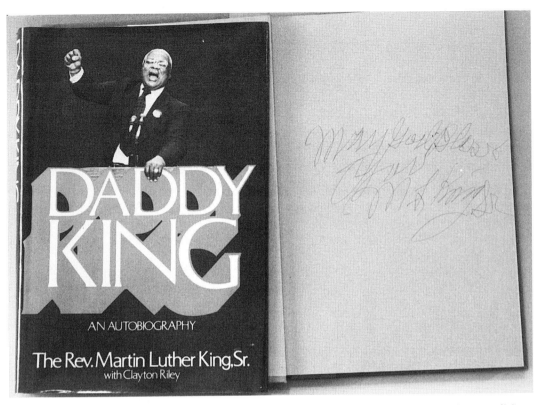

Martin Luther King Sr., *Daddy King,* autographed autobiography, 1980; near-mint condition, $150–200. Collection of Dawn and Bob Reno; photo by Bob Reno.

Some Author Biographies

James Baldwin, born August 2, 1924, in New York City, was the oldest of nine children and grew up in Harlem. As a teenager, Baldwin preached after school in a small church. He writes about that experience both in *Go Tell It on the Mountain*—his first book, a semiautobiographical novel—and his play *The Amen Corner.* One can also see the influence of the Bible on his writing.

A multitalented man, Baldwin was a novelist, essayist, and playwright. His works have been collected into books and have been highly praised. His novels and plays have often received mixed reviews, perhaps because they often dealt with the civil rights question in a separatist way not acceptable to most white Americans.

He lived in Paris for eight years and wrote *Giovanni's Room* (1956) there. That book dealt with the white world and Paris. In 1955, his collection of essays *Notes of a Native Son* established his reputation as an essayist. When Baldwin returned to the United States in 1957, he became an active participant in the civil rights struggle and stated his beliefs in his next book of essays, *Nobody Knows My Name.* On November 17, 1962, the *New Yorker* magazine awarded Baldwin almost all its editorial space for a long article on the Black Muslim separatist movement and other notes on the civil rights struggle; in 1963, the essay was published in book form as *The Fire Next Time.* His play *Blues for Mister Charlie* appeared on Broadway in 1964 to mixed reviews.

Amiri Baraka (LeRoi Jones) was born in 1934 and attended Rutgers before finishing his undergraduate education at Harvard. He served in the Air Force and then came home to work as a teacher and writer. He was the founder of the Black Arts Repertory Theatre of Harlem and acted as director of the Spirit House in Newark,

New Jersey. He changed his name to Amiri Baraka in 1965 when he became a Muslim.

Baraka's poetry attracted attention because of its intense language and imagery. His first work, *Preface to a Twenty-Volume Suicide Note,* was published in 1961. After that, he won a Guggenheim fellowship and wrote the novel *The System of Dante's Hell,* which is often studied for its style by beginning writers. This versatile writer also wrote plays (e.g., *Dutchman, The Slave,* and *The Baptism*) and edited *Black Fire,* an anthology of black literature.

Gwendolyn Brooks was the first African-American to win the Pulitzer Prize, which she received in 1950 for her poetry. Born in Topeka, Kansas, Brooks grew up in Chicago and taught at several Chicago colleges as well as at the University of Wisconsin. Her poetry reveals the African-American experience. She writes both in the traditional form and in a very lean modern form. Her subject matter varies, often focusing on women but sometimes touching on politics (e.g., her poem about Malcolm X).

Sterling Brown wrote after the Harlem Renaissance. His first and only published book, *Southern Road,* a volume of poetry, appeared in 1932. Born in 1901 in Washington, D.C., Brown went to Howard University and then entered Williams College, where he received a bachelor's degree in 1922. He earned a master's degree at Harvard the following year. During his writing career, he taught at Virginia Seminary and College in Lynchburg, Fisk University, Lincoln University, and Howard University, and was a visiting professor at many others. He acted as editor on black affairs in the Federal Writers' Project of the WPA between 1936 and 1939 and won a Guggenheim fellowship (1937–1938). After 1939, he worked on a large research project on American Blacks with the Gunnar Myrdal Group.

William Wells Brown was the first African-American to publish a novel and provides the link between slave narratives and literary works. Born in Kentucky of slave parentage, his fictional narrative of slave life in the United States, *Clotel,* is the story of a girl born to Thomas Jefferson and his housekeeper. In his later writings,

Brown revealed that he was also a slave, but some have branded that as abolitionist propaganda.

Brown served an apprenticeship to antislavery editor Elijah P. Lovejoy who was then working at the St. Louis *Times.* Later he found his way to Canada and, in his own words, "commenced lecturing as an agent of the Western New York Anti-Slavery Society." He wrote novels from 1849 to 1854, when he was in England fighting against slavery; thus some of this books were first published in London. He died in 1888.

Charles Waddell Chesnutt, born June 20, 1858, in Cleveland, has been called a pioneer of the color line (because he was one of the first Blacks to be accepted as a writer) by biographers and other writers. His work was more masterful than that of his contemporaries, and he had the distinct honor of being the first black writer to have a short story published in the *Atlantic Monthly* (August 1887, "The Goophered Plantation"). Chesnutt published more than fifty works—short stories, essays, a biography of Frederick Douglass, and three novels—between the years 1855 and 1905.

Lydia M. Child, born in 1802, was a prominent white novelist who turned to writing on behalf of black equality. Her book *An Appeal in Favor of That Class of Americans Called Africans* was published in Boston in 1833. With her husband, also an active abolitionist, she edited *The National Anti-Slavery Standard* from 1841 to 1849. Her other works include the first children's monthly periodical in the United States, books on women and their problems, and books urging the adoption of sex education. She died in 1880.

Countee Cullen, born in 1903, was known as the poet laureate of the Harlem Renaissance. He first published a collection of poetry (*Color*) in 1925, while he was still a student at New York University. Two years later, he earned a master's degree in English from Harvard and published two more books of poetry (*The Ballad of the Brown Girl* and *Copper Sun*). In 1929, he was awarded a Guggenheim fellowship, which allowed him to finish *The Black Christ and Other Poems.* He died in 1946.

Frederick Douglass, born in 1817, was separated from his slave mother when he was an infant and never knew his white father. He lived with his grandmother in Maryland until he was eight, when his owner sent him to Baltimore to live as a house servant with the Hugh Auld family. Mrs. Auld defied state law and taught Douglass how to read and write. When her husband stopped the lessons, declaring that learning would make the boy unfit for slavery, Douglass continued his learning in secret. As a teenager, he was hired out to be a ship caulker. He tried to escape in 1833 but was not successful until five years later, when he fled to Massachusetts to elude the slave hunters.

In 1841 in Nantucket, Massachusetts, Douglass told an antislavery convention about his feelings and experiences as a slave. That experience catapulted him into a new career as an agent for the Massachusetts Anti-Slavery Society. He wrote *My Bondage and My Freedom* in 1845 to combat skeptics who doubted that he could ever have been a slave. In 1882, the book became *The Life and Times of Frederick Douglass.* While on a two-year speaking tour of Great Britain and Ireland for the book, Douglass felt the weight of racism lifted for the first time and won new friends for the abolition movement.

Back in the United States, he started a newspaper, the *North Star,* and used it as his voice in the antislavery movement. During the Civil War, he advised President Lincoln on the role of black Americans in the war. He also enlisted Blacks for military service. From 1865 to 1877, he fought for full civil rights for freed men and supported the women's rights movement. Douglass was elected president of the Freedmen's Bank and Trust Company in 1874, was the first black citizen to hold high rank in the U.S. government, and held numerous political offices after 1877. He died in 1895.

W. E. B. Du Bois, a sociologist, was one of the most important black American protest leaders during the first half of the twentieth century. He was born in 1868, graduated from Fisk University in 1888, and in 1895 was the first black American

THE NEW SOUTH.

VANITY.

Down South, photos "The New South" and "Vanity" from the book; very good condition, **$40–50 for the book.** Courtesy of the Valerie Bertrand Collection; photo by Donald Vogt.

to earn a Ph.D. from Harvard. In 1897, he began contributing finely written and insightful essays to the *Atlantic Monthly.* In 1903, his writings were collected and published in one volume, *The Souls of Black Folk.*

Du Bois clashed with Booker T. Washington and took the lead in founding the Niagara Movement, precursor to the NAACP, in 1905. He also played a part in organizing the NAACP in 1909. In 1961 Du Bois joined the Communist Party, moved to Ghana, and renounced his American citizenship. He died in Ghana in 1963. Du Bois is probably best known for founding the newspaper *Crisis* (for more on this paper, see Chapter 8). He remained its editor until 1933.

Paul Laurence Dunbar, born in 1872, was the son of former slaves and the only black student in his Dayton, Ohio, high school. He was also the editor of his high school's newspaper.

Dunbar's first privately printed work, *Oak and Ivy,* was published in 1893 while he was working as an elevator operator in Dayton. He sold copies to the passengers to pay for the printing. *Lyrics of a Lowly Life* (1896) launched his literary career and national reputation. His poems were in the minstrel tradition, which was enjoying large popularity at that time.

Dunbar's short stories and sketches appeared in the *Saturday Evening Post,* as well as in other magazines, while his novels—*Folks from Dixie, The Strength of Gideon, In Old Plantation Days,* and *The Heart of Happy Hollow*—appeared during the early years of the twentieth century. Dunbar wrote seventeen books, including poetry anthologies, novels, and short story collections. He was one of the first black American writers to attempt to live off his talent and to gain national prominence. He died in 1906.

Ralph Waldo Ellison published his first book, *Invisible Man,* in 1952 and was hailed as a major contributor to American literature. The novel, a story about a southern Black who moves to Harlem, won the American Booksellers fiction award in 1953.

Born in Oklahoma City in 1914, Ellison was, at various times, a shoeshine boy, a jazz musician, and a freelance photographer. He left the Tuskegee Institute in 1936 and joined the Federal Writers Project in New York City. After his collection of essays *Shadow and Act* was published in 1964, Ellison lectured on black culture, folklore, and creative writing and taught at various universities.

Alex Haley was born in 1921 and was the author of one of the most recognized American stories every written, *Roots.* In 1977, a miniseries based on the book was shown on television, attracting one of the largest audiences in television history. Haley died in 1992 before he could see the miniseries based on the sequel to that book, *Queen,* aired on television. Haley, who began writing during a twenty-year stint with the Coast Guard, spent twelve years writing *Roots. The Autobiography of Malcolm X,* which he co-authored with activist Malcolm X, took less time, but both books were partially written during his long sea voyages.

As a result of reading *Roots* or seeing it on television, many Americans began pestering their parents and grandparents for information about their own ancestors. Haley's favorite phrase, "Find the good and praise it," also encouraged many Americans to think positively of education.

Jupiter Hammon, a slave who belonged to a Mr. Lloyd of Queens Village, Long Island, was the first Black to publish poems in America. He was probably born sometime around 1720, and his first poem, "An Evening Thought, Salvation by Christ with Penitential Cries," appeared in 1760. Most of his poetry is religious; however, one of his best known works is a prose piece titled "An Address to the Negroes of the State of New York," which he delivered on September 24, 1786.

Frances Ellen Watkins Harper, born in 1825, had her first book published in Philadelphia in 1854 when she was twenty-nine (*Poems on Miscellaneous Subjects*). She read her poems widely and was dubbed an elocutionist. Ten thousand copies of her first book were sold in the first five years. Her second book, *Moses, A Story of the Nile,* was published in 1869. Using her fame to fight for the liberation of her people, she wrote articles and letters raising questions about slavery and its effect on black Americans. In 1873, her third book, *Sketches of Southern Life,* was published, and it is notable for the language its black characters used. She frequently contributed to *Godey's Lady's Book.* She died in 1911.

Langston Hughes was born in 1902, and his career as a writer began at age nineteen when his first piece, "The Negro Speaks of Rivers," appeared in *Crisis,* a national newspaper. Five years later, Hughes's first book, *The Weary Blues,* was published, and many volumes followed after that. He wrote "Harlemese," and his sources were "street music." He has often been called an American original and has been considered one of the most important forces that showed the experience of black Americans to the rest of the world. His poetry captures the essence of jazz and is said to have been influenced by Carl Sandburg and Vachel Lindsay.

During the 1930s, Hughes became preoccupied with political militancy, and his poetry reflected his feelings. He traveled throughout the Soviet Union, Haiti, and Japan and served as a newspaper correspondent in the Spanish Civil War. During that decade, he also published collections of short stories, and in 1940 his autobiography, *The Big Sea,* was published.

When he died in New York City on May 22, 1967, Langston Hughes had twenty-seven books in print. Arthur Springarn called him the most translated contemporary American poet.

Joseph H. Ingraham, born in 1809, wrote novels that are consulted today mostly by historians. Published by newspapers during the late 1830s and 1840s, his novels were extremely popular. As a young man, Ingraham toured southwestern Mississippi and wrote his first book, *The South-West,* about what he observed there. It was published anonymously in 1835. Ingraham died in 1860.

James Weldon Johnson was born in 1871, and he published his first work of prose, *The Autobiography of an Ex-Coloured Man,* in 1912. It was not well received. By the time it was republished and gained renown fifteen years later, Johnson was a member of the NAACP. The book's reissue was partly due to the Harlem Renaissance. Johnson published a volume of black folk sermons, *God's Trombones,* and doors were opened to social events and eligibility

awards in the United States that had previously been closed to black Americans in the arts. (For more about Johnson, see Chapter 14.)

William Johnson's Diary of a Free Negro was a record that he kept for sixteen years and passed on through his family. When he died in 1938, the family entrusted the diary to two historians, who published it thirteen years later.

Sandra Kitt, a native of New York City, was born in 1947 and started writing women's fiction in 1981. She was the first African-American author to publish for Harlequin Romances, with her novel *Rites of Spring.* A librarian for the American Museum at the Hayden Planetarium in New York, Kitt holds bachelor's and master's degrees in fine arts from the City University of New York; has studied and lived in Mexico; and has worked as a graphic designer and freelance illustrator, designing cards for UNICEF and illustrating two books with Isaac Asimov. Awarded the Women of Excellence award in 1993 by Mayor David N. Dinkins of New York City, Kitt has more than a dozen novels to her credit, including *The Color of Love* (1995), *Serenade* (1994), *Love Everlasting* (1993), *Someone's Baby* (1991), *Only with the Heart* (1985), and *Adam & Eva* (1984).

James W. C. Pennington, born in 1809, was a stonemason and blacksmith. He fled slavery around 1830, aided by a Pennsylvania Quaker who sent him to Long Island, where he acquired the education necessary to teach in black schools. He received a doctor of divinity degree from the University of Heidelberg in Germany in the 1840s and studied theology in New Haven, Connecticut. He then spent some time as pastor of the African Congregationalist Church in New Haven.

His autobiography, *The Fugitive Blacksmith,* was published in 1849, and his book *The Origin and History of the Colored People,* the first major history of black people, was published in 1841. He died in 1870.

Caryl Phillips published *Higher Ground, a Novel in Three Parts* in 1989, and the book received rave reviews in the *New York Times Book Review.* The three parts of the novel are a story of slave trading in the 1800s, the story of an African-

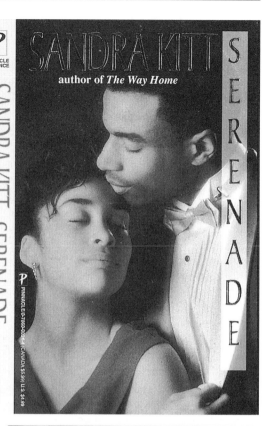

Top: Sandra Kitt, *Serenade,* paperback romance, 1994; new; *$4–5. Right:* Photo of Sandra Kitt, writer of many contemporary ethnic romances; excellent condition, *$5–10.* Courtesy of Sandra Kitt.

American prisoner (composed entirely of letters written in the 1960s), and the story of a Polish Jewish woman who was exiled in London after World War II. He is the author of three other books, including *The European Tribe,* all of which focus on the psychological, rather than external, impact of oppression on the oppressed.

Lucy Terry, the slave of Ensign Ebenezer Wells of Deerfield, Massachusetts, was one of the first African-Americans to write poetry. Her poem "Bars Fight" describes the bloody American Indian raid on the Deerfield settlement in 1746. Although she was not versed in syntax, she provided a vivid picture of the August 25 massacre of the settlers. She married a free black man and enjoyed a reputation as a storyteller, never knowing that she would be remembered 250 years later.

Sandra Kitt

Gustavus Vassa wrote a rare autobiographical account of eighteenth-century slavery titled *The Interesting Narrative of the Life of Olaudah Equiano, or Gustavus Vassa, the African*. Named Gus Vassa by a Swedish captain on one of many sea voyages, he traveled extensively, eventually exploring the Arctic. He was one of the few slaves to become educated, and he used his skills to write a journal that told of his and other slaves' trials and sorrows.

Phyllis Wheatley was born around 1753 in Senegal, Africa. In 1761 she was bought by Mr. and Mrs. John Wheatley of Boston to be a companion for Mrs. Wheatley. Mrs. Wheatley taught the sickly looking Phyllis to read and write. The black girl amazed Boston with her poetic talents. Wheatley dedicated some of her poems to a Mr. Thornton, Lady Huntington, Lord Dartmouth, and others who helped her. When Wheatley's health failed, Boston doctors suggested she take an ocean voyage. She went to England, where she published *Poems on Various Subjects: Religious and Moral* in 1773. She died in 1784.

George Washington Williams, a serious historian, published the two-volume *History of the Negro Race in America from 1619 to 1880* after researching the subject from 1876 to 1883. The work was received with excitement in scholarly circles and is regarded as the best book on black history written during the nineteenth century. Williams also wrote *A History of Negro Troops in the War of the Rebellion*.

Richard Wright wrote about the violence and opposition he experienced during his lifetime. Wright was born into a poor black family in Natchez, Mississippi, in 1908. After his father deserted the family, his mother placed Richard and his brother in an orphanage until she could save enough money to get them to their grandmother in Jackson, Mississippi. Wright left Jackson after high school and headed for Memphis, determined to be a writer. He took menial jobs to survive, borrowed books from the library, and read himself to sleep every night. While constantly studying the written word, he realized words could be used as weapons. Two years later he had saved enough to bring his brother and invalid mother to Chicago.

In 1935 he became a member of the Federal Writers Project, moving to the project's New York chapter in 1937. In 1938, Wright won a $500 prize for his book *Uncle Tom's Children*. The book brought Wright fame. The following year he received a Guggenheim fellowship as well as the Spingarn Medal from the NAACP. *Native Son,* his second book, was considered even better than his first and appeared as a Book-of-the-Month Club selection. In the next fifteen years, nearly fifty translations and foreign editions of his books ensured his fame worldwide. His third book, an autobiography titled *Black Boy* (1945), gave evidence that Wright's range was expanding. The autobiography is currently used nationwide as part of the college curriculum for human services and psychology courses as well as in the study of American literature.

After writing that book, Wright moved to Paris, where he became one of the most celebrated American expatriates. *The Outsider* (1953) was published after an eight-year silence but was not quite up to the quality of his earlier works. From then until his death in 1960, he published books that were not as well regarded as his first works. It is said that once Wright went to Europe and no longer had to fight against such strong prejudice, the anger that induced his brilliant writing cooled and so did his talent.

PRICES FOR BOOKS

Anderson, Dr. David, *The Origin of Life on Earth,* illustrated by Kathleen Atkins Wilson, winner of the 1993 Coretta Scott King Award and the 1992 African Studies Association Outstanding Book Award, cloth hardcover; 12″ × 9″; new, **$19–24.**

Andrews, E. A., *Slavery and the Domestic Slave Trade in the United States,* Boston, 1836; excellent condition, **$35–45.**

Aughey, J. H., *The Iron Furnace or Slavery and Secession,* Philadelphia, 1863; excellent condition, **$15–20.**

Barbour, Floyd P., *The Black Power Revolt,* New York, 1958; excellent condition, **$10–15.**

Benét, Stephen Vincent, *John Brown's Body,* New York, 1954; excellent condition, **$10–15.**

Big Mama's Old Black Pot Recipes, 204 recipes with folk art, folklore and biographical sketches from life in the rural South, 1800s through the Depression; new, **$12.**

Blake, W. O., *The History of Slavery and the Slave Trade Ancient and Modern,* Columbus, 1860; excellent condition, **$25–35.**

Bledsoe, Albert T., *An Essay on Liberty and Slavery,* Philadelphia, 1856; excellent condition, **$65–80.**

Bones Minstrel Gags and Speeches, very rare, Wehman Publishers, 1879; mint condition, **$100–150.**

Bowlan, Grace Duffie, and Ike Morgan, *Young Folks' Uncle Tom's Cabin,* Chicago, 1901; excellent condition, **$15–25.**

Brown, H. Rap., *Die, Nigger, Die,* New York, 1969; excellent condition, **$10–15.**

Brown, Ina Corrine, *The Story of the American Negro,* New York, 1936; excellent condition, **$12–20.**

Cable, George W., *The Negro Question,* New York, 1888; excellent condition, **$50–75.**

Cairnes, J. E., *The Slave Power: Its Character, Career and Probable Designs,* rare, 171 pages, New York, 1862; excellent condition, **$30–40.**

Caldwell, Erskine, *Tobacco Road,* New York, 1940; excellent condition, **$35–55.**

Campbell, George, *White and Black: The Outcome of a Visit to the United States,* New York, 1879; excellent condition, **$45–65.**

Carey, H. C., *The Slave Trade, Domestic and Foreign: Why It Exists and How It May Be Extinguished,* Philadelphia, 1859; excellent condition, **$25–35.**

Child, Mrs. Lydia M., *An Appeal in Favor of that Class of Americans Called Africans,* New York, 1836; excellent condition, **$80–95.**

Cleaver, Eldridge

    Post Prison Writings, Speeches, New York, 1969; excellent condition, **$10–20.**

    Soul on Ice, New York, 1968; excellent condition, **$25–35.**

Cobb, W. Montague, *The First Negro Medical Society: A History of the Medico-Cherchurgical Society of the District of Columbia,* Washington, DC., 1884–1939; excellent condition, **$40–55.**

Cohen, Octavius R., *Highly Colored,* New York, 1921; excellent condition, **$40–60.**

Cowley, M., ed., *Adventures of an African Slaver,* New York, 1928; excellent condition, **$10–15.**

Davidson, Basil, *Black Mother: The Years of the African Slave,* 1951; excellent condition, **$8–12.**

Davis, Thomas T., *Speech on Equality of Rights,* Washington, D.C., 1866; excellent condition, **$35–45.**

Dewees, Jacob, *The Great Future of America and Africa: An Essay Showing Our Whole Duty to the Black Man, Consistent with Our Safety and Glory,* Philadelphia, 1854; excellent condition, **$75–100.**

Douglass, Frederick

    Life and Times of Frederick Douglass, 640 pages, 1962 reprint; excellent condition, **$5–8.**

    My Bondage and My Freedom, New York, 1857; excellent condition, **$15–30.**

Narrative of the Life of F. Douglass: An American Slave, Written by Himself, Boston, 1845; excellent condition, **$40–85.**

Du Bois, W. E. B., *The Souls of Black Folk,* London, 1905; excellent condition, **$35–55.**

Eastman, Mrs. Harry H., *Aunt Phyllis's Cabin or Southern Life As It Is,* Philadelphia, 1852; excellent condition, **$80–100.**

Ebony, ed., *The Negro Handbook,* Chicago, 1967; excellent condition, **$7–10.**

Eldridge, Eleanor, *Slave Narrative,* 1842; excellent condition, **$150–250.**

Elliott, Reverend Charles, *The Bible and Slavery,* Cincinnati, 1857; excellent condition, **$15–25.**

Essien-Udom, E. U., *Black Nations, A Search for an Identity in America,* University of Chicago, 1962; excellent condition, **$10–15.**

Fabre, Michel, *From Harlem to Paris: Black American Writers in France, 1840–1980,* University of Illinois Press, 1991; **$36.**

Ferman, Louis, *Negroes and Jobs,* Michigan, 1969; excellent condition, **$10–15.**

Folsom, Montgomery M., *Scraps of Song and Southern Scenes,* Atlanta, 1889; excellent condition, **$25–40.**

Frazier, E. Franklin, *The Negro in the United States,* New York, 1949; excellent condition, **$10–20.**

Furnas, J. C., *Goodbye to Uncle Tom,* New York, 1956; excellent condition, **$20–30.**

Gakuo, Kariuki, *Nyumba ya Mumbi: The Gikuyu Creation Myth,* illustrated by Mwaura Ndekere, full color, paperback; 8″ × 8″; new, **$9–12.**

Gakuo, Kariuki and Valerie Cuthbert, *Beneath the Rainbow: A Collection of Children's Stories and Poems from Kenya, Volume 1, Poems by Sam Mbure,* illustrated by Samwel Ngoje, Sironka Averdung, Pat Keay, Phyllis Koinange, and John Okello, published by Jacaranda Designs, full color; 8″ × 10″; new, **$10–15.**

Gardner, Elvira, *Ezekiel,* first edition, children's book, written and illustrated by Elvira Gardner, full color, hardcover, 1937; excellent condition, **$75–100.**

Gladstone, William A., *United States Colored Troops,* 132 pages; 8½″ × 11″; new; **$19.**

Green, Lorenzo J., *Negro in Colonial New England,* Washington, D.C., 1942; excellent condition, **$55–75.**

Greenidge, C. W. W., *Slavery,* New York, 1958; excellent condition, **$10–15.**

Growing Up Black in Rural Mississippi: Memories of a Family, Heritage of Place, Walker & Co., New York, 156 pages, 1991; new, **$20.**

Halsey, Margaret, *Color Blind: A White Woman Looks at the Negro,* New York, 1946; excellent condition, **$15–25.**

Harris, Joel Chandler

New Stories of the Old Plantation, Told by Uncle Remus, New York, 1905; excellent condition, **$15–30.**

On The Plantation, New York, 1892; excellent condition, **$35–50.**

Plantation Pageants, Boston, 1889; excellent condition, **$75–100.**

The Tar Baby, New York, 1904; excellent condition, **$30–50.**

Uncle Remus, New York, 1881; excellent condition, **$125–200.**

Uncle Remus, New York, 1957; excellent condition, **$10–20.**

Uncle Remus, His Songs and His Sayings, New York, 1881; excellent condition, **$400–500.**

Uncle Remus, His Songs and His Sayings, New York, 1921; excellent condition, **$10–20.**

Uncle Remus Returns, Boston, 1918; excellent condition, **$75–100.**

Hawkins, Joseph, *A History of a Voyage to the Coast of Africa,* Philadelphia, 1797; excellent condition, **$200–250.**

Hershovitz, M. L., *The American Negro,* New York, 1930; excellent condition, **$25–30.**

Holt, Rackham, *George Washington Carver,* 1943; excellent condition, **$8–10.**

Homes, Dwight O. W., *The Evolution of the Negro College,* New York, 1934; excellent condition, **$35–40.**

Hughes, Langston, *Black Misery*, New York, 1969; excellent condition, **$15–25.**

Hughes, Langston, ed., *The Book of Negro Humor*, New York, 1966; excellent condition, **$8–10.**

Hunt, Blanche Seale, *Little Brown Koko's Pets and Playmates*, hardcover, C. E. I. Publishing Company, 1959; near mint condition, **$20–30.**

Ingraham, J. H., *The Sunny South or The Southerner at Home*, Philadelphia, 1860; excellent condition, **$50–75.**

Johnson, James Weldon, *The Book of American Negro Poetry*, New York, 1931; excellent condition, **$15–18.**

Kerlin, R. T., *Negro Poets and Their Poems*, Washington, D.C., 1935; excellent condition, **$35–50.**

King, Martin Luther, Jr., *Why We Can't Wait*, New York, 1964; excellent condition, **$20–30.**

Lincoln, C. Eric, *My Face Is Black*, Boston, 1964; excellent condition, **$8–10.**

Little Black Sambo, illustrated by Nina R. Jordan, full color and black and white, also contains *A New Story of Little Black Sambo*, hardcover, Whitman Publishers, 1932; excellent condition, **$110–150.**

Livermore, George, *Historical Research Respecting the Founders of the Republic on Negroes as Slaves, Citizens, and Soldiers*, Boston, 1863; excellent condition, **$35–50.**

Lobagola, Bata, *Lobagola: An African Savage's Own Story*, New York, 1930; excellent condition, **$35–45.**

Loring, F. W. and C. F. Atkinson, *Cotton Culture*, Boston, 1869; excellent condition, **$50–75.**

Mailer, Norman, *The White Negro*, San Francisco, 1957; excellent condition, **$20–30.**

Malcolm X, *The Autobiography of Malcolm X*, New York, 1965; excellent condition, **$35–50.**

Mann, Horace, *Slavery: Letters and Speeches by Horace Mann*, Boston, 1853; excellent condition, **$25–35.**

May, Samuel J., *Some Recollections of the Antislavery Conflict*, Boston, 1869; excellent condition, **$25–35.**

Morgan, Lewis H., *Houses and House Life of the American Aborigines*, Washington, D.C., 1881; excellent condition, **$50–55.**

Munford, Beverly B., *Virginia's Attitude toward Slavery and Secession*, Richmond, 1909; excellent condition, **$10–15.**

Myrdal, Gunnar, *An American Dilemma: The Negro Problem and Modern Democracy*, New York and London, 1944; excellent condition, **$10–15.**

The New Negro: Voices of the Harlem Renaissance, new edition of the 1925 anthology of poetry, plays, essays, introduction by Arnold Rampersad, Atheneum, 492 pages, paperback; new, **$15.**

Newcomb, B., *Sambo Minstrel Joke Book*, by famous minstrel, cover art in red, black and brown, front and back, rare, 1882; 5″ × 7″; mint condition, **$100–150.**

Nichols, Charles, *Black Men in Chains*, New York, 1972; excellent condition, **$8–10.**

Olmstead, Frederick, *The Slave States*, New York, 1959; excellent condition, **$20–25.**

Osgood, Mrs. M. A., *Little Canary Series: Black Cato Lee and Shepherd*, 1872; excellent condition, **$75–100.**

Oswaggo, Joel, *Nyalgondho and the Lost Woman from Lake Victoria*, written and illustrated by Joel Oswaggo, full color, for children and adults, paperback; new, **$9–12.**

Owen, Nicholas, *Journal of a Slave Dealer*, Boston, 1930; excellent condition, **$20–30.**

Owens, William A., *A Slave Mutiny*, 1953; excellent condition, **$8–12.**

Ownby, Ted, *Black and White;* new, **cloth: $40, paper: $18.**

Page, Thomas Nelson, *The Negro: The Southerner Problem*, New York, 1910; excellent condition, **$12–20.**

Patrick, Denise Lewis, *Red Dancing Shoes*, illustrated and autographed by James E. Ransome, first edition, Tambourine Press, New York, 1993; mint condition, **$25–40.**

Penn, I. Garland, *The Afro-American Press and Its Editors,* Springfield, 1891; excellent condition, **$8–10.**

Phillips, Caryl, *Higher Ground,* 218 pages, Viking, New York; new, **$18.**

A Picture of Slavery, published by Isaac Knapp of Boston, 227 pages, 1838; fair to good condition (lacks covers but is complete), **$12–22.**

Porter, A. F., *Nigger Baby and Nine Beasts,* New York, 1900; excellent condition, **$30–50.**

Pryor, Roger A., *A Speech of Roger A. Pryor of Virginia, on the Principles and Policy of the Black Republican Party,* Washington, D.C., 1859; excellent condition, **$60–85.**

Quarles, Benjamin, *The Negro in the Civil War,* Boston, 1953; excellent condition, **$25–40.**

Richardson, Brenda Lane, *Chesapeake Song,* award-winning writer and journalist, hardcover, Amistad, 1993; **$20–22.**

Scheer, Robert, *Eldridge Cleaver,* 1969; excellent condition, **$10–15.**

Sherrard, O. A., *Freedom from Fear: The Slave and His Emancipation,* New York, 1959; excellent condition, **$5–10.**

Simms, James A., *The First Colored Baptist Church in North America,* Philadelphia, 1888; excellent condition, **$75–90.**

Singer, Caroline, and C. L. Baldridge, *White Africans and Black,* New York, 1929; excellent condition, **$60–75.**

Songbook, *Julia Johnston's Own Colored So-Los,* Philip J. Cozans, Publisher, 107 Nassau St., Boston, ca. 1860; 2½″ × 4″; cover missing but otherwise in good condition, **$25–45.**

Spencer, Ichabod S., *Fugitive Slave Law,* New York, 1850; excellent condition, **$50–75.**

Stillwell, Paul, ed., *The Golden Thirteen, Recollections of the First Black Naval Officers,* foreword by Colin L. Powell, illustrated, 304 pages, Naval Institute Press, new, **$22.**

A Story of Our Gang, ten full-color full-page portraits, hardcover children's book, Whitman first edition, 1929; 9″ × 6½″; excellent condition, **$70–90.**

Stowe, Harriet Beecher

A Key to Uncle Tom's Cabin: Presenting the Original Facts and Documents upon which the Story Is Founded, Boston, 1853, excellent condition, **$40–60.**

Uncle Sam's Emancipation, Philadelphia, 1853; excellent condition, **$100–130.**

Uncle Tom's Cabin in 13 Monthly Parts with Illustrations by George Cruikshank, England; excellent condition, **$500–700.**

Uncle Tom's Cabin, two volumes, great rarity, Boston, 1852; excellent condition, **$19,000–22,000.**

Uncle Tom's Cabin, London, 1852; excellent condition, **$100–125.**

Tannenbaum, Frank, *Slave and Citizen in Americas,* New York, 1947; excellent condition, **$15–20.**

Taylor, Susan L., *In the Spirit,* Amistad, hardcover (Taylor is editor-in-chief of *Essence* magazine); **$15–20.**

Thompson, Julius E., *The Black Press in Mississippi 1865–1985,* 240 pages, University Press of Florida at Gainesville, 1993; **$35–40.**

A Treasury of Stephen Foster, color illustrations (some signed) include black subjects, first edition, 224 pages, Random House, 1946; 9″ × 12″; excellent condition, **$70–100.**

Van Evrie, J. H., *Negroes and Negro Slavery: The First an Inferior Race: The Latter Its Normal Condition,* New York 1863; excellent condition, **$35–50.**

VanVechten, Carl, *Nigger Heaven,* New York, 1928; excellent condition, **$10–15.**

Villard, O., *John Brown 1800–59,* Boston, 1910; excellent condition, **$20–25.**

Warren, R. P., *Who Speaks for the Negro?* New York, 1965, excellent condition, **$10–15.**

Wheeler, Opal, *Stephen Foster and His Little Dog Tray,* children's book, black-and-white illustrations, hardcover, 173 pages, 1943; 7½″ × 9″; excellent condition, **$45–75.**

Wing, Paul, *Little Black Sambo's Jungle Band* (book and record album), twenty-page text with full-color illustrations, two 45-rpm records, marked "copyright 1939, 1950 by Paul Wing"; excellent condition, **$110–150.**

PART TWO

Everyday Artifacts

CHAPTER FIVE

Advertising

Advertising, a form of communication intended to promote the sale of a product or service, first began in ancient times when a public crier roamed the streets calling attention to the sale of slaves, cattle, or imports. Yet when we talk about collecting advertising that depicts Blacks, what we are discussing, in effect, is prejudice.

Early advertising was a strong medium through which American white businessmen could express their feelings toward, and keep control over, American Blacks. Overgeneralized statements were brought to the public's eye via pictures that advertised commonly used products. These pictures, colorfully produced on boxes, cans, bottles, trade cards, and posters, portrayed Blacks in stereotypical occupations, such as cotton worker, butler, maid, cook, waitress, or laundress, or as just plain "ol' po' people." Nowhere in early advertising does one find a black family depicted as a hardworking, loving group.

Not until businessmen realized there was a black market, a black consumer, did they change their advertising principles. Thus, misconceptions about Blacks were reinforced by advertising dynamos, whose strategies remained unchanged until the 1960s.

A child growing up in the home of an average white family may not have been *taught* to hate Blacks, but more than likely the child caught the basic principle of prejudice through day-to-day living. Mother used Fun-to-Wash soap, with a Mammy on the label, to do the laundry. Mother often bought coffee in cans decorated with black figures in their native costumes. When she bought supplies to make the family clothes, her thread would come with a trade card that her daughter would have to paste in her album. ("Do all little black children have torn clothes, Mommy?") When the ads became more explicit and their characters "talked," it was always in pidgin English. Such is the manner in which prejudice is taught and maintained as a standard way of life.

Prejudice in advertising was the norm before the end of the Civil War, when Blacks were free to begin their own communities, build their own homes and businesses, and become consumers. Yet advertisers were slow to pick up on the change in the black person's buying power. During the nineteenth century, advertising began to prosper. The Industrial Revolution had a great impact on the advertising trade. The output of facto-

Green River Whiskey products; all in very good condition; *back:* tin tray, **$300–350;** *left to right:* two bottles, **$45–75 each;** store display–size bottle, **$250–300;** bottle in original package, **$125–150;** tin sign, **$300–400;** tobacco humidor, **$150–200;** cardboard tobacco box, from Green River Tobacco Company, **$100–125;** *front:* paper ink blotter; good condition, **$100–125.** Courtesy of the Leonard Davis Collection; photo by Bob Reno.

ries increased, and advertising helped to sell the bounty of products. Magazines and newspapers were sold worldwide, bringing about innovation after innovation in the way salable items were marketed in the early 1900s. Black-owned newspapers also began by buying advertising, and though their markets were smaller and the money budgeted for advertising was significantly less than the national magazines and city newspapers, the move toward pleasing the black consumer had begun.

This is not to say that advertising that degraded Blacks had stopped. Far from it! Bottles, cans, posters, and boxes still showed the black person in undignified poses, and advertisers continued to profit from the use of these symbols to advertise their products.

However, the choices were more subtle than before. The characters' features were a little less pronounced; the language quoted was a little closer to what the Northern White used on a daily basis. Instead of being depicted as slaves and strangers from a foreign land, Blacks were now being depicted as children, pets, or ignorant people who were to be pitied.

Also, just because advertisers started considering black consumers part of their audience didn't mean they were ready to accept Blacks as equals. Some advertising manuals produced from the 1880s to the 1920s, for example, encouraged advertisers to remember that the black members of their audience were not very sophisticated and would probably fail to appreciate any appeal other than low price.

Black Boy Pure Coffee tin, yellow background, shows black boy trademark, half-lb size; excellent condition, **$75–95.**

Advertisement for Paramount shoes, April 1906; good condition, **$10–12.**

During the 1920s and 1930s, consumer testing showed that advertising featuring black characters appealed both to black and white audiences. Once companies realized the sales value of racial elements in their advertising copy, more firms employed a central black figure in their advertising. Aunt Jemima became almost a legend; a black cleaning woman was used in Rinso detergent ads; and boxes of Gold Dust detergent featured a pair of nearly naked black children, known as the Gold Dust twins.

Dissatisfaction with the way Blacks were depicted in advertising began in the 1930s. By the 1940s and 1950s prominent black people began expressing their displeasure, and among their complaints was the fact that African-Americans were being used to advertise white people's products, thus making white-owned businesses rich. Further-more, the Blacks used in most ads were not made up well and were not shown in complimentary ways; for some Americans, these advertising campaigns constituted their principal impression of black people. Unfortunately, it is true that when we speak of Blacks in advertising, we speak of prejudice.

Thankfully, today's advertising is much more positive. More and more companies are hiring African-American models and spokespersons to represent their products. Comedian Bill Cosby has acted as spokesperson for industry giants such as Jell-O and Kodak; soft drink companies, such as Pepsi and Coke, have hired sports figures like Shaquille O'Neal and music legends such as Michael Jackson to sell their products. Though change has been slow, positive black role models are the norm in modern advertising.

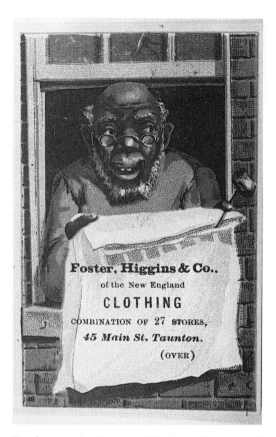

Trade card, Foster, Higgins & Co. of Taunton, Massachusetts; good condition, **$20–25**. Courtesy of Malinda Saunders; photo by Donald Vogt.

Tin sign for Sambo chocolate malted milk, 12″ × 18″; very good condition, **$100–150**. Courtesy of Rose Fontanella; photo by Donald Vogt.

Types of Collectible Advertising

ADS

Ads depicting Blacks can be found in the earliest American newspapers and are fairly common throughout the publications one may pick up at an antiques show, antiques shop, or garage sale. Usually the rare ads are also the ones that are the most degrading to black people. Although one might think that this type of ad is found only in periodicals dating before the Civil War, ads from the 1920s to 1940s are often so slanderous to black people that if they were to be printed today, a lawsuit would be levied against the periodical.

Often you can tell by the style of an ad when it was published. Knowing the differences between pre–Civil War, Civil War, Victorian, Art Nouveau, and Art Deco styles will help you to date the ad. Pre–Civil War ads were seldom illustrated; for later ads, the clothing style or type of machinery shown or historical references will help you with dating. A few other points to remember are that women were popular in ads at the time of the Civil War, company buildings were popular around 1880, and advertising using Blacks began before the Civil War and continued through the 1940s. The style of dress can give you a clue to age, as can the mode of transportation used in the ad.

Pickaninny peanut butter tins, 1-lb size, rare; excellent condition, **$250–350**; 10-lb size; good condition, **$300–350**. Courtesy of the Leonard Davis Collection; photo by Bob Reno.

Advertisement for Post Toasties, shows white children eating the product while black mammy scolds them, August 1916; excellent condition, **$10–15**.

BOTTLES AND BOXES

Parisian confectioner Nicholas Appert was, in 1810, the first to succeed in using glass bottles to preserve foods; however, paper labels were not used until much later. The most common collectible bottles depicting Blacks were not made until the turn of the century, with the bulk of such bottles produced in the 1920s and later. Utica Club Ale bottles show a young black waiter; other bottles, especially liquor bottles, may show Blacks in similar service-type positions.

The earliest advertising boxes were metal pieces that were painted or stenciled. It was not until 1850 that the Somers Brothers of Brooklyn, New York, invented a method of lithographing a design onto a metal box. Lithographed pieces are very popular and worth more if they have pictures on them.

Cardboard boxes to hold soap powder, spices, and other products began to be produced after the Industrial Revolution and were often printed by the hundreds. There are still times when a dealer or collector may come up with an unused carton of Fun-to-Wash boxes, although the collector should be warned: These advertising pieces are now being reproduced, and the copies are hard to distinguish from the originals.

CEREAL BOXES

A relatively new collectible, cereal boxes featuring black celebrities are hot! Needless to say, we are a throwaway society and—until the days of recycling—boxes, bottles, and cans of all types were just tossed into the garbage without thought. Look for the following products. Wheaties, well known for

Benne Bits brand cocktail bits, tin, red and white, 10-oz size; excellent condition, **$28–35.**

Cereal boxes, *left to right:* Urkel-Os (Ralston Purina); excellent condition, **$25–30;** Choco Maizoro (Mexican made); excellent condition, **$75–100;** Kellogg's Corn Flakes (Canadian made), back of box shows mammy mask; excellent condition, **$150–200;** Frosted Rice Krinkles (Post), back of boxes include cutout record from the Jackson 5; excellent condition, **$300–350.** Courtesy of the Leonard Davis Collection; photo by Bob Reno.

its sports celebrities series, featured the likes of O.J. Simpson and Michael Jordan, among others. Kellogg's Corn Flakes featured the photo of Miss America Vanessa Williams in 1984. The company destroyed all the boxes when the scandal broke out— she appeared in a photo layout, nude with another woman. Thus boxes with Williams on them are quite valuable today. Kellogg's Corn Flakes did a series in the 1970s that depicted everyday African-Americans in their chosen careers. Korn Kinks cereal was promoted by the H-O Company of Buffalo, New York, and sold for 5 cents a box in 1907 (the cereal was marketed from 1907 to the mid-1940s). The box featured a black child.

TINS

Tins with paper labels are difficult to find in good condition. Occasionally, as with boxes, a dealer or collector will come upon a box of unused labels. Do question their validity, but take into consideration the fact that these pieces were manufactured in bulk and often left in storage when a company went out of business or changed its style of advertising.

Rarity and condition determine the price of most tins, but shape is also a factor. For example, an unusual shape is more highly valued than the traditional round, and the roly-poly, created to resemble people, is the most desirable of all. One was a rotund black woman called mammy. Made in

Luzianne Coffee products, *left to right:* **3-lb coffee tin with bail handle, red, oldest version of tin, shows clouds behind the Luzianne lady; excellent condition, $500–600; 1-lb coffee tin, red; excellent condition, $75–100; salt and pepper shakers, red; excellent condition, $130–170; sample-size coffee tin, red; excellent condition, $200–250; 1-lb coffee tin, white; excellent condition, $500–700; Luzianne lady cookie jar; fair condition, $250–300; needle holder, paper; good condition, $50–100; sample-size coffee tin, white; excellent condition, $125–150; 1-lb coffee tin, white, Luzianne lady wears yellow skirt; fair condition, $50–75; salt and pepper shakers, green; excellent condition, $150–200; 3-lb coffee tin with bail handle, white; excellent condition, $150–175; 1-lb coffee tin, white, contemporary with brown print, 1953; excellent condition, $50–75. Courtesy of the Leonard Davis Collection; photo by Bob Reno.**

1912–1913, at least two versions of the mammy roly-poly exist.

Coffee companies often used black figures in their advertising. It appeared to be the vogue to advertise coffee by showing Blacks from the islands dressed in turbans and brightly colored clothes. Of particular note when dating coffee cans: The words *java* and *mocha* could be used by advertisers before 1906—the year the Pure Food and Drug Act was passed. After 1906 all claims had to be true, so these words generally disappeared from coffee cans. Although Luzianne Coffee cans and other items are probably the most familiar, you could spend the rest of your collecting life just trying to find all the black figures that were used to advertise coffee.

When collecting tins, it is important to remember—as with all antiques—that condition is paramount. Therefore, cleaning should be well thought out and attempted only when *absolutely necessary.*

TRADE CARDS

Colorful advertising cards, commonly known as trade cards, were given to the purchaser of articles such as shoes, thread, and household items just before and especially during the Victorian era. The cards were saved and sometimes pasted into an album that every member of the family could enjoy (see also Chapter 8).

Condition of trade cards is all-important. Rips, stains, holes, or dog-eared corners are considerations one must take into account when purchasing a card. If any one of these defects appears on the card you are about to purchase, keep in mind that its value will not be high.

Trade cards depicting Blacks started to show up in the early 1800s, printed by lithographers in Boston, New York, Philadelphia, and Baltimore. Some of the cards were fairly acceptable, but others were racist and extremely derogatory. One unusu-ally degrading trade card depicts Frederick Douglass taking Sulpher Bitters to lighten his skin.

Black trade card sales have risen dramatically in the last ten years, causing their value to skyrocket. A card that was worth $2 in 1978 could easily triple in value over as short a period as four years—an incredible price jump, even in the antiques world.

Some of the sayings on trade cards depicting Blacks are insulting, and these seem to have an increased value. The cards show large-headed, pop-eyed models in compromising or lowly positions, advertising items such as cotton seeds, coffee, and complexion creams. The Fairbanks Company

Trade card, reads "Grown with Williams, Clark & Co.'s High Grade Bone Fertilizers"; fair condition, **$20–25. Courtesy of Malinda Saunders; photo by Donald Vogt.**

made a card showing a nicely dressed white child asking a poorly dressed black child, "Why doesn't your Mama wash you with Fairy Soap?"

Rising Sun Stove Polish made a series of comical trade cards depicting the devastating effects on households that did not use their stove polish. One such card shows a black woman exclaiming, "Look yere old man! What kind o' stove blacking you call dat? I'se been rubbin' on dat stove all mornin' an' it don't gib it a polish worf a cent. You jest git de Rising Sun Stove Polish right away or dar'l be trouble. You think I got time to 'speriment with such mud?" The bottom half of the card shows the woman happily welcoming her man: "Come in, Ephraim! I'se not mad with you dis time, case yer sent me de genuine Rising Sun Stove Blacking; an it shines de stove in good shape. An' here's yer dinner all ready. Something' agin ye? No, deed I haven't; yer tink I'se an anjul to get along without good stove polish?"

TRADE SIGNS AND CIGAR STORE FIGURES

Until relatively recently, literacy rates in the United States were not high, so trade signs for city establishments, such as shoe-makers, taverns, and cigar stores, were in the form of pictures not words. Made to catch the eye of the passerby, the most common signs are the barber's pole, the hanging shoe that symbolizes the cobbler, the upraised arm holding a hammer to mark the smithy, and the watch to point the way to a jeweler or clockmaker. A tavern could be symbolized by a mug or a group of grapes, and the cigar store by a figure with a fistful of cigars or tobacco leaves.

Tobacconists' figures appeared early in the seventeenth century in England, and in America during the eighteenth century. Philadelphian William Rush, carver of wooden signs and tobacconists' figures,

made some of the earliest such figures in the United States, during the 1820s. The familiar cigar store Indian was not the only personage to grace the stoop of a tobacconist's shop. In fact, one of the earliest tobacco shop Indians was a strange combination: a black man wearing a headdress and a kilt of tobacco leaves; he was known as the "Virginian." The Englishman who carved this figure was likely trying to represent all the different people known to have a connection with the tobacco crop: the black slave who worked on the plantation, the "Virginian" who owned the plantation, and the American Indian who introduced white settlers to the growing and smoking of tobacco. The Indian was not known as a cigar store figure until the mid-nineteenth century and was a popular sign for tobacconists from the 1850s to the 1880s.

Coney Island Amusement Park advertising figure, plaster, bust of black man, about 2' tall; poor condition, $250–450. Courtesy of Rose Fontanella; photo by Donald Vogt.

Tobacconists' figures were usually carved by the same people who carved figureheads for ships, and so the figures standing in front of the tobacco shops often seemed ready to pull away from the store at any moment. Though the bulk of tobacconists' figures were Indians, there were also a smattering of figures made to resemble white people, Turks, Civil War figures, and the plantation slave (who often had a wide expanse of white shirt collar). Blackamoors were also popular during the 1870s, as were minstrels and jockeys. During the end of the nineteenth century, production of these wooden figures declined because of new ordinances that ordered the figures off the sidewalks (probably because they blocked foot traffic). Therefore, toward the end of the nineteenth century, other figures appeared as "mascots" of tobacco shops. Countertop pieces and shop window figures were made instead.

Cigar store figures of Blacks include jockeys, steamboat roustabouts, and even a portrait of Reverend Campbell. The famous detective Alan Pinkerton, who was President Lincoln's bodyguard during the Civil War, commissioned a carver to make Campbell's figure. Pinkerton had hired Campbell to fill out slaves' "freedom papers." The Campbell figure is wearing a long red coat and has a carpetbag and umbrella, according to Pinkerton's instructions.

Some Firms and Products That Used African-Americans in Their Advertising

The Aunt Jemima Pancake Flour Company used quite a few different objects in their promotions, all of which depicted the jolly black woman in her red turban. Salt and pepper shakers, cookie jars, plastic and cardboard items, even a pottery set of kitchen condiment holders made by the Weller Pottery Company, were given away in promotions. Aunt Jemima dolls were first made in 1896; later dolls included her husband, Uncle Moses, as well as daughter, Diana, and son, Wade. Premiums also included rag dolls and paper dolls, plastic syrup pitchers, trade cards, and clocks.

The Aunt Jemima image became a registered trademark in 1889, but it was not until 1893 that the company hired its first "real" Aunt Jemima. Nancy Green, a fifty-nine-year-old former slave from Montgomery County, Kentucky, acted as the trademark for almost thirty years. After she was in an auto accident, Edna/Anna Robinson took her place. Rosie Lee Moore Hall replaced Robinson and acted as Aunt Jemima until her death in 1967. It is said that Green really didn't resemble the Aunt Jemima image used on the packages, but that Robinson more closely resembled the modern symbol adopted in 1936. Today's Aunt Jemima is an updated version of the Robinson model. The Quaker Oats Company acquired the Aunt Jemima line of products in 1926 and began introducing other foods to the line. Aunt Jemima today represents almost $300 million in sales each year.

The Bull Durham Tobacco Company used Blacks in most of their advertising. One can find groups of black men engaged in card games, throwing dice, or just rocking on the porch in Bull Durham's advertising posters. These posters have been reproduced and have been seen selling for $500 and up. Buyer beware!

Coon Chicken Inn was a chain of restaurants found in Seattle, Washington; Portland, Oregon; and Salt Lake City, Utah. The restaurants existed from 1924 to 1951 and were recognizable by the large, smiling porter's face that adorned the front of each building. Patrons entered the establishment through the porter's mouth. Menus, plates, napkins, and so forth from the chain are considered highly collectible. The logo, a large smiling black porter's face, was copyrighted in 1925 by M. L. Graham.

Cream of Wheat brought us one of the most recognizable characters in advertising, the Cream of Wheat chef. His smiling face has adorned the cereal's ads and boxes from the early 1900s to this day. Earlier in this century, one could find ads for Cream of Wheat in every magazine and newspaper. "Rastus" was so popular that the

The Female American Serenade, chromolithograph print, "M & N Hanhart Litho Publishers, London"; very good condition, **$250–300.**

Reading the Crystal, by Harry Roseland, oil on canvas; excellent condition, **$18,000–20,000.** Photo courtesy of The Art and Frame Gallery, Inc.

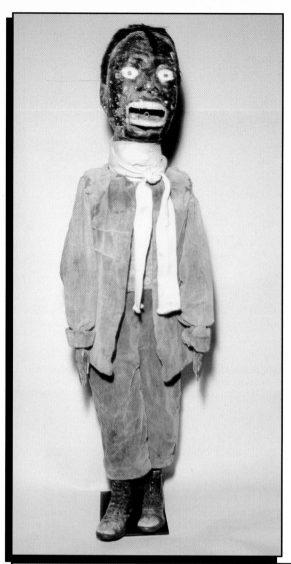

Ventriloquist's dummy, 1860–1870, used on showboat on Cumberland River, Tennessee, later used in Skeets Mayo's Blackfaced Minstrel Show in Nashville, purchased by James H. Young in 1943 from Mayo's sister, movable lower lip, paper label inside body box, wearing old clothing that appears to be original and two left shoes; very good condition, **$7,500–10,000.** Courtesy of American Eye; photo by Bob Reno.

"Dinosaur," by Charlie Lucas, Outsider Artist, plywood board with acrylic paints, painted in 1987, 12¼" × 23¾"; excellent condition, **$800–1,000.** Courtesy of American Eye; photo by Bob Reno.

Traveling puppet show, wooden case was carried on shoulder by leather strap, sides of box opened to make a "stage," paddle was placed on ground and stepped on in order to make puppet dance, late 1800s; very good condition, **$2,000–2,500.** Courtesy of Bonner's Barn; photo by Robideau Studios.

Book, *The Blackberries,* by Kemble, published by R. H. Russell, New York, cover shows three "babies" in bonnets and four figures dressed in blue dancing in the background; very good condition, **$100–150.**

Advertising figure, "The Golden Spirit," composition, possibly for a company that made rum, early 1900s; very good condition, **$200–300.** Courtesy of Rose Fontanella; photo by Donald Vogt.

Advertising figure, Euthymol toothpaste, chalk and wood, ca. 1910; very good condition, **$300–400.** Courtesy of Rose Fontanella; photo by Donald Vogt.

FairChildren New England Rag Dolls©, by Helen Pringle, six handmade dolls with detailed features and handsewn clothes; new, **$600 each.** Photography by T.R. Miller, Norton-Miller Photographs, Weatherford, Texas.

Wicker-handled "butler and mammy with feet" set, stamped "made in Japan," 1930s–1940s; all in excellent condition, *from left:* mammy biscuit jar, 8", **$1,200-1,500;** mammy cookie jar, 9½", **$1,000–1,200;** mammy salt and peppers, 5", **$100–125;** 6½", **$150–175;** butler cookie jar, 9½", **$1,000–1,200;** butler biscuit jar, 7½", **$1,200–1,500;** butler salt and peppers, 5", **$100–125;** 6", **$150–175.** Collection of Leonard Davis; photo by Bob Reno.

Ashtray, plaster, boy with crossed legs sits atop base, 1920s; very good condition, **$95–140.** Courtesy of Rose Fontanella; photo by Donald Vogt.

Toy, automaton, black male smoker, Lucien Bontemps, unmarked bisque head, hands, and arms; characterized features, set black glass eyes, pierced ears, open mouth to receive cigarette holder, black wool wig, key on mechanism (box) marked "LB," all original, rare, 24" overall, doll 16" high; excellent condition, **$1,500–2,000.** Collection of and photo by Evelyn Ackerman.

Snake Eyes dice game (*left*), 1920s–1930s; fair condition, **$35–50.** Bean-Em game, All-Fair, cardboard, bean bags thrown at exaggerated black faces, rare, 1931, 13" × 9"; very good condition, **$100–150.**

Sheet music, "The Old Cabin Home," "Compliments of J. W. Freund / Music Dealer / 11 South Side Square / Springfield, Ill."; good condition, **$75–100.**

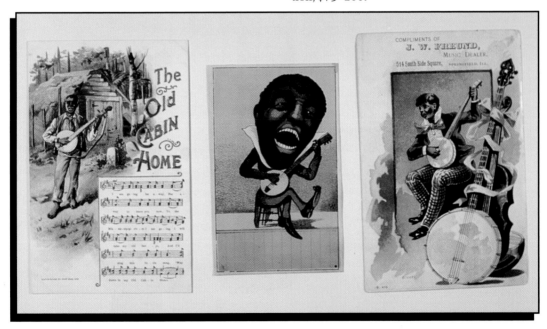

Lunchbox, Harlem Globetrotters, metal, various scenes of the team appear on all sides of the box, 1971; excellent condition, **$65–75.** Courtesy of Rose Fontanella; photo by Bob Reno.

Reproduction mammy memo pad holder, "Miss Martha Originals, Inc., Antique Repro" stamped on bottom, red dress trimmed in yellow, first of two versions made (second version had white dress), sold mostly through *Country Living* magazine in 1985 for $5–6 each, no longer produced; very good condition, **$75–85.** Collection of and photo by Mary Cantrell.

Coon Chicken Inn dinner plate, shows full face with open mouth, trademark of the restaurant, 1940s; excellent condition, **$105–135.** Courtesy of the Leonard Davis Collection; photo by Bob Reno.

company even had dolls made in his likeness as promotional giveaways (a printed and stuffed 18-inch doll was produced in 1936 and sold for 10 cents.) Puzzles and trade cards are also available. Most Cream of Wheat ads are very pleasing and are suitable for framing.

A black waiter from Chicago was the model for Rastus. He was paid $5 for the use of his image by Colonel Mapes, the general manager of the Nabisco Company, the owner of the Cream of Wheat products. The company began using his image in the early 1900s, replacing the original woodcut of a black chef on the packaging from 1894 until that time.

Famous Amos cookies, created by Wally Amos, produced a cookie jar and Christine Harris-Amos, Wally's wife, wrote a children's adventure book called *Wally Amos Presents Chip and Cookie.*

Fun-to-Wash soap powder was made by the Hygenic Laboratories, Inc., of Buffalo, New York. The boxes depicted a mammy face on the front of the box. She has a large grin and wears a scarf wrapped around her head. There are still factory cases of unused boxes, some with soap in them, on the market.

Gold Dust Washing Powder, manufactured by the N. K. Fairbanks Soap Company, showed a pair of black children running across the front of the box. A number of other objects, from figures to toys, were made in the Gold Dust twins' images. The detergent boxes are orange with black lettering and come in several sizes. Tin signs, buttons, boxes, fans, calendars, World's Fair items, trade cards, and hanging cardboard signs were also made.

The soap company was in business from 1897 to 1930. David H. Snipe of New York City acted as one of the original models for the twins. He was part of a vaudeville act and was performing on a street with his foster parents when the owners of the Fairbanks Company noticed him. In 1902, at a trade convention in Chicago, Snipes was picked to pose for the trademark. Incidentally, this trademark was the first one to have ever been registered. Edward Windsor Kemble sketched the Gold Dust twins. His pen-and-ink drawings can still be found and fetch thousands of dollars when auctioned.

In 1925, the twins appeared as radio personalities with Harvey Hindermyer and Earl Tuckerman (two white performers) providing the voices. The company was sold in the 1930s and interest in Gold Dust products declined.

Green River Whiskey used an old black man astride a mule in its advertising campaigns. The company made store display pieces, trays, signs, posters, and other advertising items as well as liquor decanters.

J. P. Alley's Hambone Cigars used a black airplane pilot on their cigar box labels. The original labels were made in the 1920s, but reproductions abound today. There is a tin sign available that depicts the pilot, but it is new—Alley did not make tin signs when it was actively doing business.

Kodak has used Bill Cosby as its spokesperson for many years. Ads that feature him can be found in newspapers and magazines as well as store display items, such as countertop signs and film display units.

Luzianne Coffee created its "coffee lady," a well-known black advertising symbol. The figure, clad in a green skirt, short-sleeved top, and head scarf, has withstood time and remains the symbol everyone associates with Luzianne. Figures, spice sets, sample giveaways, and tins can be found featuring her image. One must remember that the Luzianne lady with the green skirt is the original. There are reproductions on the market that show the woman wearing a different color skirt.

The F & F Mold & Dye Works made Luzianne salt and pepper shakers, but sold the mold. Later versions have the F & F symbol blocked out.

McDonald's featured a special series of collectible 16-ounce cups that depicted the 1992 Summer Olympics "Dream Team" basketball squad, which

included Magic Johnson, Charles Barkley, Scottie Pippen, Patrick Ewing, Michael Jordan, David Robinson, and Karl Malone.

NiggerHair smoking tobacco featured an African woman on its lithographed tobacco pails during the early part of this century. The image continued to be used even after the company changed its product name to *BiggerHair* smoking tobacco.

Pepsi's now familiar "uh-huh" commercials with Ray Charles have drawn many followers during the past couple of years. Even his backup singers, three beautiful women, have become celebrities in their own right. Subway sandwich shops served their Pepsi drinks in a 16-ounce cup featuring Ray Charles and the backup singers. You can also find all kinds of Pepsi print advertising, in-store advertising promotions (like counter signs and posters), and the cans and bottles themselves all featuring Charles's image.

Pickaninny Brand products, manufactured by F. M. Hoyt and Company, included a black girl on their labels. The small pail of peanut butter was in use in the 1920s. Prices for the pail can go as high as several hundred dollars.

Uncle Ben's Rice, a product of the Quaker Oats Company, featured a kindly looking white-haired black man as their symbol—and still does. In 1993, the company made a collectible tin to celebrate the product's fiftieth anniversary. Through the years, tin trays, tin containers, and other anniversary items have been produced.

Utica Club Soda used a black waiter holding a tray with a bottle of Utica Club perched on it. The man was usually shown on the front label of the bottles.

PRICES FOR ADVERTISING

Ad

American Tea Co., paintings, "Sambo's Love Life": "Proposal," "Wedding," and "First Child" in blue, green, red, and yellow, reads "American Tea Co." on back, ca. 1885, 7″ high × 5″ wide; excellent condition, **$175–250.**

Aunt Jemima pancake flour, from *Good Housekeeping* magazine, March 1928; near mint condition, **$10–15.**

Cream of Wheat

"Getting Up Steam," full color, June 1924; excellent condition, **$15–20.**

Nursery rhyme series—Old King Cole, magazine advertisement; excellent condition, **$20–28.**

"Oh, I done forgot dat Cream of Wheat," full color, framed; excellent condition, **$50–60.**

"What do you charge for board, sir?" black and white; excellent condition, **$12–18.**

Gold Dust Twins, black and white, May 1906; excellent condition, **$8–10.**

Listerine, from *Life* magazine, shows black family, black and white, January 1941; excellent condition, **$7–10.**

Three Bee blacking, lithograph on cardboard, shows black boy dancing in front of fellow shoeshine boys; printed by J. Ottmann Litho. Co., ca. 1882, 12″ × 17″; very good condition, **$1,500–2,000.**

Ashtray, Coon Chicken Inn, black head with porter hat and exaggerated lips; 1940–1951, 3½″ image; very good condition, **$18–20.**

Award, Dr. Pepper, reads "Perky," enameled metal plate, shows black boy holding up bottles of soda and standing on wood base; near mint condition, **$100–250.**

Bag, Aunt Jemima

Quaker Oats Co., cotton bag filled with corn meal; very good condition, **$175–200.**

Unopened bag of white corn meal; near mint condition, **$25–35.**

"Jigger Bob," paper, chromolithographed face and legs, paper clothes, with original box, which reads "Dis swell culled gent has mos' 'markable pins: When he walks foh de cake, he ev'vy times wins," 12½″; excellent condition, **$150–200. Courtesy of American Eye; photo by Bob Reno.**

Unused, paper bag for corn meal, colorful, 1960s; mint condition, **$8–12.**

Banner, Aunt Jemima

Canvas, promotional, painted in red, yellow, gold, brown, black, and white on canvas; ca. 1940, 33″ × 56″, very rare, mint condition, **$300–400.**

Cloth, used to advertise a personal appearance; excellent condition, **$350–650.**

Cotton, starched, "Coming . . . Aunt Jemima Pancakes Sat. Oct. 22 Kiwanis Pancake Day Northumberland Jr. Hi. Auditorium," 1953, 55″ × 34″, very good condition, **$550–600.**

Baseball cards, Pepsi, six cards, bottle hangers, including four black players, 1966; excellent condition, **$5–20.**

Blotter

Coca-Cola, reads "OK," shows white man on a bicycle drinking Coke with black boy serving, 1932; mint condition, **$50–250.**

Dixon & Company, comic, dark background with eyes, lips, hands and dice in white; unused, **$15–20.**

"Green River The Whiskey Without a Headache Blots Out All Your Troubles," shows black man in top hat standing holding the bridle of a horse; unused, **$15–20.**

Green River Whiskey, paper ink; excellent condition, **$100–125.**

"There'll be a Hot time in the Old Town tonight," comic, shows Old King Cole's Orchestra playing with "Neverbreak Fire Tools"; unused, **$15–20.**

Bottle

Green River Whiskey

Display bottle, amber; very good condition, **$200–250.**

Display size, glass, black and white label; excellent condition, **$250–300.**

In original package, black and white label; excellent condition, **$125–150.**

Mammy's Beverage, shows mammy on label, about 8″ high; very good condition, **$135–150.**

Bottle opener, Green River Whiskey; very good condition, **$20–30.**

Box

Amos 'n Andy, Williamson Candy Co., Chicago, Brooklyn, San Francisco, candy box, orange background, rare, ca. 1930; excellent condition, **$80–95.**

Aunt Jemima, yellow, box of buckwheat pancake batter; excellent condition, **$50–80.**

Black Boy, cigar box, shows dice, "7 & 11 always win," full color; excellent condition, **$30–40.**

Coon Chicken Inn Restaurant, cardboard chicken takeout box; excellent condition, **$75–100.**

Fun-to-Wash, shows black woman in turban and polka dot dress, yellow background with black and red lettering and design; **$20–40.**

Fun-to-Wash, Hygenic Laboratories, Buffalo, New York, cardboard, 25-cent size, 7¼″ high; excellent condition, **$20–25.**

Gold Dust, five boxes: two sample sizes and three varied sizes; good condition, **$35–75 for the set.**

Green River Whiskey/Tobacco, cardboard, tobacco box, marked "Green River Tobacco Company"; excellent condition, **$100–125.**

Log Cabin Smoking Tobacco, paper-coated wooden box with large interior label of black man outside his log cabin smoking, box: 14½″ × 7¾″ × 9¼″, label: 14″ × 8¾″; good condition, **$300–600.**

Old Virginia Cheroots, wooden cigar box, 1890; excellent condition, **$45–65.**

Overtons High Brown Powder, face powder, cardboard container, in blue, yellow, red and browns, 2½″ square; 1940s; near mint condition, **$35–50.**

Perfectos, Manufactured by F. H. Trimm, cigar box, good multicolors with wolf and word *Coon*, black boy with rifle on top, black person on side, top separate from bottom, 8″ × 5″ × 2½″; very good condition, **$125–175.**

Pickanninnies, jelly bean box, black and orange, original, 10-lb size; excellent condition, **$90–100.**

Uncle Wabash Cupcakes, Schulze Baking Co., cardboard, copyright 1924; excellent condition, **$25–30.**

Broadside, Bedwell Tobacco, shows three black men rolling barrels of Kentucky, Virginia, and Birds-Eye brands of tobacco in center oval, brand names surround the ovals, 18½″ × 14″ (excluding mat and frame); excellent condition, **$150–300.**

Button

Aunt Jemima, giveaway, shows famous Aunt Jemima face; excellent condition, **$4–6.**

Topsy Club Cool, matches the fans, shows cute black girl, 1¼″ dia.; new, **$0.83 each.**

Calendar, Brooks' & Co. Varnishes, paper; multi-paged, shows black people in "comical" scenes, rare, 1881; individual calendar sheets are 5″ × 6½″ (excluding mat), overall size is 26″ × 25¼″; near mint condition, **$300–450.**

Can

Gold Dust Twins, cleanser, cardboard canister with paper label; unused, excellent condition, **$15–20.**

Gold Dust Twins, four cardboard cans, yellow background and black decoration, shows the twins with piles of coins; 3″ dia. × 4¾″; very good condition, **$35–75 for the set.**

Jumbo Dixie Peanuts, shows black boy, tin, colorful label, 10-lb size; excellent condition, **$145–195.**

Luzianne Coffee, shows mammy, colorful label; excellent condition, **$35–50.**

Old Black Joe, grease, tin with lithographed label, 5-lb size; excellent condition, **$55–65.**

Candles, in the figure of Aunt Jemima, about 2″ tall; excellent condition, **$5–10.**

Card, "Better known as the Six Babb Brothers," original radio promotional black and white photo card, 1930s, 9″ × 11″; excellent condition, **$35–50.**

Cereal box

Frosted Mini-Wheats (Kellogg's)

Reggie Jackson, baseball player; excellent condition, **$25–35.**

Karl Malone, basketball player, excellent condition, **$25–35.**

Karl Malone, basketball player, Team USA, 1992; very good condition, **$18–22.**

Frosted Rice Krinkles (Post), the Jacksons, with actual cutout record; excellent condition, **$300–350.**

Kellogg's Corn Flakes

Basketball's 1992 Olympic "Dream Team"; excellent condition, **$40–60.**

Black grandmother, 1983; excellent condition, **$50–75.**

Willie Mays, baseball player, shown on back, autographed, 1972; excellent condition, **$250–350.**

Cereal boxes, *left to right:* **Kellogg's Corn Flakes, shows black boy with glasses; excellent condition, $45–75; Kellogg's Corn Flakes, shows Vanessa Williams; excellent condition, $100–150; Mr. T Cereal (Quaker Oats); excellent condition, $100–150; Kellogg's Corn Flakes, shows black grandmother, 1983; good condition, $50–75. Courtesy of the Leonard Davis Collection; photo by Bob Reno.**

Miss America Vanessa Williams, 1989; excellent condition, **$100–150.**

Mr. T cereal (Quaker Oats); excellent condition, **$100–150.**

Urkel-Os cereal (Ralston Purina); excellent condition, **$25–30.**

Wheaties (General Mills)

Roy Campanella, baseball player, "60 Years of Sports Heritage," 1992; very good condition, **$70–80.**

Patrick Ewing, basketball player, 1992; very good condition, **$18–22.**

Michael Jordan, basketball player, 1988 and 1992; very good condition, **$8–12.**

Willie Mays, baseball player, 1950s, autographed; excellent condition, **$50–75.**

Walter Payton, football player; excellent condition, **$50–70.**

Scottie Pippen, basketball player, 1992; very good condition, **$18–22.**

Jackie Robinson, baseball player; very good condition, **$110–140.**

Clock, Big Ben alarm clock, Aunt Jemima, 1940s; excellent condition, **$350–425.**

Clothes brush, Aunt Jemima, promotional item; excellent condition, **$8–15.**

Condiment set, Aunt Jemima, 11 pieces, including spices, salt, pepper, and syrup; very good condition, **$260–325.**

Cookie jar

Aunt Jemima, plastic, a slim Aunt Jemima in red, 1950s; excellent condition, **$450–500.**

Famous Amos, made by Treasure Craft, copyrighted in the United States, matte finish, bisque, rare; mint condition, **$250–350.**

Famous Amos cookie jars, made by Treasure Craft in the United States, *left:* **bisque, first type made, matte finish, rare; excellent condition, $250–350;** *right:* **signed by Amos; excellent condition, $200–250. Courtesy of the Leonard Davis Collection; photo by Bob Reno.**

Luzianne Coffee, ceramic, green-skirted Luzianne lady, 1940s; very good condition, **$250–300.**

Cosmetic label, Hug Me Tight sachet powders; excellent condition, **$1–5.**

Counter display figure, Green River Whiskey, shows black man with horse, rat on saddle; excellent condition, **$200–250.**

Coupon, Luzianne Coffee, used to get promotional items; excellent condition, **$18–24.**

Cup, Aunt Jemima, paper coffee cup; excellent condition, **$35–45.**

Dinner bell, Aunt Jemima; very good condition, **$40–60.**

Dinnerware, Coon Chicken Inn Restaurant, two different types: Shenango China, Inca Ware (each location had its own pattern)

Bread plate; **$75–100**

Cereal bowl; **$200–250**

Cup and saucer; **$200–300**

Custard cup; **$100–125**

Demitasse cup; **$225–275**

Dinner plate; **$125–150**

Platter; **$300–350**

Soup bowl; **$200–250**

Display

Hillbilly mechanical window attraction; electric wooden jointed black figures, including banjo player and dancer, moving figures, and pecking bird by fence on wooden platform, 20″ × 20″ × 11½″; good condition, **$1,500–3,000.**

Peachey Tobacco, made by the King Cole Co., Akron, Ohio, life-size papier-mâché black man sitting on barrel with open tobacco tin in his hand, man is dressed in three-piece suit, red-and-white striped socks, and a white hat, very lifelike; near mint condition, **$15,000–18,000.**

Pepsodent

Amos, die-cut cardboard, in black, orange, brown, and white, Amos holds Pepsodent tube, center fold, very rare, 54″ × 24″; very good/excellent condition, **$500–700.**

Andy, die-cut cardboard, in black, brown, orange, white, and green, includes Pepsodent box, center fold, very rare, 62″ × 24″; very good/excellent condition, **$500–700.**

Pug's Quality Candies, Portland, Oregon, wooden box, depicts black kids flying atop jellybean, promoting Halloween, orange and black, late 1800s; excellent condition, **$450–550.**

Sambo, die-cut cardboard piece, black skin tone, red, yellow, blue, and green decor, stands

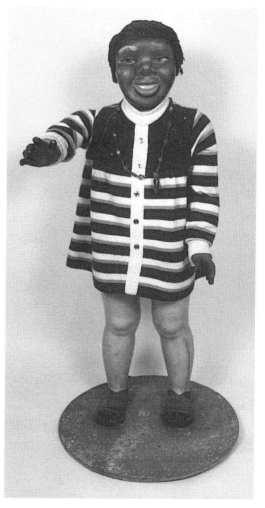

Store figurine from a New York department store, moveable, electric, head is black, but body was originally white and then painted brown, ca. 1940; excellent condition, $200–300. Courtesy of Rose Fontanella; photo by Donald Vogt.

on countertop via easel, 1940s, 14″ tall; mint condition, **$85–135.**

Smiling Sam, peanut vendor; figural head with exaggerated features, put can in head and peanuts are delivered when you pull on tongue, 12″ × 14″ × 12″; good condition, **$200–400.**

Terra-cotta statue, attributed to Arthur Strasser (who was employed by the Frederick Goldscheider Co. in Vienna, Austria), full figure of a smiling black boy sitting in a chair with bare feet crossed, once used to advertise stove blacking at Napoleon, Ohio, general store, life size, 42″ high, ca. 1890; excellent condition, **$8,000–9,000.**

Envelope, Aunt Jemima letterhead, logo in right hand corner, probably 1940s; excellent condition, **$40–50.**

Fan

Piccaninny Restaurant, two fans, cardboard with menu on backside, 1930s, 9½″ × 7″; mint condition, **$75–100 for the set.**

Topsy Club Cool, paper; new; **$3 each.**

Flue cover, mammy fortune-teller, 1880s; excellent condition, **$40–50.**

Hanger, Gold Dust, die-cut cardboard store hanger, two-sided banner, die-cut letters on top of boxes spell out product's name, rare, each piece about 7¾″ × 15½″; very good condition, **$5,500–7,500.**

Hat, Aunt Jemima

Pancake Jamboree, advertising hat, reads "Paperlynen Co. Columbus Ohio," red, tan, and brown graphics on ivory ground, 1935; excellent condition, **$65–100.**

Pancake Jamboree, paper hat, reads "Aunt Jemima's Pancake Jamboree," giveaway; excellent condition, **$5–10.**

Humidor, Green River Whiskey/Tobacco, pottery stoneware; excellent condition, **$150–200.**

Jar, Curly Top Hair Pomade, product never used, put on hair after straightening, great label in red, brown, and blue, early 20th century, 3½″ × 2″; mint condition, **$35–50.**

Key chain and tape measure, Aunt Jemima Breakfast Club, hard plastic with metal tape measure, shows Aunt Jemima in yellow plaid bandanna, late 1940s, 1¼″ square; excellent condition, **$75–100.**

Label

Black Joe, grape, 1940s, 4″ × 13″; very good condition, **$4–$5.**

Dixie Boy Fruit, Waverley, Florida, shows black boy biting into juicy grapefruit, full color; excellent condition, **$6–10.**

Florida

Three labels, show black boy eating watermelon; very good condition, **$3 for the set.**

Three labels: "Aunty," "Mammy," and "Breakfast Bell"; all in excellent condition, **$5 for the set; $12 for three sets.**

Fruit boxes, mammy, elongated octagon shape, assorted subjects; excellent condition, **$15–18 for set of twelve.**

Joe Sammy, yams, 1940s, 9″ × 9″; very good condition, **$4–5.**

Lime Kiln Club, made by J. J. Bagley, tobacco, shows black men holding court in Detroit, printed by Clay and Company; 13″ × 10″; very good condition, **$250–400.**

Log Cabin, tobacco, shows black man sitting in front of a log cabin smoking, 13½″ × 8¼″; excellent condition, **$600–1,000.**

Longwood Plantation

Syrup, can label, 1940s, 3″ × 10¼″; very good condition, **$2–3.**

Can label, three labels, shows black lady carrying pancakes with syrup, 3¼″ × 11″; very good condition, **$1 each; $6 for set.**

Negro powders, creams, perfumes, and oils, seven labels, multicolored, unused, mounted on card, assorted sizes; mint condition, **$50–75 for set.**

Lunch box

Black Dixie Kid, metal, colorful depictions of the Dixie Kid; excellent condition, **$40–60.**

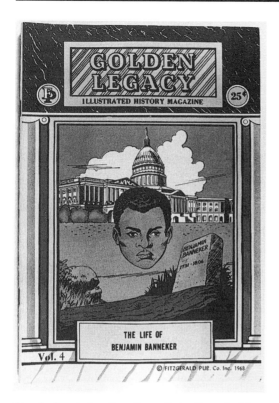

Comic book by the Coca-Cola Co., Golden Legacy series that highlighted the successes of selected African-Americans; excellent condition, **$10–15.**

Dixie Kid Tobacco, black body, colorful illustrations, tin; excellent condition, **$275–350.**

Mailing box, Aunt Jemima, premium, features portrait of Aunt Jemima in blue on white ground, 1940s, 5¼″ × 3¾″ × 1½″ deep; excellent condition, **$65–100.**

Matchbook

Coon Chicken Inn Restaurant

Individual restaurant logos on matches; **$75–100**

Regular; **$25–45**

Dinah's Shack; excellent condition, **$15–20.**

Match holder, Aunt Jemima, wall model with potholder, very good condition, **$45–65.**

Match safe, Topsy Hosiery, tin, shows black bathing beauty with black man looking down from inset near top, logo: black boy, "Topsy," rare; 3½″ × 5″; good condition, **$400–600.**

Menu

Aunt Jemima's kitchen; excellent condition, **$35–50.**

Coon Chicken Inn, shows the famous face with open mouth and the specials of the day, 12″; excellent condition, **$85–95.**

Napkin

Aunt Jemima restaurant napkin; excellent condition, **$50–75.**

Coon Chicken Inn Restaurant, marked with logo; excellent condition, **$25–45.**

Pail

Aunt Jemima, tin, colorful, 1928; excellent condition, **$30–40.**

Luzianne Coffee, tin, colorful depictions of the Luzianne coffee lady; excellent condition, **$45–65.**

Mammy's Favorite Coffee, tin, 4-lb size, 1880s; excellent condition, **$100–140.**

NiggerHair Tobacco, covered, tin, black and white depiction of African woman with ring through nose; excellent condition, **$100–125.**

Pickaninny Brand Peanut Butter, made by F. M. Hoyt & Co., Amesbury, Mass., yellow and red background, shows black baby girl in center, 1-lb size, 1920–1930; excellent condition, **$350–500.**

Paper needle holder, Luzianne Coffee; excellent condition, **$50–100.**

Paper plate, Aunt Jemima, signed by Aunt Jemima; excellent condition, **$55–75.**

Paper towel holder, Aunt Jemima; excellent condition, **$55–75.**

Pencil clips, Aunt Jemima; new, **$0.50 each.**

Photograph, Coon Chicken Inn Restaurant, black-and-white glossy of restaurant, showing famous entrance; excellent condition, **$50–60.**

Pinback button

Aunt Jemima Breakfast Club; excellent condition, **$35–45.**

Gold Dust Twins, in gold and black boxes; very good condition, **$45–55.**

Placemat

Aunt Jemima, shows the "Story of Aunt Jemima" in full color, designed by N. C. Wyeth, from first Aunt Jemima restaurant at Frontierland in Disneyland, 1955, 13¾″ × 9¾″; excellent condition, **$25–50.**

Coon Chicken Inn Restaurant; excellent condition, **$30–40.**

Plate, Hood's Sarsaparilla, lithograph on cardboard, shows white farmer with gun, black man with stick, and barking dog, all in hot pursuit of hawk swooping to catch chicken, testimonials on back of lithograph attest to numerous cures from using the product, rare; ca. 1885, 8¾″ dia.; very good condition, **$250–400.**

Poster

Charles Denby Cigars, shows black boy with box, stand-up poster; excellent condition, **$45–60.**

Coca-Cola, black family drinking the product, 1950s; excellent condition, **$195–215.**

Dixie Boy Firecrackers, multicolored, sixteen firecrackers in rare original package, complete, 28″ × 18″; mint condition, **$75–125.**

Poster for Peerless Beauty Supplies of Richmond, Virginia; good condition, $75–125. Courtesy of Rose Fontanella; photo by Donald Vogt.

Gold Dust Twins, paper, shows twins being welcomed by Uncle Sam and Teddy Roosevelt, Statue of Liberty in background, 20″ × 10½″ (excluding frame); very good condition, **$800–1,500.**

Gorton's, paper, shows foods such as puddings and pies as well as black servants taking care of white woman in hammock, setting looks like a tropical paradise, 26½″ × 20¼″; very good condition, **$250–500.**

Polk Miller's Ten Cent Liver Pills, shows stereotyped barefoot black child on logo, exaggerated ethnic features, 7½″ × 12″, 1890s; excellent condition, **$125–175.**

Red Cross Cotton, Blacks picking cotton, colorful and realistic, 1894; excellent condition, **$400–450.**

Sanford's Ginger, paper, printed by Forbes Co., shows black boy with watermelon and large bottle, 21½″ × 28½″ (excluding frame); very good condition, **$2,500–3,500.**

"Tarzan and the Mau-Maus—The most blood-thirsty tribe in Africa," bright, multicolored, shows Tarzan fighting a tiger and alligator, repairs, 40″ × 28″; very good condition, **$225–300.**

Potholder rack, Aunt Jemima, carved wood; very good condition, **$25–40.**

Recipe box, Aunt Jemima, plastic; excellent condition, **$125–150.**

Reservation card

Aunt Jemima, restaurant table card, full color, shows Aunt Jemima's face in die-cut relief, captioned "Folks . . . It's a treat to eat out often . . . Bring the whole family . . . Time for Aunt Jemima Pancakes," 1953; mint (unused) condition, **$25–40.**

Coon Chicken Inn Restaurant; restaurant reservation card, about 3″ × 5″; excellent condition, **$25–45.**

Salt and pepper shakers

Aunt Jemima, plastic, red, black, and white, about 3″ high; excellent condition, **$35–45.**

Luzianne Coffee, hard plastic, green-skirted lady, 1940s–1950s; excellent condition, **$150–200.**

Shaker, paprika, Aunt Jemima, 4″; very good condition, **$15–25.**

Shipping crate, Gold Dust, cardboard, shows multiple images of the famous twins, rare, 19¼″ × 12″ × 13½″; good condition, **$150–250.**

Sign

A & P Stores, shows white people rushing to work while black waiters prepare "ten minutes for refreshments," ca. 1886, 32″ × 22″ (excluding frame); very good condition, **$750–1,500.**

Adlers Kids, lithographed tin, shows stereotypical black boys stealing watermelons, the faces are raised (1″ deep × 2½″ wide) and made of plaster with glass eyes, muted colors, 23½″ × 19″ (including frame); good condition, **$15,000–20,000.**

Aunt Jemima, chromolithographed tin, shows Aunt Jemima on swing, colorful, 17″; excellent condition, **$45–65.**

Ayer's Pills, paper, shows the "Country Doctor," who is black and healing the child who sits in his lap with Ayer's pills ("The Best Family Physic"), depiction is serious not caricature, 28½″ × 41″ (excluding frame); very good condition, **$9,000–12,000.**

Bath Iron Works, sheet metal, life-size black man holding sign between his legs, brightly painted (perhaps second coat), illegible writing of advertising on sign, dated 1876; excellent condition, **$2,500–3,500.**

Bull Durham, paper, printed by Giles Litho. Co., "Teaching Time," shows white teacher instructing black pupils about the virtues of Bull Durham tobacco, 21½″ × 27½″ (excluding mat and frame); good condition, **$1,500–2,500.**

Charles Denby Cigars, cardboard, vivid multicolors, in wood frame with glass, 1920s, 11″ × 16″; excellent condition, **$275–325.**

Coblentz & Levy, paper, shows two fancily dressed black couples, says "Drink Black Diamond Whiskey, Rich and Mellow," extremely colorful, 15″ × 20″ (excluding frame); near mint condition, **$1,500–2,000.**

Coca-Cola

Black waiter serving white woman, "Sign of Good Taste," 1957, 20″ × 30″; good condition, **$20–100.**

Lionel Hampton, cardboard cutout, 11½″ × 15″; 1953; very good condition, **$50–250.**

Olympic winners, Jesse Owens and Alice Coachman "Quality You Can Trust," gold wooden frame, rare, 1952, 20″ × 36″; very good condition, **$250–750.**

Sugar Ray Robinson, cardboard, easel back; 1952, 12″ × 15″; very good condition, **$100–250.**

Cook's Beer, tin, black butler has large grin on his face and is handing a bottle to his white boss, 13″ × 20½″; fair condition, **$50–100.**

Derby Boot and Shoe Polish, paper, printed by Sarony, Major & Knapp, New York, a costumed merchant in a Near Eastern bazaar holds up a boot that reflects the face of a black man, who is walking by, reads "A Substitute for Blacking," ca. 1859; very good condition, **$300–500.**

Dontophile, embossed, in beautiful green, gold, red, and black; opiate for tooth pain, shows a screaming black man, "comic," 18½″ × 7½″, very rare; near mint condition, **$450–600.**

Duluth Imperial Flour, tin, shows black cook, 18″ × 25″, 1910; excellent condition, **$725–875.**

Gold Dust Twins, cardboard, Scrubbin' Tub, 28″ × 17″, dated 1921; excellent condition, **$95–110.**

Granger Pipe Tobacco, cardboard display, two-piece sign shows black butler with white child and canister of Rough Cut pipe tobacco, 29¼″ × 45″; very good condition, **$100–200.**

Green River Whiskey

Black man and horse, cardboard, framed, 1899, 42″ × 32″; excellent condition, **$900–980.**

Black man on mule, tin, classic image, original retouched frame; 40½″ × 31″ overall; fair condition, **$250–500.**

Black man with mule, tin, "Whiskey without a Headache," original frame, 33″ × 23½″ (excluding frame); good condition, **$350–600.**

Old black man and mule, paper on board, 1930, 28″ × 22″; excellent condition, **$95–115.**

Hercules Powder Co.

Winter scene, black boy hunting with muzzle-loading rifle, reads "Don't you fool me, dog!," 1920, 15¼″ × 25″ (including metal strips); excellent condition, **$460–650.**

Winter scene, two black boys, one with muzzle-loading rifle, the other pointing, reads "Dah he goes!," 1924, 15¼″ × 25″; very good condition, **$400–600.**

Lone Jack Tobacco, paper, shows four men: Turkish, black, East Indian, and Chinese with dog, all are at table smoking pipes, colorful, 12″ × 9½″; excellent condition, **$750–1,250.**

Old Harvest Whiskey, tin, self-framed, shows the interior of a black family's home with family sitting in rocking chairs, baby on mother's lap is reaching for bottle of whiskey on the table, reads "He's Gittin' Mo' Like His Dad Every Day!," 22¼″ × 16″; good condition, **$1,500–2,000.**

Pan-Handle Scrap Tobacco, cardboard, printed by Currier & Ives, shows scene of white police rousting a group of black men playing craps, 1890, 20″ × 14½″ (excluding frame); good condition, **$200–300.**

Paul Jones Whiskey

Paper over cardboard, shows black woman, huge watermelon, and child, quite colorful; excellent condition, **$600–690.**

Tin-rolled cornered classic image of "The Temptation of St. Anthony," shows mammy with watermelon and black man holding a bottle of whiskey, supposedly representing temptations for the child kneeling between them, 19½″ × 14″; good condition, **$600–800.**

Tin, lithographed, "Temptation of St. Anthony," shows black farmer with bottle, wife with watermelon, and child between, 19½″ × 13¾″; excellent condition, **$600–700.**

Picanninny Freeze, cardboard, shows black girl with watermelon, "Picanninny Freeze $.05," reproduction, full color; excellent condition, **$35–45.**

St. Louis Beef, paper, printed by A. Gast & Co., St. Louis, shows white man seated at table ready to eat and black manservant standing beside table, 10½″ × 13½″; very good condition, **$300–700.**

Swift's Washing Powder, paper on canvas, shows black couple on donkey-pulled cart, racing through a scene of animal pandemonium, black child bounces on the back with boxes of the product, 27½″ × 41½″; good condition, **$3,000–6,000.**

Topsy Smoking Tobacco, paper, made by United States Printing Co., Quincy, Illinois, colorful and large, shows a black woman holding an orange parasol and a package of the product, two sheets, reads "A Success that Succeeds! Topsy Granulated Smoking Tobacco is Always Good, The Wellman & Dwire Tobacco Co., Manufacturers, Quincy, Ill.," 40″ × 56″; excellent condition, **$45,000–50,000.**

U.S. Fur Company, shows black hunter surprised by skunk, humorous, colorful; excellent condition, **$525–595.**

Uncle Sam Range, paper, printed by Schumacher & Ettlinger Lith. Co., shows Uncle Sam with Thanksgiving meal atop the stove and political emblems such as the Liberty Lady, bald eagle, and sections of the United States, a black man is cooking the turkey, centennial dinner of 1876, 20½″ × 13¾″; excellent condition, **$5,000–8,000.**

Silverware, Coon Chicken Inn Restaurant, knives, forks, and spoons; very good condition, **$50–75 each.**

Spice set

Aunt Jemima, spice rack with spices, hard plastic, in Aunt Jemima figures, black, red, and white; excellent condition, **$500–700.**

Luzianne Coffee, six 3″ pieces, salt and pepper 5″ tall; very good condition, **$45–55.**

Store card, Briar Pipe, shows black child holding two labeled packages of pipe tobacco, 8″ × 11¼″; very good condition, **$125–275.**

Stove, Aunt Jemima, electric, premium that could be ordered from the company, red steel, about 2′ × 2′; excellent condition, **$2,500–3,000.**

Straw holder, Coon Chicken Inn Restaurant, chalkware, in the shape of the Coon Chicken logo face; excellent condition, **$250–300.**

String holder, Aunt Jemima, porcelain, wall model, 6¾″; very good condition, **$20–40.**

Sugar and creamer

Aunt Jemima, celluloid, covered; very good condition, **$32–38.**

Luzianne Coffee, figures, no lids; very good condition, **$62–68.**

Syrup jug, Aunt Jemima

Ceramic, 6″; excellent condition, **$8–15.**

Plastic; very good condition, **$20–30.**

Tape measure, Aunt Jemima, promotional; excellent condition, **$8–12.**

Tieback, Aunt Jemima, hard plastic, set of six, 1940s; excellent condition, **$30–45 for the set.**

Tins

Aunt Sally's Candy, 1-lb size; excellent condition, **$15–20.**

Diamond Match, shows black family with match dispenser, reads "You Chillun Keep Back Deah," 4½″ × 1½″ × 2¼″; very good condition, **$200–300.**

High Brown Face Powder, shows face of black girl who uses product; excellent condition, **$15–18.**

La Jean Products, three cosmetic tins, pictorial, 1930s; very good condition, **$15–20.**

De-Lite's Cocoa spice set, in original lunchbox tin, ten spices, each labeled with logo of black boy in tan and black; excellent condition, **$600–800.** Courtesy of the Leonard Davis Collection; photo by Bob Reno.

Lipton Tea

Lithograph, shows black tea pickers, 3-lb size; excellent condition, **$50–65.**

Two tins, show black workers in field, 5-lb and 3-lb sizes; good condition, **$75–150 for the pair.**

Long Tom Tobacco, made in Toronto, Canada, shows black man with funny long legs in a checkered suit, 5″ × 2″ × 3½″; good condition, **$100–200.**

Luzianne Coffee

Luzianne coffee lady wearing green dress, red background, lunch pail size; excellent condition, **$65–85.**

Luzianne coffee lady in yellow shirt, tin is white, 1-lb size; excellent condition, **$75–100.**

Luzianne coffee lady with clouds behind her, rare, bail handle, 3-lb, oldest known

Luzianne tin; excellent condition, **$500–600.**

Luzianne coffee lady drawn in brown, stylized, reads "Luzianne Coffee and Chicory," 1-lb size, 1953; excellent condition, **$50–75.**

Mammy Coffee, shows black man; excellent condition, **$95–140.**

Mammy's Favorite Brand Coffee, made by C. D. Kenny Co., shows mammy trademark, 4-lb size; excellent condition, **$65–85.**

Mammy, roly-poly, colorfully lithographed; excellent condition, **$260–365.**

Mason Shoe Blacking, black and white, shows famous black boy and boot, very early, 3″ dia.; very good condition, **$75–100.**

Negro Head Brand

Oysters, shows black man with mouth open ready to eat an oyster; red and black, 1940s–1950s; very good condition, **$100–125.**

Shrimp, shows black man with mouth open ready to pop in a shrimp, 1940s–1950s; very good condition, **$100–125.**

Sweet Georgia Brown, cosmetic tins, two large, one small, pictorial 1930s; very good condition, **$12–18 for the set.**

Uncle Ben's, show Uncle Ben and the 1992 Olympics team; commemorative limited edition; near mint condition, **$10–20.**

Uncle Joe's, cigars; excellent condition, **$35–45.**

Tobacco container

BiggerHair Smoking Tobacco, cardboard, shows black woman with earrings in both ears and through her nose, $5\frac{1}{4}'' \times 6\frac{1}{4}''$; very good condition, **$100–200.**

NiggerHair

Pail, shows African woman with ring in her nose; excellent condition, **$95–125.**

Tin, shows African woman with nose ring and earrings, $6\frac{1}{4}'' \times 5.375''$; excellent condition, **$150–300.**

Token, Coon-Chicken Inn, cardboard, size of quarter; excellent condition, **$3–5.**

Toothpick holder, Coon-Chicken Inn Restaurant, metal, in the shape of the Coon-Chicken

logo face, about $3\frac{1}{2}''$ tall; excellent condition, **$200–250.**

Towel, Aunt Jemima, cotton, colorful; very good condition, **$30–40.**

Toy, "Jigger Bob," paper; chromolithographed face and legs, paper clothes; with original box, reads "Dis swell culled gent has mos' 'markable

Zanzibar brand spice canister, tin, 1949; excellent condition, **$35–50.**

Nigger/Negro Brand food tins, *left to right:* tomatoes, unopened; fair condition, **$1,000–1,500;** oysters; fair condition, **$300–500;** shrimp; excellent condition, **$100–125;** oysters; good condition, **$100–125. Courtesy of the Leonard Davis Collection; photo by Bob Reno.**

pins: When he walks foh de cake, he ev'vy time wins," 12½", *Ron Carr Collection;* excellent condition, **$150–200.**

Trade Card

American Negroes, wedding day; very good condition, **$10–12.**

Black maid with old white man, reads "I'm a Grandpa at last . . ." of five children, five sequential cards, framed, John McGreen, Chicago, copyright 1882; excellent condition, **$75–100 for the set.**

Burdock Blood Bitters, paper, four versions, show two white kids and two black kids, the black girl is playing a banjo, the black boy is carrying a shoeshine kit, extremely colorful, framed, about 2½" × 4"; **$20–40 each.**

Mayo's Tobacco, die-cut, man with black face; excellent condition, **$15–25.**

Tray

Coca-Cola, romance series, two trays, show black couple getting married, 1970s; excellent condition, **$100–125 for the set.**

Early Times Distillery, tin charger, shows Kentuckian scene of backwoods still and black men tending to production, 24" dia.; good condition, **$500–750.**

Fairbanks Cottolene, tin, shows black mother and child working in cotton field, reads "The source of Cottolene, Best for Shortening—Best for Frying," 4⅕" dia.; excellent condition, **$150–200.**

Green River Whiskey

Tin charger, shows black man with donkey, 24" dia.; good condition, **$150–300.**

Tin server, shows black man with mule, about 8" dia.; excellent condition, **$300–350.**

Harvard Brewing Co., shows white couple seated at table and being waited on by a black man, 12" dia.; very good condition, **$100–250.**

Sheboygan; shows Indian with two black waiters, reads "Chief of Them All," company

made mineral water and ginger ale, 12" dia.; excellent condition, **$300–500.**

Treasure map, Pepsodent, Amos 'n Andy, paper, giveway for children, shows Amos and Andy and tests the child's ability to find the treasure; excellent condition, **$35–45.**

Trivet, Aunt Jemima, iron; very good condition, **$12–18.**

Whisk broom, Aunt Jemima; very good condition, **$30–40.**

Whiskey Charger, Green River, colorful curved wall piece in red, green, brown, and blue, shows detailed scene of black man in top hat holding reins of horse, reads "Whiskey Without Headache" and "She Was Bread In Old Kentucky," very rare; 24" dia.; near mint condition, **$1,200–1,500.**

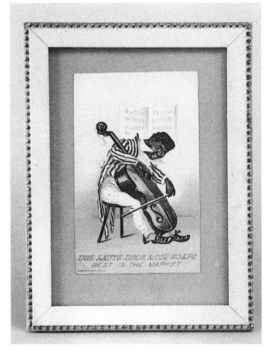

Trade card for Lautz Bros. & Co.'s soaps, printed by Eckstein & Poor Lith, New York, full-color chromolithograph, shows black man in striped tails playing a cello, framed, early 1900s; excellent condition, $18–25. Courtesy of Dawn and Bob Reno; photo by Bob Reno.

CHAPTER SIX

Dolls

The most important criterion when collecting black dolls is to decide whether or not you *like* the doll. A cherished "baby" gains more nostalgic value if she or he becomes a treasured member of the household and is passed down from generation to generation. Condition is another important factor to consider when buying a doll. Clothes and wig should be original for the doll to command top price. The wig must also not be soiled or restyled, the skin of the doll should be clean and unblemished, and if the doll has "sleep eyes," they should open and close easily.

Though you hear about antique dolls constantly setting new price records, one can begin a doll collection with a small budget. Modern black dolls can still be found at yard sales and flea markets for very little money. You may have to hunt around to find original clothes, but that exploring only serves to make collecting more interesting.

If you decide to collect black dolls, you must be prepared to compete with some of the most gregarious collectors in the antiques business. Doll collectors are more likely to go to great lengths in pursuing their "finds" than any other collectors. Doll collector clubs abound throughout the world

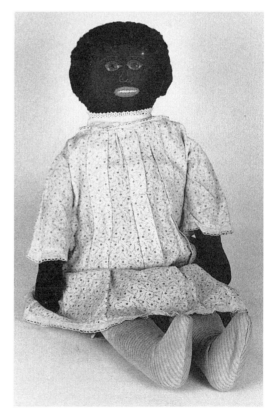

Handmade rag doll, intricately sewn facial features, including the teeth, fingers are separately sewn, calico dress with lace trim; excellent condition, **$1,500–2,000.** Photo by Donald Vogt.

and are often the best place to track down the doll of your choice.

For further information on black dolls contact the African American Doll Gallery, Attn: Erlene Reed, P.O. Box 7747, Silver Spring, Maryland 20910.

A Short History of Black Dolls in America

Although European manufacturers were responsible for most of the dolls made from early times through the beginning of the 1800s, American manufacturers produced the first commercial black rag dolls as well as stuffed and plastic black dolls.

RAG DOLLS AND HOMEMADE DOLLS

Although rag dolls are the most common nineteenth-century black dolls, one can find dolls from this time made of different materials. The novice doll collector is often pleasantly surprised by the availability and appeal of dolls made between 1900 and 1940.

Store-bought dolls were a true luxury for early African-American children. Slaves and other American girls usually had handmade dolls. The earliest homemade black dolls were extremely crude, and few have survived. They were made from bedposts with buckskin or any other fabric the makers could lay their hands on. The favorite type of doll seemed to be the rag doll. They were usually made

Five rag dolls, all dressed in gingham and head scarves; good condition, **$35–50 each.** Courtesy of Rose Fontanella; photo by Donald Vogt.

from pieces of leftover cloth and were cherished possessions of both city and farm girls. The dolls were dressed in calico, muslin, or feed bag cloth. Regional dress was usually not evident, though corn-husk and nut-head dolls were prevalent in rural areas.

From before the Civil War, dolls were made to resemble mammies. They are often holding tiny white babies, symbolizing the mammy's role in the household. Perhaps mammy herself made the doll, or her "husband" may have made it as a Christmas gift for the child. One wonders why mammies are often ample bosomed.

Interestingly, some rag dolls carry with them a bit of history as well. During the Civil War, medicines and drugs were sometimes smuggled to Confederate soldiers inside a doll's head or body, and ships carrying dolls between the North and South were accorded neutrality. It was not unusual for a black doll to be sent through enemy lines, supposedly destined for its young mistress's arms. But once the doll was inside a military camp, the Confederate doctors would take apart the doll to find the laudanum, bandages, or medicines stored within the doll's body. These dolls can still be found by collectors.

After the Civil War, black dolls began to take on richer trappings and to look more like the middle class into which these dolls would slowly move. But the transition was not a fast

Belinda and Jaspar rag dolls, Belinda was the nurse in the Raggedy Ann and Andy stories; very good condition, $100–200 each. Courtesy of Rose Fontanella; photo by Donald Vogt.

one and many rag dolls wore poor clothing until well into the twentieth century.

Eventually, rag dolls were manufactured in quantity. Their facial designs were stamped on a piece of cloth, and the bodies were cut out, sewn together, and stuffed. Though factory-made stuffed black dolls are usually found bearing a resemblance to Aunt Jemima or mammy, I have seen some that appear to be likenesses of actual children. It is eerie to find a doll with a realistic face, because these "photo" faces were often made to resemble a child who had died. But it is exhilarating as well, because these lithographed cutouts are rare and are considered a find.

OTHER DOLLS

Rubber dolls were first manufactured in 1855 by Benjamin Lee of New York; celluloid dolls were produced a decade later by John Wesley and Isaiah Hyatt. During the 1870s, a Kentucky firm made dolls' heads from a mixture that became known as "composition." Black dolls were made in all three materials and were more common after the 1920s than earlier.

In the first half of the twentieth century, character dolls eventually found their way into the kitchen, to hold whisk brooms or to be used as doorstops and toaster covers (see also Chapter 7). No matter what their

Rag dolls, dressed in 1920s fabric, most machine stitched; very good condition, **$75–200 each.** Courtesy of Carl and Jeannette Pergam of Sioux Antiques.

104

Baby girl doll, celluloid, pink dress, three braids, 1940s; very good condition, $55–75. Courtesy of Malinda Saunders; photo by Donald Vogt.

Man and woman rag dolls, in folk art genre, each has gray hair and eyebrows, man in blue-and-white shirt, woman in tan-and-brown period dress with bustle; very good condition, $3,000–4,500 for the pair. Photo by Donald Vogt.

use—toy or utilitarian—kitchen dolls are seen by collectors more as objects of folk art than as the playthings they were originally intended to be. This means that such dolls can command a high price.

Black dolls have been mass produced (along with white dolls) since the beginning of the twentieth century. Before World War I, American doll makers, unlike their European counterparts, tended to play up the comic aspects of the black dolls they made.

During the 1920s, 1930s, and 1940s, black dolls were cheaply made and often were just painted versions of white dolls. Composition baby dolls were sold during the early 1940s by major department stores. Some were jointed, some had painted faces, and some even had little tufts of hair (with tiny bows) on their heads. All were relatively inexpensive and, for the most part, modeled after white dolls.

Topsy turvy dolls, which originated as early as the Civil War, represented the best of both worlds. The doll, usually dressed in a long dress that covered her bottom half, would be black on one side and white on the other. Topsy turvy dolls were commonly made into the 1940s and can be found in rubber, plastic, celluloid, and composition. There are also some contemporary topsy turvy dolls.

Hard plastic dolls were made from the late 1940s to late 1950s. The black dolls of this era were made in the identical molds that the white dolls were made in but were finished in a brown color.

Aunt Jemima doll, molded face, arms, and legs, early 1900s; good condition, **$100–125.** Courtesy of Rose Fontanella; photo by Donald Vogt.

Vinyl dolls have been made since 1950 and are still being manufactured. The dolls are attractive, but sometimes the vinyl does not allow for the finer details that the early bisque and composition did. However, the vinyl dolls are generally made to be more representative of Blacks and give truer renditions of black people's features.

Not until the 1960s were black dolls made to represent well-known black people. Dolls made in the image of celebrities, such as Diahann Carroll (who played Julia on television in the 1970s), began to appear on the toy shelves of department stores.

Types of Collectible Black Dolls

Here are a list and descriptions of some of the commonly collected black dolls.

APPLE AND NUT DOLLS

Apple and nut dolls are truly American dolls, their origin firmly anchored in American soil. Little girls would anxiously await the day their mama was to bake one of her mouth-watering pecan pies, because they would surely get the leftover nuts to make dolls.

Once the nut was chosen for the head, other materials were used to complete the rest of the doll's body. Wood, twigs, cloth—whatever could be found—were used for the arms and legs. Once the doll itself was made, the work of making suitable clothes began. Again, whatever material was available was used.

Nut dolls became extremely popular in the South and were often made in pairs, one male and one female. Blacks were portrayed in real-life occupations: mammies, cotton pickers, farm workers, and maids are some of the characters made from nuts.

ROSA WILDES BLACKMAN DOLLS

Clay dolls were made by Rosa Wildes Blackman of Homer, Louisiana. Blackman was a white woman who made dolls during the 1940s. She is well known for her "true Southern Negro types." Some of her dolls are part of the collection at the Brooklyn Children's Museum.

BOTTLE DOLLS

Bottle dolls—the body and dress fit over a bottle, which was filled with sand or rocks to weight it—were often made by the homemaker and used as doorstops. Most of these dolls were made in the Aunt Jemima tradition, complete with apron and head scarf. They often had hand-sewn features.

Nut dolls, heads are pecans or walnuts, largest doll about 12″ tall; very good condition, **$55–75 each.** Courtesy of Rose Fontanella; photo by Donald Vogt.

DADDY'S LONG LEGS

Introduced in 1990, Daddy's Long Legs dolls are molded of wood resin composition. Although the dolls are made in molds, each is unique. The dolls are all signed by the designer and are numbered and dated. The dolls range from Doc Moses, a white-haired and moustached doctor nominated for the prestigious Doty Award in 1992, to Nettie, a beautiful African-American woman.

JOEL ELLIS DOLLS

Joel Ellis of Springfield, Vermont, made dolls out of green maple wood during the mid-nineteenth century. He patented this type of doll but did not make many because of heavy competition from imported bisque dolls. The penny wooden Ellis dolls were highly mobile because of their distinctive wooden joints. He often painted the doll's metal boots black, but sometimes the hands, also metal, were painted white.

Ellis dolls also all have curved fingers. The most common sizes are 12, 15, and 18 inches. The black Ellis dolls had painted faces and are difficult to find because the dolls were manufactured only during 1873.

FAIRCHILDREN NEW ENGLAND RAG DOLLS

The FairChildren dolls made by Helen Pringle of Aledo, Texas, will surely be the Ellis and Walker dolls of the next century. Pringle handmakes all the dolls out of stuffed cotton cloth. Their arms, legs, and heads are painted with oil paints and they are usually 32 to 36 inches tall, although a smaller version can now be ordered. They

Bottle doll, 18″ tall; excellent condition, **$50–75**. Courtesy of the Gene and Linda Kangas Collection; photo by Gene Kangas.

CARRIE LYLES DOLLS

Carrie Lyles is a dollmaker from Hyattsville, Maryland. She makes dolls out of useful objects, such as rags, sticks, and mops. She originally made faceless dolls, but now includes some with features. She sells her dolls at shows throughout the Northeast.

MAGGIE HEAD DOLLS

Maggie, a doll artist, made two types of black dolls named Nicodemus and Nicodemus Girl in 1966. The dolls are stained ceramic bisque and wear fur wigs. These dolls are marked "Maggie Head/1966" on their heads.

Rag doll, faceless, yarn braids, red calico dress with white apron, contemporary; mint condition, **$10–15**. Courtesy of the Dawn and Bob Reno Collection; photo by Bob Reno.

are seam jointed at the shoulder, hip, and knee and have applied ears. Then she hand paints the dolls' faces to resemble naive or primitive eighteenth- and nineteenth-century children's portraits. The clothing is usually antique or replicas of antique clothing. Pringle makes both male and female dolls; each has its own name, and no two are alike. Each doll is stamped with a maker's mark, signed, and numbered on the body. The price of these dolls ranges between $600 and $800. All FairChildren New England Rag Dolls are protected by design and name

SASHA MORGENTHALER DOLLS

Born in 1893 in Bern, Switzerland, Sasha Morgenthaler is the creator of the Black Sasha dolls first made in 1924. The early dolls were made of cloth, but in 1942 molds were made so the dolls could be mass produced. By 1969, the first vinyl production was released. Sara and John Doggard, friends of Sasha's, helped her produce the dolls, which were limited edition, realistic-looking dolls. They retired in 1986 and ceased producing the dolls.

LEO MOSS DOLLS

Creating beautiful black infant dolls during the turn of the century was Leo Moss's goal in life. Today his creations sell for thousands of dollars. His work is recognized by the tear on each doll's puzzled face.

PENNY WOODENS

Penny woodens were made from the early eighteenth to twentieth centuries. Because the dolls were made of wood and were sold to New Englanders (in the mid-1800s) for a penny they were called "penny woodens." Most of these dolls are under 4 inches tall, although there are taller ones with elaborate hairdos. The hair on these dolls is painted black and shows a center part. The bodies of penny woodens are jointed at the shoulders, elbows, hips, and knees, and the head shape varies with each doll. Black penny woodens are rare, but they can be found.

Man and woman rag dolls; excellent condition, $150–400 for the pair. Courtesy of the Gene and Linda Kangas Collection; photo by Gene Kangas.

TOPSY TURVY DOLLS

Topsy Turvy dolls were often black on one side and white on the other. Sometimes they were made in the form of nursery rhyme characters, such as Little Red Riding Hood on one end and the grandmother on the other or the plain and fancy Cinderellas. These dolls met the same need as rag dolls; they were econmical toys that could be made out of scraps of material. The unique feature of the topsy turvey doll was that it was two dolls in one. Topsies were made before the Civil War and are still being made today.

MARCELLA WELCH DOLLS

Marcella Welch is a self-taught artist who knows the history of making dolls better than almost any other African-American dollmaker today. Her work has been touted

Caribbean women topsy turvy doll, one side dressed in bright orange, blue, and red, other side dressed in red and blue calico, 1988; excellent condition, $20–30. Courtesy of the Dawn and Bob Reno Collection; photo by Bob Reno.

by many magazines and news programs since she began her dollmaking workshops. Welch was named 1988 Doll Maker of the Year at the Holiday Festival of Black Dolls, held at the National Afro-American Museum in Wilberforce, Ohio. Her dolls are often African in appearance, and she likes working with the three-dimensional form, creating limited-edition fabric sculptures.

Some Manufacturers of Black Dolls

Cameo Doll Products/Strombecker Doll Corp. made a 19-inch black baby doll in 1973 that they called Miss Peep. The baby resembles early bisque babies, but is all vinyl with inset brown eyes. It is marked "Cameo" on the back of its head.

Deluxe Topper Toys made a series of 6 to 6.5-inch teenage dolls. Of these, Dale, a woman wearing a minidress; Van, a football player; Dancing Dale; and Dancing Van were black. The dolls all had snapping knees and a jointed waist. The Dale dolls had rooted black hair and painted eyes, whereas the Van dolls had molded hair. The dolls were made in the early 1970s.

The Effanbee Doll Corp., a successful commercial dollmaker, was formed in 1913 by Bernard E. Fleischaker and Hugo Baum. Effanbee dolls are usually marked on the back of the head and/or on the upper back.

Among the black dolls made by Effanbee are the beautiful Grandes Dames made in 1981. The four dolls are dressed in authentic-looking turn-of-the-century costumes, complete with wide-brimmed hats and veils. In 1981, Effanbee produced a limited-edition set of 125 black versions of four of the Grandes Dames for Treasure Trove, a mail-order collectors' doll company. There are also black versions of Baby Face, Half Pint, Baseball Player, Football Player, Prize Fighter, Basketball Player, Sailor, Fair Baby, Sweetie Pie, Twinkie, Butter Ball, and Sugar Plum.

In Effanbee's 1970 catalog, almost every doll had what the company called a "Negro version." By 1971 the dolls were still being made as copies of the white dolls, but the catalog description

Rag doll with cover of *Life* magazine; excellent condition, $25–35.

listed them as "black dolls." From 1970 on, black dolls were included in every collection, but still as copies of the original white dolls. In 1980 the catalog showed a Miss Black America doll as discontinued under its International Collection line. Black Currier and Ives Skaters were issued as a special set in 1980 and Black Miss U.S.A. was the 1982 special.

Fisher Price Toys made a black cloth-and-vinyl doll in 1973 that they called Elizabeth. The doll was 14 inches tall, had rooted black hair, and painted brown eyes. It was marked "18/168630/ 1973 Fisher Price Toys" on the back of its head.

Gotz made a series of dolls called "A World for Children." One of their artists, Philip S. Heath,

created a black doll, which is worth adding to any collection.

Hasbro Toys has made black versions of quite a few of their dolls. One of the best known is G.I. Joe. In 1965, Hasbro put out a 12-inch black G.I. Joe soldier complete in combat fatigues. Soul, a black woman with an afro, dressed in wildly colored bell bottoms and accessories, was distributed in 1971. Leggy Sue was 10 inches tall and was dressed in a turtleneck evening gown; she was one of a set of four distributed in 1972.

Annette Himstedt and Hildegard Gunzel, German doll artists, have produced ethnic dolls for the current limited-edition market. The col-

111

oring, facial structure, expressions, authentic clothing, and hair have made these dolls lovely examples of African-American collectibles.

Horsman Dolls were started by E. I. Horsman in 1865. The company began producing bisque dolls shortly after it opened. Horsman's synthetic rubber and early vinyl process has always been considered among the best in the doll field. Horsman has made and distributed black versions of their dolls for the past thirty years.

Ideal Toy Corp. has been in business since 1902. They marked their early dolls with their name enclosed in a diamond and later used just the imprinted name. Often dolls were marked "Made in U.S.A." along with identifying numbers. Ideal was the first company to manufacture dolls with sleep eyes, in 1915. It was also the first company to use plastic. In 1933, this futuristic firm developed "magic skin." Ideal's baby Thumbelina was made in both black and white versions as were the Velvet dolls. Baby Belly Button, made in 1970, was all vinyl with rooted black hair and painted brown eyes.

Madame Alexander dolls, tagged as such on their body or on clothing tags, have always been noted for their beautiful costumes. Some of Madame Alexander's black dolls include 15-inch Cynthia (made in 1952), 14-inch Baby Ellen (made in 1965), and 8-inch African (made in 1966). This doll is marked "African by Madame Alexander" on its back.

Mattel, Inc. is best known as the company that makes the Barbie doll, but they have made other dolls as well and continue to be a major toy-producing firm. The Barbie doll was introduced in 1958 and Barbie's black friend Francie was introduced in 1967. In 1968, Christie was introduced. Julia, from the television show of the same name that starred Diahann Carroll, was brought out in 1970, and that same year Brad, a dark-skinned man with an afro, was put on the market.

Other black dolls manufactured by Mattel include Chatty Cathy (1962), Baby Say n See (1967), Talking Drowsy (1968), Swingy (1969), Bouncing Baby (1969), Baby Go Bye Bye (1970), Valerie (1971), Betty Beans (1973), and Peachy and her Puppets (1973).

Remco Industries had the rights to make Kewpie dolls for only two years: 1968 and 1969. During that time, they made a 7-inch black Kewpie of plastic and vinyl. It was marked "7AJLK/2/Cameo" on the head, "Kewpie" on its foot, and "Cameo" on its back. Remco also made an 18-inch doll they called Gingersnap. Gingersnap was marked: "Doll:E4/Remco Ind. Inc./1968" on the back of its head.

Sears sold a black doll from 1910 to 1940 called Chubby Kid. This Kewpie-like doll was 8 inches tall. It was made of composition and had painted features, a watermelon mouth, jointed arms, and a black mohair wig.

Sun Rubber made a 17-inch black baby doll that they dubbed Colored Sun-Dee in 1956. She was made of vinyl with brown sleep eyes and came with her own nurser. She was marked "Sun-Dee/Sun Rubber 1956" on her head.

The Treasured Customs Series produced a doll designed by Wendy Lawton called Ndeko, an African doll that is considered a fine example of the artist's work.

Uneeda Doll Co. made a few black dolls, including Littlest So Soft and Teenie Toodles. Both dolls were made of plastic and vinyl.

Vogue Doll Co. made black Ginny dolls as well as black baby dolls. They are still in business.

PRICES FOR BLACK DOLLS

Dolls Listed by Maker

American Character, Tiny Tears, dressed in panties only, 13″; very good condition, **$15–25.**

AquaTaurian, Cindy McClure's Vanessa; dressed in bonnet, bloomers, and full dress; limited edition of one thousand, 15″ tall; new, **$125–150.**

Armand Marseilles

AM Dream Baby 341, 1 4/0, black bisque head, cloth body, 9″; excellent condition, **$450–600.**

Bisque 390, brown, 30″; excellent condition, **$1,000–1,300.**

Bucilla Needlework, kit for Golliwog doll, kit is unopened, includes all cotton fabrics needed for body and clothes, rick black plush for hair, large moveable eyes, and everything needed to complete the doll, 1950s, 30″ tall; mint condition, **$65–95.**

Carole Marie Creation

Mrs. Bethune, porcelain, in the image of Mary Bethune (founder of Bethune-Cookman College in Daytona Beach, Florida), original character doll, older woman with white hair, wearing dark cape; new, **$300.**

Ms. Ann, porcelain, original character doll, wearing fox fur and large hat; new, **$250.**

Effanbee

Butterball; very good condition, **$35–50.**

Composition baby, cloth body, 12″ tall; excellent condition, **$170–225.**

Fluffy, official Girl Scout uniform; very good condition, **$25–40.**

Little Tubber, boxed, 10″; very good condition, **$25–40.**

Louis Armstrong, rubber, handpainted in brown, blue, black, and white, very detailed, trumpet and handkerchief, 16″ × 8″; near mint condition, **$125–150.**

Patsyette, chips at neck, 9½″ tall; fair condition, **$250–300.**

Girl doll, made by Eegee Toys, blue suede dress, ankle socks, shoes, black rooted hair, sleep eyes; very good condition, $25–40.

Hallmark, 229-4, nativity child; very good condition, **$10–18.**

Hasbro, plastic, dressed in baby clothes, hair seems original, 1970s; good condition, **$5–8.**

Heubach Kopplesdorf, 399, bisque, character baby, 22″; excellent condition, **$1,500–1,600.**

Horsman, Baby Bumps, 12″; very good condition, $250–300.

Ideal, Baby, 1971, 14″; very good condition, **$25–35.**

Jumeau, "Prince," African, porcelain, 1893 Paris Exposition doll, handsomely dressed in traditional African clothing; excellent condition, **$10,000–15,000.**

Madame Alexander

African woman, 8″; very good condition, **$300–375.**

Cynthia, 18″; very good condition, **$600–675.**

Ellen, baby, 14″; very good condition, **$150–200.**

French girl, 8″; very good condition, **$60–80.**

Leslie, ballerina, in box, 17″; mint condition, **$250–300.**

Pussy Cat, girl, in box, 20″; mint condition, **$90–120.**

Maggie Head

Girl, wearing jaunty hat and knee-length dress with pantaloons underneath, 16″; excellent condition, **$350–450.**

Old Man, wearing pants held up by suspenders and straw hat, playing banjo, 19½″; excellent condition, **$300–375.**

Old Woman, wearing polka dot dress with white apron, has white hair and glasses, 19½″; excellent condition, **$300–375.**

Mattel

Barbie doll

Peaches 'n Cream, 1960s; very good condition, **$40–50.**

Julia, in box, 1968; very good condition, **$45–60.**

Super Star Barbie, 1970s; very good condition, **$30–40.**

Tropical Ken, very good condition, **$20–30.**

Chatty Baby Brother, 15″; very good condition, **$85–100.**

Hush Little Baby; very good condition, **$20–30.**

Miss Martha Originals, Sonshine baby head,

vinyl, dark brown glass-like eyes, 1985; excellent condition, **$65–75.**

Sasha Morgenthaler (Sasha Dolls)

Baby Cara, vinyl, about 14″ tall; very good condition, **$150–180.**

Caleb

All original, vinyl, short black hair, white sweater, khaki pants; mint condition, **$200–225.**

Vinyl, about 14″ tall; very good condition, **$225–275.**

Cora

Vinyl, about 14″ tall; very good condition, **$225–275.**

Vinyl, short black hair, white wool turtleneck sweater and panties, red sandals, original tag on wrist, original box; mint condition, **$200–225.**

Xavier Roberts, Southern Belle, very good condition, **$260–290.**

Norman Rockwell, Wilma, limited edition, very good condition, **$325–375.**

Shindana Toys, Baby Jane, 1968; very good condition, **$25–35.**

Simplicity, transfer pattern for pickaninny doll, full color, 1947, 17″; mint (unused) condition, **$75–95.**

Simon & Halbig

1368, bisque head on nice black composition body, lips are exaggerated, wig original, large brown eyes; excellent condition, **$4,400–5,000.**

Incised "S2H 1009/DEP/St., bisque head, ball-jointed composition and wooden body with unjointed wrists, set brown glass eyes, red open mouth with teeth, pierced ears, black mohair wig, 11½″ tall, mid-1800s; excellent condition, **$500–625.**

Terri Lee Co., Brown Jerri, plastic, 20″; very good condition, **$225–275.**

Vogue

Baby Dear, signed; very good condition, **$30–40.**

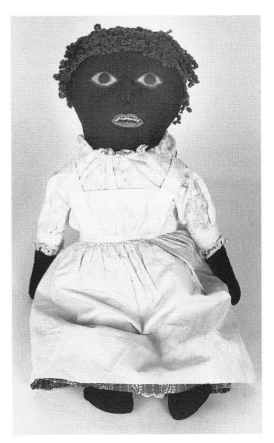

Rag doll, brown yarn hair, beaded teeth, button eyes, white blouse and apron, red-and-white dress, white slip; very good condition, **$1,200–1,500**. Photo by Donald Vogt.

Boy doll, made by Shindana Toys, vinyl, 1972; very good condition, **$50–65**. Courtesy of Malinda Saunders; photo by Donald Vogt.

Ginny

African, female, wearing brightly colored jacket, wraparound skirt and hat to match, 8″ tall; new, **$35–50**.

Ballerina, wearing pink tutu, 8″ tall; very good condition, **$40–50**.

Bride, wearing white wedding gown, 8″ tall; very good condition, **$40–50**.

Dress Me, female, 8″ tall; very good condition, **$14–18**.

Tropical, female, 8″ tall; very good condition, **$35–45**.

Mary E. Washington

Mandela, porcelain, in the image of Nelson Mandela, South African activist, gray-haired, wearing a white shirt, tie, and dark suit, one arm is outstretched, new, **$200–250**.

Medicine Woman, porcelain, with glasses, neck pouch, purse, and stick, wearing a long-sleeved print dress with a full apron; new, **$250**.

Norah Wellings, child, glass eyes, hoop earrings, 13½″; very good condition, **$185–225**.

Dolls Listed by Material

Bisque

Baby, bisque head and papier-mâché body, 34.18, brown set eyes, red painted socks, fingers damaged, 9″ tall; good condition, **$440–550.**

Baby, bisque head and papier-mâché body, marked "SHA" in circle, Germany, R. 17/0, sleep eyes, 7″; very good condition, **$165–210.**

Baby, made in Japan, 4¼″ tall; very good condition, **$20–40.**

Baby, made in Japan, 4″ tall; very good condition, **$25–30.**

Bye-Lo Baby, jointed arms and legs, gown, 4″; very good condition, **$25–30.**

Character doll, unmarked bisque head, fully jointed wood and composition body, German, set brown glass eyes, open mouth showing four upper teeth, black mohair wig; mid to late 1800s, 7″ high; excellent condition, **$250–320.**

Rag doll, machine- and hand-sewn clothes, shoe button eyes, embroidered nose and mouth; excellent condition, $150–250. Courtesy of Kristin Duval and Irreverent Relics; photo by Donald Vogt.

Girl, glass eyes, lace outfit, 11″; very good condition, **$40–50.**

Girl, jointed, three ponytails, 6″; very good condition, **$20–25.**

Pair, boy and girl, made as dollhouse dolls, rare, incised on body: "11/Germany," painted black eyes to side and molded black hair, stiff neck; jointed shoulders and hips, original clothes, 1920s, 2¾″ high; excellent condition, **$175–225 each.**

Bottle doll

Gray dress, checked apron, bandanna, earrings, 13″; very good condition, **$40–50.**

Milk bottle, mammy, original clothes, ca. 1910; very good condition, **$50–60.**

Topsy turvy, hand stitched; very good condition, **$185–230.**

Cloth

Baby, talks, glass sleep eyes, 18″; very good condition, **$125–155.**

Boy, button eyes, embroidered features, ca. 1930; very good condition, **$50–60.**

Boy, handsewn mouth and nose, oyster button eyes, made by hospital workers to raise contributions, dressed in suit and hat (machine sewn), Red Cross button on lapel says 1919, from World War I, 9″ tall (to top of hat); excellent condition, **$50–60.**

Cream of Wheat Chef, printed-on fabric, 17″; very good condition, **$65–80.**

Girl, black dress and jacket, embroidered face, human hair, mid-1800s; very good condition, **$200–250.**

Girl, blue dress, red bandana, 1950s, 10″; very good condition, **$30–40.**

Girl, felt, yarn hair, red organdy dress, felt features on face, white hat with red ribbon, 1930s, 8″ tall; excellent condition, **$55–70.**

Girl, great expression and color, fine print dress, pigtails, eyes looking left, ca. 1950, 15″; excellent condition, **$50–65.**

Girl, handsewn nose and mouth, button eyes, original dress, sometimes referred to as

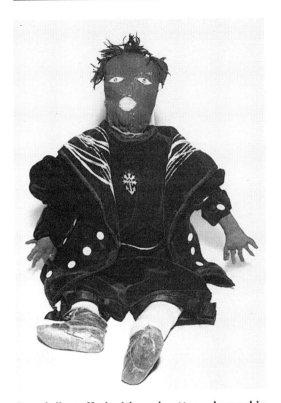

Boy doll, stuffed with real cotton, dressed in velvet sailor's uniform (uniform from John Wannamaker stores, dates to the turn of the century), real antique button shoes, hand-sewn facial features (incredible mouth and teeth), made in North Carolina, mattress ticking legs, cloth body wrapped in mattress ticking, cotton yarn hair, individually stitched fingers, straw head, 1850–1875, 32″ tall; excellent condition, $2,500–3,200. Courtesy of American Eye; photo by Bob Reno.

Beecher-type, but there is no proof she made these dolls, mid-1800s; excellent condition, **$500–625.**

Girl and boy, handmade, all original, ca. 1890, 11″; very good condition, **$300–350 for the pair.**

Girls, pair, handmade, the first has braids and handpainted face, wearing red-and-white print dress, the second is wearing blue turban and green print dress with white apron, she

has handsewn facial features, contemporary; near mint condition, **$8–15 each.**

Little Sister, manufactured ragdoll with detailed features; very good condition, **$35–50.**

Mammy

Embroidered face, red-and-white checked dress, late 1800s, 15½″; very good condition, **$85–100.**

Handsewn body and clothes, button eyes, 16½″, mint condition, **$20–35.**

Pearl eyes, earrings, kerchief, apron, 1940s, 9″; very good condition, **$50–70.**

Stuffed and hand stitched, dress in red and white; very good condition, **$50–75.**

Man, dressed in conductor's uniform, with boots and cap, stitched face, ca. 1900, 20″ tall; excellent condition, **$900–1,100.**

Man, souvenir, made by Ursuline nuns in New Orleans, hat is real silk, 3″; very good condition, **$100–125.**

Man and woman, stuffed, colorful outfits, the woman holds a cat, the man holds his hat, ca. 1900, 12″ high × 5″ wide each; fair/good condition, **$250–320 for the pair.**

Primitive oil-painted face, white with black cloth legs, replaced clothes, 15″ tall; good condition, **$300–350.**

Primitive pickaninny doll, stuffed, vivid red, green, yellow, black, one of a kind, 1920s–1930s, 6½″ × 3″; excellent condition, **$150–200.**

Rock-a-Bye Baby, manufactured, cloth body, sleep eyes, 7½″; very good condition, **$275–350.**

Topsy turvy

Cotton with hand-embroidered features, black girl wears red checkered/flowered print dress, white girl wears blue flowered dress, 1930s, 12″ tall; excellent condition, **$95–125.**

Manufactured, molded faces, colorful cloth bodies, both wear red bandannas; black girl wears pink flowered blouse, blue print

Stuffed mammy dolls, each dressed in red and white; very good condition, **$50–150 each.** Courtesy of Malinda Saunders; photo by Donald Vogt.

skirt, and ivory apron; white girl wears blue blouse and pink skirt, 1920s; excellent condition, **$135–150.**

Woman, hand-stitched facial features, lambswool hair, dress is muslin with satin ribbon trim, body is cotton, stuffed with cotton, cloth feet (no shoes), 1875–1900, 27″ tall; excellent condition, **$1,000–1,250.**

Woman, polished cotton body, red calico dress with buttons up bodice, painted facial features, hair is balls of wool, 24″ tall, 1920s–1930s; excellent condition, **$600–750.**

Woman, black stocking body, embroidered face, gray dress, white apron, pantaloons, black karakul-type hair, 20″; very good condition, **$150–200.**

Woman, wearing blue kerchief, matching skirt, button eyes, 1920s; very good condition, **$100–125.**

Woman, wearing red bandana and light blue striped dress, 1920s, 18″ tall; excellent condition, **$400–485.**

Composition

Baby

With painted eyes and mouth, 5″ tall; excellent condition, **$55–70.**

With pigtails, 1940s; fair to good condition, **$50–60.**

Girl, jointed, molded hair, three yarn braids, 14″, 1940s; very good condition, **$120–150.**

Topsy turvy, jointed shoulders, 1940s, 7″; very good condition, **$85–100.**

Nut Doll

Mammy, 8″; very good condition, **$25–40.**

Three figures, all dressed in clothing and

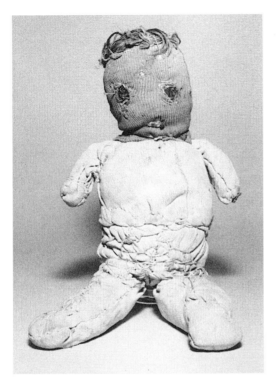

Cloth doll, possibly stuffed with pine shatts, real fisheye eyes, sock head, cotton body, made by black woman named Connor (Chincoteague, Virginia), 1920s–1930s, 12″ × 6″; excellent condition, **$200–400.**

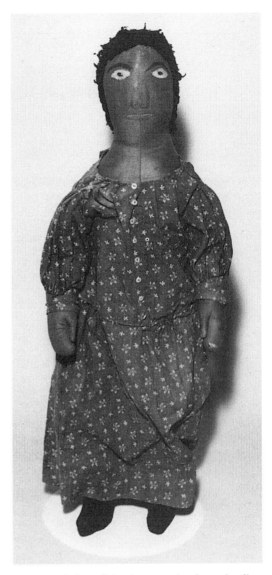

Woman doll, polished cotton body, red calico dress with buttons up bodice, painted facial features, hair is balls of wool, 1920s–1930s, 24″ tall; excellent condition, **$600–750.** Courtesy of American Eye; photo by Bob Reno.

stuffed with cotton, 8½″ tall; excellent condition, **$100–125 for the set.**

Papier-mâché

Child, jointed, hair, ca. 1885, 6½″; very good condition, **$250–300.**

Papier-mâché head with cloth body, painted, 11½″; excellent condition, **$120–150.**

Plastic

Boy, molded hair, original overalls; moveable arms, legs, and head; 1940s–1950s; excellent condition, **$225–250.**

Goo Goo Eye, original unopened package reads "Watch my eyes Blink and Wink," colorful dress; 1950s; near mint condition, **$25–40.**

Porcelain

Bride, musical, in box, 18″; mint condition, **$200–235.**

Clown, aqua-flowered outfit, in box, 22″; mint condition, **$200–230.**

Girl, with Afro wig, old, 11″; very good condition, **$150–200.**

Wax head, cloth body, mohair wig, painted eyes; 14″; very good condition, **$275–350.**

Wood

Amos 'n Andy, jointed wooden dolls, 5½″; very good condition, **$400–450 for the pair.**

Baby in quilted bunting, head is made of wood with painted features, 1986, 4″ tall; **$5–8.**

Girl, handcarved wooden face, clothes all handsewn including bloomers and scarf, real hair, 1930s, 11″ tall; excellent condition, **$100–130.**

Mammy and pappy, dressed as poor people, 1800s; 9″; very good condition, **$350–400 for the pair.**

Man carrying bag of cotton, walnut, 12″; very good condition, **$55–75.**

Walking mammy, 1940s, about 15″ tall; very good condition, **$35–50.**

Girl doll, handcarved wooden face, clothes all handsewn, including bloomers and scarf, real hair, 1930s, 11″ tall; excellent condition, $100–300. Courtesy of American Eye; photo by Bob Reno.

CHAPTER SEVEN

Kitchen Collectibles

Things that belong in the kitchen—salt and pepper shakers, cookie jars, and condiment sets—are what most people think of first when they think of black memorabilia. This is probably the easiest type of collectible to find, as well as the easiest to collect, because the pieces are accessible, affordable, and usable.

This area of collecting is as wide and interesting as its objects are colorful. Although some advertising pieces fall into this category, I have chosen to keep advertising items in their own chapter (see Chapter 5), thus more information may be obtained there (see also Chapter 9).

If you want to keep your collection limited to black Americana kitchen items, be aware that quite a few of the later kitchen pieces were made in Japan. In the first edition of this book, I tried to stay away from the Japanese items. However, because those kitchen goods were made for sale to the American public, I have included some of them in this volume. Goods made in occupied Japan and later are described in this chapter (see also Chapter 9).

Types of Kitchen Collectibles

CONDIMENT SETS

Condiment sets were made of pottery, plastic, and china and were produced throughout the 1930s to 1950s. Count yourself lucky if you find a complete set, because these items were often used every day and rarely stayed in excellent condition.

Sugar and creamers, often originally parts of a condiment set, are usually found as pairs and priced separately. If you look hard enough, you may find the rest of the matching set.

COOKBOOKS

Cookbooks in the black tradition are noticeable by the illustrations on the front cover or by the inherently black (or Southern) recipes they contain. It is worth your while to collect these books for the recipes alone; putting them into your black Americana collection may come second. Though not always easy to find, the cookbooks are usually

Condiment set, mammy pushing wagon, oil and vinegar, salt and pepper, marked "Japan," 1950, 7½" long; excellent condition, **$200–225 for the set.** Courtesy of the Leonard Davis Collection; photo by Bob Reno.

reasonably priced and make a nice addition to a shelf full of black kitchen collectibles. (Note: Companies often made cookbooks as premiums for their customers. If your cookbook advertises a certain product, the item would be an advertising collectible as well as a kitchen collectible. See my book *The Confident Collector: Advertising Collectibles* for further information.)

COOKIE JARS

Cookie jars, made from the early 1930s until today, are very popular with collectors. Many of the older cookie jars have lost quite a bit of paint due to heavy use. If the piece was enameled after it was fired, the color would not be durable.

The most common black cookie jars show the Nelson McCoy version of a mammy. Made from 1940 to 1957, the mammy sports a small head wrapped in a red bandana. She wears a voluminous white skirt with the word *cookies* emblazoned on the front. The first edition of this jar sported the phrase "Dem Cookies Sho' Do Taste Good" around the bottom of the skirt.

McCoy's 1939 Mammy with Basket of Cauliflowers is fairly rare. This jar was produced in limited quantities and was hand-painted over the glaze. Very few are found with the paint intact.

Unfortunately, the most attractive of the McCoy cookie jars, a mammy and black chef standing shoulder to shoulder, was never put into production. I have heard through the grapevine that some collectors claim to own this particular piece. If they do, it is not authentic.

Weller Pottery produced a mammy cookie jar in 1938 that was part of a set consisting of a cookie jar, covered sugar bowl, creamer, batter bowl, teapot, and syrup jug. A set in mint condition, if you could find one, would be quite valuable.

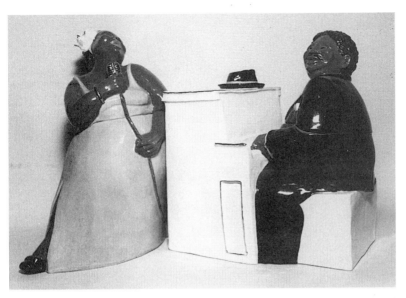

Cookie jars, Stella and Fats, by A Little Company, the Studios of Michael and Shelley Tincher Buonaiuto, limited edition, marked "#21/250," the woman wears pink and is 15" tall, the man is 14" tall, 1991–1992; mint condition, **$175–225 each.** Courtesy of the Leonard Davis Collection; photo by Bob Reno.

The mosaic mammy cookie jar was originally attributed to either the Mosaic Tile Company or the Zanesville Art Tile Company but now has been tentatively attributed to the Zanesville Art Tile Company. The patent was issued to "K. M. Gale of Zanesville, Ohio." The jar was shown in the 1944 *Patent Yearbook,* where it was called the "Mosaic Mammy" cookie jar.

During the early 1940s, the Sears and Roebuck catalog introduced a ceramic cookie jar called Sambo the Chef. It is not clear from the catalog description whether this was the same chef sold by the National Silver Company of New York during the 1940s. National also produced a mammy jar.

In 1991, F&F made a colorful cookie jar called "Rio Rita," which is a buxom black woman balancing a basket of fruit on her head. A parrot sits on her shoulder. In the few years since its introduction, the price of the cookie jar has gone from $50 to more than $200.

Cookie jar, mammy, made by Abingdon, finely decorated under glaze, well marked, she holds a flower basket, pre-1950; mint condition, **$500–700.** Courtesy of the Leonard Davis Collection; photo by Bob Reno.

123

Cookie jars, Watermelon Mammy and Watermelon Sammy, by Carol Gifford, mammy resembles the Pearl China mammy, 11" tall, 1986–1987; mint condition, **$200–250 each.** Courtesy of the Leonard Davis Collection; photo by Bob Reno.

Cookie jars have become hot items. Andy Warhol's collection, sold after his death, in 1992, went for $247,830. The field has tightened, and it is not easy to find a cookie jar for less than $200—no matter what its condition or subject matter.

GROCERY LIST AND MEMO PAD HOLDERS

Mammy figures with memo pads attached to their skirts have been made in composition, pottery, rubber, celluloid, and plastic. The grocery list holders are often rectangular pieces of wood that sometimes feature a pegboard with a list of typical grocery items. A hand-painted mammy figure or face may be found along the top. Made during the 1930s to 1950s, these items are still available and make a nice accent for a kitchen wall. The older the memo pad holder, the higher the price, although the ones made of composition or rubber are notorious for being in bad shape. The prices of these items fluctuate widely; so much so that I hesitated to add

memo pad holders to the price list for this chapter. Buy the best example you can afford and try to spend less than $65. Anything over that is too much for these common items. Hampden Novelty Manufacturing Company of Holyoke, Massachusetts, produced composition and plastic varieties of these items.

OCCUPIED JAPAN ITEMS

Since so many kitchen collectibles were made in occupied Japan, an explanation is in order. Items marked "made in occupied Japan" were made after September 12, 1945, when the Articles of Surrender ended World War II. It was not until 1947, however, that these items were imported into the United States, after the trade embargo against Japanese goods was lifted. The Japanese began to produce items they believed were salable in the United States: figurines, statues, kitchen items, bisque pieces, etc. More information about the items produced in occupied Japan is available in Marian Klamkin's book, *Made in Occupied Japan: A Collector's Guide.*

Plaque, boy eating watermelon; excellent condition, $45–60. Courtesy of Dakota Sands; photo by Donald Vogt.

Grocery list, wood with pegs, marked "I'se can't forget to remember," all graphics in black, 1940s, 9″ × 5″; excellent condition, **$24–34.** Courtesy of the Dawn and Bob Reno Collection; photo by Bob Reno.

PLAQUES

Most wall plaques of black people were made to use as kitchen accents in the 1930s, 1940s, and 1950s. Although most are plaster or chalkware, they are also available in composition, rubber, wood, and plastic. The most common kitchen plaques feature black children with umbrellas or children eating watermelons.

Watch for damage, such as flaking paint, and broken pieces that have been glued back together. The plaques are common enough that you can afford to hunt for one in excellent condition.

Most plaques are not marked with the maker's name, but they should be marked with the country of origin, if they are not

American, since most were put on the market after the 1920s.

POT HANGERS

Pot hangers, sometimes called potholder hangers, were produced in pottery, chalkware, rubber, and plastic. There are many different styles, including children, mammies, chefs, and Aunt Jemima. They were made as kitchen accents during the 1930s to 1950s and are still easily found in garage sales and flea markets at reasonable prices. If the pot hanger is an early one, expect the paint to be chipped and worn. This is not a concern if you are paying a small amount of money for the piece. If you are paying top dollar at an antiques show, however, think twice before spending more than $20 for a hanger with heavy wear.

SALT AND PEPPERS

Salt holders originated in medieval times and were eventually made in a number of elaborate designs and materials. Salt and pepper sets, however, were not introduced until the late nineteenth century. They were produced in a wide variety of shapes and

Pot hanger, chalkware, yellow and black chef; good condition, **$24–40.** Courtesy of the Dawn and Bob Reno Collection; photo by Bob Reno.

Salt and pepper, African native couple, wood, very round, male is salt, both wear hats (which screw off) and grass skirts, 4½" tall; excellent condition, **$45–55 for the pair.** Courtesy of the Diane Stary Collection; photo by Diane Stary.

sizes and were often given away as tourist mementos. The most common black salt and pepper shakers look like a mammy and a chef; they are found in many sizes and colors. Because these figures were well known and salable, reproduction shakers also exist. Other shaker sets include a mammy and chef by a stove, a bellhop holding two hat boxes, an African native with bongos, a boy on a toilet, a bellhop with suitcases, children with watermelon slices, African natives, a boy with an alligator, and African natives with stylized faces.

Salt and pepper shakers were also made to advertise products: Aunt Jemima and the Luzianne lady are two examples. See also Chapter 5.

TABLECLOTHS AND DISH TOWELS

Colorfully made out of cotton or linen, towels and tablecloths usually came in sets and were sold throughout the 1930s to 1950s. If you are lucky, you may find linens with the manufacturer's tag still attached.

Many pieces have become faded and frayed because of time, repeated washings, and use. It is recommended that you stay away from tablecloths with holes, heavily worn spots, or frayed edges. Towels may be more faded than their tablecloth "sisters," so you may allow a little more room for damage. It is important, however, to draw the line at rips and worn spots; wait for a better example.

TOASTER COVER DOLLS

Throughout the 1930s, 1940s, and 1950s, toaster dolls were made commercially and by hand and were used in the kitchen to cover appliances, such as toasters and mixers. These dolls can be found in many color combinations, and each doll seems to have a personality all its own (see also Chapter 6). Nowadays collectors use the dolls not only for their original purposes, but also in the bathroom to cover toilet paper rolls, in the bedroom as pillow accents, and as decorative pieces in a country parlor.

The price you pay for a toaster doll will depend on its age and condition. Because of the recent popularity in black Americana, these dolls are not inexpensive, and some of the older ones have been priced as high as $175, depending on whether they were machine or hand made (hand made dolls are more expensive).

Some Companies That Produced Kitchen Collectibles

Many of the companies listed here were large producers of kitchen items. Further information may be available in specialty books. Check the bibliography to find books about these companies and their products.

F&F Tool and Die Company made the Aunt Jemima and Uncle Mose items that were sold or given away as advertising promotions for the Quaker Oats Company. Items marked "F&F Tool and Die Co., Dayton, Ohio," were made only from 1949 to 1951. These particular items are more desirable and slightly higher priced than other F&F products.

The F&F Tool and Die Company also made the Luzianne coffee advertising pieces. The Luzianne lady is very recognizable, and she is available in salt and pepper shakers of all sizes and in two or three different color combinations. Reproductions are currently on the market and can be recognized easily: the original Luziannes have a green skirt and the repros don't.

McCoy Pottery was founded by James McCoy in 1899. The company has undergone many name changes through the years. It started off as J. W. McCoy Pottery. In 1903, the firm was rebuilt, and in 1909 George S. Brush took over as manager. In 1911, the name became the Brush McCoy Pottery Company, which was shortened to the Brush Pottery Company in 1925. In 1933, the company became the Nelson McCoy Pottery Company. McCoy Pottery, a division of D. T. Chase Enterprises of Hartford, Connecticut, is still in business. McCoy produced many black cookie jars.

Red Wing Potteries, Inc. began in 1936 in Red Wing, Minnesota, and closed its doors in 1967. The firm made vases and planters, among other items. A mammy clock is reputed to have been made by Red Wing, and they also made several cookie jars during the 1950s.

Shawnee Pottery was founded in 1895 in Zanesville, Ohio, and stayed in business until 1948. They made all types of household pottery and kitchen collectibles.

Weller Pottery, well known for its vases, wall pockets, and art pottery, produced a kitchen set showing the Aunt Jemima figure. The set is extremely rare and valuable.

PRICES FOR KITCHEN COLLECTIBLES

Bottle doll, cloth, homemade, black sock head with hand-embroidered features, 1820; good condition, **$195–225.**

Bottle opener

Blackface, brass; very good condition, **$55–70.**

Man and alligator, Hubley, cast iron, painted in yellow, red, green, and brown, comic image of alligator biting black man, right foot and grass is bottle opener; 4″ × 3″; very good to excellent condition, **$225–300.**

Waiter holding three steins, wood, original paint, 1900; very good condition, **$95–125.**

Bottle stopper/pourer

Boy's head, earthenware; very good condition, **$45–55.**

Butler, earthenware, butler's head is the stopper and his arm is the pouring spout, earthenware; mint condition, **$100–200.**

Broom dolls, pair, contemporary; very good condition, **$35–50 each.**

Butler brushes, pair, one green and yellow, one black and white; very good condition, **$25–30 each.**

Coaster, saxophonist, Art Deco-style figural, decal on back, green, orange, yellow, and black; 3″ diameter; excellent condition, **$35–50.**

Condiment set

African native boys (two) and native face with tongue sticking out and resting on a leaf; head comes off at middle face, and tongue is spoon, made in Japan, 1930–1950; excellent condition, **$300–350 for the set.**

African native woman's face with open mouth for salt, right eye is shaker for pepper, left eye lifts out with spoon, unmarked but believed to be from Japan, rare; 4″ × 3½″; excellent condition, **$1,000–1,200 for the set.**

Boys' head (three) on tray, bisque, two heads are salt and pepper shakers, head in the middle has spoon coming out of it, nicely done in brown, looks Austrian, 1930s–1940s;

Condiment set, two black African native men are salt and pepper, white man in cauldron is mustard pot (with spoon), made in Japan, 1930s–1940s; excellent condition, $175–200 for the set. Courtesy of the Leonard Davis Collection; photo by Bob Reno.

5½" long; excellent condition, **$550–600 for the set.**

Mammy and chef

Oil and vinegar, salt and pepper shakers, nicely hand painted; mint condition, **$80–175 for the set.**

Oil and vinegar, salt and pepper shakers, single divided bottle pours oil from one arm and vinegar from other; excellent condition, **$150–220 for the set.**

Cookie Jar

A Little Company, Edmond, man in white pants with print shirt, limited edition, 1991–1992; 20½" high; mint condition, **$175–225.**

Brayton, mammy; fair condition (hairline crack and touched up paint), **$375–500.**

Mustard set, bulbous, bodies, made in Japan, mammy is 4½" high, chef is 4" high; excellent condition, **$125–150 for the set.** Courtesy of the Leonard Davis Collection; photo by Bob Reno.

Cookie jars, Pancake Mammy and Pancake Sammy, by Carol Gifford, discontinued editions, mammy is 11" tall, Sammy is 10" tall, 1986–1987; mint condition, **$200–250 each.** Courtesy of the Leonard Davis Collection; photo by Bob Reno.

J. I. Case, 150th Anniversary Commemorative, numbered and limited; excellent, condition, **$70–80.**

F&F Plastic, mammy; very good condition, **$300–450.**

Gilner

Mammy, yellow; fair condition (hairline crack), **$800–1,000.**

Mammy's face, yellow (also made in other colors), 1940s–1950s; 11″ tall; excellent condition, **$2,000–2,500.**

Lawrence Hill, chef (pair), right: typical plain white version, left: special red, white and blue edition, each is marked inside "No Mo'," 1992; mint condition, **$150–200 each.**

McCoy Pottery

Mammy with cauliflowers; very good condition, **$475–600** (has sold for as much as **$1,200**).

Man, contemporary; very good condition, **$35–50.**

Metlox

Mammy, yellow trim; excellent condition, **$700–900.**

Topsy, depicts young Topsy sitting with her head cocked to the side; very good condition, **$350–500.**

J. C. Miller, Porsha, made by the Miller family (part of a series depicting family members), each jar comes with a little explanation and is signed "JCMiller 1991"; 13½″; mint condition, **$225–300.**

Mosaic Tile

Mammy, blue; good to very good condition, **$250–325.**

Mammy, reproduction, distributed by McCoy Pottery, handmade and hand glazed in food-safe glazes, white, yellow, marked "McCoy 93" on the bottom; 12½″ × 7″; new, **$100.**

NASCO

Chef; good condition, **$275–400.**

Mammy; excellent condition, **$225–350.**

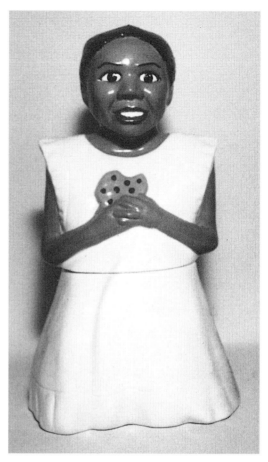

Cookie jar, Porsha, by the Miller family, part of series that depicts family members, each jar comes with an explanation and is signed, marked "JCMiller 1991," 13½″ tall; mint condition, $225–300. Courtesy of the Leonard Davis Collection; photo by Bob Reno.

National Silver Co., chef, great face and vivid blue colors; excellent to mint condition, **$200–300.**

Pearl China

Cooky, chef, 11″; excellent condition, **$350–450.**

Mammy, 1940s; 11″ high; very good condition, **$850–950.**

Rick Wisecarver

Black angel, blue dress, holding rose in lap, 1991; 11½″ tall; mint condition, **$150–250.**

Cookie jars, chefs, by Lawrence Hill, *left:* special red, white, and blue edition, *right:* typical plain white, each marked "No Mo'" on the inside, 1992; mint condition, **$150–200 each.** Courtesy of the Leonard Davis Collection; photo by Bob Reno.

Mammy

With butter churn, older lady wearing blue dress, child at side, 1989; 13½"; mint condition, **$150–250.**

With fruit, lime green dress, 1989; 13½"; mint condition, **$150–250.**

Miss America, in pink (one of a kind) with lace trim on her dress, marked "No. 1, 1991" on bottom, 14"; mint condition, **$300–500.**

"Morning Aggravation," old lady in green getting up and getting coffee, cat at feet, 1990; 11" high; mint condition, **$150–250.**

Rockingham, mammy, lid is in her belly; good condition, **$225–300.**

University of North Dakota School of Mines, Aunt Susan, #118; very good condition, (hairline crack), **$900–1,000.**

Weller

Mammy, very good condition (chip on ruffle), **$2,250–2,750.**

Mammy with watermelon, 11" tall; excellent condition, **$2,500–3,000.**

Unknown maker

African woman, bust with scarf around shoulders, 1991–1992; 10½" high; mint condition, **$200–250.**

Chef, handmade, distributed by McCoy Pottery, hand glazed in food-safe glazes; 10" high; new, **$850–900.**

Mammy, holding tray of cookies, well designed, Brayton quality, unmarked; mint condition, **$75–125.**

Washtub mammy, unmarked, came from California, 1940s–1950s; 11" tall; excellent condition, **$2,500–3,500.**

Cookie jars, Mammy at Stove, by Wihoa's Cookie Classic, handpainted by Rick Wisecarver (contemporary jar maker), each 12″; mint condition, *left:* blue, now discontinued, 1989–1990; $250–300; *right:* pink, 1991; $150–250. Courtesy of the Leonard Davis Collection; photo by Bob Reno.

Cracker jars, butlers (two), one large and one small, made in Japan; very good condition, **$775–1,000 for the pair.**

Cream pitcher, blackface, hand-painted ceramic, 1945–1950; mint condition, **$60–110.**

Creamer

Mammy Toby, brown skin tone, white dress, blue and green detailing, orange and yellow apron and sleeves, rare and old; excellent condition, **$90–125.**

Schafer & Vater, man with exaggerated features, multicolored, detailed, 19th century, Germany; 3½″ × 2½″; excellent condition, **$125–175.**

Cruets, oil and vinegar, earthenware, mammy and chef; very good condition, **$45–55 for the pair.**

Dinner bell, mammy, white dress with red details, pottery, 1930s; 4″ tall; excellent condition, **$95–150.**

Dish towel holder and wall hanging, wood, woman with googly eyes wearing real cotton plaid dress, hook for the dish towel or potholder by feet, 1940s, appears to be homemade; excellent condition, **$30–40.**

Juicer, man's head, marked on bottom and stamped "C42," European, 1900, 6″ × 4″; excellent condition, **$800–900.**

Kettle warmer, stuffed cloth mammy doll in green and white for upper body (may be turn of the century, lower dress may be later period); 16″ × 12″; excellent condition, **$150–250.**

Kitchen towels, linen, hand-embroidered, each towel shows a day of the week and mammy doing chore for that day, full color, 1930s; excellent condition, **$165–200 for the set of seven.**

Kitchenware set

Chef, cookie jar, grease pot, salt and pepper shakers, 1940s–1950s; very good condition, **$120–180 for the set.**

Chef's head, cookie jar, salt and pepper shakers, 1950s; very good condition, **$85–110 for the set.**

Mammy and chef, salt and pepper shakers, grease jar shaped as stove, bright yellow and black with gold decoration, original Woolworth's 98-cent price tag on bottom, mint to unused condition, **$150–225 for the set.**

Measuring cup set

Man's head, earthenware, large-lipped, multicolored and glazed, marked "Japan," rare, ½

132

cup, ¼ cup and ⅛ cup; largest 4″ × 2″; near mint condition, **$200–300 for the set.**

Man's head in blackface, Wales China, complete on original wooden rack, late 1940s, graduated sizes from ¼ to 1 cup; excellent condition, **$95–125 for the set.**

Measuring spoon holder, mammy, ceramic, hand-decorated underglaze, rare; mint condition, **$60–100.**

Memo holder

Mammy, chalkware; very good condition, **$130–150.**

Mammy, with pencil; very good condition, **$40–50.**

Memo holder, Mammy Memo, composition, marked "Reg. U.S. Pat. Of. Made in U.S.A. Hampden Novelty Mfg. Co. Inc. Holyoke, Mass. Pat. No. D1207," yellow turban and scarf around neck, red blouse, blue skirt, broom is pencil, 1930s–1940s; good condition, **$35–50.** Courtesy of the Dawn and Bob Reno Collection; photo by Bob Reno.

Pepper shaker, dancing boy, wears hat and carries cane, black jacket, red pants, 1940s, 4¾″ tall; very good condition, **$8–12.**

Pie bird, chef, green and red with gold spoon, early piece; mint to unused condition, **$75–150.**

Pitcher

Chef, porcelain, hand painted in green, blue, brown, and white; 4″ × 4″; near mint condition, **$150–175.**

Mammy, porcelain, hand painted in green, brown, pink, white, and blue, pre-war Japan; 4″ × 4″, near mint condition, **$150–175.**

Pitcher and creamer, porcelain, chef, hand painted in green, blue, brown, and white, pre-war Japan; 4″ × 4″, near mint condition, **$150–175.**

Plaque

Boy with umbrella and girl with umbrella (pair), chalkware, very colorful; very good condition, **$30–40 for the pair.**

Boy and girl sharing watermelon slice, pottery, colorful, hanging, 1930s–1940s, near mint condition, **$22–26.**

Cook and chef (pair), chalkware, colorful; very good condition, **$50–60 for the pair.**

Golliwog heads (pair), chalkware, heads of boy and girl with large red lips; very good condition, **$30–40 for the pair.**

Pot holder

Abolitionist, inscription in needlepoint on canvas: "Any holder but a slaveholder," depicts a black child playing ball, velvet ribbon binding, mid-1800s; 7½″ × 7¾″; excellent condition, **$350–400.**

Figural, girl, colorful; very good condition, **$18–20.**

Sambo, chalkware, yellow and black, hangs on wall; very good condition, **$35–50.**

Pot holder plaque

Children with watermelon; excellent condition, **$50–80.**

Mammy and chef

Chalkware, mammy in blue and yellow, chef in white; excellent condition, **$45–80.**

Pot holder plaques, mammy and chef, appear to be handpainted in red and white; good condition, **$35–50 each.** Courtesy of Dakota Sands, photo by Donald Vogt.

Chalkware, original green and white paint; excellent condition, **$40–70.**

Pot holder rack, Aunt Jemima, wood, carved; very good condition, **$25–40.**

Potato sack, mammy, burlap; mint condition, **$12–15.**

Recipe box, mammy; very good condition, **$18–24.**

Reminder list, wood, "We Needs Wood," original pegs; very good condition, **$80–100.**

Salt and pepper

African chief and native man, standing light brown chief, dark brown native behind cauldron, 3″ chief, 2½″ native; excellent condition, **$45–55 for the pair.**

African native couple (very round), made of wood, male is the salt, both wear hats and grass skirts, hats screw off; 4½″ tall; **$45–55 for the pair.**

African native figure with metal body wearing hoop earrings, necklace, and ankle bracelets,

carrying two ceramic drums (salt and pepper shakers), 1940s; 5¾″ tall; mint condition, **$60–75 for three pieces.**

African native man and woman, faces painted on square shakers, salt is side view of woman with flower in hair, pepper is native man with earrings and bone through nose; salt 2¾″ tall; pepper 3″ tall; very good condition, **$35–50 for the pair.**

African native men, ceramic, heads only, light brown and white, bone in nose; 3¼″ tall; excellent condition, **$45–55 for the pair.**

Babies in basket, girl wears yellow panties, white blouse with green trim and bed jacket with gold detailing and wine trim, boy wears blue shorts, white shirt with green trim and gold detailing, basket also has gold detailing, uncommon set; excellent condition, **$100–150 for the pair.**

Bellboys, one holds phone, the other holds pad of paper, orange hats and jackets, gray pants, light-colored faces; each 3½″ tall; very good condition, **$35–45 for the pair.**

Boy and girl

African native boy and girl, boy sitting with hands up in air, girl laying on stomach, head propped on elbows, brown bodies, black hair, girl wears green fig leaf; 2½" boy, 1½" girl; excellent condition, **$45–55 for the pair.**

Boy wearing white shirt and white pants with green stripes, girl in white and red polka-dotted dress and turban; 2¼" boy, 3" girl; excellent condition, **$125–150 for the pair.**

Boy with large slice of watermelon, little girl in short red dress, ceramic, 1940s; 4½" boy, 4" girl; excellent condition, **$65–75 for the pair.**

Caribbean boy and girl, boy (pepper) in white shorts, yellow hat and carrying guitar, girl (salt) in a yellow skirt marked "Curacao," 4⅓" boy; 3" girl; excellent condition, **$65–75 for the pair.**

Heads only, bald-headed boy, girl with yellow straw hat, hand decorated underglaze; mint condition, **$50–110 for the pair.**

Salt and pepper, boy and girl with huge pieces of watermelon, two sets: watermelons are pepper shakers and children are salt-shakers, each 4½"; excellent condition, $95 per set. Courtesy of the Diane Stary Collection; photo by Diane Stary.

Sitting, boy in blue outfit, girl in pink dress; 3" boy, 3¼" girl; excellent condition, **$35–45 for the pair.**

Sitting back to back with heads lifted to sky as if singing, girl wears red-and-white dress, apron, and scarf, boy wears blue pants, blue, green, and beige shirt; 4" tall; new, **$35–45 for the pair.**

Boy on alligator; very good condition, **$30–45 for the pair.**

Boy on toilet; very good condition, **$35–65 for the pair.**

Boy with melons; very good condition, **$60–70 for three pieces.**

Boy's head with watermelon, hand painted underglaze; mint condition, **$40–70 for the pair.**

Butler and maid, pottery, brown skin tone, woman in plaid dress with deep rose bandanna, butler in black jacket, 1930s, range size, 5" tall; excellent condition, **$150–200 for the pair.**

Chef

Ceramic, 5"; very good condition, **$15–25 for the pair.**

Round faces with tall chef's hats, wood tops, glass bottoms; 3¾" tall; very good condition, **$35–45 for the pair.**

Children

Eating watermelon, yellow hats; 3¼" tall; new, **$15–20 for the pair.**

Googly-eyed kids in turbans, Goebel, Germany, brown skin tone, deep orange, white, navy blue, and yellow, 1930s, 3½" tall; excellent condition, **$125–150 for the pair.**

Kissing on a bench (three pieces); very good condition, **$125–155 for the set.**

Kissing, pottery, white with gold trim, exaggerated features and braids, 1950s, 3" tall; very good condition, **$65–80 for the pair.**

On ears of corn; very good condition, **$70–90 for the pair.**

Girl with drum, white skirt and red belt, the letter S embossed on the bottom of her skirt, black, red, and white drum is pepper shaker; 6¼″ girl, 1½″ drum; excellent condition, **$125–150 for the pair.**

Mammy

Nodding mammy with melon; very good condition, **$130–150 for the pair.**

Pearl China, large; very good condition, **$200–230 for the pair.**

Pineapple mammy face, cartoon quality, brown skin, extremely colorful, pottery; 4″ tall; excellent condition, **$65–85 for the pair.**

Wine color dress, white aprons with cherry gold trim; 3½″; very good condition, **$40–50 for the pair.**

With gold tooth, high-grade ceramic, pink and green glaze on white background with gold tooth and highlighting; mint condition, **$50–100 for the pair.**

Mammy and chef

Big-eyed, red highlights, gold decoration; mint condition, **$50–80 for the pair.**

Black suits with bright orange appointments; mint condition, **$40–60 for the pair.**

Blue with gold trim, sold as tourist mementoes, 1950s, 5″ chef, 4¾″ mammy; excellent condition, **$24–32 for the pair.**

Decorated with bittersweet, ribbons and gold; mint condition, **$50–100 for the pair.**

Gold decoration on white ground, souvenir of Washington, D.C.; mint condition, **$35–80 for the pair.**

Green dots underglaze with lots of gold; mint condition, **$50–100 for the pair.**

Herby and Spicey, black suit with red hats and utensils, original hanging tag around neck, rare; unused to mint condition, **$50–100 for the pair.**

Mammy and Moses, F&F Plastic, old; table size; unused to mint condition, **$30–40 for the pair.**

White with gold decoration, marked "Souvenir of N.Y.S. Thruway"; mint condition, **$40–60 for the pair.**

With two table-size Peppys, Pearl China Co.; all mint condition, **$150–300 for the set.**

Man with two bottles protruding from his pockets, brown skin, brown clothes, the bottles (pink and green) are salt and pepper shakers; 6¼″ tall; excellent condition, **$75–95 for the pair.**

"Mandy's Pickaninnies," pottery, brown boy holds basket of apples, girl holds bouquet of flowers, from recently discontinued Mandy set; mint condition, **$85–100 for the pair.**

Salt and pepper, nodding African native with watermelon slice, unmarked; good condition, $100–150. Courtesy of Dakota Sands; photo by Donald Vogt.

Noah and the Ark, very colorful; new, **$40–50 for the pair.**

Nodder (rare), three-piece set, nude female forms holder, nodding head and melon slice are the shakers, 1930s–1950s, 3½"; excellent condition, **$175–225 for the pair.**

Salty and Peppy

Pearl China; 4½"; very good condition, **$25–35 for the pair.**

Salty is female and Peppy is male, faces of two black chefs in hats marked with names, both have dark brown skin, red lips, and gold earrings, each 5¼" tall; mint condition, **$125–150 for the pair.**

Woman's head, pottery, Art Deco, aqua, glazed with brown detailing; 3½" tall; mint condition, **$75–100 for the pair.**

Salt dip spoon, sterling silver, Johnny Griffin figural bust, ca. 1910; 2¼" long; excellent condition, **$95–125.**

Saltshaker

Black child, Ceramic Arts Studio; very good condition, **$30–35.**

Mammy

Black dress with white apron and red turban, 1950s, 4" tall; very good condition, **$8–12.**

Ivory dress with red polka dots and green trim, green turban, sitting, 1930s; 3" tall; excellent condition, **$8–12.**

Scrub-pad holder

Girl's head, unusual; very good condition, **$135–160.**

Mandy, Brayton Laguna, ceramic, well marked on bottom; mint condition, **$150–250.**

Shopping list, on board, mammy face at top, holes mark various items; very good condition, **$35–45.**

Pearl China kitchen items, marked "Pearl 22 kt. gold, U.S.A." on bottom in gold shell; excellent condition, *back row left to right:* cookie jars, each 11", mammy, **$600–800;** mammy with watermelon, **$5,500–7,500;** Cooky (chef), **$350–450;** *middle row:* two sets of salt and pepper shakers, Peppy and Salty, each 7" tall, white, **$225 for the set,** yellow, **$200–225 for the set;** *front row:* salt and pepper shakers, Peppy and Salty, yellow, 4", **$75–100 for the set.** Courtesy of the Leonard Davis Collection; photo by Bob Reno.

Spice jar set

Chef, original wood rack, red bow ties are handles, colorful; 10½" × 5¼" overall; excellent condition, **$175–225 for the set.**

Mammy, six pieces; very good condition, **$75–85 for the set.**

Mammy or chef personalities, five shakers, wood rack, 1940s; excellent condition, **$185–225 for the set.**

Spoon rest with watermelon slice shaker (doubles as a pie bird), mammy, good decoration under-glaze; mint condition, **$50–100.**

String holder

Butler, earthenware, full figure; 6½"; excellent condition, **$300–350.**

Mammy

Earthenware, plaid dress; mint condition, **$295–325.**

Green-and-brown striped dress, original cold-painted face; near mint condition, **$115–250.**

Red turban and dress of black squares with orange dots, not reproduction; 6¾" × 3½"; very good condition, **$90–110.**

White apron and floral dress; excellent condition, **$150–225.**

String holder, ball of twine is placed in the head, string comes out the mouth, hand-made; excellent condition, **$350–400.** Courtesy of Malinda Saunders; photo by Donald Vogt.

Sugar and creamer, plastic, mammy, original colors, white sugar and creamer with mammy attached (standing straight, same height as the sugar and creamer, possibly serving as a handle), limited supply; excellent condition, **$5–6 for the set.**

Sugar bowl, Weller, mammy, white body with mammy head cover, most desirable black set, original label on bottom; mint condition, **$100–200.**

Sugar container, porcelain, hand painted in green, blue, orange, brown, and white, head comes off, pre-war Japan, 4" × 4"; near mint condition, **$150–175.**

Sweeper, bread crumb, earthenware, mammy; very good condition, **$30–40.**

Tablecloth, Southern plantation and its activities, linen, red, green, yellow, purple, and black, 1940s, 52" square; very good condition, **$85–100.**

Tea towel, embroidered linen, black boy eating melon with his dog watching, 1940s; very good condition, **$45–55.**

Thermometer, Diaper Dan, boxed, 1949; 5"; very good condition, **$85–95.**

Tin, Aunt Dinah; 4½"; very good condition, **$30–35.**

Toaster doll

Blue-and-white dress, button eyes, hand-sewn features; very good condition, **$38–48.**

Red dress, 1950s; excellent condition, **$30–45.**

Rubber face, yellow dress and bonnet; very good condition, **$30–40.**

Toothpick holder, antique milk glass, boy with ethnic features in fancy clothes, was originally painted black, 3¼" × 3½"; very good condition, **$155–185.**

Toothpick holder and creamers, Schafer & Vater, Germany, happy feet toothpick holder, two of three sizes of the grotesque creamer, early 1900s; excellent condition, **$150–250 for the set.**

Towel

Aunt Jemima, cotton, colorful; very good condition, **$30–40.**

Chef with lobster; very good condition, **$25–35.**

String holders, *left to right:* mammy, ceramic, apron pocket for scissor, string comes out the mouth, 7″; excellent condition, **$350–400**; mammy, chalkware, yellow turban, 8″; excellent condition, **$300–350**; mammy, chalkware, 8″; excellent condition, **$225–250**; butler, ceramic, 6½″; excellent condition, **$300–350**. Courtesy of the Leonard Davis Collection; photo by Bob Reno.

Teapot, African native man sitting on elephant, mounted on stand (not original), available in different sizes, made in Japan, 1930s–1940s, 9¾″; excellent condition, **$125–150 with cups, $100–125 without cups**. Courtesy of the Leonard Davis Collection; photo by Bob Reno.

Wall pocket

 Chef, Hollywood Ceramics, pottery, brown-skinned chef wearing white sits on yellow wood-burning stove, 5½″ × 4½″; excellent condition, **$95–125**.

 Chef and stove; very good condition, **$55–75**.

 Mammy, earthenware, marked "Coventry-made in the USA," very rare; mint condition, **$70–175**.

 Mammy head, Coventry; very good condition, **$50–65**.

 Moors (pair), Royal Copley, porcelain, man and woman, glazed, 1950s, 8″ × 4½″; excellent condition, **$450–500 for the pair**.

Toaster dolls, plastic faces, commercially made; excellent condition, **$50–75 each.** Courtesy of Rose Fontanella; photo by Donald Vogt.

CHAPTER EIGHT

Paper Ephemera

Ephemera is defined as anything that has temporary interest or value. Most paper goods, such as newspapers, magazines, posters, playbills, postcards, greeting cards, postage stamps, and trade cards fall into this category. Note that some ephemeral items are covered in other chapters. For example, most posters and playbills as well as related newspapers and magazines are in Part Four ("Entertainment") and newspapers, magazines, and slave documents are in Part Three ("Historical Artifacts").

To obtain a clearer view of the field, one must explore publishing and advertising and become familiar with the personalities (or subject matter) one is interested in collecting. For example, if you want to collect ephemera about black Americans during the Civil War period, you should learn about the newspapers and magazines of that day, the politicians in power, the household trends, the military, and so on. (Again, be sure to see the chapters devoted to these areas.)

Ephemera is one field that infringes on all the other areas of collection. There are clubs, antiques shows, and shops devoted to ephemera. To find sources in your area, consult your local antiques or collecting trade papers.

How to Collect Ephemera

Because paper does not withstand the test of time, it is most advisable to keep your collection in acid-free mats or, if possible, period frames. Trade card, greeting card, and postcard collectors can file their collections in albums made especially for that purpose. These albums can be found in most large stationary or department stores.

Remember that gluing your collection into a scrapbook decreases its value. Furthermore, if you chose to sell all or part of your collection, you would have a hard time doing so if the individual items were glued.

Condition of paper goods is important, but don't pass up a newspaper or other article with information or photos of black Americans because the piece is a little dog-eared. The older the newspaper (or paper article), the more likely it is to be brittle or damaged. Remember to take into consideration the definition of ephemera when collecting: "anything that has temporary interest or value."

Postcard, "Two Loving Hearts," comic, full color; very good condition, $6–8. Courtesy of Malinda Saunders; photo by Donald Vogt.

Types of Ephemera

The following discussion describes some of the broad categories of ephemera.

BROCHURES

Most companies created brochures to advertise their products. Stores also printed brochures for special sales, to list their goods, or to advertise the store itself. See also Chapter 5.

CALENDARS

Calendars have been made of paper, as well as other materials, and many calendars have had photos or illustrations of black people on them. Even calendars that are missing a page or two are desirable to col-

lectors because these items are so often thrown away.

GREETING CARDS

Cards have been made for every occasion. One might collect cards relating only to a specific holiday (i.e., Christmas or Valentine's Day) or collect any type of card illustrated with a black personality. The earlier comic greeting cards are becoming more and more scarce, thus are highly collectible.

MAGAZINES

By the end of the eighteenth century, some one hundred magazines had appeared in the United States. Each offered entertainment and/or uplifting information for the

Greeting card, "To my Valentine," in original mailing box, woman's head is composition, clothes are paper, was sent to Miss Hazel V. Brown and postmarked California 1905; very good condition, $75–100. Courtesy of American Eye; photo by Bob Reno.

average white American citizen. Magazine publishing did not have a solid base in the United States until after the Civil War.

During the mid–nineteenth century, illustrated magazines became more common. *Leslie's Weekly* and *Harper's Weekly* were the forerunners in this new phase of the magazine industry. During the Civil War, *Leslie's* had as many as twelve correspondents at the front and was able to give a good pictorial record of the war. *Leslie's* and *Harper's* are sources for stories (fiction as well as nonfiction) about Blacks during this time. Though few of the actual magazines found are perfect and intact, one can often find etched covers and frontispieces that have been matted and framed, among them well-done views of Blacks during the Civil War and Reconstruction. The magazines often ran articles about slavery and different points of view on the subject. Humorous stories and scenes of black life were also subjects of interest in these early magazines.

Once the British repealed the advertising tax in 1853, advertising in magazines became more common. *Harper's* did not want advertisers to invade its pages until the 1880s, and some magazines did not allow advertisers until the mid-twentieth century. This fact made a difference in the amount of revenue the magazines procured, but it also had a secondary effect: It allowed the magazines to maintain higher standards without bowing to the wishes of advertisers who were designing ads derogatory to black Americans.

Today, the interplay between a magazine and its advertisers is complex. If a magazine publishes an article offensive to its advertisers, it can lose thousands of advertising dollars. Conversely, an offensive advertisement can result in lost readership or an outcry against the company and the magazine from consumer groups. But until Blacks began to own businesses, including magazines and newspapers, advertising was

Magazine cover, *Harper's Weekly*, New York, *Bond and Free,* Saturday, December 27, 1873; very good condition, **$25–35**. Photo by Donald Vogt.

the domain of white businesspeople, and all too often these people took actions that perpetuated rather than countered myths and misconceptions about Blacks. Once Blacks entered the business world, they could slowly chip away at the subliminal prejudices contained in some ads. Advertis-ing continues to have a very strong impact on the magazine publishing industry.

Black political and scholarly journals usually do not need to cater to advertisers, even though they are often published by the same companies that put out mass-market magazines. Prominent black journals through the years have included the *Journal of Negro Education, Phylon,* and the *Quarterly Review of Higher Education among Negroes.*

News and photo magazines, such as *Time* and *Life,* began to appear in the first half of the twentieth century. These magazines summarized the news, expanded it, made it more concise, or made it more attractive. They supplemented newspapers by presenting information in a glossier or more varied format. *Life* magazine began publishing in November 1936 and was printing a million copies within a couple of weeks. The "digest" format that was started by *Reader's Digest* in 1922 was used by *Negro Digest* and *Jet* in the subsequent decades. Many of the news magazines, including those catering to the general public, published the work of black reporters and photojournalists in their earliest issues (see the biographies of Bruce Davidson and Danny Lyon in Chapter 3).

3. MY OLD LOG CABIN.

Photograph postcard, "3. My Old Log Cabin," linen, full color; very good condition, $8–10. Courtesy of Malinda Saunders; photo by Donald Vogt.

Blacks were finally becoming the photographers and writers instead of just the subjects.

The middle of the twentieth century brought about the decline of magazine publishing's most expansive phase. Many of today's magazines, including those aimed at black Americans, tend to be moving away from general interest, toward specialization. An August 5, 1990, article in *The New York Times* stated that "at least 25 black-oriented magazines are competing for a national readership" in the U.S. market. Three such magazines are *Jet, Ebony,* and *Essence.*

Though magazines have a hard time getting and keeping advertisers in today's economy, they continue to be produced because of low overhead costs. Desktop publishing has enabled people to create magazines without the financial burdens of printing and personnel. Still, there are expenses, and advertising helps defray some of the costs. The problem these new black-oriented magazines are running into is an old one—convincing advertisers that there is a market and a value in advertising in the black media.

NEWSPAPERS

The first black newspaper, *Freedom's Journal,* was published by Samuel Cornish and John B. Russwumn in New York City on March 16, 1827. It was followed twenty years later by Frederick Douglass's newspaper, *The North Star* (which was renamed in 1830: *Frederick Douglass' Paper*). Douglass, a famous abolitionist, dedicated himself to pleading the American Black's case before a mostly uncaring public (see also Chapter 4). *Freedom's Journal,* renamed *Rights for All* in 1823, ceased publication in 1830.

Other black newspapers that had some impact on the reading public included New York's *Colored American* (1837); Albany, New York's *Elevator* (1842); *Genius of Freedom* (1842), also a New York paper; and New York's *Ram's Horn* (1847).

Cartoon, full color, early 1900s; very good condition, $18–22. Photo by Donald Vogt.

The number of black-owned newspapers in the United States rose from 10 in 1870 to 20 in 1880, reaching 154 in 1890.

In 1850, *The Voice of the Oppressed* was born in Ohio. William H. Day and Dr. Charles H. Langston acted as that paper's first editors. The newspaper changed its name in 1851 to *Clarion of Freedom*, but it folded within the year. Day went on to publish *The Aliened American* (1853), but publication ceased in 1855. Another Ohio paper was *Herald of Freedom*, published by Peter H. Clark.

California's first black newspaper, *Mirror of the Times*, was founded by Mifflin W. Gibbs in 1855. He actively fought against inequality in Sacramento, where he lived, as well as throughout California. He was struck by gold fever in 1858, headed for Canada, opened a store, and entered politics in the James Bay district. Later, Gibbs got a law degree and became a city judge in Little

Rock, Arkansas. He eventually was named U.S. consul in Madagascar. Gibbs wrote his autobiography, *Shadow and Light* before he died in 1903.

The *Waco Spectator*, published by nineteen-year-old Albert Parsons, a Confederate veteran, aroused some anger in 1868, because the paper defended black people and underdogs. The *Spectator* went under, and Parsons headed for Chicago where he became a leader in the Knights of Labor and spoke out for the anarchist cause. In 1887, Parsons and three of his comrades were hung for their beliefs. Another newspaper published during this period, *The Texas Freeman*, was edited by Emmett J. Scott, a debonaire twenty-five-year-old who became Booker T. Washington's right-hand man.

After the Civil War, black journalism grew rapidly and several periodicals joined the ranks of the political press. By the turn of the century, black America was experiencing a surge of upward mobility, and the newspaper industry catered to this population. W. M. Trotter, editor of the *Boston Guardian*, was one of the most noted of the early black editors. He often found himself at odds with Booker T. Washington and was considered quite a radical. The *Chicago Defender*'s editor, Robert Abbott, was known for his efforts in mass circulation and his distinctly different use of headlines.

Although the black press was concerned with keeping the black public informed of black views, it also reported its feelings on issues of the day. Periodicals became a powerful political tool and were often the targets of violent acts in response to radical editorials or unpopular remarks by outspoken editors. Eventually, black business leaders formed political and economic organizations such as the National Association for the Advancement of Colored People (NAACP) and the National Negro Business League to give themselves more power. In the early days, however the black reporter often had a difficult time.

During the post–Civil War era, one of the most prominent black journalists was T. Thomas Fortune. Fortune attended Howard University but never finished, having left his studies to marry. He learned the newspaper business at a number of eastern newspapers before editing *The Globe,* a black daily. Along with Booker T. Washington, he formed the National Negro Business League in 1900. The black press supported black self-help groups, but also kept the black public informed on vital community issues, such as education and police protection.

During the world wars, black journalists and their periodicals backed the United States during its time of need. After World War I the black press turned its focus on civil rights. Roy Wilkins, a journalist in the Midwest in the 1920s and 1930s, was recognized by the NAACP for his work to further the cause. Some newspapers were so adamant in their beliefs that the Justice Department threatened them with sedition charges in 1942. It became increasingly difficult for those papers to find newsprint.

After World War II, with the increasing popularity of radio and television, all newspapers suffered. White papers, stronger metropolitan dailies, and national magazines began to hire top black journalists to cover the black community. The smaller black papers did not have enough power to hold their employees, nor could they offer them the salary of the larger papers.

Adam Clayton Powell founded and edited the *People's Voice* in 1942. He became well known for promoting views on equal opportunity, for printing features on important African-Americans, and for relating stories about improving the black rights. By the 1950s, the combined weekly circulation of 210 black newspapers was estimated at 2,500,000. The Atlanta *Daily World,* considered the country's leading black daily, had a total circulation of 29,000.

During the late 1960s and early 1970s, black newspapers began to rally and the National Newspapers Publishers Association, which represented more than 30 black papers, began to schedule workshops that served to put black journalism back on a better financial level. Today there are almost 150 black newspapers. The dailies the *Atlanta World* and the Chicago *Daily Defender* have circulations of more than thirty thousand.

POSTAGE STAMPS

The first African-American to be honored with his image on a postage stamp was Booker T. Washington. The year was 1940, and others soon received the same honor (George Washington Carver in 1948 and Frederick Douglass in 1967). In 1978, the Black Heritage series began recognizing distinguished African-American citizens on postage stamps. The thirteenth stamp in the series honored Ida B. Wells, journalist and founder of the NAACP, and was released in 1993. Wells, born in 1862 to a Mississippi slave family, died in Chicago in 1931.

The Black Heritage stamps are issued each February to mark Black Heritage month. Abolitionist Harriet Tubman graced the first in the series, issued on February 1, 1978. Others include Martin Luther King Jr. civil rights activist (1979); Mary McCleod Bethune, founder of Bethune-Cookman College in Daytona Beach (1985); Sojourner Truth, social reformer and women's rights activist (1986); Jesse Owens, Olympic athlete (1990); Jackie Robinson, baseball player (1982); Scott Joplin, ragtime musician; Roberto Clemente, Puerto Rican baseball player (1984); and Duke Ellington, jazz musician extraordinaire (1986).

Other stamps with a black American theme include the 1973 *Porgy and Bess* stamp, the 1940 stamp that commemorated the seventy-fifth anniversary of the abolition

Photograph, postcard, "27. Weighing Cotton," plantation owner weighs cotton while workers look on; very good condition, $8–12. Courtesy of Malinda Saunders; photo by Donald Vogt.

of slavery (the stamp depicts President Lincoln and a slave and is the subject of a Thomas Ball statue); and the centennial anniversary of the Emancipation Proclamation stamp, released in 1963.

Stamps from African countries are fascinating, often depicting masks, fetishes, sculptures, or paintings. Stamps issued by Chad have shown rock paintings of various native animals. Ethiopia, Swaziland, and Mauritania have also printed stamps featuring rock paintings. Masks of all kinds are depicted on postage stamps from Guinea, Zaire, Mali, Liberia, Ivory Coast, Upper Volta, and Cameroon. The great variety of art stamps available makes collecting African stamps a very hot area.

Another type of collectible postage stamp is made in a foreign country to depict U.S. black culture. Quite a few countries, especially those in the Caribbean, have created stamps that feature black Americans such as Duke Ellington, Charlie Parker, Michael Jackson, Bill Cosby, Ralph Bunche, Roberto Clemente, Nat "King" Cole, Ella Fitzgerald, Jackie Robinson, Whitney Houston, Al Joyner, Martin Luther King Jr., Eddie Murphy, and Malcolm X.

To find stamps, attend the shows that cater to philatelists. Also contact the American Philatelic Society, which now has more than fifty thousand members. For other information on collecting black postage stamps, contact the Black American Philatelic Society, c/o Walt Robinson, 9101 Taylor Street, Landover, MD 10785 or the Ebony Society of Philatelic Events and Reflections, P.O. Box 548, F.D.R. Station, New York, NY 10150-0548.

POSTCARDS

Postcards could not be mailed in the United States until 1873. It is thought that the first picture postcard was not mailed until 1893. Following the Civil War, postcards of black military, farmers, and workers were made with regularity, and they are considered desirable in today's market. The black subjects of the early hand-tinted postcards were depicted in their normal habitat as well as in typically black American scenes. As with all early black American ephemera, postcards usually showed blacks and black culture in a derogatory light. Postcards that simply show a black work group, cowboys, or minstrels are often more valuable to a collector because they depict the "professional" Black of that era.

The heyday of the picture postcard ranged from 1900 to World War II. The use of postcards as tourist mementos widened their appeal, and many have ended up unused and unposted in postcard albums and collections. This was also the era when black "comic" postcards were in style. Here's a typical example: A cards shows a large black woman, with her back to us. The card reads, "I'se a lil behind in mah writin'." The linen-like photograph postcards that began to be circulated in the 1920s showed such scenes as a black mother picking lice out of her children's hair or an old black man driving a mule touted as the "only transportation in Atlanta." It was also during this period that cards depicting black cotton workers and Blacks eating watermelon were common. Derogatory postcards were being produced up to the time of the 1960s civil rights movement.

POSTERS

Posters with a black American connection that were circulated before and immediately after the Civil War were usually slave auction posters or wanted posters. These early posters were often letter pressed and not as big as today's posters. Because newspapers were bought only by those who could afford—and could read—them, posters were used as a way of spreading news of an upcoming event. Slave auctions were advertised this way during the early days of the United States, but these early posters are rarely found intact.

More commonly found are later posters demanding the recovery of runaway slaves or Civil War soldiers (see also Chapter 12). Plantation owners often advertised large rewards for the return of their "property," which may have encouraged the bounty hunter to keep the poster as proof that the offer had been made and to ensure that payment for return of the slave was made.

SLAVERY-RELATED EPHEMERA

While some ephemera collectors concentrate on one form of paper collectible,

Postcard, "Eve stole first and Adam second . . .," linen, full color, comic, 1907; very good condition, $12–15. Courtesy of Malinda Saunders; photo by Donald Vogt.

Postcard, "A Watermelon Feast," linen, full color, framed, 1920s; excellent condition, $15–20. Courtesy of the Dawn and Bob Reno Collection; photo by Bob Reno.

such as newspapers or postcards, other collectors prefer to focus on a particular topic and collect various types of ephemera related to that topic. Focusing on slavery allows a collector insight into an important and underdocumented era of U.S. history.

The history of the colonies in the New World cannot be divorced from the history of slavery. Transatlantic trade of African blacks by Puritan merchants brought wealth to early New Englanders. Boston and Newport prospered from the trading of slaves, which can be traced back as far as 1638. Because New England did not have a plantation economy, the black population was relatively small—fewer than 17,000 slaves were based in New England out of a total of 660,000 living in the colonies. In the seventeenth century, 887,500 slaves were imported to many regions of the burgeoning nation. An all-time high of 7 million was reached in the eighteenth century.

Ulrich B. Phillips, a professor at the universities of Wisconsin, Michigan, and Yale, wrote two books (in 1918 and 1929) on the economics of slavery. He based most of his argument on the prices of slaves and prices of cotton. He believed there was a direct relation between the economy of slave labor and the rise and the production of cotton in the United States. In the beginning, slaves were used to farm tobacco, sugarcane crops, and other such Middle to Deep South farm crops. Once cotton became the largest produced item on the plantations, the value of the slaves who worked to produce that crop grew. Phillips proved that the ratio of slave to cotton prices "rose by over sixfold between 1805 and 1860, a change of this magnitude clearly indicated to Phillips that, by the last decade of the antebellum era, slaves were overvalued—that is, priced too high to permit an investor to earn a normal rate of profit" (see Fogel and Engerman, 1984, in the "Bibliography"). But slaves were desired not only because they were able to produce crops, but also because they were symbols of a plantation owner's social status and wealth.

The Caribbean island countries started to abolish slavery in 1804, when Haiti led the way. Other countries followed suit throughout Central and South America, including the British, French, and Danish colonies. The United States was last to outlaw slavery.

When emancipation finally came, it did not signal an end of trouble for Blacks or even an end to slavery. Quite a few plantations were known to have owned slaves longer than they should have after emancipation. Sometimes Blacks themselves decided to stay at the plantation, often because they were looking for other members of their families. Unfortunately, life for African-Americans did not improve just because they were emancipated. Most free Blacks had a difficult a time getting a job, buying land, marrying, and as noted, finding their families and their roots.

Reconstruction, which started in 1863 and continued through 1877, marked the unfinished revolution of slaves and abolitionists. Both former slaves and southern whites were unprepared for the responsibilities that freedom gave to a people who had no experience in providing for themselves. And Blacks could not simply forget their past imprisonment of slavery and mistreatment.

According to Eric Foner's *Reconstruction: America's Unfinished Revolution,* "between 1865 and 1870, the black population of the South's ten largest cities doubled, while the number of white residents rose by only 10%." Smaller towns, from which Blacks had often been excluded as slaves, experienced even more dramatic increases.

Blacks had difficulties finding a way to make a living and support their families. Most former slaves did not want to work as field laborers, the most available jobs. Black women who had domestic responsibilities as slaves used their skills to become cooks, seamstresses, laundresses, and nannies. Some Blacks who tried to grow their own crops also experienced frustrations. They usually had to rent land or had shares in the land, but they did not own it. And the land they were able to farm was most likely of marginal fertility. See also Chapter 13.

Newspapers, magazines, and other forms of public communication in the nineteenth century, such as posters and handbills, certainly addressed the issue of slavery and, as such, are collected as ephemera. Some newspapers, such as *The Liberator* and the *Anti-Slavery Standard,* were founded specifically to speak out against slavery. The chilling and dehumanizing attitudes of the slave era are often more clearly revealed, however, in the incidental documents of the time—bills of sale, tax documents, and the like. I have included many such documents in this chapter (categorizing them in the price list as documents, letters, and so on). They demonstrate how ephemera often has historical value.

TRADE CARDS

Trade cards began to appear as early as the late seventeenth century and carried advertisements for businesses of all kinds. They reached their peak of excellence in the nineteenth century, when they were often embellished with vignettes illustrating the trade the card advertised. Many of the cards were beautifully inscribed using copperplate engraving. See also Chapter 5.

PRICES FOR PAPER EPHEMERA

Booklet

Boston slave riots, original illustration of slave Anthony Burns on the covers, because of this trial, many states passed personal liberty laws that blocked the Fugitive Slave Law regarding runaway slaves, important and rare and includes photocopies of the history of the trial whereby the United States Army had to intervene with Boston citizens trying to stop the Rev. Cutter Morris from taking Burns back into slavery, printed in Boston, 1854; very good condition, **$25–35.**

Montgomery Alabama—Pamphlet and Poetry by Eve Merriam, 1956; excellent condition, **$20–25.**

Broadside, slave reward, printed broadside on thin, delicate paper, states William T. J. Richards, administrator for James Richards, offers a $100 reward for Abram, "who is about 30 years old, 5 feet from 8 to 10 inches high, and weighs from 175 to 180. His complexion is dark, though not black, and hair long for a Negro. He is a very shrewd fellow, and there is reason to believe he is attempting to get to a free state . . . ," printed in Richards' Ferry, Culpepper County, Virginia, on September 24 (no year stated in description); 8½″ × 6½″; good condition, **$1,000–1,200.**

Calendar

A Journey Into 365 Days of Black History, noted events in the history of Blacks around the world for every day of 1993, for every month an historic photograph and essay about notable black men and women from early recorded history to the present day, printed on high-quality enamel paper; 13¼″ × 12″ (13¼″ × 24″ opened); mint condition, **$11–15.**

Homecoming: The Paintings of William H. Johnson, a tribute to one of America's most important but neglected painters, a selection of paintings recently on exhibition at the National Museum of American Art in Washington, D.C., printed on high-quality enamel paper; 13¼″ × 12″ (13¼″ × 24″ opened); mint condition, **$11–15.**

South African advertising, embossed leather top portion features African woman in traditional dress milling corn, "EBE South Africa" marked on table, 1979; 11″ × 17½″; excellent condition, **$60–75.**

Cartoon

Field hand leaning on a stump with hoe in hand and fields in background, caption reads "The innocent cause of the war"; very good condition, **$4–8.**

"Hambone's Meditations" by Alley, pasted in typing manual, 55 pages plus inside flaps, all date from mid-1940s–1960s; 10¾″ × 8½″; excellent condition, **$150–200.**

"The Housekeeper," three-picture cartoon showing boy fishing where "No Fishing Allowed," November 1905; excellent condition, **$5–7.**

"The Latest Contraband of War," black field hand without shoes carrying hoe, caption reads "Whar Is Massa Jeff Now, dat's what's de matter"; very good condition, **$4–8.**

"Southern Currency," cover, slaves escaping northward in droves, star in the north says "Come Along Colored Pussons"; very good condition, **$4–8.**

Comic book, *Golden Legacy,* full color, Fitzgerald Pub. Co., Inc., 1970

Frederick Douglass, Part Two; excellent condition, **$9–12.**

Joseph Cinque and the Amistad Mutiny; excellent condition, **$9–12.**

Men of Action—White, Witkins, Marshall; excellent condition, **$9–12.**

The Saga of Toussaint L'Ouverture and the Birth of Haiti; excellent condition, **$9–12.**

Currency, $10 note from the Central Bank of Alabama, very attractive with large pictorial scene of slaves picking and carrying cotton,

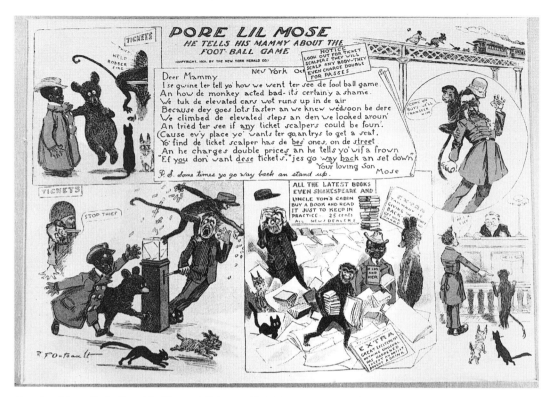

Comic, *New York Herald,* "Poor Lil Mose," 1901; very good condition, **$35–50**. Photo by Donald Vogt.

portrait of George Washington, overall view of Montgomery City, pre–Civil War; very good condition, **$12–18**.

Document

Auction notice

"Administrative Sale" detailing how eight slaves will be sold in Hancock County, Mississippi, by order of the court, manuscript, large lettering at the top, nicely done, dated December 26, 1855, 8″ × 14″; very good condition, **$35–45**.

Listing slaves, with children, sold on the steps of Solomon Johnson's residence in Hancock County, Mississippi, and listing the mother and her three children, all selling for $870, also listing an amount for three other children including a young boy who sold for $893, total sale, $2840, manuscript, dated 1854; very good condition, **$28–38**.

Bill of sale

For a 36-year-old slave woman, a seamstress and a cook, washer and ironer, and a six-year-old child, free from all defects and claims, signed by several witnesses, purchaser Owen McGovern, in English and French with embossed Notary seal, multipaged, dated Nouville, Orleans, March 1853; very good condition, **$38–50**.

For "Negresse Mary Griffin" warranting that "this slave to be free of all claims and sound in mind and body," beautifully written in French on bluish paper with a high linen content, blue-green ink, "from the City of Nouvell Orleans," dated 1849; excellent condition, **$32–45**.

Lists two black men about 20 years old, details their physical features and describes them as being of sound mind and body, amount received for them at auction, from Memphis, Tennessee, dated 1852; very good condition, **$32–42.**

Printed and written in French from the French quarter of old New Orleans, watermarked paper showing large American eagle and large 1853 date, rare, 2 pages, dated 1858; very good condition, **$28–38.**

Bond, South Carolina, $50 bond printed in red and black on white, illustrated masthead showing Blacks in a cotton field and steamboats on a river, early train and state seal, dated 1870 by the Charleston Board of Trade, 16″ × 20″; very good condition, **$25–50.**

Contract

To allow sale of slave to pay debts, auction to be held at the court house, slave valued at $1200; planter resided in Gallatin, Tennessee, one page, Memphis, Tennessee, dated 1859; quarto; very good condition, **$20–30.**

To hire slave, printed (which is rare), filled-in spaces are handwritten, March 18, 1837; excellent condition, **$400–450.**

Court document describing how a black woman from Jackson County, Mississippi, was accosted in 1858 by a black man who went to her cabin and asked for something to eat, then attacked her, sketch shows her with two children at log cabin door, handwritten, rare; very good condition, **$350–400.**

Court order

City and County of New York, declares Henry Smith to be a freedman, September 30, 1814; excellent condition, **$500–550.**

County of Fulton, Kentucky, describes the claim of a widow to three of her deceased husband's slaves—Kizzy, Scilla and Susan (young girls), the widow wants the slaves (in addition to the two slaves she already owns) for her dowry upon her remarriage, dated 1856; very good condition, **$33–43.**

Statement of slave ownership, court found that it was illegal to keep a hired-out slave after the original owner died, the holder of the slave had to pay a fee to the heirs of the original owner, includes cross examination

questions, manuscript, in ink, Shelby County, Tennessee, both sides dated 1844; 3″ × 18″; very good condition, **$20–35.**

Estate

Appraisal, concerning estate of J. Jackson, naming, on the reverse side of the first page, 18 slaves for a total value of $10,000, ages ranging from one to 47, with the 47-year-old slave valued at $700, including the swearing in of judges who appraise the estate, in manuscript, Prairie County, Arkansas, dated 1856; very good condition, **$20–30.**

Last will and testament

Instructing the decedent's lawyers about the methods for freeing his many slaves: "Phebe is to remain a slave until my death and my wife's . . . then she will be set free, my boy Jacob to be free on the 25th Dec. 1858 . . . ," details about all of his many slaves, rare item, three pages, dated 1836; very good condition, **$38–48.**

Stating the decedent's wishes that "his old Negro wench" can choose on her own who she will live with after his death, his other slaves he wills to his children, North Carolina, dated 1827; very good condition, **$25–35.**

Settlement of a Washington, D.C., estate, including slaves, possibly household slaves, the decedent is willing the slaves "free from defects and from other debts" to her children in Missouri, slaves described in detail, dated 1831; very good condition, **$33–43.**

Genealogy, from a black family named Mattingly listing "the servants" births, deaths, names, years, etc., 1848–1860, 6″ × 12″; very good condition, **$15–25.**

Hiring notice

Details the conditions to hire a group of slaves, they will have to be furnished clothing of "good yarn," yarn stockings, wool hat, a good blanket, and the taxes paid by those who will hire them, early laid paper stock, no date, 1830s; very good condition, **$28–38.**

Renting of two slaves for $75, a woman and a child for one year, renter will pay taxes and supply clothing, including bonnets, stockings, and shoes, handwritten, many signatures, 1858; good condition, **$25–40.**

Work authorization to hire Blacks who were idle and hired out by their owners to those who could not actually own a slave, to work the land belonging to orphans of a deceased man, from Hinds County, Mississippi, dated 1858; very good condition, **$18–28.**

Impressment of slaves, original, preprinted, lists a slave's name and states he was received from a slave owner and that he is to work on the fortifications at and near the city of Richmond, signed by Chief Engineer G. Lamb, dated 1862, also a photocopy of a South Carolina order for all slaves to work for the military defense; very good condition, **$30–40 for both.**

Inventory

> From New Orleans, preprinted, in columns, listing names of households, the number of slaves in each household, and each slave's value, also listing whether owner has income over $1000, furniture valued over $500 and value of carriages, etc., blue paper, 1850s; 15″ × 20″; very good condition, **$35–40.**
>
> Lists Hiram Mounger's property, including 34 slaves, 22 bales of cotton in store, 12 mules, 200 cattle, and 165 hogs, manuscript, ca. 1855 or earlier; 3″ × 11″; very good condition, **$22–32.**
>
> Printed masthead stating "etat de La Louisiane, Ville de La Nouville—Orleans," from the register of property, lists three slaves with details as to name, age, and health, on blue paper, one page, dated New Orleans, 17 Dec. 1850; legal size; excellent condition, **$32–45.**

Marriage license, for two freed slaves, "Henderson Carter (colored) and Rebecca

Marshall (colored), state of Georgia, January 10, 1870"; excellent condition, **$175–200.**

Medical blood-letting account, lengthy doctor's account of attendance to a family, including the family's slaves, noting that he bled and administered concoctions many times during the course of nearly a year, neatly written, dated 1830; 8″ × 14″; fine condition, **$21–35.**

Sales receipt

> For one slave, preprinted, man had been turned over to the government, includes his assignment to work on city fortifications, signed by J. Lamb, Government Agent, dated at Richmond, Virginia, November 12, 1862; very good condition, **$25–40.**
>
> For one-half slave, details of sale for slave "equal to one half or 40 pounds money," manuscript, signed by William Bride, dated 1799; very good condition, **$9–15.**
>
> For slaves, statement concerning acceptance of slaves named Ambrose and Charlotte who both belonged to Littleberg Camp, Upham County, Texas, dated 1851; very good condition, **$20–30.**

Tax assessment

> Lists taxed items of the Todd estate (related to President Lincoln), including land, a horse, and two slaves, signed by John Morton, Sheriff, small, dated 1808; very good condition, **$10–20.**
>
> Virginia plantation, value of the land and two-story houses, including forge and iron furnace and other land and furnaces, plus 14 slaves, all male, between 14 and 50 years of age, land valued at $18,000 and slaves at $5600, dated 1815; very good condition, **$24–34.**

Tax receipt, preprinted, states that slaves are to be taxed as personal property, i.e., "horses, slaves, clocks, watches . . . ," states that it was completed for a "free Negro" and lists the "White titheable county levy and poor rates," printed just prior to the Civil War; very good condition, **$8–18.**

Greeting card

"A . . . A . . . Ah me! Goin' away"; very good condition, **$7–10.**

Birthday card, comical, boy taking bath, 1920s; very good condition, **$3–5.**

Christmas card, boy in manger with several children around the crib, inside reads "What Child Be Dis?"; new, package of twelve, **$8.**

Valentine card

Child peeking out of box, heart-shaped; excellent condition, **$7–10.**

"From Many Lands," chromolithograph, shows girl, Tuck; very good condition, **$10–15.**

Journal, *First World an International Journal of Black Thought,* cover includes robot-like bust in silhouette with white cutouts of the United States, Africa, and South America for eyes and nose and a keyhole cutout for mouth, January/February 1977; excellent condition, **$20–35.**

Letter

Personal; states that now is not a good time to buy slaves because prices are so high, in Texas a number one boy sold for $1125 but in Tennessee boys go much cheaper and "if Lincoln is elected the price of Negroes will be flat as ever," mentions cotton crops and a great fire in the city, in ink, with envelope, three pages, from New Orleans, dated September 23, 1860; very good condition, **$25–35.**

Political content

About hanging the pro-Lincoln abolitionists, states that the writer's people had so far hung 50 white men and several black men but that they didn't like to hang Blacks because they were worth too much money, talks of joining a regiment and marching to Mexico, comments on the upcoming elections, thinks the state of Texas will vote for Breckinridge; in ink, letter and envelope postmarked Richmond, Texas, dated August 1860; large size; very good condition, **$30–40.**

By well-educated Union soldier about Lincoln's address to Congress, "the great point of restoration of the federal union and no compromise to slavery. . . . I favor the President, that plan embraces the restoration of the Union, the preservation of the Constitution and the Emancipation of the slaves"; in ink, four pages, dated Falmouth December 8, 1862; 8″ × 11″; very good condition, **$25–35.**

Postcard, "Ah tries to be puhlite an' nice . . . ," comic; very good condition, $10–15. Courtesy of Malinda Saunders; photo by Donald Vogt.

155

History of Grace Jackson, a slave born in Fredericksburg, sold with her brother and sent to New Orleans with a slave gang, written by eyewitness to her father leading her by the hand, this letter was used to raise funds in Boston to help the freed slaves; in ink, nine pages, dated 1866; very good condition, **$25–35.**

Horace Mann's letters on the extension of slavery into California and New Mexico and the duty of Congress to provide for trials of accused fugitive slaves, 32 pages, dated July 8, 1850; very good condition, **$22–32.**

Slave transaction

Details dispute in which a woman accepted a slave to work for her in return for a piece of jewelry; later, the original owner wanted the slave back and was refused; in ink, two pages, Lawrence County, Alabama, dated 1839; very good condition, **$15–25.**

Details sale of land and houses, with one place unsold, writer is asking if they can put up slaves of equal value in place of the cash needed to buy the last piece of property, much more, in original envelope, hand stamped with a Washington City postmark and "PAID" in circle, sent to Maryland, letter dated 1851; very good condition, **$32–42.**

Details the receipt of a slave who has just been "put in the county jail" and for the receiver of the letter to come get him as soon as he can because the slave was not received in good condition, the letter writer is willing to swap for another slave or other compensation, "even take on a girl"; in ink, rare item, from Lexington, Kentucky, 1852; 8″ × 11″; very good condition, **$45–65.**

Magazine (see also Chapters 13, 14, and 15)

Black World, formerly *Negro World,* cover shows highly polished, ornate, African mask on an ray-burst background with captions "Africans in Africa" and "Africans in the Americas," a Johnson Publication, May, 1970; excellent condition, **$10–17.**

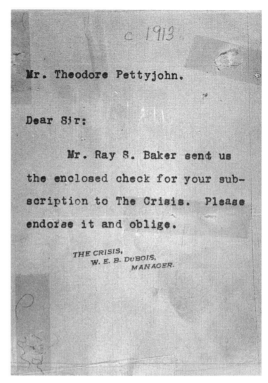

Letter, to "Mr. Theodore Pettyjohn," from "W. E. B. DuBois, Manager" of the *Crisis* (the first black newspaper), ca. 1913; fair condition, **$145–175.** Courtesy of the Valerie Bertrand Collection; photo by Donald Vogt.

Look, special issue *The Blacks and The Whites,* January 2, 1969; excellent condition, **$25–30.**

The Messenger, sketch of woman's face on cover, March 1924; excellent condition, **$25–30.**

Saturday Evening Post, includes an article titled "Slavery in Delaware," February 15, 1862; good condition, **$17–25.**

Yankee Notions, cartoon-filled issue, cover is cartoon of black contraband being questioned by do-gooder preacher, also Civil War cartoons, over 20 pages, 1864; very good condition, **$15–20.**

Magazine article

Collier's, "He Has No Time to Hate" by W. O. Saunders, about Laurence E. Jones, one page, August 30, 1924; excellent condition, **$8–12.**

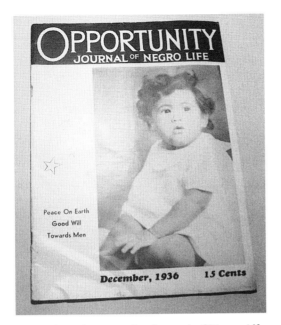

Magazine, *Opportunity: Journal of Negro Life,* picture of baby on cover, December 1936; excellent condition, $20–25. Courtesy of Rose Fontanella; photo by Bob Reno.

Saturday Evening Post, "The Boll Evil" by Garet Garrett, illustrated with pictures of black people picking cotton, eight pages, December 29, 1934; excellent condition, **$10–15.**

Magazine page, advertising Little Brown Koko rhyme contest, $75 first prize, in color, 1941, 10³/₄″ × 14″; excellent condition, **$35–50.**

Map

Africa, hand colored, vertical, very attractive, 1864, 15″ × 22″; very good condition, **$12–20.**

Slave states, overall map of the United States with shaded areas showing area of rebellion in 1861 and 1864, from *Harper's Weekly,* dated 1864, 11″ × 15″; very good condition, **$12–20.**

Newspaper (see also Chapters 12, 13, 14, and 15)

Colonization Herald, Philadelphia, masthead motto reads "The Americans are successful in planting free Negroes on the Coast of Africa: A greater event probably in its conse-quences than any that has occurred since Columbus set sail for the new World," various articles about slaves, September 25, 1844; good condition, **$18–25.**

Connecticut Courant, Hartford, includes "A Negro Riot at Charleston, S.C.—Colored & White Democrats Attacked & Beaten by Colored Republicans," article on page 3, September 14, 1876; very good condition, **$16–22.**

Daily Graphic, illustration of man in KKK costume on horse with black man hanging onto horse's tail, full front page, April 25, 1877; good condition, **$20–40.**

Daily National Intelligencer, Washington, D.C., "Fifty Dollar Reward" for runaway slave woman, "$10 Reward" for runaway slave woman and her son, front page ads, December 2, 1837; very good condition, **$19–28.**

Deseret Evening News, Salt Lake City, Utah Territory

"The Answer of the Commissioners Regarding Negro Exclusion" article on front page, March 11, 1889; very good condition, **$14–20.**

"Three Negroes Hung" article on front page, March 16, 1889; very good condi-tion, **$14–20.**

Dover Enquirer, verbatim report of the famous speech by William H. Seward on slavery and the Kansas situation, full front page, dated March 8, 1860; very good condition, **$4–8.**

Harper's Weekly, New York

Colored Troops under General Wild, Liberating Slaves in North Carolina, illus-tration, full and complete issue, Saturday, January 23, 1864; excellent condition, **$25–50.**

Mustered Out, illustration, reads "colored volunteers at Little Rock, Arkansas," full and complete issue, Saturday, May 19, 1866; excellent condition, **$25–50.**

Negro Sportsmen in Louisiana, full front illustration, two black men duck hunting,

February 18, 1888; good condition, **$14–20.**

Negroes Driven South by the Rebel Officers, two-page center spread, full and complete issue, Saturday, November 8, 1862; excellent condition, **$25–50.**

One of the First Fruits of the Victory, full front page illustration by Thomas Nast, white man and black man shaking hands, also included in issue is full-page illustration "The World's Exposition at New Orleans," which shows black people, November 22, 1884; good condition, **$16–20.**

Independent Republican, Montrose, Pennsylvania, includes "Lamar & His Imported Slaves," a letter from Charleston, S.C., on page 2, April 7, 1859; good condition, **$7–12.**

Lancaster Journal, Pennsylvania, "$200 Reward" for two runaway slaves ad on back page, November 1, 1805; good condition, **$18–25.**

Leslie's, "Courtship to Marriage," December 22, 1900; very good condition, **$20–30.**

The Liberator, Boston, famous anti-slavery newspaper published by William Lloyd Garrison, giant illustrated masthead showing slave auction and freed slaves heading for the Gate of Emancipation, news of the antislavery movements, letters to Garrison, General Banks and his efforts to release slaves, four pages, never bound, dated April 8, 1864; excellent condition, **$8–12.**

National Anti-Slavery Standard, New York

"A Fugitive Slave, Kansas" illustrated slave ad on page 2, front page article titled "Southern Non-slaveholders," August 30, 1856; good condition, **$22–28.**

Antislavery focus in articles about Lincoln's assassination, April 22, 1865; good condition, **$245–300.**

New England Palladium, Boston, "Negro Slavery" article on page 2, July 30, 1802; very good condition, **$8–12.**

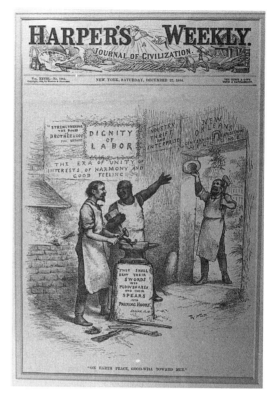

Magazine cover, *Harper's Weekly,* **New York,** *On Earth Peace, Good-will toward Men,* **Saturday, December 27, 1884; very good condition, $25–35. Photo by Bob Reno.**

New York Herald, includes "Cotton Trade—The South & The Institution of Slavery" article on page 2, October 28, 1849; very good condition, **$9–15.**

New York Journal & Patriotic Register, includes "$15 reward for runaway Negro Man named Cull" article on front page, April 3, 1793; good condition, **$21–30.**

The New York Times, article

"The Abolition of Slavery the Price of Foreign Recognition," January 6, 1865; good condition, **$17–25.**

"Prisoners Captured—A Guerrilla Hanged—Thousands of Slaves Set Free," January 9, 1864; good condition, **$26–35.**

"The Slave-Trade," on page 5, January 17, 1861; very good condition, **$8–12.**

Photograph postcard, "Comrades," linen, full color, with derogatory message from the sender; very good condition, **$8–12.** Courtesy of Malinda Saunders; photo by Donald Vogt.

"They Must Regulate Negro Suffrage Themselves," on front page, October 23, 1865; very good condition, **$10–15.**

Pennsylvania Packet, Philadelphia, regarding "Acts" from Virginia including "An Act to repeal part of any act directing the trial of Slaves Committing Capital Crimes," four pages, January 28, 1789; good condition, **$56–65.**

Protestant & Herald, Frankfort, Kentucky, includes "Religious Instruction of the Blacks in Georgia," article on front page, January 18, 1844; good condition, **$14–20.**

The Star, Raleigh, North Carolina, "$100 Reward," ad on front page, woodcut of black man running, May 29, 1812; good condition (laminated), **$12–18.**

Weekly Register, including a chart listing the number of slaves in Southern states and many in Northern states, including U.S. and world news as well as the slave census, 20 pages, 1811; very good condition, **$10–20.**

Postcard booklet

"Greetings from Dixieland," 20 full-color and captioned views of life in the Old South, 1937 souvenir; mint (unused) condition, **$35–50.**

"Greetings from Dixieland," contains 18 scenes, including some with slaves picking cotton; good condition, **$15–25.**

Postcard

"At the Old Cabin Door," Richmond, Virginia; very good condition, **$5–10.**

Boy riding turkey, linen, full color; very good condition, **$5–8.**

"Compliments of the Fifth Dimension," color photograph; excellent condition, **$6–8.**

"Cotton Ginning Day," road with carts of cotton, linen, full color; very good condition, **$10–12.**

"Cotton picking in the South," color photograph, 1950s; very good condition, **$6–8.**

"Goliath was struck out by David . . . ," comic, linen, full color; very good condition, **$12–15.**

"A Good Crop in Dixieland," boy getting hair cut; very good condition, **$5–10.**

"Honey, next to myself, I love you," comic illustrated by Twelvetrees, full color; very good condition, **$6–8.**

"Honey, we'se waitin' fo' you all in beautiful Florida," two babies sitting on pelican's back, linen, full color; very good condition, **$12–15.**

"I wasn't born to labor," boy leaning against cotton bale, linen, full color; very good condition, **$12–15.**

Photograph postcard, "Sunday Morning in Dixieland," linen, full color; very good condition, **$8–10.** Courtesy of Malinda Saunders; photo by Donald Vogt.

Photograph postcard, linen, shows workers picking cotton, full color; very good condition, **$6–8.** Courtesy of Malinda Saunders; photo by Donald Vogt.

"I'm in it with both feet," man with chicken in hand and feet in a trap, color, 1933; excellent condition, **$10–15.**

"I'se waitin' fo' you here down south," linen, full color; very good condition, **$12–15.**

"If dat don't fetch her, nothing will," dandy waving straw hat; excellent condition, **$12–15.**

"Mischief brewin'," four children, linen, full color; very good condition, **$8–10.**

"Olde time method of cooking as used at Boscobel Farm up to 1905," photo; very good condition, **$7–10.**

"Out on Bale," boy sitting on top of bale of cotton, full color, linen; very good condition, **$15–20.**

Postcard, "Rebecca went to the well with a pitcher . . .," linen, full color, comic, 1907; very good condition, **$10–12.** Courtesy of Malinda Saunders; photo by Donald Vogt.

Postcard, "Lawsy me! What a peculiar little boy," comic; very good condition, **$10–12.** Courtesy of Malinda Saunders; photo by Donald Vogt.

"Rapid transit at West River, Maryland"; very good condition, **$6–8.**

"Rapid transit in Middlesex County, Virginia," photo; very good condition, **$6–8.**

"Romeo and Juliet in the Cotton Field/ Souvenir of the Sunny South," foldout; very good condition, **$40–50.**

"Seben come Leben," boys tossing dice, linen, full color; very good condition, **$12–15.**

"Seven-Up," children standing in row outside cabin door, linen, full color; very good condition, **$12–15.**

"Sleighing in Old Virginia," linen, full color; very good condition, **$12–15.**

"Smiling Soft in Dixieland," smiling little girl on pile of cotton, linen, full color, framed, 1920s; excellent condition, **$15–20.**

Southern products, baby sitting in basket of cotton, photo; very good condition, **$6–10.**

"Thanksgiving Greetings," woman plucking turkey, linen, full color; very good condition, **$12–15.**

"That strain again," man with homemade violin, singing, linen, full color; very good condition, **$12–15.**

Three children eating chicken, photo; very good condition, **$10–15.**

"Three of a Kind," three boys sitting on a fence, linen, full color; very good condition, **$12–15.**

"Waitin' fo' Mah Sweetheart," linen, full color; very good condition, **$18–20.**

"Wanted: someone to play wif mah Chickun preferred," linen, full color; very good condition, **$12–15.**

"Well! Who'd A thunk it?," linen, full color; very good condition, **$15–20.**

"Who said watermelon?," linen, full color; very good condition, **$12–15.**

Woman sitting in front of fire, photo; very good condition, **$6–8.**

"You doan want none of my lip hey?" two dapper gents talking to each other, each has very exaggerated features, full color; excellent condition, **$12–15.**

Poster, antislavery, "The Negro Woman's Lamentation," ca. 1775, approximately 20″ × 24″; very good condition, **$250–300.**

Postcard, "I'se ah comin', sugah-lump," linen, full color, comic; very good condition, **$15–18.** Courtesy of Malinda Saunders; photo by Donald Vogt.

CHAPTER NINE

Pottery, Porcelain, and Glass

This chapter covers pottery, porcelain, and glass items other than those found in the kitchen. Through the years, American, European, and Asian companies have produced figurines, plates, jugs, statues, and other recreations of African-American faces and figures. If you don't find the information you need in this chapter, see Chapter 7.

Pottery and porcelain are both types of ceramic ware. There are four basic categories of ceramics: earthenware and stoneware, both of which are made of clay fired at high temperatures and considered forms of pottery; porcelain, which is a type of stoneware that is transluscent; and bisque, which is unfired pottery or porcelain. As you can tell, these categories overlap and can cause confusion to new collectors. To add to the confusion, pottery also refers to jars, vases, pitchers, and similar vessels handmade from clay.

Ceramic decoration also has its own terms and methods. Cold paint is color added to a piece after it has been fired. Glazing, which makes the surface of a piece shiny, is technically a glass coating that seals the porousness of a piece. Polychrome decoration is decoration involving more than one color.

Glass is also covered in this chapter, though less extensively, because there are fewer figural items available in glass. Glass also has its own lexicon and varieties of materials and manufacturing methods.

Before you begin collecting ceramics or glass, you may want to do some research. The best way to learn is to go out in the field and talk to dealers and collectors. There are also plenty of books that cover this subject in depth. For further information about particular companies or items, refer to the books listed in the bibliography. You might want to check a general price guide, such as *Warman's American Pottery and Porcelain* or *Warman's Glass,* or you might prefer a more specific one that focuses on your taste in collecting. There are many books devoted to specific makers of ceramics and glass. These books often show photos of each design in a company's line to help you better identify specific pieces, as well as their age and their value.

Types of Items Collected

The following are descriptions of particular types of ceramic collectibles.

CERAMIC FIGURINES

Ceramic figurines depicting black figures have been made for more than a hundred years, but some collectors believe the only ones on the market are those made in Japan. Though the Japanese ceramic pieces are easiest to find, other companies also produced black figurines or ceramic scenes featuring Blacks. Even Hummel has created some pieces that include black figures in the scene as well as some individual black figures (for example, "Silent Night with Black Child"). Lladro was the first to introduce black brides and grooms (although their figurines are considered porcelain). They also

Figurine, bisque, Moor boy, by Andrea Company, paper label attached, hand painted, reproduction of 1930s piece, marked "Made in Japan," 1950s, 7″ tall; excellent condition, **$90–125.** Courtesy of the Lewis and Blalock Collection; photo by Bob Reno.

have done American Indian figurines and a Black Heritage Collection. (A free brochure is available from Black Heritage Collection, 43 West 57th Street, New York, NY 10019.)

Other companies that make ceramic figures include Gatlan U.S.A., who has created plates, figurines, and other collectibles that focus on sports stars. Duncan Royale has introduced the Ebony Collection, which features religious figures, musicians, and professionals. Others include figurines from Sarah's Attic, which reflect black life before 1950 (write Sarah's Attic Forever Friends Collector's Club, 126 ½ West Broad, P.O. Box 448, Chesaning, MI 48616); the Alex Haley Remembers series (write Alex Haley Remembers Collectors Society, P.O. Box 3333, Tazewell, TN 37879); Etcetera Collections; the Constance Collection; "All God's Children," by Miss Martha Originals and Miss Martha's Collection for Enesco (write Miss Martha Originals, P.O. Box 5038, Glencoe, AL 35905); the Blackberry Bonnet Collection, by Debbie Bell Jarrett of North Carolina; and Simple Wonders for Artaffects.

Not all figurines depict positive images of black people. Because figurines reflect the times in which they are made, one can find figurines that exaggerate black features, portray stereotypes, and with explicit derogatory sayings or messages.

When collecting figurines, you should check the piece for detail painting (the finer the details, the better the piece). Make sure none of the paint is chipped or scratched and that there are no signs of breakage (watch for lines around the neck of a figure or around the hand and finger areas). Check to see whether the artist signed and numbered the piece (dates are important too), and look for a company logo.

HANDMADE POTTERY

Most of the early American pottery that came out of the South was created by slaves.

Figurine, plaster, "The early bird catches the worm," degrogatory, great color, vestiges of a menu on the bottom (e.g., "fried clams," "frappe"), signed and dated 1951; good condition, $75–95. Courtesy of Kristin Duval of Irreverent Relics; photo by Donald Vogt.

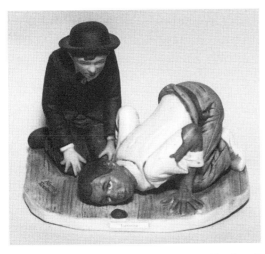

Figurine, bisque, *Listening*, Norman Rockwell design made by and marked on bottom "1980 David Grossman Designs," made in Japan; near mint condition, $125–150. Courtesy of the Lewis and Blalock Collection; photo by Bob Reno.

Slave pottery is not what I would call attractive, but rather bizarre. Even pottery that slaves made for their own private use frequently depicts skulls or grotesque faces. In nineteenth-century Georgia and the Carolinas, slaves were employed in plantation potteries, and the jugs they made in their free time were often tagged "voodoo pots," "slave jugs," or "grotesque jugs"—which is how they look. It is not known what purpose, if any, these jugs fulfilled. Most early folk pottery produced in the South bears the slave's mark. Though only about fifty black potters can be identified, perhaps researchers will eventually be able to name more.

Dave the Potter (also called Dave the Slave) was the only slave we are aware of to sign and date his works. He first made large storage jars, some holding more than forty gallons. He often inscribed his jars with couplets such as "Great and Noble Jar / Hold Sheep, Goat, and Bear"; "Dave Belongs to Mr. Miles / Where the oven bakes and the pot biles"; and "Pretty little girl on a virge / volca[n]ic mountain how they burge." His work is included in *By the Work of Their Hands* by John Michael Vlach.

Most of the distinctive decorative pottery, like grotesque jugs and miniature head vessels, came from the Edgefield district of South Carolina. Robert Farris Thompson, a noted expert, says that these stylized face jugs resemble some made in the Bakongo region of central Africa. He states that the facial features have some of the same aspects.

Earthenware produced in that area of Africa (called *m'vungo*) bears the same distinguishing facial features as the Edgefield pottery. Some of the African pieces had a single canted spout, as do some of the Edgefield pieces. Vessels of this type are still made in the West Indies and are called "monkeys" or "monkey jugs." The earliest jugs produced by American slave potters resembled water jugs that were made in Africa. Later stoneware clay versions are similar to the African ones.

MAJOLICA

Made during the Victorian era, majolica is a highly glazed earthenware created in Europe. Herbert Minton, an Englishman, refined the practice in 1850 and was well known for his figural pieces. Some of Minton's creations included tall, regal Blacks, who were exotically attired, wore jewels, and carried ornamental pots on their heads (these figures were called *blackamoors*). Humidors and tobacco jars held a gentleman's smoking materials.

The finer black pieces were, for the most part, produced in England, but America's potters did produce some majolica—though human figures were rare. The blackamoor and black child and adult figurals produced in Europe are recognizable because of their beauty and realistic facial features. Historians have noted that getting skilled labor in American potteries was difficult, which probably explains why the quality of European majolica pieces is so much higher than the American examples.

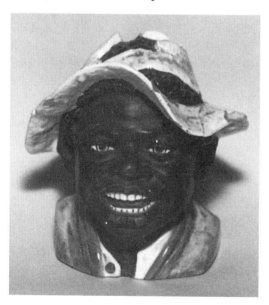

Tobacco jar (humidor), majolica, man with Johnny Griffith look, hat lifts off, 1890s; excellent condition, $650–750. Courtesy of the Lewis and Blalock Collection; photo by Bob Reno.

Some of the black figural majolica pieces were marked; others were not signed but were instead marked with a series of numbers and letters (these corresponded with the maker's records). When you see pieces marked with these numbers, note if there are three sets of numbers—the third set of numbers usually indicates the year of manufacture.

Majolica went out of favor after the turn of the century and was no longer a giveaway (the A&P supermarket company offered majolica as a premium) or in stock in the better department stores.

PORCELAIN COLLECTOR PLATES

Porcelain collector plates have been produced for a number of years in Europe and are now collected in the United States. China produces most of these plates today, manufacturing them with a process called underglazing. The bigger companies that produce these plates—the Bradford Exchange and Hamilton Mint, for example—are now producing plates with an eye on the African-American consumer. The Black Heritage Series of postage stamps has been reproduced on plates by artist Thomas Blackshear. He also has done multiracial clowns and is currently producing a line called "Innocent Wonders."

Though the choices of black collector plates are still limited, there are more now than in the past, some plates depicting sports figures (i.e., Magic Johnson and Kareem Abdul Jabaar), while others focus on children or home scenes.

TERRA-COTTA

The Frederick Goldscheider Company of Vienna, Austria, established in 1885, made some terra-cotta black statues and busts. Several, attributed to Arthur Strasser who was employed by the firm, featured black youths. One outstanding piece was a full-figure statue of a boy wearing a hat, jacket, short pants, and a big smile; he was seated on a stool. It was designed to be a fountain for an exposition and was later used to advertise stove blacking at a Napoleon, Ohio, general store.

TOBACCO JARS (HUMIDORS)

Ceramic tobacco jars decorated with black figures are considered highly collectible. Examples exist in majolica and porcelain. These jars are so popular that in 1993 the Society of Tobacco Jar Collectors was formed in Nashville, Tennessee. The group viewed an exhibit of figural tobacco jars, the first such exhibit in the United States, which included 180 jars loaned to the U.S. Museum of Tobacco Art and History by museums and private collectors. Members of the group hail from Europe, the United States, and Japan. For more information about the group or a sample copy of *Tobacco Jar Newsletter,* contact Sandie Goodman, 3021 Courtland Boulevard, Shaker Heights, Ohio 44122. You might also write to the Tobacco Institute in Washington, D.C., for more information.

PRICES FOR POTTERY, PORCELAIN, AND GLASS

Ashtray

Earthenware

African woman, put cigarette in the tray and smoke comes out of her mouth, old stock, 6″ tall; very good condition, **$8–12.**

Genie, comic face, smoke comes out ears, hand painted in red, black, gold and green, 5″ × 3½″; excellent condition, **$125–175.**

Satchmo, hand painted in black, brown and yellow, modeled after Louis Armstrong, smoke comes out the eyes, Japan; 4″ × 4″; near mint condition, **$75–100.**

Porcelain, boy in humorous pose hugs fish, multicolored, Japan, 5″ × 4″; mint condition, **$125–150.**

Bank, earthenware, chef, penny bank, nicely decorated, rare form, 1950s; mint condition, **$50–100.**

Bell, earthenware, mammy, red and green cold paint, rare, early; mint condition, **$45–100.**

Bells, porcelain, set of two mammies in full skirts, good detail; mint condition, **$50–100 for the pair.**

Bottle, glass, miniature peach cordial brandy bottle in figure of a black man, painted white and black, dark brown liqueur gives color, original label, 1920s; 4″ × 2″; excellent condition, **$60–90.**

Bust, chalkware, man wearing red turban and earrings, 1950s; about 10″ tall; excellent condition, **$18–25.**

Calling card holder

Majolica, figural, African man wearing brown floppy hat, yellow-trimmed maroon coat and tattered blue pants, 19th century; 27″ tall, **$3,300–3,600.**

Majolica, figural, African woman in turban and yellow dress, wearing pink jewelry and holding brown and yellow basket in her outstretched arms, her braceleted foot rests on brown bale, her other foot on mottled green, yellow and brown base, 19th century; 27″ tall; excellent condition, **$3,300–3,600.**

Majolica, figural, young man in European dress; excellent condition, **$75–300.**

Dish, bisque, Nippon, high relief, part of series of four, the only black subject, uniquely designed figure, extremely rare, 1900–1925; excellent condition, **$250–350.**

Glass bottle with woven basketweave peel overlay, stopper is black clay head, bulging features, painted, 1930s–1940s, 12½″ tall; excellent condition, **$75–100.** Courtesy of American Eye; photo by Bob Reno.

Figurine

Bisque

Boy eating watermelon, hand painted in blue, red, green, brown and black, inscribed, "Germany"; near mint condition, **$250–300.**

Choir children, two white children and one black child, all three are connected at sleeves, marked "Japan"; 6″ tall; very good condition, **$120–130.**

Girl with frog in her dish, detailed and painted in red, green, blue and black, 19th century; 4″ × 3″; near mint condition, **$150–225.**

The Little Sucker, baby with bottle, marked "Made in Germany," 1930s–1940s; 4½″ tall; excellent condition, **$325–450.**

Little Black Dandy, young man with cigar sitting on chair, hand painted in brown, black, blue, gold and green, Germany, 19th century; 6″ × 3″; near mint condition, **$175–225.**

Moor boy, Andrea Company paper label, hand painted, marked "Made in Japan," 1950s reproduction of 1930s piece; 7″ tall; excellent condition, **$90–125.**

Cookie jars, pottery, chef and mammy, by Artistic Pottery, blue and brown versions; good condition, **$300–500 each.** Courtesy of the Leonard Davis Collection; Photo by Donald Vogt.

Musicians, set of five, hand painted in black, white, red and gold, Japan; mint condition, **$175–250 for the set.**

Nodder, boy holding chalkboard, head nods, marked "Germany," early 1900s, 3″ × 6″; excellent condition, **$275–325.**

Chalkware

Boy on his knees, red shirt and blue overalls; approximately 8″ tall; excellent condition, **$45–60.**

Country couple, smiling well-dressed man, woman carrying two baskets, painted, probably made in Europe; 12³⁄₄″ high; **$350–400 for the pair.**

"Way Down South," boy eating watermelon on base, vivid colors, very detailed, original paint; 2¹⁄₂″ × 4″; near mint condition, **$125–175.**

Clay, woman with head cocked coyly to one side and resting against finger, blue dress with white apron, red polka-dotted turban, signed "Evans" on back, marked "1987," 8″ tall; mint condition, **$75–125.**

Earthenware (see also Majolica)

African native, cartoonish, exaggerated features, big-lipped, in orange, red, black, brown, blue and green, Occupied Japan; 5″ × 3″; near mint condition, **$50–75.**

Blackberry Bonnett Collection, by Debbie Bell Jarrett, detailed, hand painted and numbered, accompanied by certificate of authenticity and copy of the Blackberry Bonnett Gazette, which gives the history of each figurine, limited edition, each approximately 6¹⁄₂″ tall

Angela in straw hat; new, **$55.**

Baby Netty sign; new, **$45.**

Benjamin Banneker with telescope; new, **$55.**

Gabrielle with tulip; new, **$55.**

Malia in bonnet; new, **$55.**

Naomi with nosegay; new, **$45.**

Nicodemus with bag; new, **$45.**

Figurine, porcelain, *Uncle Tom,* by Staffordshire, shows Uncle Tom holding Little Eva, made in England, ca. 1880, 10″ tall; excellent condition, $750–900. Courtesy of the Lewis and Blalock Collection; photo by Bob Reno.

Phyllis Wheatley with feather quill; new, **$55.**

Pompey the Drummer Boy; new, **$55.**

Prissy with flag; new, **$55.**

Young Pharoah; new, **$55.**

Boy with violin, hollow, possibly handmade, 1960s; 5″; near mint condition, **$60–90.**

Boys (two) and baby in box, one boy is playing with a snake, the other is feeding a baby alligator, when box is opened, a frog swallowing the baby is visible, Germany, early 1900s; excellent condition, **$100–200 for three pieces.**

George Washington Carver, Hallmark; 7″; mint in box, **$30–45.**

Musicians, set of three jazz musicians with instruments, hand painted in orange, red, black and brown, Japan; each 3½″ × 2″; mint condition, **$50–75 for the set.**

"Silent Night with Black Child," Hummel, HUM #31; mint condition, **$20,000–25,000.**

Majolica

Girl and boy, girl lying on stomach, boy lying down with watermelon, 1890s; each 6½″ long; excellent condition, **$750–800 for the pair.**

Nubian slave with basket on head standing in front of wooden box which is open (probably for pipe and tobacco), lovely soft colors; near mint condition, **$350–400.**

Plaster, fisher boys, carnival, very heavy, ca. 1920, 12″ tall; excellent condition, **$50–75.**

Porcelain

African men (pair), one sitting and playing drums, the other playing flute; excellent condition, **$20–25 for the pair.**

"Ben," Bright Eyes Nature Craft, sits on log and strums banjo, numbered 307, signed "Bright Eyes Nature Craft, England, made in 1990"; excellent condition, **$100–125.**

Billikin (the god of things as they ought to be), rare black version, Germany; excellent condition, **$250–350.**

Boy on potty, contented smile, hand painted in red, white, and black, glazed kerchief and pants, early, 4″ × 2½″; excellent condition, **$125–150.**

Clown, aqua flowered outfit; 22″, mint in box, **$200–230.**

Clown, yellow outfit; 16″, mint in box, **$100–130.**

Hallmark

Nativity child, no. 229-4; very good condition, **$10–18.**

Santa, no. 801-5; very good condition, **$20–25.**

Lladro Black Legacy Collection, set featuring black men, women, and children in educational, religious, recreational, musical, and family scenes, delicate quality, Spain; mint condition, **$75–1,600 each.**

Minstrel band, black children musicians, hand painted in red, yellow, green, and blue, nicely detailed, marked "Occupied Japan," 3″ × 1½″; near mint condition, **$125–150.**

Miss Martha Originals by Martha Holcombe in Alabama

"All God's Children," set, handcrafted smiling, playful children, numbered and signed, certificate given at time of purchase, All God's Children Collectors' Club, these figurines are dramatically expressive of the African-American experience in the South and American history generally; mint condition, **$70–90 each.**

"I'm Not Showin' Off," Childhood Games Series, second issue, open edition, first available spring 1993; 4½″ high; new, **$40.**

"Moses," boy standing against cracker jar, signed "Martha Holcombe," marked "181," 1987; excellent condition, **$100–125.**

Shoeshine boy, Occupied Japan, 5″; very good condition, **$80–100.**

Incense burner, porcelain, child on potty; excellent condition, **$125–140.**

Match holder or match striker (see also smoking stand)

Bisque

Boy in front of box that holds matches, 1880s, England, 4½″ tall; excellent condition, **$475–690.**

Cigarette holder/match striker/ashtray, majolica, figure of black artist, 1890s; excellent condition, **$450–550.** Courtesy of the Lewis and Blalock Collection; photo by Bob Reno.

Cigarette holder/match striker, majolica, woman holding basket, 1890s; excellent condition, **$650–750.** Courtesy of the Lewis and Blalock Collection; photo by Bob Reno.

Man, multicolored, striker on seat of man's pants, Germany, late 1800s, 4″ × 3½″; excellent condition, **$225–300.**

Three boys trying to climb into three sets of pants, pants are marked "ashes, cigarettes, matches," made in Japan, 3½″ tall × 5″ long; excellent condition, **$35–45.**

Majolica

Boy in hat sitting on side, cigarette holder and match striker, 1890s, 8″ tall; excellent condition, **$650–800.**

Boy sitting on bridge eating corn, match striker only; excellent condition, **$75–300.**

Plate

Earthenware, "Little Tommy Tucker," Staffordshire, blackface; excellent condition, **$45–60.**

Porcelain

Ron Hicks, African-American Family Series, Heirlooms of the Heart, 25K

One-On-One, father helping son to learn how to skate; new, **$35–40.**

Precious Gifts, happy mother, daughter, and younger son in modern kitchen; new, **$35–40.**

Clarissa Johnson, nationally known artist, bonded 22K gold, limited edition, numbered

No. 1, bust of black clown with big bow tie, sepia; new, **$48**

No. 2, three- or four-year-old black boy standing on wooden box leaning down to kiss black girl sitting on the box, sepia; new, **$48.**

No. 3, white-haired black woman sitting in Victorian chair holding little black girl, sepia; new, **$48.**

No. 4, bust of young black mother cuddling her newborn, sepia; new, **$48.**

No. 5, young black ballerina in sitting position; new, **$48.**

Shelf rests (pair), terra-cotta, each is a detailed, life-size head of a black man, brown, self-hang-

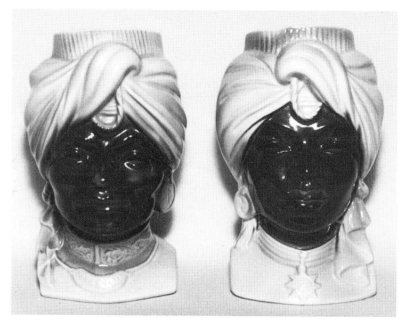

Wall pockets, glazed china; Moor man and woman, each marked on back "Royal Copley," 1950s, 8″ × 4½″; excellent condition, **$450–500 for the pair.** Courtesy of the Lewis and Blalock Collection; photo by Bob Reno.

ing, 12″ × 9″ × 8″; near mint condition, **$300–400 for the pair.**

Shelf sitter or plaque, earthenware, watermelon boy, hand painted in brown, green, pink, blue, Occupied Japan; 4″ × 2″; near mint condition, **$75–100.**

Smoking stand, bisque, figural, chimney sweep, hand painted in green, yellow, orange, brown and pink, holds cigarettes, ashes and matches, rare, Germany, 19th century; 5½″ × 4″; near mint condition, **$275–350.**

Stein, majolica, figural, African man smoking pipe and wearing golden earrings; excellent condition, **$75–300.**

Tobacco jar (humidor)

  Bisque

    Baby sitting in top hat, numbered on bottom, Austria, mid-1800s, 6″ tall; excellent condition, **$600–800.**

    Boys jumping out of barrel, black, yellow, red, green, and brown, possibly German, 6½″ × 4″; near mint condition, **$300–400.**

Tobacco jar (humidor), majolica, Moor woman, signed on bottom in pencil "from Lee Lichtenstein to J. L. Heintz, dated 1894"; good condition (missing lid), **$300–350;** with lid, **$450–575.** Courtesy of the Lewis and Blalock Collection; photo by Bob Reno.

Glass, boy, painted in red, white, and black with brown glass head, screw-on cap holds coffee or candy, rare, $4\frac{1}{2}'' \times 6''$; excellent condition, **$400–500.**

Porcelain, jockey, multicolored, detailed cap is humidor, Germany, 19th century; near mint condition, **$250–350.**

Vase

Earthenware, Brayton, mammy, brown skin, rare, incised mark "Brayton Laguna Calif. K 29," $7\frac{1}{2}''$ tall $\times$ $4\frac{3}{4}''$ diameter (base); excellent condition, **$275–325.**

Porcelain, black head vases (pair), Occupied Japan, 6''; very good condition, **$115–130 for the pair.**

Whiskey decanter, glass, African native woman leaning back on her haunches, made in Italy, 1950s; excellent condition, **$20–30.**

Whistle, earthenware, hand painted in white, black and orange, blow through head, rare, early, $3\frac{1}{4}'' \times 1\frac{1}{2}''$; very good condition, **$150–200.**

Vases, majolica, Moor boy and girl, 1890s, 8" tall; excellent condition, $750–900 for the pair. Courtesy of the Lewis and Blalock Collection; photo by Bob Reno.

CHAPTER TEN

Toys

If you are lucky enough to afford the luxury of collecting black toys, you have selected a field that spans well over two centuries and includes articles made of an assortment of materials, in diverse ways and manners. And don't be alarmed by my comments about prices; there are still areas of toy collecting that can be satisfying even with a small pocketbook. The better buys are high in price, but toys made in the twentieth century, especially plastic ones, are still reasonable enough for the average buyer to afford. You must hunt for these lesser-priced items and get them into your collection quickly, however, because toys tend to rise in price the moment a new owner purchases them.

Because you will be collecting items made of tin, cast iron, wood, and paper, the methods for preserving and caring for each toy will be different, and you should take the time to learn about each one. You should also take into consideration how to display your collection. Because these items don't need to be stored at specific temperatures or to be protected from normal house dust, the task is a pleasurable one. Remember, however, that paper toys will not stand the

abuse that the others will and special care must be taken to preserve them.

Displaying your toys can be one of the most interesting things about collecting them. Who could resist a fireplace mantel full of movable tin toys, a cabinet displaying iron banks, or a bedroom lined with shelves that hold the prettiest of the automatic toys? There's always an interesting way to display the playthings of children. For more ideas, check the magazines that currently tout the collecting craze. They usually have a section devoted to the way various people display their antiques, and many ideas can be adapted or borrowed for your own home.

Toy collectors have always been attracted to toys that depict black characters. Prices have skyrocketed with recent interest shown in the category, and black toys now command prices between $50 and $300, with rare examples reaching into the thousands.

Don't buy a toy you aren't familiar with unless it is cheap enough to allow you the luxury of researching its background later. What you may think is a perfect piece may have one or more essential parts missing, and as you know, that fact will decrease the

Figures, African natives, made by Schoenhut, part of Safari Set, late 1800s; excellent condition, **$200–300 each.**

value of anything that is considered antique or collectible.

Cast-iron toys have been reproduced (as have cast-iron banks) and the buyer should be extremely comfortable with the piece's originality before plunking down a sizable amount of money. Nothing is more heartbreaking than to pay a high price for what you believe to be an antique, only to find out later that it is a cheap reproduction. (For more information, see the Appendix.)

Papier-mâché (a combination of paper, paste, oil, and resin) is one of the materials used to make toys that one might add to a black collection. The process was largely used in the latter part of the nineteenth and early twentieth centuries. This material is hard to store, as it does craze and crackle with age, but the items made are usually fine and worth collecting. Some of the papier-mâché toys you might find are dolls, scissor toys, rolypolys, and nodders.

Most toy dealers and collectors will agree with me when I say that you should buy the best example you can afford. If you're like most collectors, there will probably be a day when you want to upgrade your collection by selling off the lower-end items. You may become frustrated and disappointed

if you cannot sell your toys because they are damaged or not all original. They may have seemed like bargains when you bought them, but in the antiques world there are few bargains you won't have to pay for sometime in the future. My husband calls such bad buys *gronks*. By his definition, a *gronk* is a thing that excites you momentarily—enough to give away your hard-earned money to own it—but grieves you endlessly, because you can't sell it for the amount you paid for it.

Information about specific toys not covered in this chapter—and there will be a lot because the field is seemingly endless—can be obtained from books that are specifically geared to toys or even a specific type of toy (see the Bibliography). Museums (such as the Margaret Woodbury Strong Museum in Rochester, New York, and the Brooklyn Children's Museum in New York City) and dealers whose specialty is toys are also good sources of information. There are antiques shows that feature just toys and dolls. See also Chapter 2. If you take the time to wander around such a show and ask questions, chances are you will come out much more knowledgeable about black toys than when you went in.

Types of Collectible Toys

AUTOMATA

Automatic devices go back as far as the ancient Romans, who developed a device that opened temple doors. Clocks were popular in the thirteenth-century Mongol court and continued their popularity throughout the sixteenth and seventeenth centuries. The eighteenth and nineteenth centuries saw the introduction of figures that moved as a music box played.

An American firm, E. R. Ives of Bridgeport, Connecticut, made automated dolls that included one called "Uncle Tom" and another called "Heathen Chinee." Black automata are fairly rare so that when a collector finds one, he or she has reason to be excited. Most of the good automata can be found in toy museums, such as the Shelburne Museum in Vermont.

Clockmakers often made automated toys as well. Some of these toys are not marked with the maker's name.

BANKS

In almost every collection of black items, there is sure to be a still or mechanical bank that depicts black people as they were seen by whites in the late 1800s. The days after the Civil War found much of the white country angry about the Black's newfound freedom, yet they were not able to do much about it. Still, bigotry, prejudice, and racial tension crept into everyday life, even in items made for children. The Freedman's Bank, for example, was a political antiblack comment made after the Civil War. The bank shows a black bank teller taking money while thumbing his nose.

Ethnic bias began cropping up in bank manufacturing circles from 1860 on. Blacks were not the only ones against whom white Protestant Americans were prejudiced. The

Bank, mechanical, "Stump Speaker," cast iron, man drops coin into suitcase, American; excellent condition, **$1,500–1,750. Courtesy of Evelyn Ackerman; photo by Evelyn Ackerman.**

Chinese, Irish, and Jews were also attacked. Banks were made depicting Chinese as sneaky thieves, Irishmen with pigs, and Jews as greedy businesspeople. But the Blacks were by far the most stereotyped. There are ten versions of the bust bank, all with the stereotypical big lips, large, bulging eyes, and kinky hair. And there are more than twenty other mechanical banks always portraying black people as the butt of some obvious joke. The bank "Bad Accident" depicts the black farmer as ignorant and slow.

However, one bank called "Darktown Battery," designed by James Bowen and manufactured by the Stevens Company, depicts three black baseball players and makes no derogatory comment on Blacks. Ironically, this bank was made before black baseball players were allowed to participate in the Major Leagues!

The banks that are considered collectible usually hail from the Victorian era. They were made of iron and were decorative. The first iron banks were stills, but once the simple spring action brought life to a bank, more and more intricate movements became popular, causing a peak in mechanical bank sales to be reached before the end of the century. Cast-iron mechanical banks are purely American products. It seems that ingenious Americans, with their love for competition and capitalism, wanted a more interesting way to save those pennies, dimes, and nickels.

Banks produced in the years after the Civil War reflect the social, political, and cultural views of the times. They show historical events as well as predictions of technological advances. The height of popularity of mechanical banks spans a sixty-year period from 1870 to 1930.

Some Companies that Produced Ethnic Versions of Mechanical and Still Banks

It should be noted that most companies did not mark their banks. Unless you know which companies produced certain banks, you will have a hard time attributing the right maker to the right bank. There are several very good books on the market that can point you in the right direction.

Charles A. Bailey of Cobalt, Connecticut, is the bank designer whose name one sees most often. He was responsible for at least twenty-nine designs, but his banks are difficult to find nowadays because of the fragile spring mechanism he favored.

Articulated dancing figure, "Rag Time Jim," paper figure dressed in top hat, tails, and spats, factory made, marked "MVM, 261 W. 37th St., New York," 1920s–1940s, 21½" tall; excellent condition, **$40–50.** Courtesy of American Eye; photo by Bob Reno.

J. & E. Stevens of Cromwell, Connecticut, was the most prolific of the bank manufacturers, producing the first mechanical bank and many others after that, working over a period of fifty years. It began manufacturing still banks during the late 1860s and ceased producing all types of banks in 1928. Some of the ethnic banks produced by this prolific firm are among the most popular and most recognized by collectors in this field. "Bad Accident," "Dentist," "Darktown Battery," "I Always Did 'Spise a Mule," "Jolly Nigger," and "Horse Race" are some of them.

Jerome B. Secor of Bridgeport, Connecticut, manufactured the most valuable mechanical bank of all time, the striking "Freedman's Bank." It was the only bank made by Secor and is thought to have been made for only five years (1878–1883). The bank is advertised in an 1880 circular for sale for $4.50—expensive even then. Because only a few of these banks are still available, they are extremely valuable. Prices of $100,000 and up have been reported. A full-page color photo of the bank is shown in Carole Rogers's book *Penny Banks: A History and a Handbook.*

Weeden Manufacturing Company of New Bedford, Massachusetts, produced tin windup mechanical banks such as "Weeden's Plantation." The company, known for its toy steam engines, began producing tin mechanicals in the late 1880s. Though "Weeden's Plantation" is fairly easy to find, often the figure of the dancer on the left side of the cabin is missing.

Other manufacturers include Shephard Hardware Manufacturing Company of Buffalo and Rex Kyser and Rex of Philadelphia.

Some Collectible Banks

"Bad Accident," manufactured by J. & E. Stevens during the 1890s, is 6 inches tall. A black man sits in a cart drawn by a mule. Behind a bush hides a black boy who, after the coin is dropped between the driver's feet, darts in front of the donkey causing it to rear, the driver to tilt back, and the coin to drop into the bottom of the cart. The words "Bad Accident" are printed on the base, facing the back of the bank. If you find this bank with the letters facing the front of the bank, you have found a rare version.

"Darktown Battery," manufactured by J. & E. Stevens, is 7 1/4 inches tall. The bank shows three black baseball players: pitcher, hitter, and catcher. After the coin is placed in the pitcher's hand, a lever is pressed behind the catcher. The pitcher pitches the ball, the hitter turns his head to watch it go by, the catcher catches the ball, the coin enters the catcher's body and is deposited into the bank. The bank is unusual because all three figures have movable parts. The words "Darktown Battery" appear on the base of the bank.

"Darky Fisherman," attributed to Charles A. Bailey, was made in the 1880s and is 4 1/4 inches tall. It is an extremely rare lead bank. At the base

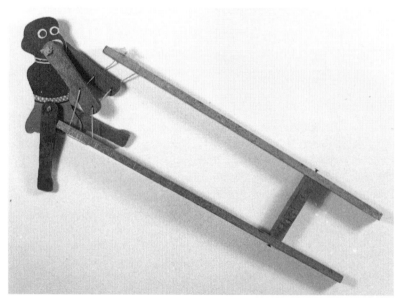

Flipover toy, wooden sides and legs, paper body; very good condition, $22–30. Courtesy of Malinda Saunders; photo by Donald Vogt.

of the bank, near the boy's feet, are the words "Dis Pond Am De Boss Place to Fish." The boy stands at one end of the bank, holding a fishing pole with a fish on its end. When a coin is placed in the slot in the "pond" and a lever at the boy's right elbow is pressed, the fish emerges and pushes the penny into the bank.

"Dentist," manufactured by J. & E. Stevens in the 1880s, is 6½ inches tall. The bank features a black man who is seated in the dentist's chair. The dentist, who is white and sports a large moustache, is bent over his patient. When a coin is placed in the dentist's pocket and a lever pressed next to his foot, the tooth is extracted, the dentist falls back, the patient topples off his chair, and the penny slides into the gas bag behind the dentist.

"Freedman's Bank," manufactured by Jerome Secor, is 10¾ inches high. One of the most beautiful, as well as rarest, of all mechanicals, the bank is made out of wood, cloth, and metal. It features a black man with a wide smile, dressed in a flowered outfit resembling a clown's, complete with red bow tie and starched collar. He stands behind a wooden box on turned legs. On the front of the box is a plate marked "Freedman's Bank."

The bank must first be wound, then a coin is placed on the table, and a lever on the side of the bank is pressed. The man's left hand slides the coin into the opening. His right hand raises to thumb his nose at the viewer as he simultaneously nods his head.

"Horse Race," manufactured by J. & E. Stevens, is 4¾ inches tall. The bank shows a circular platform with two archways, one on each end of the platform. A black man in short blue pants stands in the middle of the circle next to a raised slot. When the coin is dropped into the slot, the horses begin to revolve around the platform. The base of the bank is yellow and orange, one horse is white and the other is brown. This bank was made in another version besides the one described: It is taller and the coin trap is in the bottom.

"I Always Did 'Spise a Mule," manufactured by J. & E. Stevens, was patented April 22, 1879, and April 27, 1897. There were two versions of this bank. The earlier one shows a rider being tossed from a kicking mule. The later, and more common, version shows a black man seated on the ground in front of what appears to be a very reluctant mule. When the coin is placed on the tray beneath the figure, the mule spins around and kicks over the black man. When the man falls, the coin is deposited into the bank.

"Jolly Nigger," manufactured by Shephard Hardware and J. & E. Stevens, was patented November 14, 1882, and is 6¾ inches tall. This mechanical bust was the only American-made "Jolly Nigger." A plate on the back of the bank shows the patent date. The bank depicts an exaggerated face of a black man. The man wears a

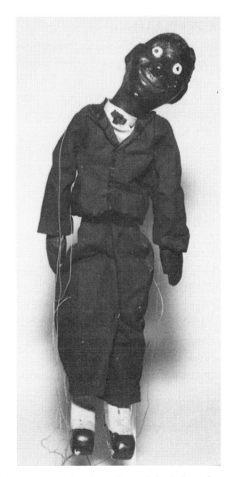

Puppet, wooden hands and feet, hand-sewn black-and-white tux with spats, composition head, handmade, 1920s–1930s, 18″ tall; excellent condition, $500–700. Courtesy of American Eye; photo by Bob Reno.

red shirt. When a coin is placed in his hand, the arm lifts to deposit the coin in his mouth and his eyes roll.

"Weeden's Plantation" was manufactured by Weeden Manufacturing and stands 5¼ inches tall. Construction of the bank is tin and wood with a clockwork mechanism. The bank looks like a small shack. In front of the shack sits a black banjo player on the right with a black dancer on the left. On one side of the shed is labeled "Jig Dancin,'" and the other, "Pete Jones, Banjo Lessuns, One Cent." The mechanism is wound with a key, the coin is inserted at the side of the shack, and the banjo player and dancer perform.

BOARD GAMES

Most board games involve a starting point and an ending point; the participants compete in a race for the finish. The games are often accessorized with dice, counters, and paper money. Board games made to feature black playing pieces were extremely derogatory in nature. Often the central black character was being chased by an animal or another (white) human being, and usually the object of the game was to catch the black person. Whichever way you played, the Black lost.

Some of the companies that manufactured board games were Parker Brothers Co. (Salem, Massachusetts), W. & S. B. Ives, the McLoughlin Brothers, and Milton Bradley (Springfield, Massachusetts). The Bradley and Parker companies are still in the business of producing board games.

Twentieth-century board games are sometimes marked with their copyright date on the outside box cover. They will also have the maker's name marked there, and that information will help you to research your board game's origins.

CARD GAMES

One can find an indeterminate number of card games that feature black people as card decorations or that were designed to be played under specific directions. Often such card games were distributed on railroad lines to keep the travelers occupied.

MECHANICAL TOYS

In the first third of the twentieth century, major department stores, such as Sears, Roebuck and Company and Montgomery Ward, sold mechanical toys that portrayed black people in an unfavorable light. Toys such as "Musical Negroes," "Alabama Coon Jigger," "Mammy's Black Boy," and "Dude Negro" were advertised in their catalogs as "amusing" and "fascinating." For the most part, these mechanical toys were made of tin and were fairly colorful. (See also Banks and Tin and Cast-Iron Toys, in this chapter.)

PULL TOYS

One of the earliest and most interesting pull toys is a lithographed paper-on-wood boat on wheels that was made by the W. S. Reed Company and patented in 1881. The boat was 17 inches long and held a group of smiling black men who played various instruments and whose arms and bodies moved as the toy was pulled. The side of the boat is labeled "Reed's Latest Sensation— Pull for the Shore."

Another such toy was made by N. N. Hill Brass Company around 1900. Made of brass, the toy features a bronze alligator on wheels. Atop the alligator sits a black boy in a blue jacket, yellow pants, and red hat. When the toy is pushed or pulled, the bell (or gong) underneath the alligator sounds.

PUZZLES

Jigsaw puzzles had relatively large pieces and simple shapes in Victorian days. The idea of early puzzles was to pass on knowledge in an interesting way. Because of that, puzzles often related to history and geography. Later in the nineteenth century, works of art were more popular subjects for puzzle makers.

Figures, "Humpty Dumpty Circus Negro Dudes," made by Schoenhut, both one-part and two-part heads shown, late 1880s; excellent condition, **$200–300 each.** Courtesy of Evelyn Ackerman; photo by Evelyn Ackerman.

Puzzles depicting black subjects became common during the latter part of the nineteenth century and beginning of the twentieth. Subjects were characters from books (Sambo); cartoon characters; and real-life, stage, screen, and television personalities (Amos 'n Andy).

TABLE GAMES AND TOYS

Table games and toys include rolling and tossing games, which were extremely popular in the Victorian era. Bean-toss games often incorporated black faces or figures as the target at which the bean bag or ball would be thrown.

Such games of Victorian vintage are rarely found in mint condition. However, they were made well into the mid-twentieth century, and you may be able to procure some of the later ones in good condition. These games did take a lot of abuse so the chance of obtaining a large collection of mint pieces is slim.

TIN AND CAST-IRON TOYS

Because tin was lightweight and easy to work with, toys made of that material first appeared in quantity in the early nineteenth century. The United States, Connecticut in particular, took the lead in this new field. As early as the 1820s, tinsmiths in Connecticut were making whistles and bubble pipes. Factories sprang up to produce tin toys within a decade.

Francis, Field and Francis, a Pennsylvania firm, was documented as producing black tin toys in 1838; the firm continued a decade later under a different name: the Philadelphia Tin Toy Manufactory.

Clockwork toys were made by George W. Brown and Company in Forestville, New York. The firm began in 1856 and changed its name to Steven and Brown in 1869 (merging with J. & E. Stevens, see p. 177). The new company made a number of black tin toys, but its specialty was wheeled horse-drawn vehicles.

Clockwork toy, dancer, wood, made by LaGrove & Webb, New York, jointed man, original clothing, mounted on wooden box with grain-papered cover, original label and directions, listed in Blair Whitton's *American Clockwork Toys*, patent 143,082 on September 23, 1873; 7" × 3"; excellent condition (minor soiling and paint removal), **$1,200–1,500.** Courtesy of American Eye; photo by Bob Reno.

Toss game, "Aunt Sally," made by F. H. Ayres, Ltd., London, colorful face with hole in nose to hold pipe, dressed in scarf and ragged clothes, original box with pine sticks (which were thrown to break pipe), from the Schneiders of Hallowell, Maine, late 1800s to early 1900s; excellent condition, **$500–700.** Courtesy of American Eye; photo by Bob Reno.

An interesting pair of clockwork toys was made in the 1870s by the Ives Company. The toys were drums and on top of each drum was a wooden dancing figure: a black woman and a black man, each dressed in colorful clothes.

A livelier clockwork toy is "The Cane-walkers." Two Blacks—described as "colored society people"—dance around comically. When first shown in the 1890 Ives catalog, the dancers were sold (wholesale) for $36 per dozen. It would be practically impossible to find one of these toys at that price today!

Ives appears to have made more black clockwork, tin, and iron toys than any other manufacturer of its time, and many other toys besides the ones discussed here can be found for your black toy collection.

Another example of a fine clockwork toy was made by the Automatic Toy Works in 1875. The toy, 10 inches in height, was a black suffragette woman standing on a box. The woman bends forward, straightens up, and bangs her fist on the podium in front of her. (Ives made a similar toy featuring a black stump speaker in 1882.)

Automatic also produced a toy featuring an old black fiddler seated on a stool, playing his instrument. He is dressed in a morning suit, which consists of checked pants and a velvet coat. His hand moves the bow back and forth across the violin's strings.

The period between 1840 and 1890 seems to have produced the finest of black American tin toys, but companies such as the Marx toy firm continued to produce imaginative toys in the early 1900s and led the way with windup tin toys.

The Gong Bell Company advertised a toy in their 1883 catalog that showed a black man kneeling on an iron cart. The man was ringing a Liberty Bell. Could the slave have been celebrating his freedom? This combination of tin and cast iron was expensive to produce, thus the toy is rare.

In the period after World War II (1945–1952) toys began to be made in occupied Japan and Germany. These toys, stamped with the maker's mark and the words "Occupied Japan" or "U.S. Zone Germany," are easily identifiable. Before 1900, there were a number of people involved in toy making, but the items were not allowed to be marked with the maker's name, because the middleman's job (or "jobber") would have been eliminated.

Cast-iron toys were not made as prolifically as were tin toys. They were enjoyed in the United States during the late nineteenth and early twentieth centuries. J. & E. Stevens was a prominent manufacturer of cast-iron toys, cap guns, banks, and small tools. Also in the field were the Ives firm, Hubley Manufacturing Co. (Lancaster, Pennsylvania), and the Kenton Hardware Company (Kenton, Ohio).

Gray iron was used because it was sturdy and could be painted. Once the molds were made, companies turned out identical cast figures and used standard parts, making it easier to put the toys on the mass market.

One such toy was the popular horse and buggy. Kenton Company made a phaeton in the late 1800s that was 18 inches long and featured a lady with a dog in the rear and a black coachman in formal white uniform in front.

Cap pistols were often made in animated figures, including Punch and Judy, Chinese figures, Irish figures, and black figures.

Some American Manufacturers of Toys Depicting Blacks

Chein Industries, Inc. of Burlington, New Jersey, started making toys in 1903 and is still in business. The company's specialty is tin banks and toys. It has also made reproduction rolypolys. It stopped making toys in 1977.

Edward Ives worked in Plymouth, Connecticut, from 1825 to 1930. In 1872, the firm became known as Ives and Blakeslee. It specialized in window displays, clockwork toys, horse-drawn vehicles, and trains.

Marx Brothers of New York began making toys in 1921 and continues to be one of the best-known toy manufacturers today. The company made tin and windup toys as well as many other kinds of playthings.

The A. Schoenhut Company was founded by a German immigrant named Albert Schoenhut. He opened his toy business in 1872 in Philadelphia and began making lathe-turned, hand-painted wooden toys. His factory-made toys often came in sets and replaced the customary, hand-made wooden toys.

The Stephens and Brown Manufacturing Company of Cromwell, Connecticut, was in business from 1869 to approximately 1880. During that time it made tin and iron toys and banks.

The Strauss Company of New York manufactured clockwork and tin windup toys from 1900 to 1920.

PRICES FOR TOYS

Articulated dancing figure

"Dancing Rastus," plywood and pine, marked "R. Marion Stuart, 2245 Baxter Street, Los Angeles, Calif. Patent Pending," painted white, red and black figure, articulated body, 1930s; 13½" tall × 4½" × 10"; excellent condition, **$750–1,000.**

Man, all wood, painted black, red, and white, bowler hat, from Schneiders, Hollowell, Maine, early 20th century; 12" high × 31" long paddle; excellent condition, **$750–1,000.**

Man on contemporary stand, all pine, articulated legs and feet, moving arms, painted yellow legs, white features and green and soft yellow body; 22" × 5" × 4½"; excellent condition, **$300–500.**

Man with cork top hat, articulated wooden hands and feet, painted face, clothing is hand-stitched red-checkered cotton, 1890–1910; excellent condition, **$200–300.**

"Sambo," cardboard, dressed in red, white, and black with spats and a bow tie, original illustrated packaging, 1940s; 11"; mint condition, **$18.**

Automaton, man smoking, Lucien Bontemps, unmarked bisque head, hands, arms, exaggerated features, set black glass eyes, pierced ears, open mouth to receive cigarette holder, black wool wig, key on mechanism (box) marked "LB" (Lucien Bontemps), all original, rare French musical mechanical piece; 16" high doll, 24" overall height; excellent condition, **$1,500–2,000.**

Bank

Mechanical

"Always Did 'Spise a Mule," J. & E. Stevens Co., cast iron, jockey atop a mule about to buck, brown base, designed by James H. Bowen, 19th century; 8¼"; excellent condition; **$1,000–1,400.**

"Always Did 'Spise a Mule," J. & E. Stevens Co., cast iron, jockey atop a mule about to buck, red base, designed by James H. Bowen, 19th century; 8¼"; excellent condition, **$1,700–2,000.**

"Always Did 'Spise a Mule," J. & E. Stevens Co., cast iron, man sitting on bench with mule in front of him, yellow base (rare); excellent condition, **$3,700–4,200.**

"Bad Accident," J. & E. Stevens, cast iron, upside down letters, depicts man driving mule-drawn cart, ca. 1891; excellent condition, **$4,500–5,500.**

Black man in minstrel costume, cast iron, put coin in his chest, push a lever, and he tips his hat and deposits the coin, red coat with tails, white pants with blue stripes, yellow hat, and white shirt, tin; 7½" high; excellent condition, **$800–1,600.**

"Book of Knowledge," cast iron, man riding mule, 1950s; excellent condition, **$90–120.**

Boys stealing watermelon, cast iron; excellent condition, **$4,500–5,500.**

"Darktown Battery," J. & E. Stevens Co., cast iron, one man pitching, one catching,

Bank, mechanical, "Jolly Nigger," good condition, $300–500. Photo by Donald Vogt.

one holding bat, colorful, designed by James H. Bowen; near mint condition, **$10,000–12,000.**

"Darky in Cabin," cast iron, ca. 1885; no trap, trip level off, otherwise good condition, **$150–175.**

Mammy, cast iron, feeding dish; excellent condition, **$450–500.**

Sharecropper, cast iron; excellent condition, **$30–65.**

"Stump Speaker," cast iron, man drops coin into suitcase; excellent condition, **$1,500–1,750.**

"Stump Speaker," Shepard Hardware Co., cast iron, man with exaggerated features, wears small top hat; excellent condition, **$4,700–5,200.**

"Thrifty Tom's Jigger Bank," Ferdinand Strauss Corp., cast iron, no box included; excellent condition, **$1,595–1,700.**

"Two-Faced Negro," cast iron; 3″; excellent condition, **$100–150.**

"Weeden's Plantation," cast iron, two men on stage, one with banjo, other dancing; excellent condition, **$600–700.**

Still

Baby in cradle, cast iron; 3⅞″; excellent condition, **$1,000–1,200.**

Boy, cast iron, nodder, eating watermelon, souvenir of Biloxi, Mississippi; excellent condition, **$60–90.**

Boy, cast iron, nodder, sitting between two oranges marked "Florida," 6″; very good condition, **$90–125.**

Chef, ceramic, penny bank, nicely decorated, rare form, 1950s; mint condition, **$50–100.**

Boy's head, cast iron, double-faced; excellent condition, **$240–275.**

Double face, cast iron, silver paint; 4″; excellent condition, **$80–100.**

Girl, chalkware, nodder, girl wears blue dress, bank at side; very good condition, **$165–180.**

Banks, mechanical, "Dinah," made by Saalheimer & Straus, England, coin goes in her hand, *left:* short-sleeve version, *right:* long-sleeve version, ca. 1900; excellent condition; **short sleeve: $400–800; long sleeve: $300–500.** Courtesy of the Leonard Davis Collection; photo by Bob Reno.

Man on slide, cast iron; 6″; excellent condition, **$45–65.**

Man's head with turban, pottery; excellent condition, **$45–65.**

Jackie Robinson, tin, dime register, 2″; excellent condition, **$60–80.**

Sharecropper, cast iron; excellent condition, **$100–135.**

"The Young Nigger," cast iron, painted blue, red, pink, black and white, coin slot in back of head, title on back "known as the Jolly N's son," rare; 5″ × 3½″; very good condition, **$275–350.**

Battery-operated dancer, "Dan Jigger," with microphone, boxed; very good condition, **$400–450.**

Blocks, "Acrobatic Balance Toys," Anchor Toy Co., Springfield, Missouri; wood, figural block set depicting porter with black skin, features impressed in gold, toothy grin, and side-glance googly eyes; includes five die-cut wooden figures, original in box; 1920s; each figure measures 5¼″ tall; mint condition, **$175–225.**

Clockwork or mechanical toy

"Alabama Coon Jigger," Ferdinand Strauss, lithographed, windup, man in black jacket, yellow vest, red tie and red pants, 10″ tall; excellent condition, **$500–600.**

"Alabama Coon Jigger," Lehmann, Oh-My Windup, 1912; very good condition, **$295–335.**

"Amos 'n Andy Fresh Air Taxi," Louis Marx, lithographed tin, windup, red car with one man driving, the other wears a green jacket and sits in back seat; excellent condition, **$1,000–1,500.**

"Amos Walker," Louis Marx, lithographed tin, Amos in his taxi hat; good condition, **$175–300.**

"Auto Uncle," tin, windup, man with three-wheeled cart and umbrella; excellent condition, **$500–600.**

"Automatic Boxers," Ives, two men in very tattered clothing, patented December 26, 1878, by William Maguire; 11″ tall; very good condition, **$4,700–5,300.**

Banjo player, Jerome B. Secor, cast iron banjo, gray cloth jacket with gold trim, orange checkered pants, original label, ca. 1876; excellent condition, **$23,000–26,000.**

Banjo player in green jacket, top hat and checkered pants; excellent condition, **$525–625.**

"Black Dandy," Gunthermann, tin, man in top hat, green jacket with white-and-red pants, red shoes, sits on rolling soapbox-type cart that moves, hand painted; good condition, **$950–1,050.**

"Bones Player," Jerome B. Secor, red-and-black plaid cloth jacket, horizontally striped pants, ca. 1876; excellent condition (clothing apparently not original), **$11,500–13,000.**

"Boy on Velocipede," Stevens & Brown, hand-painted tin and cast iron, red jacket, horizontally striped pants, patented January 25, 1870, by Arthur M. Allen, rare; excellent condition, **$5,000–6,000.**

"Charleston Trio," Louis Marx, lithographed tin, windup; man, boy, and dog, one man dances, other plays fiddle, 1921; mint condition, **$1,050–1,200.**

Dancing couple

Gunthermann, appears to be iron, hand painted, heavyset women in yellow dress with red trim, smaller man dressed in tails; good condition, **$1,200–1,500.**

Man and woman dancing on stage, bell rings in background, rare, variation of J. M. Cromwell Toy patented March 28, 1865; very good condition, **$3,700–4,200.**

Dancing figures, D.A.A. Buck Co., West Cheshire, Conn., figures are composition, box depicting porch and two men and one women; one man is sitting and playing banjo, man and woman dancing; as crank is turned, banjo player moves his arm in strumming motion and couple dances; hand crank, paper label, rare, patented March 19, 1889; 9″ wide × 6½″ tall; excellent condition, **$5,000–7,500.**

Dancing man

Automatic dancer, jointed man in overalls and plaid shirt, paper-covered wood background depicts Southern scene, patented September 23, 1873, by Henry L. Brower; very good condition, **$1,200–1,600.**

"Dancer," Ives, grayish green jacket and orange knickers, hangs from marionette-type hook, patented March 30, 1886, by Charles A. Hotchkiss; very good condition, **$2,000–2,500.**

Dancer, windup, man moves up and down and dances in realistic fashion, original plaid jacket and brown striped pants, patented by Brower, early 19th century; 9½" tall × 7¼" wide; good condition, **$1,000–1,500.**

Dancers, lithographed tin, windup, two dancing men, background is Southern scene with people picking cotton and playing banjo; 8¾" tall × 6½" wide; very good condition, **$600–1,200.**

"Dancing Bojangles," windup, boxed; very good condition, **$60–80.**

Dancing women

Dancers, Ives, two wooden dancers on top of box, ca. 1880; 6¼" wide × 10" high; very good condition, **$800–1,400.**

"Double Negro Dancers," Ives, two jointed and dressed wooden female dancers atop box, patented February 17, 1874, by W. L. Hubbell; 9½" tall; excellent condition, **$1,200–1,600.**

Clockwork dancing man, "Coon Dance," wooden jointed figure wearing straw hat and red neckerchief, hand-painted face, windup, unknown origin, 13" × 7½" × 3¾"; excellent condition, **$400–600. Courtesy of American Eye; photo by Bob Reno.**

Clockwork dancing man, "Tap Dancer," celluloid, windup, man stands on corner of Lenox Avenue and 125th Street, has key, marked "Made in Occupied Japan," 1950s; excellent condition, **$750–900. Courtesy of the Lewis and Blalock Collection; photo by Bob Reno.**

"Dare Devil," Lehmann, lithographed, windup, man in cart pulled by bucking zebra; 6¹/₂" long; excellent condition, **$325–450.**

Drummer, Schuco, windup, man playing drums; very good condition, **$125–175.**

"The Giant," Ives, tall man in red knickers and gray jacket, extremely rare, 1890s; 14" tall; excellent condition, **$7,500–9,000.**

"Ham & Sam," Ferninand Strauss, lithographed, windup, banjo player in red checkered jacket and blue checkered pants, piano player, colorful, 7¹/₂" tall; good condition (some repair), **$325–500.**

"Ham 'n Sam," Linemar, windup, two men, one plays piano while other dances, original box, 5¹/₄" × 4³/₄" wide; excellent condition, **$1,750–2,250.**

"Jazzbo Jim," Ferdinand Strauss, tin, windup, 1921; very good condition, **$675–725.**

Mammy, Lindstrom, lithographed tin, ruffled cap, exaggerated features, "Mammy" printed on white apron, 7¹/₂" tall; good condition, **$100–150.**

Man, Louis Marx, lithographed tin, exaggerated features, red jacket and yellow-and-black striped pants; good condition, **$300–400.**

"Old Aunt Chloe, The Negro Washerywoman," Ives, green-and-white plaid cloth capelet and apron, red dress, stands on early painted and stenciled box, original packaging; excellent condition, **$21,000–23,000.**

"Old Black Joe," Ives, cast iron shoes on rollers, man in red plaid trousers and tails, patented September 21, 1875, by Arthur Hotchkiss; excellent condition, **$2,400–3,400.**

"Old Uncle Tom, The Fiddler," Ives, man in checkered pants and black tails, early painted and stenciled box; excellent condition, **$6,500–8,000.**

"Our New Clergyman," Ives, articulated figure on red stenciled box marked "Preacher" in front of red stenciled round pulpit, preacher in black jacket, white shirt, red-and-white checkered trousers; mint condition with original box, **$6,500–8,500.**

"Political Stump Speaker," Ives, articulated man in brown cloth jacket, red checkered pants, straw hat, cast iron table; excellent condition, **$6,000–8,000.**

"Red Cap Porter," Ferdinand Strauss, lithographed tin, windup, man pulling cart; 7" long; excellent condition, **$750–850.**

"Stepin' Tom" walking toy, Sturdy Mfg., comical man painted in red, white, yellow and black, signed "Stepin' Tom—Sturdy Mfg.," 1920s; excellent condition, **$100–150.**

"Sweeping Mammy," Lindstrom, lithographed tin, original box; 8" tall; excellent condition, **$300–400.**

"Tambourine Player," Jerome B. Secor, red-and-black plaid cloth jacket, gray pants, scarf around neck, extremely rare, ca. 1876; excellent condition, **$35,000–40,000.**

"Tombo-Alabama Coon Jigger," Lehmann, chromolithograph, tin, windup, cowboy standing on top of a box; excellent condition, **$450–550.**

Typical Mississippi river scene with man in tattered pants and jacket, wood backboard with lithographed paper scene, Brower patent, early 19th century; 6¹/₂" wide × 9" tall; excellent condition except for clothes, **$4,000–6,000.**

"Woman's Rights Advocate," Ives, articulated woman in red-and-white dress with white apron; mint condition, **$9,500–10,500.**

Dart board, Sambo, Wyandotte, bright multicolored lithograph of numbered targets, 1930s; 23" × 14"; excellent condition, **$100–150.**

Dice toy, Alco Britain, black head, round, green, brown, red, yellow, and black, depress head and dice spin around; near mint condition, **$75–100.**

Figure

African native

Saalheimer & Strauss, man with exaggerated features wearing earrings and a toothy grin, Germany, 1910–1930; excellent condition, **$4,500–5,000.**

Teddy's Adventures series, two-part head, jointed shoulders and hips, sash costume;

7 3/4" high; normal wear, good to very good condition, **$2,000–2,600.**

Band of musicians (six), lead; very good condition, **$75–100 for the set.**

Boy drummer, black cotton hair over tin, grass skirt; 5"; very good condition, **$75–95.**

Girl, nodder, sitting in rocker; very good condition, **$165–180.**

"Hustler Black Boy and Donkey," wood, painted in green, yellow, white, red, and black, donkey's head and boy's arms move up and down, rare; 11" × 6"; very good condition, **$225–350.**

"Kobi," celluloid, man's head, face, moving eyes, 1920s; very good condition, **$110–125.**

Mammy and child, Kyser & Rex Co., mammy in red dress with white full apron, child on lap has mouth that opens and closes, patented October 21, 1884; excellent condition, **$8,000–9,000.**

Man, nodder, coolie hat, sitting in yoga position, very good condition, **$100–150.**

Man, nodder, hand painted in orange, blue, and other colors, exaggerated mouth, spring legs, prewar; near mint condition, **$95–150.**

"Shuffling Sam," wood, primitive; very good condition, **$95–115.**

Fireworks, "Smoking Sambo," Tipp Fireworks Co., fireworks in Sam's mouth light; very good condition, **$38–55.**

Game

"Bean Em Game," All-Fair, cardboard, bean bags thrown at exaggerated black faces, rare,

Figures in outhouse, pine and plywood, one man hands the other toilet paper, painted, handmade, 1930s–1950s, 9" × 6"; excellent condition, $200–300. Courtesy of American Eye; photo by Bob Reno.

1931; 13″ × 9″; very good condition, **$100–150.**

"Cake Walk Game," Anglo-Canada Game Co., cover art shows five men waiting to dance with two young women; very good condition, **$2,000–2,200.**

Comic, conversation cards, Ottman USA, cardboard, multicolored, word game with fine graphics on box, ca. 1910; 5½″ × 7½″; excellent condition, **$250–350.**

"Little Black Sambo," Cadaco-Ellis, copyright 1951; very good condition, **$50–200.**

Fireworks holder, "Smoking Sambo," made by Tipp Fireworks Co., Tippecanoe City, Ohio, directions included, fireworks were put in the mouth and then lit; very good condition, $75–100. Photo by Bob Reno.

"Poor Jenny," contents and box; very good condition, **$75–95.**

Sambo shooting target, child's; very good condition, **$50–80.**

"Snake Eyes," wide-eyed picture on box, cards and chips; very good condition, **$22–30.**

"The Jolly Darkie Target," lithographed, 1890s; very good condition, **$150–190.**

"Watch on De Rind," All-Fair, Churchville, New York, three children holding and eating one large piece of watermelon; 11½″ × 11½″; excellent condition, **$200–350.**

"Watermelon Frolic," I. M. Yunger, slice of watermelon to be put in boy's hands or mouth, 13 slices on this particular version, framed, copyright 3304—1900, published by E.I.H. New York; 25″ × 45″; excellent condition, **$2,000–2,500.**

Jack-in-the-box, bisque head in pine box, European, originally from Ron Carr collection, ca. 1900 (perhaps earlier); 2⅝″ square; excellent condition, **$300–500.**

Jumping jacks, wood box covered with printed paper, two heads (made of papier mâché) on springs, one is white with painted blue eyes, the other is brown with painted black-and-white eyes and very red mouth, heads are covered with cheap glazed cloth, unmarked, probably from Germany; 4⅞″-wide box; very good condition, **$500–600.**

Pinball machine, "Minstrel," Gottlieb and Co., bells, lights; very good condition, **$1,200–1,500.**

Playing cards

"Amos 'n Andy Card Party," cardboard lithograph, cards, tally and score cards with all the characters, complete, firm box, very rare, ca. 1930; 6″ × 8″; near mint condition, **$300–400.**

"Golly," lithographed double deck, one deck shows two kittens surprised by Golliwog jack-in-the-box, other deck features two Pekinese dogs surprised by clown rag doll, both decks complete, original double-hinged box; mint condition, **$135–160 for the set.**

Woman with basket of cotton, boxed; very good condition, **$6–8.**

Pull toy

"African Mailman," Lehmann, lithographed tin, ostrich pulls man driving small cart, man dressed in green cap and jacket, yellow cart, 7" long; very good condition, **$275–300.**

Boy, tin, pull the string and eyes spin, 1910; 2½"; very good condition, **$25–30.**

Cart, cast iron, man sitting on alligator on top of cart, bell rings when toy is pulled, iron, ca. 1890; excellent condition, **$2,500–3,500.**

Cart, Hubley, cast iron, two wheels, man drives cart; 5½" × 2"; very good condition, **$185–200.**

Puppet

Civil War officer, carved wood, marionette, painted head, hands and feet, fine detail, ca. 1900; 24½" high; very good condition except for the fragmented Navy wool uniform, **$1,000–1,300.**

"Clippo presents Lucifer," Fleischaker and Baum, New York, string, 1938; very good condition, **$195–225.**

Dancing man, articulated, jointed arms, legs and hips controlled by strings, yellow, red, white, black, and brown; 19" × 8"; mint condition, **$35–50.**

Jim Crow, black hand-carved head, from Punch-style puppet shows, costume in orange, purple, blue, gold and black, rare, ca. 1870; 18" × 6"; excellent condition, **$425–500.**

Man in oilcloth top hat, polka-dotted full-sleeved shirt, black pants, red socks and black oilcloth slippers, hand-sewn eyes, nose, mouth, eyebrows, cloth hands, handmade, 1920s–1930s, from Ron Carr Collection; excellent condition, **$200–300.**

Minstrel, possibly Al Jolson; 27" tall; very good condition, **$350–500.**

Puzzle

"Amos 'n Andy," jigsaw, Pepsodent premium, 1932; very good condition, **$55–65.**

"Amos 'n Andy, Lightnin' Brother Crawford and Kingfish at O.K. Hotel"; very good condition, **$75–95.**

Puppets, hand held, the one on the left is Mohammed Ali (Cassius Clay), 1950s–1960s; good condition, $35–65 each. Courtesy of Rose Fontanella; photo by Donald Vogt.

"Little Black Sambo," wood; very good condition, **$20–30.**

Record dancer (dances when record spins)

"Dancing Sam," original box; near mint condition, **$150–300.**

Puppets, marionettes, plastic faces, grotesquely designed, man on bottom is dressed in fur to resemble a gorilla; good condition, $50–75 each. Courtesy of Rose Fontanella; photo by Donald Vogt.

"Ragtime Rastus and Boxing Darkies," wooden figures, original box with directions, patented March 18, 1915; two boxers: 4½" tall, Rastus: 5½" tall; excellent condition, **$200–400.**

Ring toss piece, "Garden Aunt Sally," wooden painted face, toss rings into pipe in her mouth, cotton bonnet and dress, an improved edition of an old game, very portable for picnics, etc., ca. 1890; face 15" high × 5" wide; excellent condition, **$250–350.**

"Shooting Gallery," Brinkman Baby Rack USA, tin, shows babies with exaggerated faces, painted in red, orange peel and black, original label, very rare, 1915; 15" × 5" × 7"; excellent condition, **$600–800.**

Smoking toy, paper and tin lithograph, blow smoke into the hole and tap, smoke rings come out, blue, yellow, black, red, and green, late 1800s; 2¼" diameter; near mint condition, **$75–100.**

Steam-operated toy, "Happy Jack and Happy James Tap Dancers," tin lithograph, two figures dance like Charlie Chaplin, names are written on curtains in background, marked "WK," "Made in Germany," and "D.R.G.M.," colorful and rare; 6½" tall × 7" wide × 3" deep; near mint condition, **$2,000–4,000.**

Toss game

Bean-bag, face, eyes and mouth pop out; very good condition, **$250–300.**

"Black Chuck," stands up, ca. 1890; very good condition, **$50–75.**

"Jolly Darkie," Milton Bradley, cardboard, toss ball into mouth, painted in bright colors, 1890; 15" × 8"; near mint condition (box top missing), **$200–300.**

"Sambo," colorful, tin; very good condition, **$125–150.**

Toy theater, Playette Theater, cardboard, "Little Black Sambo," 1942; 18" × 12"; very good condition, **$28–35.**

CHAPTER ELEVEN

Miscellaneous Everyday Artifacts

There are some black collectibles that do not fit into one category comfortably, and some that might have deserved their own chapters had there been enough information to fill more than a couple of pages or enough interest to dedicate a chapter to the subject. This chapter, therefore, encompasses all these miscellaneous everyday items.

Perhaps your specific area of interest is covered in this chapter, perhaps it is not. As you know, the field of collecting black memorabilia is vast and can hardly be contained in one book, though I have tried to at least mention everything I've come across in the past decade. At the very least, the following information should whet your appetite for more.

Avon Collectibles

During the years it's been in business, Avon has manufactured some items that depict African-Americans, such as plates, dolls, Christmas collectibles, perfume and cologne bottles, and ads. The plates, made from 1985 to today, show scenes from everyday life, such as 1988's plate titled "A Mother's Work Is Never Done." It shows a small black girl pretending to be a mother. (See also Chapter 9.) Several Avon dolls have been made, including a porcelain one called "Adama from Nigeria"; its box is imprinted with information about Nigeria and the influence Nigerian artists had on the rest of the world. Another series of dolls is called "Tender Memories," and the 1990 version shows two black children. A bottle, which was made to hold two ounces of cologne, depicts a black child, who is of one of the children found in Disney's "It's a Small World" ride.

Clocks

Figural clocks, such as the female figure of Topsy, were designed around 1870. The clock faces were normally situated in the figure's stomach, and the figure's eyes were designed to roll back and forth with each tick of the clock. Clauncey Jerome, a clock manufacturer who worked in various parts of Connecticut, was known to have made most of the figural clocks available.

In an 1895 catalog, novelty clocks (resembling later alarm clocks) with scenes on the face of the clock are listed. The figures in

Clocks, Sambo (clock in banjo) and Topsy (clock in skirt), made by Waterbury Clock Co., winking eyes, ca. 1870; excellent condition, **$1,500–3,500 each.**

these clocks had moving parts: black female figures scrubbed clothes; black males played the banjo.

Commemorative Items

Plates, cups, plaques, and other items are made to celebrate special dates or occasions. A picture, title, and date usually appear on these items. Normally made by collector-plate firms, commemoratives of Blacks are becoming more common and should continue to rise in value. Each piece is usually marked with a maker's name and serial number or edition number. For example, "Limited edition of 3,000/number 159" would mean that the plate was the 159th one made in a run of 3,000.

Medals also fall into this category. Keep your eye out for state centennials, special occasions, and events. Medals are sometimes created for these events, and if you get them when new, they'll only increase in value.

Golliwogs

The term *golliwog* refers to a fuzzy-haired black figure with exaggerated lips and eyes. Created during the mid-1920s, most golliwogs were pins given away by the Golden Shred Company, but golliwogs are still manufactured in England today. Golliwogs are often found as the top of perfume or cologne bottles (made of frosted or satin glass) and were featured in ads for the perfume they represented. These figures also decorated children's china sets. Miniature golliwog bronzes were made, and the figures wore red, white, and blue outfits. Keep a watch out for the current golliwog collectibles being produced in England.

Iron Collectibles

ANDIRONS

The andirons produced in America until the early 1900s were generally less ornate than the French and English styles, and a number of andirons were made in the form of black people or characters. The most commonly seen figures are jockeys, but sailors, "Mammy" and "Pappy" forms, and other "personalities" can also be found. This type of andiron was usually made in the South, often at the same foundries where slaves worked to design iron balustrades and railings for southern homes. Most andirons were manufactured during the early to middle 1800s, but prime examples of these decorative fireplace pieces were also made during the latter part of the century.

When buying andirons, be wary of any with brightly colored paint. If the andirons were used in a fireplace, as originally intended, the paint should be fairly faded and chipped by now. Any andirons with bright paint were probably repainted at one time and should be treated like any other repaired antique, i.e., the price should reflect the repairs.

DOORSTOPS

Doorstops were commercially made around 1775 to keep open doors that incorporated the new rising-butt-type of door hinge. Although the first examples were molded in earthenware, other doorstops were cast in iron, bronze, and brass. Doorstops—or door porters—became familiar objects in

Andirons, black sailors standing with legs apart, painted, mid-1800s; good condition; $1,000–1,500 for the pair. Photo by Bob Reno.

Victorian homes. They often were made to look like celebrities of the time, animals, or familiar characters such as Punch and Judy. The black mammy doorstop remains one of the most collectible.

The most common doorstop material was metal, which was usually cast with a flat, hollow back. However, some of the early examples were cast in the round. Lacquered brass doorstops were popular until about 1850, and the cast-iron form was common from about 1820 on. When production of doorstops increased, the makers began to add paint or a bronzed finish as extra decoration.

Because of the recent vogue for collecting them, prices of doorstops are now at an all-time high. Since interest in these items is so high, it is important to be cautious about the price of the piece, its condition, and whether or not it is a reproduction. Unfortunately, the market has been flooded with repros. As in the past with items such

as iron banks, companies try to take advantage of current trends by making new examples of antique collectibles. Certainly, the new items fill a need for those of us who don't care to spend the money these pieces are currently commanding; however, if you are looking for something that will become more valuable as time goes by, reproductions are not the way to go. (For more information on reproductions, see the Appendix.)

The most common black doorstop is the mammy. She is seen in many different colors and sizes and can be found at just about any antiques show. Besides the mammy, there are many other black doorstops. Some are pretty rare, but it you hunt diligently, you may be able to find one of the butler doorstops or even a child eating watermelon. Black doorstops were also made to resemble jockeys and musicians, among other figures.

HITCHING POSTS

The hitching post, used to secure visitors' horses, was first made during the 1860s. When a farmer drove into town, he looked for a hitching post because the post was the mark of a good store. Companies such as J. W. Fiske and Mott Ironworks made most of the posts supplied in the horse-and-buggy era.

The cast-iron post succeeded the wrought-iron one, and the earliest posts were usually topped with a horse's head that held a ring for the reins. Human figures were introduced as hitching posts during the mid-nineteenth century when iron foundries began to explore new fields. Jockeys, Sambos, footmen, and stable boys were some of the figures representing Blacks. The jockeys and footmen wore brightly painted clothes, and people who could afford a hitching post placed it in front of their home. The hitching post became a status symbol of sorts. The better the post, the better the home it represented.

Iron figures, Gold Dust Twins, advertising giveaway, twins are wearing hula skirts and playing banjos; excellent condition, **$150–300. Courtesy of Rose Fontanella; photo by Bob Reno.**

Although the black slave boy is probably the most common of all posts, it is not the oldest. The 25-inch so-called darky hitching post is considered to be the oldest. The black male is dapperly dressed in spats, cap, checkered vest, and squarish pants. The figure stands on a wood or concrete base and has one hand outstretched and the other in its pocket. Two or three variations of this figure can be found, each slightly different, according to the time it was manufactured.

The jockey is another familiar form of the hitching post. Usually 46 to 48 inches high, the jockey was the elite of the posts, being found outside hotels, estates, restaurants, and other places of gentlemanly leisure. Commonly called "Jocko," this statute has endured a bit of controversy during its time. The story of how the Jocko statue came into being is an interesting one that goes back to the Revolutionary War. Because the Second Continental Congress had refused black recruits, the black volunteers went to the British side. Washington decided after that point that it would be wiser to let American Blacks serve with his army. One of these was a twelve-year-old boy named Tom Graves who was given the mission of holding a lantern to signal to Washington the whereabouts of his horses. Throughout the snowy night, the boy stood holding the lantern and the horses. He froze to death doing so and Washington honored his loyalty by having a statue of the boy holding the lantern erected at his home, in Mount Vernon.

After the 1950s, the Jocko statues were considered a symbol of racism, and a lot of them were painted white.

Jewelry

Various pieces of jewelry have been made in the image of black people. Some of

Jewelry, pin, wood and plastic, inspired by Josephine Baker, 1930s–1940s; excellent condition, **$125–175.** Courtesy of Rose Fontanella; photo by Bob Reno.

the most popular in today's market are those made to resemble a Blackamoor. Dealers have finally discovered the value of a pin, bracelet, necklace, or earrings created to reflect a black image, and thus prices have skyrocketed. Jewelry pieces are a hot collectible and one can get carried away.

Suggestions from dealers who handle jewelry include watching for hallmarks that indicate whether the piece is gold or silver, buying from reputable dealers, and limiting yourself to certain items (e.g., Bakolite pieces or jewelry from a certain decade).

Johnny Griffin Collectibles

In the mid-1800s an unknown artist painted the face of a black youngster in warm, soft colors. Since that time, a number of different articles have been made in the image of "the boy with the torn hat," or Johnny Griffin. Brass ashtrays, spoon holders, pipe racks, souvenir spoons, chalkware

Hanging plaque, brass, Johnny Griffin ("Boy with the torn hat"); excellent condition, $45–65. Photo by Donald Vogt.

Lawn figure, concrete, boy with watermelon; good condition, $150–200. Photo by Donald Vogt.

busts, humidors, toothpick holders, and many other items have been made to resemble Johnny Griffin.

Lawn Items

Water sprinklers in the form of black boys; lawn ornaments depicting black children; and flower pots, planters, and thermometers that show black themes are all collectible lawn items. See also the section on hitching posts earlier in this chapter.

Some of the items made during the 1930s to 1950s—such as the lawn sprinkler—may still be found at flea markets and garage sales, but they are becoming increasingly scarce. Beware of the dealer who tries to sell you a wooden lawn sprinkler as a piece of "folk art." Most of these articles were commercially made in large quantities and should not in any way be considered art objects.

Masonic Collectibles

Prince Hall's lodges (called Negro Masonic Lodges) were first chartered in 1784 by England's Grand Lodge, an association of international lodges. The Masons, a secret fraternal order, asks its members to believe in the existence of a Supreme Being and in the immortality of the soul. Their measures wear a ring, which shows the Masonic symbol; the symbol is also on other pieces of jewelry.

Hall, whose father was an English leather worker and whose mother was a free woman of African descent, became part of Lodge No. 441 at Castle William in Boston Harbor on March 6, 1775. Fourteen other African-Americans were installed that night. Prince Hall became master of African Lodge No. 459 in Boston in 1784. The lodges in the United States rejected the legitimacy of Hall's African lodges, and according to a running argument in the summer issues of *Maine Antique Digest* in 1993, some Masons still don't accept the possibility that a miniature portrait of a black man wearing the traditional Mason necklace is authentic.

Textiles and Sewing Collectibles

Condition is of the utmost importance when buying textiles of any kind. Collectors should watch for pulled threads, because if one thread is pulled, many more will follow. Also smell the cloth for obvious odors, such as animal urine, mold, or mildew. Check for stains, rips, and tears. Textiles are difficult to repair, and if a repair needs to be made, it should be done only by an expert.

Care of your textiles is of equal importance. Never hang a quilt by pounding nails into it. Instead, baste a sleeve onto the back of the quilt, then insert a pole or strip of wood into the sleeve. Then you can hang the quilt by the pole or wood instead of from the fabric itself. The same care should be taken with any kind of needlework.

Store any quilts or needlework not currently being displayed in acid-free tissue in a closet or hope chest. Wrapping the item is also a good idea; then if you need to move it or take it out of storage, you won't be pulling on the fabric directly, which could damage it (especially if the fabric is older than you are). If you store the item in a bag,

make sure you use a bag especially meant for fabric (e.g., a sweater bag); fabric needs to "breathe" so that it doesn't become damaged from trapped moisture.

And, finally, do not send quilts and textiles to the dry cleaners! I've heard many horror stories from people who wanted to preserve Grandma's handiwork and thought a professional would do a better job cleaning it than they would. Sometimes the item comes back in pieces, sometimes it doesn't come back at all, and most often, the harsh chemicals a dry cleaner uses weakens the stitching as well as the fabric itself.

QUILTS

Quilts can be traced from slavery to the present, from Harriet Powers to the contemporary work of Pecolia Warner, Sara Mary Taylor, and Pearlie Posey. Most black families have a quiltmaker somewhere in its past (or present) who exercised artistic ability while creating something to keep the family warm. It has been estimated in recent years that African-American quilts number somewhere around eight hundred thousand, a number that is considered by the experts to be on the low side.

Since most of the slaves in the early years of the United States worked in the South on cotton plantations, it is not surprising that the women of the family were accomplished spinners and weavers. They used their homespun materials to make sweaters, socks, coats, and blankets as well as quilts. Slave narratives show that one of the chores women looked forward to was making "pretty quilts." Elvira Boles of Texas cut timber and split rails during the day but had enough energy when she got home at night to create quilts—perhaps the most beautiful things in her life. Slave quilts, as they are called by today's collectors, were often created by the light of a single candle, and the woman created quilts for both white families and their own.

For generations, country women have engaged in the social phenomenon commonly known as the "quilting bee." Julia Banks, an ex-slave from San Antonio, Texas, commented that quilting bees were a social occasion for slaves, a time when they could celebrate a few moments away from the drudgery of their lives.

Quilt, browns, tans, and blues, filled with cotton and seedpods, made by Mrs. Jernigan Saunders, Brundidge, Alabama, squares and triangle-pieced circles, backed with homespun, 1860–1880; about double size; excellent condition, **$400–600.** Courtesy of American Eye, photo by Bob Reno.

African-American quilts have some distinctive qualities, as do their makers. Each is individual and striking, yet there are ways by which the quilts can be identified as being made by black Americans because this is one area where the women knowingly incorporated African designs or patterns into their quilts. If one looks back in African cultural history, it is quite easy to see that Ashanti weaving patterns were copied by African-American quilters.

Experts tend to disagree about quilting styles used by African-Americans. *The Afro-American Tradition in Decorating Arts* states that the system black women used for quilting was "significantly different than [that] used in Anglo-American quilts. Blacks used a distinctive improvisatory style to overturn the rules of geometry, balance and order commonly expected in the design of a quilt top." Other experts state that the quilts made by black women looked no different than the ones made by whites and that the only difference was its maker.

Nothing but hand-picked cotton went into the best Southern African-American quilts. Most quilts were hand sewn, though some early black quilts were sewn on a machine (the sewing machine was invented in 1846). Often the yarn used to make quilts would be taken from materials the maker had available: feed, tobacco, and flour sacks.

Appliqué, commonly practiced in Africa, seemed to influence Southern black quiltmakers, such as Harriet Powers, who often used this technique in the designs. Appliqué, a fabric motif sewn on a piece of base fabric, created a new design over the original, plain quilt.

Strip quilts have been compared with Ashanti and Ewe woven textiles from Ghana. Strip, or string, quilts were commonly made by African-American quilters who lived on the eastern seaboard, from Maryland south to Georgia and inland to Mississippi. Strip quilts were made, as their name suggests, from straight strips of various types of fabric. Sometimes the quiltmaker used pieces of cloth from old or wornout clothing. The preference for red and yellow in black American quilts is thought to have also come from Ashanti preferences for the same colors in their woven cloth.

In the June 1993 issue of *Maine Antique Digest,* David A. Schorsch Inc. advertised a drawing by Marriet McGreath of Montpelier, Indiana. The drawing (pencil on paper, 15½ by 20 inches) depicted a country auction with all black participants. Of special interest to me was the quilt being held up in the center of the drawing. The quilt was stated to be an "African-American bird quilt." It featured a crow in the middle, surrounded by other birds, which also appeared to be crows. I began to wonder about the significance of that quilt and whether the artist was black or white (especially because the Blacks in the drawing have exaggerated features and appear cartoonish). Having sold the drawing to a dealer, Schorsch was reluctant to give me any further information or the price for which it sold. I have no additional information about African-American bird quilts, but the quilt appeared to me more of a symbol of Blacks (the crows) within McGreath's drawing than a representation of an actual quilt.

Quilt patterns were handed down from generation to generation, often accompanied by hand-wrought embroidery samplers. The style of black American patterns is more informal and less complex than that used by the Amish or Southern white quilters. Most patterns are geometric and include the popular Sawtooth, Wedding Ring, Rising Sun, and Lone Star designs. The crazy quilt was extremely popular because many quilters (black and white) often had only small scraps of material to work with. The random assemblage of odd-shaped pieces that make up the informal crazy quilt design seemed perfectly suited to the resources at hand.

Quilt, made by Marie Crawford, signed, dated 1979, crib size; excellent condition, $125–135. Courtesy of the Mary Cantrell Collection; photo by Mary Cantrell.

Most noticeable in African-American quilt designs are the following. Strips are used to form the basic quilt design. The use of large-scale quilt designs in bright contrasting colors is common. If a pattern could be considered a bit offbeat for its time and/or if the quilt looks as if it were not "planned," then chances are the quiltmaker was black.

Some Biographies of Quilters

Bertha Bachus appeared in a film that was put together by the Center for Southern Folklore (in Memphis) to record the oral histories of people who have shaped Southern tradition and culture. Bachus lives near Hernando, Mississippi, where she has spent most of her 70 years making quilts. She put her eight children through school by working as a seamstress and quilter. She decided to make quilts to record her family history when she got lonesome one year after her family returned to their own homes after Thanksgiving. She put each of her children into that first quilt (made during the 1970s), using the materials of the day (for example, old blue jeans were used for their pants) and copying the fashion styles as well (for example, the children had Afro hairdos and wore bell-bottom pants).

Luzia Combs, brought from the Guinea Coast to the United States during the beginning of the Civil War, was one of the first known black quilters. Combs raised her own sheep, sheared them, carded the fleece, spun the wool, then dyed and wove it to make her own fabric. With this homespun material, Combs made quilts, using a brightly colored striped pattern in an African color scheme (bright red-orange, lavender, blue, and light orange).

Harriet Powers, a slave, made some of the finest black American quilts known to exist. Her quilts are now in collections in the Smithsonian Institution and the Museum of Fine Arts in Boston. Her "Bible Quilt" (ca. 1895, owned by the Smithsonian) is 68 by 105 inches and consists of fifteen squares in which she tells the story of the Bible from Adam and Eve to the Crucifixion of Jesus. Power's 1898 explanation of a quilt now owned by the Museum of Fine Arts reveals religious and astronomical symbols that are meant to be warnings to the sinful.

It is thought that her quilting style was a derivative of textiles made in Dahomey, Africa, where brightly colored fabrics were appliquéd on a dark background. The appliqué work in Power's Bible quilts has also been compared with Fon appliquéd textiles.

Powers was born a slave in Georgia in 1837 and died near Athens, Georgia, in 1911. She exhibited her first Bible quilt in 1886 at the Cotton Fair in Athens. She refused to sell the quilt to University of Maryland scholar Gladys Marie Fry at any price, but when she was in need of money four years later, Powers contacted Fry and sold it to her. Through following visits and conversations with Powers, Fry discovered the meaning behind each detailed square of the quilt and also realized that Powers had put herself, her beliefs, and her emotions into her quilt designs, which she believed to be the "darling offspring" of her brain.

Other quilt artists are discussed in a brochure published by the Study of Southern Culture, University of Mississippi. The authors, Maude Southwell Wahlman of the university and Ella King Torrey, give general information about black quilts and biographies of specific quilters.

SAMPLERS AND NEEDLEWORK

Embroidered pieces of linen were produced in the New World since its early European colonization. Early samplers are rare because the materials used were fragile and the passage of time has taken its toll.

The embroidered designs on the samplers of the seventeenth and eighteenth centuries were meant to teach young girls a wide range of stitches as well as the letters of the alphabet and the numerals. Most samplers were dated and signed once completed and were often worked on for a long period of time. Samplers reached their height of popularity between 1830 and 1870.

Although it is difficult to determine whether any particular signature on a sampler belongs to a black American, there are often distinguishing earmarks in the sampler itself. The most obvious clue is black figures worked into the overall design, a practice that was common in samplers made shortly after the Emancipation Proclamation of

1862. However, if a sampler is signed but has no distinguishing black earmarks, the best way to validate it is by researching the family name. Don't be surprised if your research turns up an old white Southern family—remember that slaves often took on their master's surname.

If you are unsure about the sampler's date, measure the piece. Early samplers were narrow, usually less than 8 inches wide; wider ones did not appear until the looms on which cloth was made got wider. The samplers made in the late eighteenth and early nineteenth centuries were wider than they were high. The thread is also a giveaway to the age of the piece: eighteenth-century samplers used wool thread; silk thread was used thereafter. Most black samplers were made using cross stitch, and the stitching is often long, uneven, and crude.

Do not expect to find black samplers made before 1800. They are extremely rare. The Connecticut Historical Society in Hartford holds a piece of needlework done by Prudence Punderson (1758–1784) titled *The First, Second and Last Scene of Mortality.* The scene shows a cradle attended by a young black girl. A woman is shown in the center of the piece and a small coffin is to the left.

Needlepoint pieces made just after the Civil War often include a saying that celebrates freedom, for example, "We's Free." Many of these pieces can be found in a variety of conditions, sizes, and craftsmanship. Note that some of these items may be modern reproductions. Expect to find a wide range of prices.

SEWING ITEMS

A little-known area of black memorabilia, sewing items have just recently been coming to the forefront as a viable collectible. Now, more than ever before, dealers are approached at antiques shows by buyers looking for sewing items, but I have yet to be approached by someone looking for sewing items that could also be considered black Americana. Perhaps now is the time to start collecting these objects. If you do not have too much display space and would like to collect small black collectibles that are still reasonably priced, sewing items may be for you.

Tape measures depicting black figures are available: they were made in metal, plastic, ivory, and celluloid. The celluloid ones are easiest to damage so you may come on some examples that won't be in the best condition. Pin cushions are also available in many shapes, like mammies, children, and figures with watermelons. Emeries are more difficult to find, yet they have been made in black faces. Neat little sewing caddies can be purchased to hold other black sewing items, such as pincushions or "Frozen Charlottes." (See also Estelle Zalkin's books on sewing collectibles for further information.)

Tourist Trade Items

For many years, items from historic sites or large cities have been stamped with the name of the place and sold as mementos of the visit. Many southern business establishments and towns have had tourist items made. Dinner bells, dolls, and "kitchen" souvenirs were sold to vacationers or travelers.

One thing that seems to hold true for souvenir articles—no matter what they are or where they're from—is that they were cheaply made. Still, the category is an interesting and varied one.

PRICES FOR MISCELLANEOUS EVERYDAY ARTIFACTS

Ashtray, child on potty, metal; very good condition, **$45–60.**

Ashtray/card holder, brass, Johnny Griffin; very good condition, **$275–325.**

Bell hook, celluloid, Johnson Hat Company, man in top hat; very good condition, **$15–25.**

Bookends, mahogany, African woman's face with neck piece; excellent condition, **$20–25 for the pair.**

Brush, shaving, wood, mammy, figural handle; very good condition, **$18–25.**

Card holder

Bellhop, full figure, floor standing; 32″; very good condition, **$245–280.**

Boy, standing, in toga; very good condition, **$1,550–1,700.**

Cigarette lighter, chrome, Ronson, woman bartender with exaggerated lips mixing a drink, late 1920s; very good condition, **$500–650.**

Clock

Alarm

"Blackface" reproduction, child on knees with right hand up; very good condition, **$275–325.**

"Little Black Sambo," electric, white clock with picture of Sambo in middle, 1950s; excellent condition, **$175–200.**

Animated

Man, metal and wood, Lux Mfg. USA, eyes move with second-hand movement, painted black, red, white, green, and brown, rare, 8″ × 4″; near mint condition, **$500–650.**

Andirons, black butlers, iron, mid-1800s; excellent condition, **$1,500–2,000 for the pair.** Photo by Donald Vogt.

Figure, iron, drunk man with dog, 1950s; excellent condition, $175–210. Courtesy of Bold Soul for the Black Memorabilia Museum, photo by Bold Soul.

"Sambo," cast iron, winking eyes, ca. 1860; excellent condition, **$1,500–1,700.**

Banjo player, painted metal; 16″; very good condition, **$825–900.**

Mammy, Red Wing; very good condition, **$240–260.**

Commemorative collectibles, 1-oz. silver, art bar series, 1974

Sammy Davis Jr., obverse: "Peace / & Love" / (bust of Davis, frontal) / (signature of Sammy Davis Jr.), one of four in Super Star Signature Series, two thousand minted; excellent condition, **$35–40.**

New Orleans jazz band, obverse: (New Orleans Jazz Trio), one of 50 in the "America the Beautiful" series; excellent condition, **$35–40.**

Golliwog pinback; very good condition, **$15–20.**

Golliwogs, variety of clothing types and figures; 2″ tall; excellent condition, **$38–45 each.**

Humidor

Boy standing by a sugar barrel with a cat on top, bronze; excellent condition, **$1,100–1,500.**

Boy with pipe in mouth; very good condition, **$100–130.**

Woman, gold earrings, headdress; very good condition, **$100–130.**

Jewelry

Bracelet

African-looking charms, black metal on woven bracelet, 1970s; excellent condition, **$65–85.**

Bakelite charms on woven bracelet, 1930s; excellent condition, **$95–110.**

Egyptian-looking faces on Bakelite background, 1930s; excellent condition, **$100–125.**

Chatelaine, two pins joined by chain, one is woman with headdress (atomizer), other is

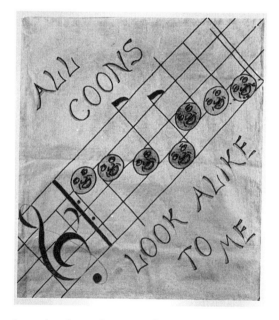

Laundry bag, homemade, with extremely derogatory saying; good condition, $45–55. Courtesy of Rose Fontanella; photo by Donald Vogt.

Inkwell, man sitting between inkwells, American, early 1800s; excellent condition, **$1,500–2,000.** Courtesy of the Lewis and Blalock Collection; photo by Bob Reno.

rhinestones and black "pearls," 1950s; excellent condition, **$350–375.**

Cuff links

African faces, jet colored with gold accents, 1950s; excellent condition, **$95–115 for the pair.**

Boy's face and alligator, sterling silver, 1960s; excellent condition, **$100–125 for the pair.**

Earrings

Blackamoor faces, white metal, screw-on, 1960s–1970s; excellent condition, **$85–100 for the pair.**

Blackamoor faces with orange and purple, metal, clip-on, 1950s; excellent condition, **$85–100 for the pair.**

Egyptian faces, early plastic, clip-on, 1940s–1950s; excellent condition, **$60–75 for the pair.**

Necklace, Bakelite on black strand, African man playing the drum, 1930s; excellent condition, **$60–75.**

Necklace/locket, holds perfume, woman's face, 1950s; excellent condition, **$100–115.**

Pin

African face with turban, rhinestones and green stones that look like emeralds, 1920s–1930s; excellent condition, **$250–275.**

African native, full figure in dancing position holding feather, 1920s–1930s; about 3″ long; excellent condition, **$165–200.**

Blackamoor face with turban, made by Har, well-known jewelry maker, 1950s; excellent condition, **$350–400.**

Golliwog, enamel painted over gold-toned metal, boy in red pants and blue jacket holds sword, 1½″ tall; excellent condition, **$45–60.**

Man's face with red polka-dotted turban, wears an earring, looks like a pirate, 1940s; excellent condition, **$110–125.**

Porter-style figure, Bakelite, red and black, legs move, 1930s–1940s; excellent condition, **$150–175.**

"Walk with Truth," pewter, signed and created by Inge Hardison, sculptor, made to resemble Sojourner Truth; (the original 24″ sculpture was presented to Nelson Mandela by Governor Cuomo in New York City on June 20, 1990); new, **$35–75.**

Pin clip, grotesque black face with red trim, 1940s; excellent condition, **$65–85.**

Ring

African face, gold and ebony, possibly made in Italy, 1950s–1960s; excellent condition, **$225–250.**

Head of African woman with earrings in unusual V-shaped setting, solid gold, 1970s; excellent condition, **$300–350.**

Set

African drums and native heads, Bakelite, bracelet, necklace and earrings, 1930s; excellent condition, **$325–350 for the set.**

African native faces, copper and ceramic, jade color, pin and earrings, 1940s; excellent condition, **$185–200 for the set.**

African native faces with large earrings, white metal and Bakelite, bracelet, necklace and earrings, 1940s; excellent condition, **$325–350 for the set.**

Blackamoor figure, sterling silver, pin and clip-on earrings, 1930s; excellent condition, **$450–600 for the set.**

Jewelry box, wood, boy shaking dice, 6″ × 3″; very good condition, **$60–80.**

Johnny Griffin collectibles, souvenir spoon, sterling silver, made by Charles W. Crankshaw, watermelon painted inside spoon, boy's face on handle, "Atlanta" on back of spoon; very good condition, **$50–70.**

Lamp, African natives, one man, one woman, both have bowls in laps, 1950s; **$85 for the pair.**

Lawn figure, wood, girl; very good condition, **$95–120.**

Lawn sprinkler, boy, attaches to hose; very good condition, **$100–145.**

Letter opener, boy holding alligator, red, white, black, and brown, pencil head pulls out, Germany, 1800s; 7″ × 1½″; near mint condition, **$250–350.**

Match holder and ashtray, brass, porter carrying bags; very good condition, **$65–80.**

Jewelry, pin, ceramic face, basketweave hat, 1930s–1940s; excellent condition, **$125–150.** Courtesy of Rose Fontanella; photo by Donald Vogt.

Jewelry, pin, wood, African woman wearing earring, exaggerated features, 1930s–1940s; excellent condition, **$125–150.** Courtesy of Rose Fontanella; photo by Bob Reno.

Figurine, plaster, woman (originally carried a flag), base is numbered on bottom front, about 9″ tall; good condition, **$125–175.** Courtesy of Rose Fontanella; photo by Donald Vogt.

Party favor, cardboard and paper, shows people partying, 1950s; very good condition, **$13–18.**

Quilt

African pictorial, appliqued with dolls, lizards, people, other animals in blocks, each block is different, all hand stitched, 1930s–1940s, king size; near mint condition, **$700–1,000.**

Made by Mrs. Thrashy from Hogansville, Georgia, summer quilt, circle and rectangle design, calicos, stripes and flowered materials, backed with flour sacks, 1920–1930; excellent condition, **$300–500.**

Quilting book, *Southern Quilts: A New View,* by Bets Ramsey and Gail Andrews Trechsel (EPM Publications, McLean, Virginia), paperback, traces history of Southern quiltmaking and the meaning it has had for quiltmakers, describes the impact of the crafts movement in America and resulting respect given handmade objects, 1991; new, **$24.95.**

Sewing collectibles

Buttons, depict girl (match The Topsy Club Cool fan listed on p. 92); 1¼″ diameter; new, **$0.83 each.**

Embroidery, cakewalking couples, inscribed "leave your razors at de door," multicolored, framed, 1890s, rare; 22″ × 18″; near mint condition, **$250–350.**

Planter, plywood with milk glass insert, two men holding box, red shirts, blue pants, label taped on bottom reads "Clayton C. Wagner," 1940s–1950s; 8½″ long × 3½″ tall; excellent condition, **$50–75.** Courtesy of American Eye; photo by Bob Reno.

Quilt, homespun fabrics, filled with cotton and seedpods, made by Mrs. Jernigan Saunders, Brundidge, Alabama, square patch, backed with navy plaid homespun, 1860–1880; about double size; excellent condition, **$400–600.** Courtesy of American Eye; photo by Bob Reno.

Emery bag, mammy-faced emery bags are usually made of silk or rayon with painted or embroidered features; very good condition, **$25–50 each** (slightly higher with original box or card).

Needlepoint

Abolitionist pot holder, child playing ball in needlepoint, inscribed "Any holder but a slaveholder," on canvas, velvet ribbon binding, mid-1800s, 7½″ × 7¾″; excellent condition, **$350–400.**

Male and female dancing figures, "We's Free," excellent condition, **$775–1,000.**

Pin holders (two), found fabric on tin food cans, one has hand-stitched eyes, nose and mouth, other has painted facial features, made by Marie Rogers of Washington, D.C., 1992; excellent condition, **$10–15 each.**

Pincushion

Maid, lace apron, rooted hair; 7″; very good condition, **$15–25.**

Mammy; very good condition, **$22–40.**

Sampler, cross stitched, woman and man outside house, ca. 1890; 7½" × 8½"; excellent condition, **$895–1,000.**

Sewing caddy, Aunt Jemima, pincushion on lap; very good condition, **$32–50.**

Sewing kits, usually cut out of felt in the shape of a full-figured mammy or young girl, embroidered, pockets for thimbles, opens to hold needles and pins; very good condition, **$25–45 each.**

Tape measure, celluloid, case depicts man; very good condition, **$100–140.**

Sign, "Colored and White Rest Rooms," white glass, black lettering, signed "B & J Signs," 1929; excellent condition, **$125–135.**

Smoking stand

Bellhop, carved mahogany, three-dimensional, painted brown, black, blue and white, rare; 39" × 14"; near mint condition, **$300–400.**

Butler, wood; appears to be new, **$78–85.**

Porter carries baggage which is brass cigar holder and match holder, wood and brass, painted white, black, brown, and red; 9" × 4"; excellent condition, **$175–250.**

Thermometer, cork, boy peeking out from side, 1940s; 5" tall; good condition (thermometer is broken), **$15–35.**

Tie rack, Flemish Art Co., New York, two boys, ties in hands, "I rather guess we use some sense, We hang our neckties on dis fence!"; very good condition, **$65–80.**

Tip tray, boy eating watermelon in red, green, white, brown, and yellow, scalloped edges, very detailed, 1800s, 3¼" × 2¼"; excellent condition, **$175–250.**

Toothpick holder, metal, two boys eating watermelon; very good condition, **$35–50.**

Tourist trade

Dinner bell, mammy

Wood head, painted, cotton dress goes over bell, Charleston, South Carolina, 3½" high; mint condition, **$12–18.**

Wood, painted, "from Olney Inn," souvenir; very good condition, **$22–28.**

Salt and pepper shakers, mammy and chef, green with red trim, marked "Mount Vernon, VA"; 5" tall; excellent condition, **$50–65.**

Toothpick holder, silver plate, New Orleans Centennial Exposition, December 1884; excellent condition, **$75–95.**

Tourist trade, grocery list, wood, reads "We Needs ?," marked "Groton, Mass.," mammy wears red turban and red-and-black polka-dotted dress, 1940s–1950s, 11" × 7"; excellent condition, $28–40. Courtesy of the Dawn and Bob Reno Collection; photo by Bob Reno.

PART THREE

Historical Artifacts

CHAPTER TWELVE

Militaria and Related Collectibles

Black militaria hasn't really been dealt with in other books about collecting black items. Many items in this area are scarce and, as such, found only in museums or private collections. If you keep your definition of military collectibles broad, however, you'll find much worth collecting.

Military and war collectibles run the gamut from Civil War discharge papers to photographs of some of the great black soldiers. Broadsides printed during the Revolutionary and Civil wars asked for runaway slaves to be captured and brought back to their masters—some of those slaves had run away to join the army. Daguerreotypes of black soldiers are highly valued by collectors (see also Chapter 3). Information about the first black troops was printed in early newspapers (see also Chapter 8), but photographs of the whole troop are rare. Books like *Army Life in a Black Regiment* by Thomas Wentworth Higginson (originally written in 1870 and reprinted in 1983 as part of the Collector's Library of the Civil War) will give you in-depth information about the day-to-day trials the black soldier endured. Posters made during World War I are the most attractive of any American war-time posters. Artists such as Will Bradley, Maxfield Parrish, Charles Dana Gibson, and Howard Chandler Christy are among some of the American illustrators responsible for the marvelous artwork depicting black fighting men on posters between 1880 and 1920.

Although the information is not strictly military or war related, I have included brief discussions of Blacks who rode as cowboys and those who considered themselves American Indians. Both groups played significant roles in the establishment of the United States as a nation, and collectibles relating to these lesser-known aspects of black history are in demand.

One might keep in mind that military collectibles include all the paper documents drawn up on behalf of the armed forces, the clothing the men and women in the armed forces wore, the weapons they carried, the badges and medals they accumulated, and photographs and artwork of them in their military uniforms.

Your imagination and knowledge of black militaria will steer you to the areas easiest to collect. From there, you must rely on dealers and collectors' associations to find the items you want to complete your collection.

A Short History of African-Americans in the Military

In 1715, the British used black soldiers against the Natchez Indians in the Yemasee War, because the Indians had killed white settlers in a previous attack, yet spared the African-Americans. Black soldiers who had fought for South Carolina were publicly thanked by that state in 1747.

Though there were black soldiers in the Revolutionary War, President George Washington fought to get them removed from military duty by issuing an order on November 12, 1773, which instructed recruiters not to enlist Blacks. The British army, however, welcomed both freed Blacks and slaves, which put the American army in an awkward position. Therefore, the army decided to pay slaveowners who provided slaves to fight in any future wars.

Approximately five thousand African-American soldiers fought in the Revolutionary War, one-sixth of the total amount of Americans fighting against England. Most were northerners and some black troops existed. Because some slaves resented not being given the right to die for their freedom, a few chose to organize their own armies or regiments (e.g., Denmark Vesey, Nat Turner, and Gabriel Prosser).

The Naturalization Act, passed by Congress in 1790, meant to extend citizenship to all free white persons. However, when, in 1794 and 1795, amendments to this act were being considered, Samuel Dexter of Massachusetts suggested that "aliens be required to renounce possession of slaves forever before being naturalized" (see *Military Necessity and Civil Rights Policy*, p. 21). During the debate that followed, James Madison and William Giles of Virginia said that their state wanted to renounce slavery as soon as possible, but that it might be premature to discuss it in public. Twenty-eight voted in favor of Dexter's resolution (almost all northerners), which was defeated by the sixty-three votes against it.

Due to this resolution, black males were still not accepted into the military, and when Congress began organizing the militia in 1792, only white males between the ages of eighteen and forty-five could enlist. Though Congress continued to control the militia, the navy used African-Americans aboard ship (in the lowliest positions) whenever it felt the necessity. It was reported that some black sailors served courageously during the Naval War with France (1798–1800) and the War of 1812.

In 1804, free Blacks presented a petition to William C. Claiborne, the first governor of the Louisiana Territory, proposing that their services be accepted by the American government. Claiborne, having heard from Henry Dearborn, the secretary of war, that Claiborne might have the corps serve in a diminished fashion, presented them with a standard on January 21, 1804. The act enraged whites and a general militia law was passed in 1805 which, once again, restricted service to all "able-bodied white male citizens ages sixteen to fifty."

In 1811, Claiborne's black militia companies helped to suppress a slave revolt and won the respect of some of his constituents. Though the government never changed the militia law to permit the use of black soldiers during the War of 1812, as noted, some Blacks did serve in that skirmish. Various acts put into effect during the period 1794–1814 all stated that able-bodied men were to be accepted into the national army—though none of these acts mentioned color.

Between the War of 1812 and the Civil War, free men of color fought in New Orleans against the British (430 of them, as a matter of fact) and won praise from everyone concerned for their loyalty, courage, and perseverance. Free men of color who were veterans were asked to participate in commemorative ceremonies held in 1851 and were present when a statue of Andrew Jackson was unveiled in 1856. Certain proponents of bringing Blacks into the military voiced their opinions and brought to light the loyalty freed Blacks showed their country.

In 1853, Henry Highland Garnet proposed that free Blacks must be citizens to be included in the militia. His proposal was adopted, and Blacks in Massachusetts petitioned for a law that would permit them to enlist in the regular militia or to create their own black militia. They were unsuccessful. The debate continued, and raised it head again in 1860 when Blacks petitioned the legislature—this time to remove the word *white* from the state militia law. The bill lost, by a close call; the vote was seventy to eighty-six in the House.

When the Civil War began, this incongruity became more evident when northern blacks were denied the right to fight in what was, essentially, *their* war, their battle for freedom. Black men begged to be allowed to enlist, but were refused, told that this was "a white man's war, fought to preserve the Union." Slaves fled to the north to join the Union Army and to fight for their freedom. The Union Army, not knowing what to do with all their new black recruits, declared them "chattel of war," and in some cases, slaves were even returned to their masters. By late 1862, the Militia Act was passed and President Abraham Lincoln consented to enlist Blacks. As a result, more than two hundred thousand black soldiers fought in the Union Army and Navy and played a critical part in winning the war. The 54th Massachusetts Regiment (recently portrayed in the movie *Glory*) is particularly remembered for its valiant fight to control a fort on the coast of the Carolinas.

Newspaper illustration, *Harper's Weekly,* New York, "Negroes Driven South by the Rebel Officers," two-page center spread, full and complete issue, Saturday, November 8, 1862; excellent condition; $25–50. Courtesy of Timothy Hughes, Rare and Early Newspapers; photo by Bob Reno.

After the Emancipation Proclamation was passed in 1863, the War Department initiated the Bureau of Colored Troops. Blacks were still paid less than white soldiers until the all-black 54th Regiment served for a year without pay rather than accept the lower wage. By the end of the war, twenty-two black military personnel received the Congressional Medal of Honor; 156,000 black troops had fought with the Union Army; and 39,000 had served in the Union Navy.

Four troops were formed in 1866 when Congress authorized the organization of black regiments: the 9th and 10th Cavalry and the 24th and 25th Infantry, and all were made up of black soldiers. These men were sent out west, making up 20 percent of the cavalry stationed there; they became scouts, fought American Indians on their own territory, and protected the newly formed territories of the west. Black soldiers patrolled the area

from the Mississippi to the Rockies and from the Canadian border to the Rio Grande—often crossing the Mexican border to "get their man." Though some white officers refused to serve with black men, others did without a problem. In fact, not many people know the reason General John J. Pershing was nicknamed "Black Jack": He got the nickname after he led the 10th Cavalry in Nebraska, at San Juan Hill, and in Mexico.

The Buffalo Soldiers, dubbed that by the Native Americans they fought, were peacetime volunteers stationed in Texas and the Indian Territory in the west in 1871. The troops were all black regular soldiers. They got their name because of the color of their skin and their toughness on the battlefield. Henry O. Flipper, the first black officer, was a graduate of West Point (the first black graduate) and was assigned to the 10th Cavalry in 1877. A limited-edition print by

"MUSTERED OUT" COLORED VOLUNTEERS AT LITTLE ROCK, ARKANSAS.—[SEE PAGE 318.]

Newspaper illustration, *Harper's Weekly*, New York, "Mustered Out," depicts "colored volunteers at Little Rock, Arkansas," full and complete issue, Saturday, May 19, 1866; excellent condition, $25–50. Courtesy of Timothy Hughes, Rare and Early Newspapers; photo by Bob Reno.

Kwasi Asante depicts Flipper in battle. The Heritage Foundation, Inc., is the company responsible for the print, and they are leading the plan to get a stamp made to honor Lieutenant Flipper.

Though the soldiers fought fairly, the people they protected often did not appreciate that fact. One such citizen murdered a black soldier and then the two men who came to arrest him for his crime—yet a jury of his peers declared the white murderer not guilty. It should also be noted that even though the assignments given to black soldiers were the most dangerous and challenging, their rate of desertion and number of court-martials were far fewer than that experienced by the all-white troops.

The 9th Regiment, organized in 1866 in New Orleans and stationed in Texas near San Antonio, was under the command of Colonel Edward Hatch. Hatch eventually became a general and commanded certain troops of the regiment at Fork Stockton. The regiment's main objective was to help open and protect the mail route from San Antonio to El Paso. In 1875, the regiment transferred into New Mexico and for the next five years it was involved in some important affairs (mainly against American Indians). During the 1890s, when the Indians' Ghost Dance activities were at their peak, the 9th Regiment rode more than one hundred miles to relieve the 7th Cavalry. Artist Frederic Remington immortalized the event in his drawing *Captain Dodge's Colored Troops to the Rescue.*

The 10th Regiment of the cavalry consisted of two field officers, one company officer, and sixty-four unassigned recruits by the end of 1866. The founder of the unit, Colonel Benjamin Grierson, was a former music teacher, and under his command the 10th Regiment became one of the most intrepid and hardest-fighting military units (it also had a great band!). It established headquarters at Fort Riley, Kansas from August

1867 to April 1868. The men's job was to protect the Union Pacific Railroad and any exposed settlements. In 1869, the headquarters was moved to Camp Wichita in Indian Territory, and the regiment's orders were to protect the country from Indians as well as to keep the Native Americans within their reservations. The unit was attacked several times by Kiowa and Naconee Indians and eventually moved to Fort Gibson in 1872. Troops split from the regiment during 1874 and 1875 to fight against the Kiowas and Comanches. Portions of this regiment passed over and back across the Mexican border during 1876 to 1880, until regimental headquarters were once again moved, this time to Fort Davis where it remained until 1885. This regiment was largely responsible for Geronimo's capture and the surrender of his band of renegades. General Pershing led the troop for more than a decade, and the 10th Regiment was the subject of many drawings by Frederic Remington.

The 24th Regiment of the infantry could not claim any honors and had only a short history, due to the lack of government consolidation. Organized in 1869, the 24th consisted of the 38th and 41st Regiments. Ronald S. Mackenzie headed the regiment as colonel. It was stationed in Texas from 1869 to 1880, but did not see much action. In the fall of 1880, the regiment moved to Indian Territory; in 1888, it moved to the Department of Arizona; and by 1892, the companies had been distributed to different posts.

The 39th and 40th Regiments were combined to create the 25th Regiment in 1869. The regiment had a full complement of officers and 1,045 men. By the end of its first year, 532 men had been discharged because their service time was up, which left about 500 men in the regiment. The regiment moved to western Texas, establishing its headquarters at Fort Davis in 1872. It built and repaired military posts, telegraph lines, and roads, and skirmished with and scouted for American Indians. The 25th Regiment moved from fort to fort throughout the Dakotas, Minnesota, and Montana from 1880 to 1888. In 1888, headquarters and four companies were in Fort Missoula; the other four companies made their bases at Fort Shaw and Fort Custer. By 1890, the work of the 25th was pretty much done.

Eleven black soldiers won the Medal of Honor during the final frontier days. They included Sergeant Emanuel Stance, Sergeant George Jordan, and Sergeant Moses Williams, all from the 9th Cavalry.

In 1898, during the Spanish-American War, the all-black 9th and 10th Cavalries were the first to lead the charge of the Rough Riders up San Juan Hill. Teddy Roosevelt had high praise for the soldiers he called "smoked Yankees" as did the white soldiers who fought with them; however, two years later, Roosevelt was quoted as stating that the black soldiers were "of course, peculiarly dependent on their white officers." A newsreel, filmed by Lincoln Motion Picture Company in 1918, featured the 10th Cavalry of Fort Huachuca, Arizona. This unit also fought during the Mexican War, and in 1916, Troops K and C of that unit were nearly wiped out during a battle called the Carrizal Incident.

During the period from 1898 to 1902, black soldiers began to regularly write editors of African-American newspapers, and those editors published the men's letters on a regular basis. Some of the letters are reprinted in *Smoked Yankees and the Struggle for Empire: Letters from Negro Soldiers, 1898–1902.* Their letters describe Cuba, the suffering the soldiers experienced, the battles they valiantly fought, their despair that although they had fought for their country prejudice toward them had increased, the horrendous conditions they encountered in Puerto Rico, their wounds (both physical and mental), and the incongruities they suffered as a result of the color of their skin. Yet in all the letters printed in that volume, one thing is common: the pride these soldiers had in being able to fight for their country.

During World War I, the 369th Infantry was an all-black unit that produced Sergeant Henry Johnson and Needham Roberts, both awarded the French *croix de guerre* for aborting a surprise German attack. However, Blacks were not allowed to join the marines and served in the navy only in the lowest capacities. Prejudice and discrimination ran high, and black soldiers found they were treated better in Europe than in their home country. Although some black soldiers (e.g., Johnson and Roberts) performed feats of heroism during World War I, they came home to great racial tension and were sometimes even hanged in their uniforms.

One ironic fact is that the gas mask, one of the tools used by Americans during World War I, was invented by a black scientist from Cleveland, Ohio, named Garrett A. Morgan. I'm sure that when he invented it he had no idea it would end up being used against his countrymen.

During World War II, approximately half a million black soldiers, sailors, and marines served in battle. Though they were still discriminated against, Blacks now served in every branch of the service. Serious race riots resulted from the treatment African-Americans got, both in the service and at home. One in particular took place in 1943 in Detroit. By the time the riot was over, twenty-nine Blacks and nine Whites were dead, plus almost a million dollars' worth of property had been demolished. The event spurred President Harry Truman to sign an executive order in 1948 that demanded that all members of the armed services receive "equal treatment and opportunity."

The Negro Soldier, a movie produced in 1944, documented the actions of black military up until that time, including black Minutemen who participated in the battles at Lexington and Concord, black sailors who fought with Admiral Perry at Lake Erie, the Massachusetts 54th Regiment of the Civil War, the 9th and 10th Cavalries, the 34th Infantry at San Juan Hill, and the actions of black troops throughout World War II. In 1945, another movie documentary called *The Negro Sailor* was produced by the U.S. Navy Department and follows the story of Bill Johnson, a black sailor, from the time he gets drafted to his duty aboard a destroyer, which is manned largely by black sailors.

The next war in which black military people fought was the Korean War, and reports stated that there was some reduction in inequalities. Black soldiers made up 385 units in military service and more than 200,000 served in those units by 1951. However, by the end of the Korean War (1953), only 88 of those units remained in the army. As much as Harry Truman wanted the inequalities to lessen, they did not, and by the time soldiers fought in Vietnam, discrimination and prejudice had heightened. Only 15 percent of the total number of military people in Vietnam were African-American (approximately 22,000), but in 1966, 22.5 percent of troops killed in action were black. That statistic proves that most Blacks who fought in that war fought on the front lines, in the combat zones.

It must come as no surprise that black soldiers were concerned about who was the true enemy: their white counterparts or the North Vietnamese. In one account of the Vietnam War, David Parks (the son of the well-known photographer, Gordon Parks) voiced his confusion about dealing with his white roommate, a young man from Mississippi "as quiet as a tombstone" and the white officers who treated him so shabbily that he began to feel ashamed. He stated in his diary that if you "show any sign of intelligence ... you've had it."

During the Vietnam War, Martin Luther King Jr. was murdered, and black soldiers reacted with violence and passion to the devastating event. Stories of fiery crosses being lit in Da Nang and Ranh Bay aired on the evening news. There was one thing black soldiers shared with their white counterparts in the Vietnam War: None of them were welcomed home as heroes, even though quite a few of the African-American soldiers *had* become heroes overseas, serving as tunnel rats or participating in full-blown combat.

Since that time, there has actually been an increase in the number of African-Americans joining the armed services, and General Colin Powell presents living proof that some African-Americans have been able to advance to even the highest positions.

African-American Cowboys

After the emancipation, the institution of sharecropping and the fact that blacks were still not able to advance themselves economically caused a black migration to the north and west. Black cowboys were not a rarity. They drove cattle, scouted, and mined for gold right next to their white counterparts. Blacks founded towns in Oklahoma, such as Boley, Langston, and Summit.

After the Civil War was over, five thousand of the cowboys who helped drive cattle up the Chisholm trail were black. They used skills learned in slavery—or freedom—to help carve the West. Some were law-abiding men; others were not. Whatever the case, the men who rode the trail found less discrimination there than in "civilized" towns. Black cowboys broke the toughest stallions, rode the roughest trails, and seldom earned top jobs—ranch owner, foreman, trail boss—on the ranch, which were reserved for whites.

Nat Love ("Deadwood Dick"), born a slave in 1854, found opportunity in the wild west. At fifteen, he left his family and headed for Kansas. He lived a life a lot of boys dream about and few achieve. Love knew the West,

Cowboy poster showing Bill Pickett, "The Bull Dogger," full color, about 24" × 20", framed and matted; excellent condition, **$1,000–1,200.** Courtesy of Leonard Davis collection; photo by Bob Reno.

the emptiness of a prairie night, the excitement of a cattle drive, the life of an Indian (he was adopted by a tribe), and the friendship of such western luminaries as Bat Masterson. Love wrote his autobiography in 1907, telling of rodeos and shooting contests, long trail drives, and the love of a Spanish maiden. All cowboys, like Love (nicknamed Deadwood Dick after becoming the champion roper at Deadwood City in Dakota Territory), saw their way of life go under in front of the "iron horse" (the railroad).

Cherokee Bill, born in Fort Concho, Texas, was the son of a 10th Cavalry soldier. His mother brought him up to stand up for his rights. Unfortunately, Bill's parents broke up, and when his mother remarried, Bill, at the age of twelve, was pushed out of his new home. He became a scout, first with the Cherokee Nation and later with the Creek and Seminole Indians. Somewhere along the line he went bad and joined an outlaw gang. He became a wanted criminal, a deadeye shot with a gun, and was sentenced to die before his twentieth birthday.

Ben Hodges, a resident of Dodge City, was a card player who supported himself through his gambling winnings. His father was black and his mother Mexican; but Hodges claimed his ancestry to be Spanish. He used this lie to claim land in Texas and his fast tongue convinced others to join him. Before anyone knew what had happened, Ben swindled a bank president and talked the railroads into believing he was important enough to receive a free pass. His glib manner got him out of many tight situations—including jail (he was charged with stealing a herd of cattle).

Hodges continued to live this way until he asked the governor to make him a livestock inspector. The men he had cheated and swindled demanded the governor say no. Thus Hodges did not become a law man, but continued to live in Dodge City until he died; he is buried in the local graveyard.

Another black westerner, Isom Dart, lived during the latter 1800s, dying in 1900 at the age of fifty-one after being shot in the back. Born an Arkansas slave in 1849, Dart foraged for Confederate officers in the Civil War years, then worked in the Southwest as a rodeo clown. He finally settled in Colorado after a period of rustling cattle. People who knew him reported his unequaled ability to handle a horse as well as his loyalty toward friends. Even when Dart was arrested in Wyoming for rustling cattle, he could not bring himself to leave the deputy hurt when their buckboard ran off the road. Instead, Dart stayed with the deputy and gave him first aid. Then he took the deputy to the hospital before turning himself in at the town jail.

By 1890, half a million black people had settled Texas and Oklahoma alone. Violence was not uncommon in that wild area of the

United States. Black town marshals such as Dick Shafer (as well as white ones) were shot and killed. Cowboys—black and white—became heroes (and villains).

Britton Johnson, a black cowboy who became a legend, was considered a crack shot. In 1864, his wife and baby son were carried off by Comanche and Kiowa raiders. Johnson tried to recapture his family, but twenty-five warriors attacked and killed him and three fellow cowboys.

African-Americans Considered to Be American Indians

One of the first black men in the West had actually gone there as a slave of Lewis and Clark, the explorers. York was invaluable to the expedition, helping the other members of the group with his hunting, fishing, and swimming skills. After the journey, Clark freed York, and he went back West—eventually becoming the chief of an Indian tribe.

Other African-Americans worked with Native Americans as interpreters (e.g., Abraham, who interpreted for the Seminoles when they negotiated with the U.S. govern-ment in 1825), and some simply decided (after having been accepted) to become members of an American Indian group because life was safer there. Quite a few slaves integrated with the Seminole tribe in Florida (Ben Bruno, for example, ended up being a leader in the tribe) and then fol-lowed along when the tribe was forced to travel to Oklahoma. This period, called the Seminole Wars, is described in history books as a serious Indian war, but others have called it a "Negro insurrection." Florida governor William Duval warned Seminoles in 1826 against believing "what the Negroes say."

Jim Beckwourth, as skilled in "Wild West" tools and trades as Kit Carson, lived with and was adopted by the Crow Indians. He became a leader of the tribe after marry-ing the chief's daughter and leading the Crow in raids against their enemies, the Blackfeet. He was also responsible for discovering a pass through the Sierra Nevadas and led the first settlers through; the pass became known as Beckwourth Pass.

The Choctaw tribe included more than five hundred Blacks, according to a survey done in 1831 by the U.S. Army; and the Pamunky Indian tribe of Virginia was made up almost solely of Blacks.

PRICES FOR MILITARIA AND RELATED COLLECTIBLES

Pre–Civil War

Pamphlet, *Services of Colored Americans in the Wars of 1776 and 1812,* by William C. Nell, state-by-state accountings of black participation, "Published in Efforts to Half The Prejudice Against the Colored Race," original wraps, forty pages, Boston, 1852; excellent condition, **$18–28.**

Civil War

Document

    Confederate estate personal property document valuing one slave at $1,200 and listing all the household goods and livestock, possibly an Alabama document, dated 1862; very good condition, **$23–35.**

    Memorial discharge, James H. Bryan, 4th Regiment, U.S. Colored Troops, Infantry Volunteers, dated May 1865; very good condition, **$385–500.**

    Mustering out roll, 13th Regiment U.S. Colored Infantry, Company I, Captain William Dougall, November 1863, lists all transactions as well as some black soldiers and why they did not return (e.g., "lost through neglect"), two pieces, five pages; excellent condition, **$500–600 for both.**

    Naval document, signed by C. C. Carpenter, Asiatic Squadron from the USS *Baltimore* (Carpenter served on steam frigates *Merrimac* and *Roanoke* during the Civil War and was credited with stopping many slave ships, including the *Mohawk* with five hundred slaves, and the *Echo* with three hundred slaves), 1904; very good condition, **$12–22.**

    "Power of Attorney for Free Black," preprinted with revenue stamp applied, granting power of attorney for a "free colored man" of the 4th Regiment Colored Troops, "X" signature, dated July 4, 1865, 8″ × 11″; very good condition (small water stain), **$8–12.**

    Servant's pay, concerning an officer with the 10th Illinois Volunteers who is getting pay for his black servant, Jack Mitchell, signed by Surgeon A. M. Speen in charge of the hospital where the injured officer is bedridden, preprinted, large size, dated 1864; very good condition, **$6–10.**

Envelope, "The Contraband of War," slaves with picks and axes coming into the Union lines, multicolored design; unused/excellent condition, **$4–8.**

General Order

    #67, regarding the court martial of Chauncey D. McCoy who threatened black officer Lieutenant James Murphy of Company K, 3rd Arkansas Volunteers, signed by George A. Holloway, assistant adjutant general, seven pages; excellent condition, **$12–15.**

    #79, No. 8, regarding Wesley Ellis, "a colored man" owned by John P. Ellis who was enlisting as a volunteer in the U.S. Army and was stopped by John Ellis, this happened in the "county of Lincoln, and State of Missouri, A.D. 1864," signed by George A. Holloway, assistant adjutant general, six pages; excellent condition, **$20–30.**

    #177, regarding Assistant Surgeon Christian Miller of the 8th U.S. Colored Troops who did not take care of his troops by providing their comfort or food and who was found intoxicated and unable to do his duties, order to be dismissed with the loss of all pay, one page, October 1, 1864; excellent condition, **$3–5.**

Government report of a military murder, includes investigation regarding the murder of Lieutenant White, a member of the 7th U.S. Colored Troops by southern men in 1863, eight pages, dated 1874; very good condition, **$6–10.**

Hard card print, copper-plate etching, *The Supply Train,* by famous artist Edwin Forbes, black teamsters moving a long wagon train of army supplies and white Union officers leading the way, fairly rare edition, dated 1876, 13″ × 18″; excellent condition, **$20–30.**

Letter, autographed

To General Butler from Abraham Lincoln, about wages to Blacks, 1862; very good condition, **$6,500–8,000.**

To the governor of Virginia from General Robert E. Lee, about free Blacks; very good condition, **$1,600–1,800.**

Newspaper article

Harper's Weekly, "Gen. Thomas Addressing the Negroes in La. on the Duties of Freedom," on front page, also "The Negro Troops in the Southwest," November 14, 1863; very good condition, **$32–40.**

The Liberator, news of escaping slaves, an eyewitness account of the horrors of a Civil War battlefield, and Lincoln and the slaves, great masthead, May 6, 1864; excellent condition, **$9–15.**

New York Herald, "Desperate Charge by the Rebels on the Negro Regiments: The Negroes Break in Confusion, Rally & Drive the Rebels Back," about the Civil War, June 14, 1863; very good condition, **$19–28.**

New York Times

"Call for 500,000 Negro Troops," August 30, 1863; fair condition, **$10–15.**

"Enlistment of Negroes in Delaware" and "Patriotic Message from Gov. Cannon," includes some information about Blacks enlisting in the military, on front page, August 13, 1864; very good condition, **$24–35.**

"Negroes Flocking in Great Numbers to Join His [Sherman's] Army," March 11, 1863; good condition, **$25–35.**

"Negroes to be Armed and the Lands of Rebels Assigned to Union Volunteers," April 3, 1863; good condition, **$24–30.**

"Reception of Negro Troops" and "Great Enthusiasm Among the Colored People," October 11, 1865; very good condition, **$28–38.**

Newspaper illustration, *Harper's Weekly*, New York, "Colored Troops under General Wild, Liberating Slaves in North Carolina," full and complete issue, Saturday, January 23, 1864; excellent condition; $25–50. Courtesy of Timothy Hughes, Rare and Early Newspapers; photo by Bob Reno.

Richmond Examiner, "The Negro Troops on the Southside," single-sheet issue with war news, rare to find mention of black troops in Confederate papers, June 3, 1864; good condition, **$165–190.**

Newspaper illustration, *Harper's Weekly,* New York

20th U.S. Colored Troops, half-page, March 19, 1864; good condition, **$43–50.**

The 55th Mass. Colored Reg. Singing John Brown's March in the Streets of Charleston, full-page print, March 18, 1865; very good condition, **$65–80.**

Patriotic Cover

Black man polishing boots, caption reads "by golly massa Butler, I like dis better dan workin in de fields for old Sesesh massa"; very good condition, **$5–8.**

Jeff Davis visiting sick and bedridden slaves, with bottles of medicine in the background, caption reads "Oh! Massa Jeff, Dis Sesesh Fever Will Kill De Nigger," Classic Comic; very good condition, **$6–10.**

Large work gang of black men approaching a white Union officer with dialogue in large lettering, addressed to General Butler, very colorful American flag behind the general; very good condition, **$6–10.**

Union, big scene of slaves taking cotton bales to market, inscription at bottom of cover in ink "envelope bought in 1862, m.v.t.," unused; excellent condition, **$10–15.**

White master holding up a baby slave, caption reads "Him fader's hope, Him moder's joy, Him darling little contraband boy," in blue; very good condition, **$5–8.**

Wide scene of a dancing boy smoking a large cigar, caption reads "Dis Chile's Contraban'," in blue; very good condition, **$5–8.**

Woman running with young child; very good condition, **$5–8.**

Photo cards, "Blacks in the Military," Civil War set, the Picture Bank Archives, twenty cards; each card 4″ × 6″; new, **$25 for the set.**

Poster, "Black Military Recruitment," linen, ca. 1862; very good condition, **$1,250–1,500.**

Print

"Black Military Recruitment," lithograph, Union soldiers at camp, 1863; very good condition, **$500–600.**

Civil War battle, black soldiers taking the fortification of Fort Wagner and white soldiers leading them over the top, graphic with exploding shells, dated 1867, 8″ × 9″; very good condition, **$9–15.**

The Massacre at Fort Pillow, by "H.W.," hand-to-hand battle with unarmed black soldiers being bayoneted by Confederates with white officers standing by watching, dated 1864; 11″ × 15″; very good condition, **$12–20.**

Sculpture, wood, buffalo soldier, saddlebag pouch over his shoulder, painted blue, yellow, brown, and white, 1940s–1960s, 12½″ tall; excellent condition, $50–75. Courtesy of American Eye; photo by Bob Reno.

World War I

Photo cards, "Blacks in the Military," World War I set, the Picture Bank Archives, twenty cards; each card 4″ × 6″; new, **$25 for the set.**

Photograph, soldier in oval, convex glass frame, sepia; approximately 24″; excellent condition, **$350–400.**

Portrait, oil on canvas, soldier named Burrell who died in France in 1918, framed; approximately 22″ × 28″; excellent condition, **$600–700.**

Prints (two), *True Blue* and *Welcome Home,* lithographs, multicolored, patriotic black family images, detailed and high quality; 16″ × 20″; near mint condition, **$325–400 for the pair.**

Toy soldiers, gun metal, painted, four male and one female, from World War II era; about 2″ high; excellent condition, **$60–70.** Courtesy of Rose Fontanella; photo by Bob Reno.

CHAPTER THIRTEEN

Political Memorabilia

Political memorabilia traditionally encompasses campaign material (both for the electoral process and concerning public policy) as well as items related to particular politicians. Specific items include buttons, bumper stickers, broadsides, cartoons, posters, newspaper and magazine articles, T-shirts, photographs, autographs, books, and other documents. But for collectors of black memorabilia, the definition of *political collectibles* must be broadened because during much of America's history, African-Americans were not assumed to be part of the public policy arena. African-American political history must include any effort made by black Americans to become and be treated as full citizens, and so all items relating to that struggle are covered here. If you don't find an item you're looking for listed in this chapter, please check Chapters 4, 8, or 12.

Though collecting political memorabilia has been popular for some time, few are focusing on collecting only items that relate to black activists, leaders, and politicians. You should still be able to find inexpensive items for those politicians who are still alive or in office, though collectibles relating to

politicians from the Civil War period through the 1950s are more rare and will come at a higher price. You should be aware that condition is paramount and that these items may be difficult to find because they were often discarded by the truckload after a campaign ended.

A History of African-Americans in Public Life

In the following sections I discuss the memorabilia produced by the world of politics. Since the social struggles African-Americans have undergone generally spring from the political attitudes of the day, I have also included memorabilia spawned by slavery, the civil rights movement, the NAACP, and other social organizations or struggles.

FREEDOM FROM SLAVERY

For most African-Americans before the Civil War, the only way to participate in public life was to escape from slavery. Slaves often risked their lives by fleeing or revolting. There are many individual stories of such bravery and a few historical figures whose efforts are well known.

Harriet Rose Tubman (1823–1913), famous as the "conductor" of the Underground Railroad, also served as a nurse and spy for the Union troops in the Civil War. Tubman organized the Underground Railroad, freed herself and her family, and then traveled south nineteen more times to free other slaves.

Nat Turner was born a slave in 1800 and was executed on November 11, 1831. He was a preacher and considered to be the instigator of the Southhampton Insurrection. Turner believed he had a vision and that black people were to rise up and slay their oppressors. With seven friends, he murdered his master and five members of the family while they lay sleeping in their beds. The next day, Turner's group had grown to forty-five and had massacred thirteen men, eighteen women, and twenty-four children. His actions resulted in

Magazine cover, *Golden Legacy*, published by Coca-Cola, shows Harriet Tubman, 1967; excellent condition, **$10–15. Photo by Bob Reno.**

stricter slavery codes. William Styron, author of *The Confessions of Nat Turner* (1968), used a document that Turner dictated while waiting for his execution as the basis for his Pulitzer Prize–winning novel.

It is not so well known that some slaves attempted to obtain their freedom by legal means. Abda, a mulatto slave who belonged to Thomas Richards of Hartford, Connecticut, was the bastard son of a black woman and a white man. He ran away in 1702 and lived with Captain Wadsworth, also of Hartford. Richards sued Wadsworth for the return of his property and was answered by Abda's countersuit for damages. Abda claimed that because of his white blood his enslavement was illegal. Abda was declared free by the Inferior Court of Common Pleas in Hartford in 1704.

Other slaves, including Adam, the slave of Judge Saffen of Boston, and Caesar, who belonged to Richard Greenleaf of Newburyport, Rhode Island, followed Abda's example and won their cases.

Some blacks, such as Cambridge, Moore, Caesar Prescott, Caesar Jones, and Caesar of Griswold, Connecticut, earned their freedom by serving in the colonial or Revolutionary armies. Also freed during the Revolution were slaves who were owned by Tories and runaway slaves such as Crispus Attucks.

In rare cases, black Americans were simply allowed to live in freedom. This, too, is a little-known aspect of African-American history. Joseph Burnett II, known as "Bus Bus," was a free black landowner and the first free black slaveholder in New England. He lived during the late eighteenth century.

Paul Cuffee was a free Black of mixed parentage who in the first quarter of the nineteenth century became famous as a merchant, philanthropist, and colonizer. Cuffee was also a staunch Quaker and helped in the building of a new meetinghouse for the Friends. He was the first Black to attempt the resettlement of freedmen in

Africa. In 1815, he helped found the Friendly Society of Sierra Leone and took thirty-eight freedmen to Liberia at his own expense. When Cuffee died, he left an estate estimated at around $120,000.

Prince Hall was born in 1748 of a white English father and a mulatto mother in Barbados. He came to Boston in 1765. While he sought the means to improve the status of Blacks, he worked for the emancipation of Massachusetts slaves. Hall began the Negro Masonry of the United States in 1787 with African Lodge No. 459, after he had been denied admission into the white Masons' lodge. (There are at least two versions of Hall's story; see Chapter 11 for more information.)

POLITICS OF THE LATE NINETEENTH CENTURY

The Civil Rights Act gave slaves citizenship in 1866, and in June of that year Blacks got the right to vote. Black men started entering politics and began making a decisive difference in the way an election would turn. The first black man to hold public office in the United States, John Mercer Langston, had a legal background (he defended Edmonia Lewis, the sculptor mentioned in Chapter 1, when she was accused of poisoning two white classmates at Oberlin College).

It was not an easy time for Blacks to participate in public life. During the late nineteenth century, disgruntled white former slave owners formed the Ku Klux Klan and other anti-Black organizations and unleashed their fury on the black population. Reconstruction-era political cartoons lampooned such sensitive issues as emancipation, freedom, voting, and citizenship. Cartoonists such as Louis Maurer attacked black candidates for their beliefs—attacks that often helped their opponents.

Thomas Nast, the best known political cartoonist of his day, advocated freedom for African-Americans and backed the Republican Party. One of his cartoons in *Harper's Weekly* showed the goddess Columbia asking herself, "Shall I Trust These Men . . ." (a group of Confederate rebels) "And Not This Man?" (a handicapped black veteran). The first black U.S. senator, Hiram Revells of Mississippi, was pictured in a Nast cartoon of 1870 taking his seat in the Senate, greeting the Republican politicos surrounding him. Revells filled the office vacated by Jefferson Davis, the Confederacy's president. If you begin to collect political cartoons of this era, you might like to read *Thomas Nast: His Period and His Pictures* by A. B. Paine or *The Art and Politics of Thomas Nast* by Morton Keller.

SOUTH CAROLINA—A RUSTIC ELECTION SCENE—PLANTATION HANDS TRAVELING TO THE POLLS.

Illustration, Frank Leslie's newspaper, "True Blue Democrat Club," November 18, 1876; very good condition, $15–25. Photo by Donald Vogt.

POLITICS OF THE EARLY TWENTIETH CENTURY

The twentieth century started off more positively than the nineteenth did. African-Americans like Booker T. Washington began to be instrumental in the politics of the United States. Washington was the chief black adviser of presidents Theodore Roosevelt and William Howard Taft. He did not have the full support of the black community, however, because he favored conciliation as the way for Blacks to gain equality. Many belittled his work and called him such names as "Pope Washington," the "Benedict Arnold of the Negro Race," the "Great Traitor," the "Great Divider," and the "Black Boss."

W. E. B. Du Bois, the leading civil rights champion of his generation, was one of Washington's critics. A professor at Atlanta University, he brought his Niagara Movement out of the college arena and into the arena of racial politics. The movement was dedicated to civil rights, voting rights, equal educational opportunities, job opportunities, and human rights in general. The Niagara Movement was the forerunner of the National Association for the Advancement of Colored People (NAACP), formed in 1910.

James Weldon Johnson is credited for much of the NAACP's expansion and growing influence because he joined the staff in 1916 and became the organization's first black executive secretary in 1920. He helped transform the NAACP from a white-led organization to a black-dominated organization. He led membership drives, created a respectable lobbying force within the halls of Congress, and strengthened the NAACP until it celebrated victory in the school desegregation cases of 1954.

At the same time that black political life was changing, labor unions started to gain power. Washington was opposed to labor unions, and many Blacks were excluded from membership in them. Some people, however, took steps to make sure that the black people who worked in certain industries were protected.

In the mid 1920s, for instance, A. Philip Randolph began spreading his message through his magazine, the *Messenger*. Randolph used the magazine as a tool to help form the Brotherhood of Sleeping Car Porters, one of the first unions whose membership largely consisted of black workers. Randolph fought against one of the strongest companies in the United States, the Pullman Company, even though he didn't have a dime of his own. Randolph was a socialist, which at the time was considered un-American. But his efforts on behalf of African-American laborers definitely paved the way for future labor organizations, both black and white.

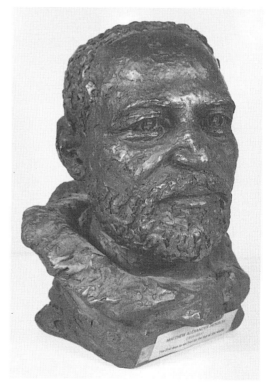

Bust, Matthew Henson, first black man to reach the North Pole; excellent condition, **$50–75**. Courtesy of the Valerie Bertrand Collection; photo by Donald Vogt.

EDUCATION

Mary McLeod Bethune is best known as an educator, and founded Bethune-Cookman College in Daytona Beach, Florida, which is known as one of the best black schools in the United States. A strong proponent of education and the black women's club movement, she was also involved in politics.

In 1930, President Herbert Hoover invited her to his White House Conference on Child Health and Protection. President Franklin Roosevelt appointed her to serve as director of the National Youth Administration's (NYA) Division of Negro Affairs. She served the NYA from 1936 to 1944, granting funds to students who could not otherwise have continued graduate study.

Charles Hamilton Houston is noted as the chief strategist of the NAACP campaign against educational discrimination that resulted in the celebrated *Brown v. Board of Education* decision in 1954. In that decision, the Supreme Court found that segregation in education was unconstitutional. Houston was well respected among African-American leaders. He was called "Mr. Civil Rights" and was an expert in constitutional law as well as a litigator in educational, labor, and housing rights cases. He worked in legal activities and as a civil rights leader from 1929 to 1950.

Women have been quite strong in the field of education. Some of the best known include the following. Marguerite Ross Barnett, president of the University of Houston, appointed in 1990, was the first Black as well as the first woman to lead that institution. Johnnetta Betsch Cole was the first black woman president of Spelman College; Marva Collins founded Chicago's Westside Preparatory School; and Gloria Scott was the second woman chief administrator of Bennett College in Greensboro, North Carolina, and served as national president of the Girl Scouts U.S.A.

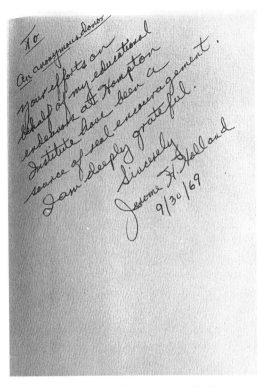

Autograph, Jerome H. Holland (died January 1985), who had a forty-five-year career in government, education, and business, dated September 30, 1969; excellent condition, **$45–75. Courtesy of the Valerie Bertrand Collection; photo by Donald Vogt.**

THE CIVIL RIGHTS STRUGGLE

In the second half of the twentieth century, the struggle for civil rights affected all African-Americans. In the widest sense, the fight for civil rights encompassed all attempts to overcome discrimination, including the NAACP's struggles for equality, attempts to bring more Blacks into politics, and the struggle for certain social movements to make their needs known (such as the Southern Christian Leadership Conference (SCLC), the Black Panthers, the Black Muslims, feminists, and others).

The Voting Rights Act of 1965 eliminated discriminatory voter registration practices in several southern states with large black populations and distinctly influenced how leaders in this country were chosen. During this period, racially related riots broke out in the Watts district of Los Angeles, as well as in some Detroit neighborhoods.

Martin Luther King Jr. and the SCLC tried to calm the volcanic eruptions that took place during this period of the civil rights struggle. Blacks rallied around King, following him to Birmingham and Selma, Alabama, where they marched with him across the Pettus Bridge on March 7 on their way to the state capital, Montgomery. They wanted to present a petition to Governor George Wallace. When the marchers were put down by state troopers, volunteers of all colors and backgrounds flocked to Selma and offered their help. King and the SCLC went on to raise the consciousness level of most African-Americans in a positive way.

Not all black activists followed King, however. Young racial extremists and extremist groups gained strength—for instance, H. Rap Brown, Stokely Carmichael, Floyd McKissick, and the Black Panthers (a revolutionary group founded in 1966 to protect residents of black ghettos from police brutality). While King was trying to peacefully solve problems that had existed for most of America's history, other African-Americans believed that the only way the problems would be solved was by meeting violence and anger with violence and anger.

Malcolm X fought for the rights of the black underclass, attempting to bring respect to African-Americans through the Muslim faith, his militant politics, and his belief that education was the most important thing for his people. His style was totally different from that of Martin Luther King Jr., but the two leaders shared many of the same beliefs and goals.

The feminist movement also boasted some important black leaders. One of the earliest was Annie J. Cooper, who died in 1964. She was active in the civil rights era, expressing her views of justice and equality for women alongside her views of racial equality.

Angela Davis also fought for both women's rights and civil rights. She became associated with the NAACP and then in the late 1960s became involved with the Student Nonviolent Coordinating Committee, the Black Panthers, and the Communist Party.

In 1970 Davis was accused of being a co-conspirator in a gun smuggling that resulted in four deaths. When she was caught, she was kept without bail while a movement for her release echoed throughout the world. After she was acquitted of murder and conspiracy charges, in 1972, she began speaking on behalf of the National Alliance Against Racist Political Expression. She was awarded the Lennon Peace Prize in 1979.

Other active black feminists of the late 1960s, 1970s, and 1980s include Aileen Clark Hernandez, the first black president of the National Organization for Women; Queen Mother Audley Moore, a civil rights activist, women's rights activist, and pan-African nationalist for nearly eighty years; and Flo Kennedy, a lawyer, feminist, and civil rights activist.

CONTEMPORARY POLITICS

In recent years there have been many influential African-Americans in politics. In 1968, Shirley Chisholm was the first black woman to be elected to the U.S. Congress, and in 1972 she was the first woman and first black to seek a presidential nomination. In 1984, Jesse Jackson was the first major black presidential candidate when he sought the Democratic nomination, and he ran again in 1988. Cardiff Collins was elected to the U.S. Congress in 1973 as a representative from Illinois and was the first woman to serve as leader of the Congressional Black Caucus. In 1966, President Lyndon Johnson appointed Robert Weaver the first black secretary of the Department of Housing and

Photograph, autographed, Ralph Bunche, 1950 Nobel Peace Prize winner; excellent condition, not priced. Courtesy of Mildred Franklin.

Urban Development and nominated Thurgood Marshall to the U.S. Supreme Court in June 1967. President George Bush appointed Dr. Louis Sullivan secretary of human services in the 1980s. In 1990, Douglas Wilder of Virginia became the nation's first black governor. Black mayors have included Marion Barry, mayor of Washington, D.C.; Thomas Bradley, elected mayor of Los Angeles in 1973; Andrew Young of Atlanta (1981); and Coleman Young, three-time mayor of Detroit in the 1970s and 1980s.

Some Biographies of Political Activists and Politicians

Sadie T. M. Alexander was, in 1927, the first black woman admitted to the Pennsylvania bar. She also served as chair of the Philadelphia Commission on Human Relations, was the secretary of the New York Urban League, and was appointed by President Harry Truman to the U.S. Commission on Civil Rights.

Mary McLeod Bethune, born in 1875, was the founder and president of Bethune-Cookman College. She also served as adviser to President Franklin Roosevelt, was president of the National Council of Negro Woman, and is considered by some to be the most influential woman in black American history. She died in 1955. (For more about Bethune, see "Education" earlier in this chapter.)

Thomas Bradley was elected the first black mayor of Los Angeles in 1973. He was a popular politician who has been credited with building L.A.'s confidence, keeping racism to a minimum, and helping to rebuild the downtown area. In 1982 he ran for governor of California unsuccessfully.

Stokely Carmichael is credited with popularizing the phrase "black power." He joined the Congress of Racial Equality (CORE) in 1960, hoping to integrate public accommodations in the South. After he graduated from Howard University in 1964, he joined the Student Nonviolent Coordinating Committee (SNCC) and became its leader. After he resigned from the SNCC, he joined the Black Panthers, but he differed with Eldridge Cleaver's views and resigned shortly afterward. In the late 1960s, Carmichael moved to Guinea. In the early 1970s, he returned to the United States to speak about his pan-African ideology.

Eldridge Cleaver, former minister of information for the Black Panther Party, was an ardent follower of Malcolm X. Cleaver wrote *Soul on Ice,* a well-known collection of letters and essays that probed the modern black psyche. After fleeing a U.S. prison sentence in 1969, Cleaver traveled the world, living in Algeria for a while. He returned to the United States in 1979, a born-again Christian, to speak for the country he had previously criticized.

Angela Davis, a Birmingham, Alabama, native, took an active political role in the Black Panthers, the SNCC, and the Communist Party in the mid to late 1960s. Hired to teach at UCLA, she was fired because of FBI information that she was a Communist Party member. In 1970, her legally owned guns were part of a shootout in a courtroom, and she became a fugitive. Arrested two months later, she spent sixteen months in jail, came to trial for murder and conspiracy, and then was acquitted. She helped organize the National Alliance Against Racist and Political Repression.

Medgar Wiley Evers joined the NAACP in 1954 and soon became Mississippi's field secretary. He fought for equality through voting and economic boycotts. His assassination in 1963 spurred black political activism in Mississippi and helped to rush civil rights legislation through Congress.

Dick Gregory, a comedian and civil rights activist, was arrested quite often during the 1960s and 1970s for his nonviolent acts of protest. He ran unsuccessfully for mayor of Chicago and for president of the United States. Today, he records, writes, and gives lecture tours.

Jesse Jackson has been a major force in American politics since the civil rights era. He worked with Martin Luther King Jr. in the 1960s and was with King when he was assassinated. Throughout the 1970s, Jackson became an even more influential figure in black politics and tried to follow in King's footsteps. He ran for the Democratic nomination for president with a platform he calls the Rainbow Coalition. During the Gulf War and uprisings in South Africa, Jackson represented the United States on several diplomatic missions.

John Jones traveled from North Carolina to Chicago to make his fortune as a tailor and also acted as a "station" on the Underground Railroad. He fought against his state's black laws with his money and his talent, publishing a pamphlet in the early 1860s called *The Black Laws of Illinois and a Few Reasons Why They Should Be Repealed.* In January 1865, the state revoked its black laws.

Martin Luther King Jr. believed in bringing about change through nonviolent civil disobedience. His type of consciousness-raising came at a time when America's Blacks needed a leader to pull them together and give them direction.

With his eyes on progress and his heart full of hope, King worked through the churches of the South, right into the hearts and souls of black people. Black people pulled together in support of King's ideals in marches, boycotts, and sit-ins.

King stimulated people, such as Rosa Parks, the woman who refused to give her bus seat to a white passenger. Her actions called attention to a great injustice, and the U.S. Supreme Court outlawed Alabama's bus segregation laws on December 20, 1956.

In early 1960, King made his first connection with John F. Kennedy, then a senator. When Kennedy ran for the presidency, King urged Blacks to vote for him, and it was the first time in history that the black vote was instrumental in putting a president in office. Kennedy received 75 percent of the black vote and went on to fight for the civil rights bill, though the bill was not passed until after Kennedy's assassination.

Martin Luther King Jr. was assassinated in 1968. Today a holiday is devoted to him and many items have been made to commemorate his strong, yet too short, life.

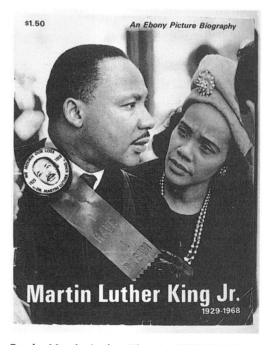

Book, *Martin Luther King Jr., 1929–1968,* by the editors of *Ebony;* very good condition, **$100–200. Courtesy of the Valerie Bertrand Collection; photo by Donald Vogt.**

John Mercer Langston, a lawyer and diplomat, was admitted to the Ohio bar in 1854 and became the first black elected official in the United States when he was elected clerk of Brownhelmn Township in 1855. He also acted as inspector general of the Freedmen's Bureau in 1868, taught law and became vice president of Howard University from 1869 to 1876, and was named minister to Haiti in 1877. When he returned to the United States in 1885, he served as president of Virginia Normal and Collegiate Institute and then was a Republican congressman for Virginia from 1890 to 1891.

John Roy Lynch was born into slavery at the Tacony Plantation, Louisiana, in 1847 and remained a slave until 1863. In 1866 he became a photographer, and later he was a congressman from Mississippi. He gave a most profound speech on the Civil Rights Act of 1875, and in 1884, Theodore Roosevelt named him chairman of the Democratic National Convention. Presidents James Garfield, William McKinley, and Benjamin Harrison often sought his advice. He died in 1939.

Malcolm X became well known in the 1950s and 1960s as a spokesman for the Black Muslims. In 1964 he left the movement and traveled to the Middle East and Africa, where he met with Islamic practitioners who moderated his extremist views. He was assassinated in the Audubon Ballroom in Harlem in 1965. His career has recently enjoyed a resurgence of interest due to Spike Lee's powerful movie *Malcolm X.*

Adam Clayton Powell Sr. was a clergyman before he founded the Urban League (in 1910) and became a member of the first board of directors of the NAACP. He is the father of Congressman Adam Clayton Powell Jr.

Philip Randolph organized the Brotherhood of Sleeping Car Porters in the 1920s after fighting the Pullman Company for twelve years. When Randolph planned a march on Washington to fight discrimination in the car industries, President Franklin Roosevelt created the Fair Employment Practices Committee to see that his executive order to stop discrimination would be enforced.

John Rock, a Boston doctor and lawyer, in 1858 became the first African-American admitted to practice before the U.S. Supreme Court. As far as we know, he was also the first person to say "Black is beautiful."

Mary Church Turrell, born in 1863, was the co-founder and first president of the National Association of Colored Woman. She represented black American women at three international conferences and was active in civil rights as well as in the desegregation of Washington, D.C.

Booker T. Washington was born a slave in Hale's Ford, Virginia, in 1856. His determination to get an education led him to walk several hundred miles to Hampton Institute to enroll in 1872. He graduated from Hampton three years later and taught in Malden, West Virginia. He entered Wayland Seminary in Washington, D.C., and later returned to Hampton to teach American Indian boys. In 1881, he was appointed principal of a small school with thirty students called Tuskegee Institute. He brought the institute to worldwide attention and was invited to be the spokesman for Blacks at the Atlanta Exposition in 1895. Presidents Theodore Roosevelt and William Howard Taft sought his views and advice on Blacks in America.

Washington organized the National Negro Business League in 1900 and also participated in organizing the General Education Board and the Phelps Stokes Fund. He advised black people to work out their problems by helping themselves improve. He felt that this would slowly lead to an improvement of the masses and would eventually erase prejudice. He died in 1915.

Andrew Young joined Martin Luther King Jr. in 1961 and became his trusted confidante. In 1972, Young was elected a representative for Georgia. President Jimmy Carter eventually convinced him to leave Congress to take the position of ambassador to the United Nations. In 1979, Young left that post after an uproar about his secret meeting with a representative of the Palestine Liberation Organization. Young became mayor of Atlanta in 1981, when that city was having major economic and social problems.

Coleman Young, three-time mayor of Detroit in the 1970s and 1980s, had a close relationship with the Carter administration. Young had a long and interesting career, with jobs ranging from being an electrician with the Ford Motor Company to working with the Negro Labor Council.

PRICES FOR POLITICAL MEMORABILIA

Autograph, Gerrit Smith, famous reformer and statesman and supporter of John Brown of Kansas, rare; very good condition, **$15–25.**

Book

Pryor, Roger A., *Speech of Roger A. Pryor of Virginia, on the Principles and Policy of the Black Republican Party,* Washington, D.C., 1859; excellent condition, **$60–85.**

Scheer, Robert, *Eldridge Cleaver,* 1969; excellent condition, **$10–15.**

Booklet

Chase, Samuel P., "The Repeal of the Missouri Prohibition," speech before the Missouri Senate on February 3, 1854, against the repeal of the Missouri Compromise that forbade slavery north of the 36th parallel, 30 pages, original printed wraps; very good condition, **$18–28.**

Hayden, Tom, *Revolution in Mississippi,* concerns beginning of civil rights movement, 1961; excellent condition, **$10–15.**

The History of SNCC, illustrated with black-and-white photographs throughout, 1966; excellent condition, **$15–20.**

The Missionary Register, a survey of worldwide Protestant missionary stations, concentrating on the African Blacks taken on board slave ships, reports that slavers take an average of fifty thousand slaves per year, tells how it is done and the cruelty involved, map of Sierra Leone, 64 pages, dated January 1836; very good condition, **$10–20.**

Wilson, Henry, speech, extension of slavery, concerns the president's message, the extension of slavery into the territories and the support of the newly formed Republican Party, 16 pages, printed in Washington, D.C., 1857; very good condition, **$15–25.**

Bumper sticker, "Jesse Jackson for President"; good condition, **$10–20.**

Campaign button, "Dick Gregory for President," mint condition, **$15–25.**

Commemorative plate, "In Memoriam, Dr. Martin Luther King, Jr., 1929–1968"; very good condition, **$10–15.**

Congressional newspaper, *Congressional Globe,* printed just before the Civil War and during the time of slave problems in the territories, southern speeches and debates, actual word-for-word confrontations, 16 pages, dated 1859; very good condition, **$5–10.**

Document, autographed

John Roy Lynch, signed as auditor of the United States, 1890; very good condition, **$20–30.**

Mary McLeod Bethune; excellent condition, **$200–225.**

Doll, black man attached to cork and wood sign, reads "It's up to you," derogatory; very good condition, $75–125. Photo by Donald Vogt.

Engraving, *President Lincoln Entering Richmond,* by Thomas Nast, February 24, 1866; very good condition, **$90–105.**

Focus cards

Commemorates the lives and accomplishments of African-Americans, including Frederick Douglass, Harriet Tubman, George Washing-ton Carver, and others, 19 cards; new, **$5–10 for the set.**

Martin Luther King Jr., his life and times, 16 cards; new, **$5–10.**

Government document

Detailed report concerning the Freedmen's Inquiry Commission, the hardships brought about by the slaves' emancipation, setting up land and homes for them, and much more, 110 pages, 1864; very good condition, **$9–12.**

"Report of Slavery in the District of Columbia," about the absolute abolition of slavery in the District of Columbia, e.g., to retract the Compromise of 1850 wherein it was legal to own slaves in Washington, 22 pages, dated March 1862; very good condition, **$9–15.**

Submitted by Lincoln to the Congress concerning suppression of the African slave trade, letters from Seward and others about Cuba and the slave routes out of Africa, the ships involved, ideas, etc., 28 pages, dated 1864; very good condition, **$9–15.**

#148, emancipation and colonization document, black emancipation and return to Africa as a means of gradually ending slavery in the South, good history of American slavery, 83 pages, dated 1862; very good condition, **$8–12.**

Journal, *First World: An International Journal of Black Thought,* cover includes robotlike bust in silhouette with white cutouts of the United States, Africa, and South America for eyes and nose and a keyhole cutout for mouth, January–February 1977; excellent condition, **$20–35.**

Letter, autographed

Angela Davis, dated August 5, 1978; excellent condition, **$25–35.**

Malcolm X; good condition, **$300–400.**

Magazine

Ebony, Dr. Martin Luther King Jr. and Coretta King walking hand in hand, on cover, September 1968; excellent condition, **$25–30.**

Life

Angela Davis, "The Making of a Fugitive," September 11, 1970; excellent condition, **$20–25.**

Coretta King, "He Had a Dream," on cover, September 12, 1969; excellent condition, **$20–25.**

Martin Luther King Jr., "Week of Shock," April 12, 1968; excellent condition, **$25–30.**

Medgar Evers's widow consoling son during funeral service for Medgar, on cover, June 28, 1963; excellent condition, **$25–30.**

"The Savage Season Begins," the beginning of the march in Alabama, March 19, 1965; excellent condition, **$20–25.**

Newspaper

The Anti-Slavery Standard

Filled with stories of horrible treatment of slaves, the slave trade and how to end slavery, fairly rare issue, published by the Anti-Slave Society of New York, a national organization, dated 1842; excellent condition, **$10–20.**

News of Reconstruction and southern treatment of ex-slaves, including horrible cruelties, rare, dated 1866; very good condition, **$8–12.**

The Liberator, European opinions about Lincoln and the history of Lincoln's administration, slaves buried alive at Fort Pillow, and other articles, dated July 22, 1864; very good condition, **$9–15.**

Pamphlet, religious, distributed by the Society for the Diffusion of Political Knowledge, giving examples of slavery in the Bible and how it is a sin to hold a person in bondage, etc., printed, 16 pages, ca. 1861; very good condition, **$6–10.**

Engraving, *Emancipation,* by Thomas Nast, *Harper's Weekly,* New York, January 1863; very good condition, **$60–85.** Photo by Donald Vogt.

Photograph

> Jesse Jackson, autographed, late 1970s; very good condition, **$50–65.**
>
> NAACP Wartime Conference, July 12–14, 1944; excellent condition, **$175–225.**
>
> Shirley Chisholm, autographed; mint condition, **$15–25.**

Plaque, slave ship depicted on numbered coin made of nickel silver, tag on back of plaque relates 15 facts concerning the slave ship and its cargo, framed in pine; 18″ × 15″; new, **$30–40.**

Sign, tin, anti–civil rights, pregnant black woman saying "I went all the way with LBJ 1964," painted red, white, and black, rare; very good condition, **$125–200.**

T-shirt, Malcolm X, generated by movie produced by Spike Lee; new, **$15–20.**

Slave ball and chain, iron, rare, 1860s; excellent condition, **$1,000–1,500.** Courtesy of Bold Soul of the Black Memorabilia Museum; photo by Bold Soul.

PART FOUR

Entertainment Memorabilia

CHAPTER FOURTEEN

Music and Dance Memorabilia

The Collectibles

Collectible items in the music and dance arena include sheet music, photographs, posters, and even toys.

SHEET MUSIC

Whether the songs were written by black artists or illustrated with black personalities, sheet music is highly valued by collectors today. Make sure your piece is in good condition, with no bent corners or rips, when considering the price you should pay. Since most sheet music was used rather than stored, you must expect *some* wear; however, any excessive wear definitely lowers the value of your piece.

Sheet music was decorated as early as the fifteenth century, when monks handlettered songs for the Church. The pieces considered collectible today consist of songs issued from 1820 on. The introduction of a better way to print the covers of sheet music not only made them more attractive but added to the salability of the music. Between 1820 and 1900, an estimated one hundred thousand different music covers were sold in the United States. By the mid-nineteenth century, sheet music had reached its peak, and by 1870, standards had deteriorated. When World War I broke out, the quality

Sheet music, "Moonlight on the Melon Patch," very good condition; **$25–40**. Photo by Donald Vogt.

243

had diminished to the point that covers were poorly drawn and garishly decorated.

The age of sheet music can usually be discerned by the size of the picture on the cover. If it is small, chances are the piece is old. Larger pictures with the title in decorative type came into fashion around 1870. Color was added as early as 1840, and chromolithographs were first used in 1843.

Sheet music of the nineteenth and early twentieth centuries is a valuable source of information on fads, historical events, and the general mood of the day. Sheet music announced the first all-professional baseball team, the Adams Express Company's continent-spanning services, the tragic Johnstown flood, the popularity of the high-wheeled bike, and the prejudice toward "men of color."

Some of the best covers were made before the 1930s. Especially collectible are pieces of sheet music illustrated by Currier and Ives,

Louis Prang, Winslow Homer, and Sarony. Other desirable artists include James Montgomery Flagg, Pfeiffer, Wholman, Archie Gunn, Norman Rockwell, and Frederick S. Manning.

PHOTOGRAPHS

When buying any photographs, you need to be sure they are not ripped, do not have bent corners, and are not faded (see also Chapter 3). Most music, dance, stage, and film stars have publicity photos made up to send to prospective promoters, producers, and fans; therefore, they are relatively easy to find. Autographed photos of personalities are obviously more valuable than unsigned ones; however, most contemporary stars do not *personally* autograph their photos but have someone on their staff do the job. If the photo is personalized, the chances that the autograph is real are better than if the photo is simply signed with the personality's name.

OTHER COLLECTIBLES

Because singers and dancers often appear in movies and plays, their names and likenesses may be featured on lobby cards, playbills, or posters, each of which is discussed in more detail in Chapter 15. Lunchboxes and toys (discussed in Chapters 10 and 15) may also occasionally depict famous singers or dancers.

TYPES OF AFRICAN-AMERICAN MUSIC

FOLK MUSIC

African-American music began with folk music, whose roots are recognizable in the slave experience and are also associated with work, social activity, and the church. Jazz, the second most important music contribution of the African-American, was the music of cabarets and vaudeville houses.

Sheet music, the works of "Tom the Blind Negro Boy Pianist"; very good condition, $20–35. Photo by Donald Vogt.

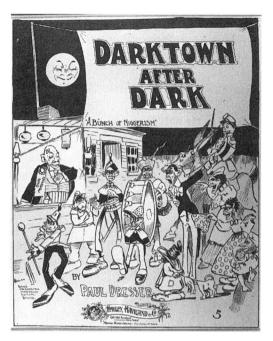

Poster, *Darktown after Dark,* by Paul Dresser; excellent condition, **$40–60.** Photo by Donald Vogt.

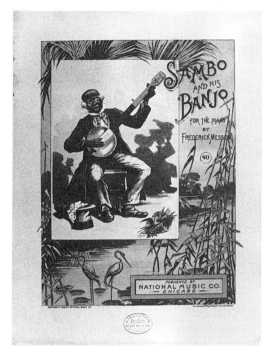

Sheet music, "Sambo and His Banjo," mid to late 1800s; very good condition, **$25–45.** Courtesy of Jim Bollman of the Music Emporium; photo by Donald Vogt.

Slave Songs of the United States (1867) is the oldest collection of black American songs and serves as the foundation of the study of African-American music. The white northern editors who produced the book were attracted to the beauty of the music, but they did not understand its origins or the conditions that produced it. Consequently, the editors did not grasp the music's extraordinary overtones, topical references, and double meanings, as the following examples illustrate.

The song "Blue Tail Fly," also known as "Jimmy Crack Corn," probably originated with blackface minstrels, but it was taken up by slaves. It tells of the slave's delight should his master suffer an untimely death. "All the Pretty Horses," an authentic slave lullaby, reveals the bitter feelings of black mothers who had to watch over white children and neglect their own; "Go Down, Moses" told of the slave's feeling of persecution. The song is said to be about Harriet Tubman who, as one of the "conductors" of the Underground Railroad,

was nicknamed Moses. The song "Steal Away" was sung at many black meetings as a signal to those slaves who were to begin their dangerous journey northward; "Follow the Drinking Gourd" was a song about the Big Dipper, the stars that pointed north and to freedom.

SPIRITUALS

The spiritual makes use of scriptures and religious ideas. It was popular after 1865 with Christians who felt a deep attachment to God. It is often thought that spirituals were not as popular with the slaves in the eighteenth century as they were with sheet music collectors in the nineteenth century, because the slaves had other music that was more expressive of their lot. One possible reason that spirituals gained popularity was the slaves' fear of punishment by white masters. Spirituals did not represent a threat to the masters as did, say, work songs.

Black Americans who sang spirituals were expressing their sadness and emotional upheaval at having to leave their homelands and learn a new culture, language, and way of life. The title of a spiritual often shows the underlying message in the song. "We'll Soon Be Free" tells of jailed Blacks. Songs speaking of religion gave working slaves the only solace they knew. One can gauge the misery of the slave and the oppression he or she felt by tracing the mood of the song.

The Jubilee Singers (1874) was a collection of sixty-one songs, the first collection to contain spirituals exclusively. The majority of the songs are sorrowful—"Nobody Knows the Trouble I See, Lord," "From Every Graveyard," "I'm a Rolling Thro' an Unfriendly World," and "We'll Die in the Field."

According to *Papers of the Hymn Society of America,* spirituals may be classified into three groups: the call-and-response chant, the slow, lone-phrase melody, and the syncopated,

segmented melody. The spirituals that are sung on stage today by trained choirs lack much of their original sound. The spirituals' true sound does not show predetermined harmony that adheres to music theory rules.

WORK SONGS

Blacks turned to work songs for companionship and as a way to ease the boring repetition and back-breaking effort of their labors. The songs often dealt with the slave's mean white boss or with topics familiar to all the workers, such as living conditions, people in the community, and family. Often the songs would give a rhythm to the work of laying ties on the railroad, digging ditches, or carrying bales of cotton. The leader would pace the song accordingly until the job was done.

Work songs, documented as unique in the post–Civil War years, were primarily men's songs. Women working in the kitchens or fields more often than not sang hymns or blues.

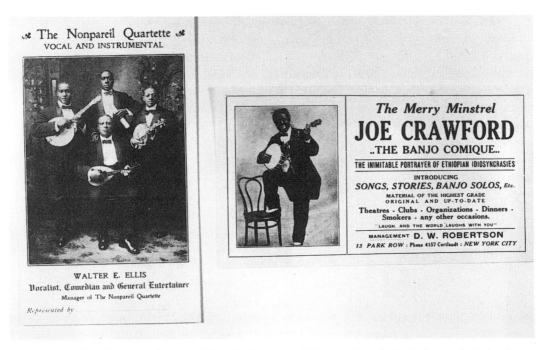

Show ad and business card, *left:* ad for the Nonpareil Quartette minstrel show, *right;* business card for Joe Crawford "the Banjo Comique"; very good condition, **$50–75 for both.** Courtesy of Jim Bollman of the Music Emporium; photo by Donald Vogt.

THE BLUES

Blues had its roots, as already noted, in early slave laments and developed in the levees and deltas of the Mississippi. It then extended along the rivers throughout the Midwest. They are songs of the individual and of slavery and postslavery experiences.

The blues song was original a solo, and it has remained so. The text is important to the music, and the usual pattern is to repeat the first line, follow with an antecedent phrase, then add a third line.

GOSPEL MUSIC

Gospel music is, in a sense, the spiritual of the twentieth century. It is a music that achieves its effects through the singing and its beat. Sometimes it sounds like the blues, sometimes like rock, sometimes like jazz. The main difference between spiritual and gospel music is that gospel music is accompanied by the piano and/or other instruments. Thomas A. Dorsey is thought to have been one of the primary forces in gospel music.

JAZZ

Jazz, despite all the fabrications, half-truths, and general misconceptions about it, is basically black music. Black people gave jazz its language, syntax, heart, and vocabulary, the roots of which spring from African rhythms and European harmonies and the African-Americans' feelings about their place in the social, racial, economic, and cultural conditions of the South. Although jazz expresses happiness, love of life, and ebullience, it remains protest music.

New Orleans is famous as the nursery of jazz, and by 1900, it was the black musical center of the South. By the turn of the century, jazz was being played by brass and marching bands who "ragged" music rhythmically and improvised their tunes. The Creole Jazz Band, led by King Oliver, is perhaps the best known group from the first

Poster/flyer, Oriental Club of Amherst, a black men's club, 1904; $20–30. Courtesy of the Valerie Bertrand Collection; photo by Donald Vogt.

period of jazz. Louis Armstrong, a King Oliver sideman, is the best known single player, though many others followed him, and some are still creating new types of jazz.

RAGTIME

Ragtime, the music of the first twenty years of the twentieth century, was essentially piano music played hard, brightly, cheerfully, and in a machinelike way. Scott Joplin, James Scott, Artie Matthews, and Louis Chauvin were among the most important black American ragtime musicians.

The Harlem Renaissance in the 1920s gave black Americans a place uniquely theirs in the history of American music. Duke Ellington, Eubie Blake, Noble Sissle, Paul Robeson, Charles Gilpin, Josephine Baker, and Florence Mills made their names on stage and in music. By the 1930s, the social songs were replaced by the growing popularity of blues and jazz.

Magazine, *Jazz Record,* Scott Joplin on cover, "Nov. 1947"; excellent condition, **$20–25.** Courtesy of Rose Fontanella; photo by Bob Reno.

SOME BIOGRAPHIES OF AFRICAN-AMERICAN MUSICAL ENTERTAINERS

Marian Anderson, born in 1902, first sang in the Union Baptist Church in Philadelphia as a child. Her voice thrilled her listeners and her five-foot, nine-inch regal presence captured attention—especially in 1939, when Eleanor Roosevelt arranged for Anderson to appear at the Lincoln Memorial, despite the fact that the Daughters of the American Revolution had denied the singer the right to appear at Constitution Hall. It wasn't until 1955, when Anderson was fifty-seven years old, that she was able to make her Metropolitan

Opera Debut. She published her autobiography, *My Lord What a Morning* in 1957.

Louis Armstrong was born in 1900 in New Orleans. He has been called the greatest jazz trumpet player in music history. In 1922, Armstrong was asked by King Oliver to play second trumpet in his Chicago-based band. He made a series of records with Oliver's Creole Jazz Band, including *Canal Street Blues.*

Armstrong broke the convention of three-instrument lines in jazz bands by introducing the solo jazz trumpet. He also introduced "scat" singing to millions of listeners who would not usually have listened to jazz. (Scat is a vocal in which meaningless syllables substitute for words.) He was a band leader, singer, musician, film star, and comedian as well as a composer; his songs include "I Wish I Could Shimmy Like my Sister Kate" (with Clarence Williams), "Wild Man Blues" (with Jelly Roll Morton), and "Gut Bucket Blues." He died in 1971.

Charles "Buddy" Bolden was one of the black musicians who originated jazz in the Storyville section of New Orleans in the late 1800s. He organized the first jazz band in 1897 and won the title "King" by popular acclaim.

Harry Thacker Burleigh was born in Erie, Pennsylvania, on December 2, 1866, and died in Stamford, Connecticut, on September 12, 1949. He was a baritone who also composed. He transcribed more than two hundred songs and arranged black spirituals. After studying under Antonin Dvorak at the National Conservatory of Music in New York City, he taught Dvorak American black music. In 1916, Burleigh won the Spingarn Medal for the highest achievement by an American black.

Edward Kennedy "Duke" Ellington was born in 1899 and became one of the most eminent jazz musicians of the twentieth century. He was a composer, pianist, and jazz orchestra leader. As a child he studied piano and at seventeen began to play professionally. He developed his "jungle style" with the help of his band, which consisted of musicians such as Bubber Miley and Tricky Sam Nanton. Ellington led a band from 1927 to 1932 at Harlem's Cotton Club. During the 1940s, he composed concerts and appeared at Carnegie Hall in New York City. The band made world tours in the 1950s, while Ellington was also composing motion picture soundtracks for such movies as *Anatomy of a Murder,* directed by Otto Preminger. Duke is also known for "religious jazz." His "In the Beginning God" was performed at St. Michael's Cathedral in England, in New York City, and in German churches in 1966. *Music is my Mistress,* his autobiography, was published in 1974, the year he died.

Ella Fitzgerald, born on April 25, 1918 in Newport News, Virginia, sang in New York in her early teens and made her recording debut in 1935 on the Decca Label when she was seventeen.

She has the distinction of having the longest singing career of any American, working through the 1940s as a band singer, through the 1950s as a single singer, and then doing classics from the late 1950s to today.

Newport Gardner, the slave of Caleb Gardner of Newport, Rhode Island, was given music lessons and then excelled as a teacher. He opened a music school in Newport where he taught both black and white students. In 1791, he won $2,000 in a lottery and bought freedom for himself and his family.

Johann Christian Gotlieb Graupner became known as the father of "Negro songs." He sang "The Gay Negro Boy" and accompanied himself on the banjo on December 30, 1799, at the Federal Street Theater in Boston, Massachusetts.

Elizabeth Taylor Greenfield, born in 1809, was nicknamed "the Black Swan." Her soprano voice won world acclaim. She died in 1876.

William Christopher Handy, born in 1873, was a composer whose best known work is the classic "St. Louis Blues." From 1903 to 1921 he conducted his own orchestra, even though he was struck blind at the age of thirty. Handy was one of the musicians who worked through the ragtime-to-jazz transition period, drawing on black folklore melodies and adding harmonizations to those tunes as he worked out his orchestral arrangements. He introduced an element of blues into the popular ragtime, writing songs such as "Memphis Blues," a campaign song for Mayor Edward "Boss" Crump of Memphis in 1911, and the popular "St. Louis Blues" in 1914. Because he was forced to publish "St. Louis Blues" on his own, Handy formed his own publishing company and directed it until late in life. His firm published studies of African-American musicians as well as anthologies of black spirituals and blues. Handy's autobiography, *Father of the Blues,* was published in 1941. He died in 1958.

Billie Holiday, born Eleanora Gough McKay in Baltimore on April 7, 1915, made her singing debut in 1931 at a Harlem nightclub; she recorded her first album two years later. In 1935, she was recognized as a jazz singer, and for a few years after that, she toured with Count Basie and Artie

Shaw. Although she broke from the bands in 1940 to become a solo nightclub act, she never severed her affiliation with jazz. Holiday's voice and diction remained superb even when her heroin addiction overtook her. Music critics believed her best years to be 1936 to 1943, when she recorded with saxophonist Lester Young. *Lady Sings the Blues,* her autobiography, was published in 1956. She died in New York City on July 17, 1959. In 1972, Diana Ross starred in the movie version of Holiday's book.

Lena Horne appeared in her first black-cast film, *The Duke is Tops* in 1938. The movie was shown to an all-white audience, which applauded throughout its showing. Horne, born in 1912 in Brooklyn, entered show business as a chorus line dancer at the Cotton Club in Harlem. She achieved fame as an actress and singer in such films as *Panama Hattie, Cabin in the Sky, Stormy Weather, Swing Fever,* and *Ziegfeld Follies.* She continues to perform today and is best known for her vocal skills.

Photograph, autographed by Lena Horne; excellent condition, not priced. Courtesy of the Valerie Bertrand Collection; photo by Donald Vogt.

Mahalia Jackson, born on October 26, 1911, in New Orleans, became a great gospel singer whose religion was an intense part of her life. She sang at the age of five in her father's choir and became familiar with singers such as Bessie Smith. At sixteen, she went to Chicago and began singing in Baptist churches. After 1945, her fame spread throughout the United States and her recordings of "Move On Up a Little Higher" and "Silent Night" were very successful.

James Weldon Johnson was born in Jacksonville, Florida, on June 17, 1871, and died in Wiscasset, Maine, on June 26, 1938. He was well known as a poet, a diplomat, and an anthologist as well as an accomplished musician and composer. He and his brother John wrote the black national anthem "Lift Every Voice and Sing" and together the brothers wrote more than two hundred songs for the musical stage. In 1906, President Theodore Roosevelt appointed Johnson as U.S. consul in Puerto Cabello, Venezuela. In 1912, Johnson's novel *Autobiography of an Ex-Coloured Man* was published anonymously. The book was reissued in 1927 under his name and got a better reception than it had its first time out.

The Jubilee Singers from Fisk University introduced black spirituals to the musical world in 1871. Included in their large repertoire were such songs as "Steal Away to Jesus," "Freedom Over Me," "Nobody Knows the Trouble I See," and "Swing Low, Sweet Chariot."

Florence B. Price, born in 1888, was the first black woman composer to achieve national recognition. She won the Wanamaker Foundation Award for her *Symphony in E Minor* in 1925. She died in 1953.

Bessie Smith, born in 1898, became one of the greatest female blues singers of the early twentieth century. She was inspired and helped by "Ma" Rainey, the first of the great blues singers. Clarence Williams, a representative of Columbia records, discovered Smith and helped her record her first single in February 1923. Smith made well over 150 recordings and starred in the movie *St. Louis Blues* in 1929. The movie, banned then, is now preserved in the Museum of Modern Art in New York City. Although Smith was known during the 1920s as "The Empress of the Blues," when the style of popular music changed, she did not change with it. She became an alcoholic and lost control of her career; she died on September 26, 1937.

A History of African-Americans in Dance

The first dancers to perform on the stage or in movies were tappers or "shufflers." People like Bojangles Robinson and Peg Leg Bates began to put class into the moves, creating and choreographing tap dances done in tuxedos, rather than in overalls or minstrel outfits. Today's dancers also learned from these early performances, as Sammy Davis Jr. freely admitted. Some of the best tap dancers in the world have performed at places like the American Museum of Natural History and at dance festivals held on an annual basis (e.g., the Colorado Dance Festival in Boulder).

Other types of dance are brilliantly represented by black troupes, such as the Alvin Ailey American Dance Theatre, which performs regularly in New York and is considered the foremost interpretative dance company. Alvin Ailey is a well-known choreographer who has trained more than three generations of dancers; he formed the company in 1958 to showcase works related to African-American heritage. This troupe performs modern as well as classic dances. The Ailey Theatre has spawned such stars as Judith Jamison, who now runs her own troupe called The Jamison Project.

Another dance company of note, The Garth Fagan Bucket Dance Company, located in Rochester, New York, plays to sell-out crowds. Its founder, Garth Fagan, is noted for creating a variety of works and receiving raves from the critics for his repertoire.

The Dance Theatre of Harlem, headed by Arthur Mitchell, is the premiere black ballet company. Mitchell founded the company in 1971, declaring that he wanted to teach "young black people the art of classical ballet, modern and ethnic dance."

A fairly new event on the dance scene, the Black Dance Conference, gives dancers a chance to network. Each year a different dance company sponsors the conference.

Some Biographies of Dance Personalities

Cab Calloway, a dancer and actor in the films made in the 1940s made his first black film, *Hi-De-Ho,* in 1942.

Lincoln Perry was born in 1889 in Key West. He selected the stage name "Stepin Fetchit" because he won money on a horse named Step and Fetch It. During his dancing and singing career, he changed his name several more times and even got into trouble with the law. He made it on the vaudeville circuit and eventually made it to Hollywood with a part in *In Old Kentucky.* He appeared in numerous pictures, but lost his pull in Hollywood in 1952.

Bill ("Bojangles") Robinson, the creator of the word *copasetic,* began his life in 1878 in Richmond, Virginia. While working at a stable, he began learning how to tap dance and started dancing for spare change before the age of ten. In 1908, he began his vaudeville career, and in 1914, a friend gave him the nickname "Bojangles." He starred in the movie *Hello Bill* in 1929, his first film. Though Robinson earned (and spent) about $3 million during his sixty-six years in the business, he died in November 1949, almost destitute.

PRICES FOR MUSIC AND DANCE MEMORABILIA

Book

    Hughes, Langston, *The First Book of Jazz,* New York, 1955; very condition, **$20–25.**

    Johnson, James W., ed., *The Second Book of Negro Spirituals,* New York, 1926; very good condition, **$12–16.**

    Marsh, J. B. T., *The Story of the Jubilee Singers, with Their Songs,* Boston, 1881; very good condition, **$20–25.**

    Singer, Barry, *Black and Blue the Life and Lyrics of Andy Razaf,* foreword by Bobby Short, includes classics: "It's Make Believe Ballroom Time" and "I'm Gonna Move to the Outskirts of Town," illustrated, 444 pages, New York, Schirmer Books; new, **$28.**

Cassette tape

    Amazing Grace, Aretha Franklin, New Wax Unlimited; new, **$12–15.**

    Golden Greats, Mahalia Jackson, New Wax Unlimited; new, **$9–12.**

Commemorative collectible, one ounce silver, art bar series, 1974

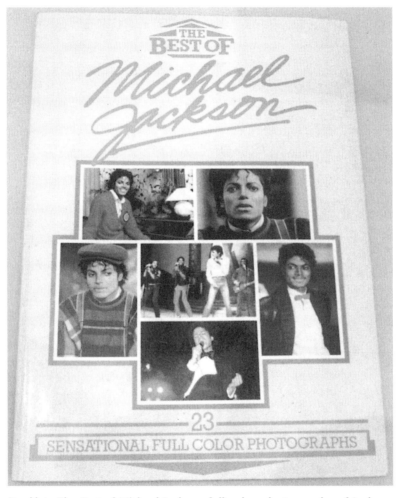

Booklet, *The Best of Michael Jackson,* full color photographs of Jackson from his childhood up to 1984; excellent condition, **$25–30.** Courtesy of Rose Fontanella; photo by Bob Reno.

Louis Armstrong, single issue, "Satchmo/ 1900–1971," reverse: "Silver Creations, Ltd.,/Limited Edition 4000"; excellent condition, **$40–50.**

Ella Fitzgerald, "Birth / of the / Blues / 1974"; excellent condition, **$35–45.**

Charlie Pride, bust, "Music City / Mint / Nashville / Tennessee," only 100 struck, rare; excellent condition, **$115–125.**

Compact disc, *R. Nathaniel Dett: Piano Works,* performed by pianist Denver Oldham; excellent condition, **$15–20.**

Compact discs/cassettes, *Althea Waites Performs the Piano Music of Florence Price, Sonata in E Minor, The Old Boatman, Cotton Dance,* and *Dances in the Canebrakes,* Cambria Records; new, **compact discs: $15–18 each; cassettes: $12–15 each.**

Doll, Louis Armstrong, Effanbee USA, hand painted in brown, blue, black, and white, very detailed, trumpet and handkerchief, rubber; 16″ × 8″; near mint condition, **$125–150.**

Dress-up set, Michael Jackson, 1984; excellent condition (in original package and wrapper), **$45–50.**

Hotel menu, autographed by Duke Ellington, ca. 1940; very good condition, **$12–15.**

Magazine, *Saturday Evening Post,* includes "Harlem's White Father," by Maurice Zolotow about the Four Ink Spots and Mo Gale, their manager, September 27, 1941; excellent condition, **$10–15.**

Medal

Cannonball Adderly, bronze created as cover art for his last album, *A Big Man Is Judged by Others—Not One's Self,* includes Cannonball's signature, 1976; excellent condition, **$60–70.**

Marian Anderson, "Marian Anderson / 'He's Got the Whole World in His Hands,'" U.S. Mint, 1980–1984; mint condition, **$30–35 for bronze; $235–250 for gold.**

Louis Armstrong, 1-oz. silver, excellent artwork, Franklin Mint; excellent condition, **$45–75.**

Count Basie, nonprecious "white metal," "Jazzfest June 1–7, 1969," 33 mm; mint condition, **$12–14.**

Sidney Bechet, bronze, shows two hands playing a soprano saxophone, Paris Mint; 68 mm; mint condition, **$65–70.**

Ray Charles, bronze, to honor the "King of Soul," in French and Braille, Paris Mint; excellent condition, **$65–75.**

Duke Ellington, 1-oz sterling silver, special commemorative issue, Franklin Mint, 1974; 39 mm; mint condition, **$45–55.**

Fisk Jubilee Singers, 1-oz. silver, quality artwork, Franklin Mint; excellent condition, **$45–75.**

W. C. Handy

Excellent quality artwork, 1-oz. silver, Franklin Mint; excellent condition, **$45–75.**

For civic and musical achievement, "De Soto, Jackson, Handy / Memphis / Sesquicentennial," reverse: "Shelby Memphis County Tennessee, United States Mint, 1969," 1⁹/₁₆″; mint condition, **bronze: $20–25, silver: $35–45.**

Mahalia Jackson, 1-oz silver, quality artwork, Franklin Mint; excellent condition, **$45–75.**

James Weldon Johnson, 1-oz. silver, quality artwork, Franklin Mint; excellent condition, **$45–75.**

Scott Joplin, 1-oz. silver, excellent quality artwork, Franklin Mint; excellent condition, **$45–75.**

Charlie "Bird" Parker, bronze, "The Immortal," shows Parker playing the saxophone, reverse: "Bird lives / 1920 / 1955 / Charlie Parker Memorial Foundation," shows a bird in flight, designed by Hallmark, sold at a May 13, 1973, benefit concert, 1¼″ and 3″; mint condition, **$18–20.**

Bessie Smith, 1-oz. silver, excellent quality artwork, Franklin Mint; excellent condition, **$45–75.**

Thomas "Fats" Waller, 1-oz. silver, excellent quality artwork, Franklin Mint; excellent condition, **$45–75.**

Sheet music, "Unforgettable," with picture of Nat "King" Cole, copyright 1951; excellent condition, **$30–40.** Courtesy of Rose Fontanella; photo by Bob Reno.

Photograph

Chuck Berry, three autographed, one in purple ink; very good condition, **$30–50 for three.**

Fats Domino seated at piano, autographed; 8″ × 10″; very good condition, **$6–8.**

Duke Ellington, autographed; very good condition, **$20–25.**

Minstrel troupe, on elaborate stage, sepia, framed without glass, 1890s; 20″ × 10″; near mint condition, **$100–150.**

Puzzle, Michael Jackson, 1980; excellent condition (in original package and wrapper), **$45–50.**

Record album

Art Songs by Black American Composers, composers include John Work, Florence Price, Howard Swanson, William Grant Still, Margaret Bonds, Undine Moore, and others, recorded by the University of Michigan, includes songbook, two-album LP set; new, **$16.**

Black Composers Series, CBS, music written by African-American composers in the 18th, 19th and 20th centuries, performed by major international symphony orchestras, LP only, nine-album set reissued by the College Music Society; new, **$48–55.**

Nat King Cole, *Forgive My Heart;* very good condition, **$20–25.**

Fats Domino, *Counting Boy* and *If You Need Me;* very good condition, **$6–8 each.**

Duke Ellington

With his orchestra, *Creole Love Call,* Victor, ca. 1927; very good condition, **$15–20.**

With the Jungle Band, *Mood Indigo,* Brunswick, ca. 1930; very good condition, **$18–22.**

Record album cover, MGM Records, Inc., close-up painting of bust of Sammy Davis Jr., with polka-dotted bow tie, and Count Basie facing away from each other, overlay at lower front center of a small colorless pencil sketch of three-quarter-length view of same pose, caption at top reads "Sammy Davis Jr. & Count Basie," 1973; excellent condition, **$20–35.**

Sheet music

"Ah Wants to Die from Eatin' Possum Pie," 1922; very good condition, **$8–12.**

"And They Called It Dixieland"; very good condition, **$35–45.**

"Angel Eyes," Nat King Cole; very good condition, **$8–10.**

"The Colored Major," march and two-step; very good condition, **$35–45.**

"Coontown Troubles," 1909; very good condition, **$15–20.**

"Darktown Strutter's Ball," 1917; very good condition, **$20–25.**

"Kingdom Coming," Civil War music by Henry Work, five pages, dated 1862; very good condition, **$12–20.**

"A Little Bit o' Honey," oval of mother and child; very good condition, **$12–15.**

Sheet music, "Mandy Lou," words and music by Thomas S. Allen; very good condition, **$25–50.** Photo by Donald Vogt.

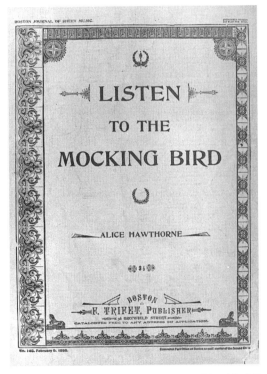

Sheet music, "Listen to the Mockingbird," by Alice Hawthorne, song was originally written by and credited to Richard Milburn (a black man), after 1855 all sheet music for this song bears Hawthorne's name; very good condition, **$25–50.** Courtesy of the Valerie Bertrand Collection; photo by Donald Vogt.

"My Babe from Boston Town," words and music by George M. Cohan, labeled as "coon song"; very good condition, **$25–35.**

"Old Black Joe," 1906; very good condition, **$10–15.**

"The Pepsodent Hour," Amos 'n' Andy; very good condition, **$20–25.**

"Uncle Jaspar's Jubilee"; very good condition, **$125–175.**

"Zip-a-Dee-Doo-Dah"; very good condition, **$15–25.**

Video cassette, *Give My Poor Heart Ease,* interviews and performances by B. B. King and James "Son" Thomas, Parchman Penitentiary work chants and Wade Walton's barber shop boogie-woogie, color, 20 minutes; new, **$40.**

CHAPTER FIFTEEN

Movie, Television, and Theater Memorabilia

The Collectibles

Collectibles in the arena of black movies, theater, and television include items such as lunch boxes, photographs, playbills, and toys.

LUNCH BOXES

Some of the best known television series and entertainment personalities have been depicted on lunch boxes. Some themes are *Julia,* the Diahann Carroll television show that first appeared in 1968; *Fame,* the late 1970s television show that featured Debbie Allen as a dance teacher; the Harlem Globetrotters, an exhibition basketball team; Bill Cosby's *Fat Albert and the Cosby Kids,* a cartoon show that began in 1972, and many black sports stars.

The metal lunch boxes, which are the older versions, are more valuable than the plastic or vinyl ones. Look for wear on the corners, scratches, and missing handles or snaps. If your lunchbox also includes a matching thermos, you are in luck. Prepare yourself for prices that may, at first, seem unreasonable. These are hot collectibles and in much demand.

PHOTOGRAPHS

Most entertainers have publicity photographs made to send to promoters, producers, and fans. Autographed photos are, of course, more valuable than unsigned ones; but many modern photos are signed not by the star but by a member of his or her staff. See Chapter 14 for more information about publicity photos and Chapter 3 for general information about photography.

PLAYBILLS AND LOBBY CARDS

Though few contemporary playbills and lobby cards are found (for some reason, they are not made in the quantities today that they once were), the older examples are easier to collect than posters (see below), because they were often made of cardboard rather than thin paper, thus better withstanding the test of time. The rarity and condition of the card and the popularity of the character(s) decide the price.

POSTERS

Entertainment posters vary in price, depending on the popularity of the event, the rarity of the poster, and its age. Naturally, a poster made in the early days of black film-making will be more difficult to find than one that stars, for example, Eddie Murphy. Many video stores keep out of date posters, which they either give away or sell very cheaply. A collection of such posters can be started for little or no money by paying attention to when the store changes its displays.

TOYS

Made to depict favorite movie and television characters, toys are often overlooked by collectors who are focusing on a certain personality. Dolls, board games, and windup toys can often be found at yard sales and flea markets. Look for the ones still in their original boxes (see also Chapter 10).

Poster, Harry Clapham's Minstrels, about 18″ × 24″; very good condition, **$125–150.** Courtesy of Rose Fontanella; photo by Donald Vogt.

A History of African-Americans in the Movie Industry

Blacks have participated in some manner in the movie industry since its beginning in the late nineteenth century. The silver screen's negative portrayal of African-Americans during the period from 1900 to 1940 was protested by black newspapers, performers, and organizations. Some of those who protested realized the only way to make a change in the industry was by building their own film companies.

One of the first to take this step was William Foster who, in 1910, created the first comedies to star only African-Americans. Soon afterward, the Los Angeles–based Lincoln Picture Company produced *Realization of a Negro's Ambition* (1916), the first film in which Blacks were not stereotyped.

The Lincoln Motion Picture Company, organized in Los Angeles in 1916, became the first in the motion picture industry to make and distribute realistic black films

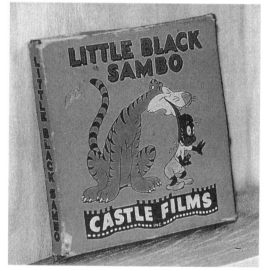

Film, *Little Black Sambo,* ca. 1940s, 8 mm; good condition, **$275–295.** Courtesy of the Mary Cantrell Collection; photo by Mary Cantrell.

instead of degrading burlesque or comedic farces. The company's first feature films were shown in California, Nebraska, Missouri, and Alabama. Lincoln's president, Noble M. Johnson, also starred in some of the films the company released, including *The Trooper of Company K* and *The Law of Nature,* before resigning in 1918. His resignation eventually led to the company's demise, though the company did not discontinue its operations until 1923.

Other companies soon followed Lincoln's lead, and from 1910 to 1950 more than 150 independent film companies sprang up across the nation. Only 75% of those companies actually produced films and only approximately 35% of those companies were owned exclusively by black filmmakers. These companies grew rapidly during the Roaring Twenties, experienced a decline in operation during the Depression (as did most American businesses), then experienced a revival after World War II.

In 1919, James Smith opened the first black-operated casting office in Los Angeles, and by 1921, more than three hundred theaters across the United States showed black films as well as vaudeville shows. As successful as this might sound, things still weren't easy for black filmmakers. For example, a film titled *For His Mother's Sake,* in which Jack Johnson starred, was banned in Ohio because Johnson had been convicted of "white slavery."

By 1924, there were enough black actors to organize the Colored Actors Union in New York City, even though a survey proved only 50% of theaters that catered to black patrons were actually owned by Blacks. That was also the year Oscar Micheaux's movie *Son of Satan* was banned in Norfolk, Virginia.

One of the first newspapers to inform the black movie industry, *The Actor's News,* began publishing in New York in 1925.

The 1930s were a turbulent time, with many fits and starts in the industry. Though

some of the best known black stars began working during this decade, it was also a decade when many films met with resistance in such film-popular cities as New York City and Los Angeles.

After withstanding many years of abuse and degradation at the hands of independent white filmmakers, black actors and filmmakers decided to give themselves a hand up—they started writing more of their own movies and creating better roles as well as respectable stories. Before the 1930s, the only filmmaker of note who had created tasteful black films was Oscar Micheaux. He was responsible for approximately 10% of Black-cast films produced between 1915 and 1950. His company, the Micheaux Film & Book Co. in Chicago, produced its first film, *The Homesteader,* in 1918, the year the company was formed. Micheaux endured all kinds of problems during his filmmaking years, including bankruptcy and having some of his pictures banned. In 1931, *The Exile,* his first sound picture, was prevented from being shown in New York City in 1932; in 1938, *God's Stepchildren* was banned from RKO Regent Theatre in New York City.

Micheaux's talent highlighted the controversial subjects his films discussed; his first film was *Within Our Gates* (1920). This film contained a scene depicting the lynching of a black man and was first shown at Hammon's Vendome Theatre in Chicago. However, its debut had originally been stalled by the Chicago Board of Movie Censors, who claimed its showing might result in a race riot. Though the house was packed when the film opened, no riots occurred. Many reviewers and theaters refused to comment on the picture or to show the movie, but Micheaux did not stop making movies.

Some of Micheaux's other films include *The Gunsaulus Mystery* (1921), starring Evelyn Preer, Dick Abrams, Lawrence Chenault, and L. DeBulger; *The Dungeon* (1922); two versions of *Birthright,* a silent film in 1924 and a talkie in 1939, which starred Ethel Moses, Alec Lovejoy, and Carmen Newsom; *The House Behind the Cedars* (1924); *A Daughter of the Congo* (1930); *Temptation* (1936); *The Notorious Elinor Lee* (1940); and *The Betrayal* (1948).

Micheaux wrote books as well as films, including *The Wind From Nowhere, The Case of Mrs. Wingate, The Forged Note, The Story of Dorothy Stanfield,* and *The Masquerade.* He died at age sixty-seven in 1951 in Charlotte, North Carolina.

During the 1940s, Blacks spent hundreds of millions of dollars going to the movies. All of America wanted to escape the realities of war by sitting in dimly lit theaters, watching light movies like *Hi-De-Ho.* By the end of the 1940s, some of the industry's greats, like Micheaux, retired, stepping aside for new talent.

After World War II, the NAACP voiced their dismay with the way African-Americans had been depicted in films and called for major changes. The industry listened and started producing films such as *Intruder in the Dust, Pinky, Lost Boundaries,* and *Home of the Brave* (all done in 1949). Finally, black problems took center stage in the movie world.

The 1950s saw the emergence of many black actors who, like Sidney Poitier, were dignified and intelligent and did not dance or sing. Poitier, along with Ossie Davis, Louis Gossett Jr., and Ruby Dee proved to be critically acclaimed dramatic actors. The 1950s also presented Dorothy Dandridge whose beauty and tragic suicidal death served to highlight her roles in *Porgy and Bess* and *Carmen Jones.*

The 1960s, an age of rebellion and change, saw black films and actors take on a radical, tough, and militant mood. Films such as *Shaft* (1971) and *Super Fly* (1972) led to a whole list of film lookalikes. Many of these films were commonly called *blaxploitation.*

By the end of the 1970s, filmmakers came to the fore to produce other types of black films. Unfortunately, many films cast black performers, who had once had leading roles, into supporting positions for white leads. For example, Billy Dee Williams's roles in *Nighthawks* (1981) and the Star Wars movies.

The tide once again turned in the 1980s. Powerful, critically acclaimed films such as *The Color Purple* (1985) and the big hit *She's Gotta Have It* (Spike Lee's 1986 low-budget film) were being produced. Lee was the first independent black filmmaker to produce movies black patrons could relate to. His *Do the Right Thing* was a look into the lives of black and white residents of Brooklyn. He starred in the film and also promoted it heavily, taking it to the Cannes International Film Festival in France. By 1990, there was no doubt that Spike Lee would have an impact on black filmmaking for a long time.

The 1980s and 1990s also introduced Eddie Murphy and Richard Pryor, both comedians-turned-actors and both true box office superstars. Other black actors of note include Whoopi Goldberg, Gregory Hines, Louis Gossett Jr., Danny Glover, and James Earl Jones.

Some Biographies of Movie Personalities

Louise Beavers first starred in Million Dollar Productions' all-black casts of *Life Goes On* and *Reform School* and then went on to become what America thought of when they pictured a maid or mammy. Though she considered her greatest movie to be *Imitation of Life,* she also starred in *Uncle Tom's Cabin, Dr. Monica, She Done Him Wrong* and *Ladies of the Big House.* She died in 1962 in Los Angeles.

Harry Belafonte, a multitalented actor and singer with strong political beliefs, was born in 1927 and became one of Hollywood's black leading men in the 1950s. During the 1960s, he was involved with the civil rights movement and was a close friend of Martin Luther King Jr. Belafonte held off his entertainment career during this time; when he returned it was to produce and act in *Angel Levine* and *Buck and the Preacher.* Belafonte also made a number of appearances on television, including *The Ed Sullivan Show* and specials like *Tonight with Belafonte.* His daughter, Shari Belafonte, is also an actress.

Clarence Brooks was born in San Antonio, Texas, in 1895. He starred in many films after his first production, *Realization of a Negro's Ambition* in 1915, but he might best be known as one of the founders of the Lincoln Motion Picture Company. He starred in all Lincoln's films except one.

Diahann Carroll, born in 1935 in New York City, started her career as a model before blossoming into a singer and actress. She has played Broadway, nightclubs, television, and movies. Her series *Julia* (1968–1971) was very popular; look for the dolls that were made in that character's image. Carroll won a Tony in 1962 for her performance in *No Strings.*

Ralph Cooper, a very popular actor in the 1930s, first appeared as a singer and dancer in New York's Apollo Theatre in about 1920; he also performed as an emcee and band leader. Cooper's first Hollywood break came in 1936 when he was called in to replace Bill Robinson in *White Hunters.* Even though he didn't actually get that part (he didn't fit the public's stereotype of a black man), he did end up getting a role in the movie; unfortunately, his scenes were edited out. Cooper starred in the first all-black gangster talkie, *Dark Manhattan.* The movie broke all house records at New York's Apollo Theatre. During his career, he helped organize Million Dollar Productions and starred in many gangster roles before tiring of that image in 1939. Cooper's other talents included screenwriting, acting as a radio show host, and producing *Harlem Spotlight,* a successful East Coast television show.

Dorothy Dandridge, born in 1922 in Cleveland, Ohio, started in show business at a young age, singing, dancing, and acting with other members of her family. She also appeared at the Cotton Club in Harlem, debuting in the black-cast film *Four Shall Die* when she turned eighteen.

During the 1950s, she sang in nightclubs and starred in *Bright Road* with Harry Belafonte. Her role in *Carmen Jones* (1955) won her an Oscar. Dandridge died in 1965 of a drug overdose.

Sammy Davis Jr. appeared in his first film, *Rufus Jones for President,* in 1933. After that time, he appeared in numerous films as a singer, dancer, and actor. Known as a member of the Rat Pack, along with Frank Sinatra, Dean Martin, and Peter Lawford, Davis was a longtime favorite of the Las Vegas club scene. His star did not shine in only music, acting, or dancing—his brilliance made him an all-round, well-loved entertainer. His last film, *Taps,* was also the last time he danced on screen. He also hosted two television shows and made innumerable television appearances from the 1950s through the 1980s. He died in 1990.

Whoopi Goldberg, comedian, movie star, television actress, and theater performer, was born Caryn Johnson in New York City in 1950. She had theater roles in *Jesus Christ Superstar* and *Hair* in the 1970s, then moved on to improvisational theater in the 1980s. Goldberg eventually brought her comedy show to Broadway and also taped it for a television special in 1985. Her movies include *The Color Purple* (1984), the box-office smash *Sister Act* (1992), and *Ghost* (1990), which won her an Oscar. Goldberg also had a featured role in television's *Star Trek: The Next Generation* (1987–1995).

Louis Gossett Jr., born in 1936, graduated from New York University and began acting on stage in the 1950s. During the 1960s, Gossett did some television, and in 1970, he made the break into movies. In 1977, he played Fiddler in the television miniseries *Roots.* He won an Oscar as Best Supporting Actor for his 1982 role in *An Officer and a Gentleman.*

Noble Johnson, born in 1881 in Colorado Springs, was one of the first and most important African-American actors. In his first film, *The Eagle's Nest,* Johnson played an American Indian, and he continued playing nonblack roles until he organized the Lincoln Motion Picture Company. He starred in a long list of films after resigning as president of the Lincoln Motion Picture Company in 1918.

Hattie McDaniel, born in 1898, was a radio and film actress and the first black female to win an Academy Award. McDaniel won for her supporting role in *Gone with the Wind* in 1939. She also played the title role in the early television series *Beulah.* She died in 1952.

Thelma ("Butterfly") McQueen, best known as Prissy in *Gone with the Wind,* was born in Tampa, Florida. Early in her life, she proved she could dance and sing and soon became part of the "Butterfly Ballet," which is where she got her nickname. She had strong convictions and was once out of work for more than a year because she refused to accept maid roles. McQueen also worked on radio and had a club in Augusta for preteenagers. She later became a nurse.

Mantan Moreland, born in the late 1800s, was a voracious actor and appeared in more than three hundred roles on screen, including the Charlie Chan series. His trademark line, "Feets, do your stuff," is still mimicked today. He also appeared in various television shows, including *The Bill Cosby Show.* He died in 1973 in Hollywood.

Eddie Murphy, born in 1961, is one of the modern superstars of both stage and screen. He began as a comic, playing to sell-out crowds before he reached his twenty-third birthday. He was one of the stars of the *Saturday Night Live* television show, and like many of his *SNL* colleagues, he was able to move on to great success. Some of his hit movies include *Beverly Hills Cop* (three films in the series) and *Forty-Eight Hours.* His personal appearances have been turned into best-selling videos and albums, for example, *Raw.*

Clarence Muse, born in 1889, had a long and productive movie career beginning in 1929 when he appeared in the second talkie, *Hearts in Dixie,* and continuing through to *Car Wash* in which he appeared at the ripe old age of eighty-six. A multitalented person, Muse acted on stage, sang, composed a number of songs, acted as a dialogue and acting coach, and worked on radio. He was awarded an honorary doctor of humanities degree from Bishop College in 1972.

Sidney Poitier, actor and director, has been called the most important black actor in Hollywood. Born in 1927 in Miami, the youngest child of seven, Poitier grew up poor and was influenced by his parents' Bahamian background. At sixteen, he left home and headed for New York, where he became a member of the American Negro Theatre. He landed some roles in the 1940s, including a small one in *Lysistrata* in 1946. In the 1950s, Poitier's career blossomed and by 1958, he was nominated for the Oscar for Best Actor for his role in *The Defiant Ones.* He became the first black actor to win an Oscar, for his role in *Lilies of the Field* (1963). During the 1970s, his most well known film is *To Sir, With Love,* in which he plays a British schoolteacher. After that film, his acting career took a downward turn. In the 1980s, Poitier turned to directing, creating films such as *Stir Crazy* (1980).

Richard Pryor, born in 1940 in Illinois, became a comedian early in life. He dropped out of high school to join the army and then went on to play nightclubs, learning his trade from the ground up. He appeared on television variety shows and starred in several films, before turning to the Las Vegas scene. In 1970, he took a two-year break from his career, coming back to television in the mid to late 1970s. Pryor made a series of movies (e.g., *Stir Crazy*). In 1980, he survived near-fatal burns, caused from free-basing cocaine. Though he makes selected public appearances, he suffers from multiple sclerosis, which significantly restricts his entertainment activity.

Noble Sissle was the first black performer (with Eubie Blake) to star in a motion picture with sound in 1923.

Cicely Tyson, born in 1938, worked as a model and appeared in New York theater before turning to television in the 1960s. Her role in the 1974 film *Sounder* won her an Oscar nomination for Best Actress; she won an Emmy for her portrayal of Jane Pittman in the television special *The Autobiography of Miss Jane Pittman.*

Melvin Van Peebles, director, actor, composer, and writer, is considered the most important black director since Oscar Micheaux (although Spike Lee fans may disagree). His first movie, *Story of a Three Day Pass,* was shot in 1967 and won Van Peebles some acclaim, but his 1971 film *Sweet Sweetback's Baadasssss Song* became a legend. Van Peebles went on to direct two Broadway shows and also did a film version of *Don't Play Us Cheap.*

A History of African-Americans in Television

Televisions started showing up in American homes in 1950, and the first weekly sitcom to feature a black actor was *Beulah* (1950–1953), starring Ethel Waters. She was not the first black face on the tube, however. Bob Howard, an entertainer who hosted his own short (fifteen-minute) program, had aired from 1948 to 1950 on CBS's *The Bob Howard Show*. In 1950, Hazel Scott, a jazz pianist, starred three nights a week on the *Hazel Scott Show*.

The next sitcom to make an impact, *Amos 'n' Andy* (1951–1953), had originally been a radio show (see also "A Brief History of African-Americans in Theater"). Satire and parody was the name of *Amos 'n' Andy's* game—a situation for Blacks on TV that would not change until the series *I Spy*, starring Bill Cosby. Between the 1950s and 1960s, various black stars were featured on sitcoms and were interviewed on programs like Edward R. Murrow's *Person to Person*.

The 1960s saw a shift toward more realistic African-American characters on television. The change began slowly with featured black performers appearing among the regular casts of several television series. *I Spy* was the first show to feature a white and a black actor on equal footing—or *seemingly* on equal footing. That trend continued until 1968 when Diahann Carroll broke the mold of Blacks being secondary characters in her series *Julia*. The late 1960s also introduced *Room 222* (1969–1974), with Lloyd Haynes and Denise Nicholas; and *The Bill Cosby Show* (1969–1971), on which Cosby played a gym teacher.

In the early 1970s, *The Flip Wilson Show* (1970–1974) and *All in the Family* (1971–1983) repopularized the type of black comedy that was seen in the early days of movies. The 1970s also became a period to showcase black comedy shows like *Sanford and Son, Good Times, What's Happening!,* and *The Jeffersons*. The decade also brought important TV movies to the small screen: *The Autobiography of Miss Jane Pittman* (1974), *Roots* (1977), *King* (1978), and *Attica* (1980). This time period also saw the beginning of some television series with good, realistic parts for black actors, such as *Fame*.

Then came Bill Cosby—again. This time he starred in the incredibly successful *Cosby Show*, which he also created, carving major avenues for all black actors. Cosby's television family was funny, but not in a degrading way. Though it was criticized for being too idealistic, the show did make a major television breakthrough for all blacks.

Poster, ad for a minstrel show, colorful, about 36" tall × 20" wide; excellent condition, **$1,500–2,500. Photo by Bob Reno.**

In the 1990s, new television shows emerged that gave black actors their juiciest roles yet. Some of these shows are *I'll Fly Away; Home Front; Homicide,* with Andre Braugher as Detective Frank Pembleton; *Under One Roof,* with James Earl Jones; *NYPD Blue;* and *Deep Space Nine,* which features black Commander Sisko.

Some Biographies of Television Personalities

John Amos, born in New Jersey in 1939, is best known as the father, James Evans, on the television series *Good Times.* He has been acting since the early 1970s, and though most of his credits are from television series, he also was the older Kunta Kinte in the TV miniseries *Roots* and has appeared in several movies.

Eddie "Rochester" Anderson, best known for his role as Jack Benny's valet in his television show, was born in 1906 into a show business family. He started performing in his teens and worked as a song-and-dance man with his brother Cornelius. In the 1940s, Anderson also appeared in movies.

Bill Cosby, one of the most highly successful television stars in the history of the business, was born in Philadelphia in 1937. He started as a club comedian at the age of twenty six, trying television two years later. He costarred on the television series *I Spy* in the 1960s, then did a number of other television shows during the 1970s before hitting paydirt with *Fat Albert and the Cosby Kids,* a children's cartoon series. Cosby has acted as spokesperson for a number of products including Kodak, Jell-O, Coca-Cola, and Ford, keeping himself in the public eye with his well-done commercials. He also acted in a number of movies during the 1970s and 1980s before *The Cosby Show* became one of the best-loved family situation comedies on television. Cosby also has several best-seller books and comedy albums to his credit.

Phylicia (Ayers-Allen) Rashad, best known as Claire Huxtable, Bill Cosby's wife on *The Cosby Show,* was born in 1948 and is the older sister of dancer Debbie Allen. Rashad, a graduate of Howard University, came to Broadway to understudy in the 1982 musical *Dreamgirls.* She has guest starred in other television movies and has a few television movies to her credit.

Oprah Winfrey, often called the richest woman in television, has hosted talk shows and also acted in movies and on television. She won an Oscar nomination for her supporting role in *The Color Purple* (1985). She began hosting the TV talk show *People Are Talking* in 1977, and in 1984 she hosted *A.M. Chicago,* which eventually was renamed *The Oprah Winfrey Show.* Winfrey, known for her candor, has become a spokesperson for abused women, gaining the public's trust through her personal experiences.

A Brief History of African-Americans in Theater

The first minstrels were white performers who "corked" their faces to travel in blackface minstrel shows. An Englishman visiting America in 1822 was the first person to introduce black stage characters. Charles Matthews studied the dialect, character, history, and actions as well as the songs and lore of black American life. During one of his acts, he used a song called "Possum up a Gum Tree," which is thought to have been the beginning of blackface minstrel shows. Minstrel shows continued through the early 1800s with such white performers as Thomas D. Rice, George Washington Smith, and J. W. Sweeney, who used black songs and dances in their routines.

When Harriet Beecher Stowe's *Uncle Tom's Cabin* came to the stage, the comical minstrel characterization of black Americans all but disappeared. But black characters were still played by whites who corked their faces. It was not until the late 1800s that traveling acting troupes began to advertise the inclusion of "real Negro" actors. Between 1850 and 1910, black minstrels

Photograph, *Showboat,* shows Paul Robeson, Irene Dunne, Hattie McDaniel, and unidentified actress, 1940s; excellent condition, **$15–20.** Courtesy of Rose Fontanella; photo by Bob Reno.

such as Thomas Greene Bethune ("Blind Tom"), the Luca family, Horace Weston, and the Hyer sisters performed on the American stage, some going on to head troupes that traveled all over the world.

By the 1920s, black minstrel shows began to take a back seat to the up-and-coming institution of vaudeville. Performers, such as Amos 'n' Andy started out in vaudeville, then worked their way on to radio, and later, television. In fact, most of the black actors who worked on stage after the 1920s also worked in the movie or television industry.

Some Biographies of Theater Performers

Amos 'n Andy started out as a vaudeville team named Sam 'n Henry. When they were put on nationwide radio, they changed their name to Amos 'n Andy. Their radio show was successful from 1926 to 1956, at which time they starred in a hit CBS TV show. In 1930, they starred in their own movie, *Check and Double Check,* but audiences were disappointed to see their favorite radio characters on screen in blackface. Many collectible articles were made in the Amos 'n Andy images.

Pearl Bailey, born in 1918 in Newport News, Virginia, began performing while still a child. She appeared in the nation's top all-black theaters, as a comic as well as a singer who half-sang, half-talked her songs. She debuted on Broadway in *St. Louis Woman* in 1946 and eventually appeared in a number of movies. In the 1950s, she appeared on television's *The Ed Sullivan Show* and even hosted her own variety series in 1971. She also wrote two autobiographies: *The Raw Pearl* (1968) and *Talking to Myself* (1971).

Josephine Baker, born in St. Louis, Missouri, on June 3, 1906, died a famous French stage person-

265

ality and naturalized French citizen in Paris on April 12, 1975. Baker was a member of a Philadelphia dance troupe at age sixteen, and at seventeen she joined the chorus of a Boston show, and then became part of the floor show of the Plantation Club in Harlem. She crossed the ocean in 1925 to dance in La Revue Negre and at the Theatre des Champs-Elysees in Paris. She had starred in a light opera and made *Zou-Zou* and *Princess Tam-Tam* before World War II, but Baker devoted herself to working with the Red Cross and Resistance during the war years. In 1940, she was recruited to spy for France. As a result of her actions, she was awarded the Croix de Guerre and the Legion of Honor with the rosette of Resistance. In 1949, her book *Memories* was published. She first retired from the stage in 1956 but starred in *Paris* in 1959, returning to New York theater in 1973. She died of a massive cerebral hemorrhage in 1975 and was buried with a twenty-one-gun salute from the French government in Monaco.

Anita Bush, called the mother of "Negro drama," was born in Washington, D.C., but grew up in Brooklyn. She formed her own vaudeville troop in 1910, after playing small parts in the theater. In 1912, an injury ended her dancing career, and she returned to New York to organize the Anita Bush Players, which started out at the Lincoln Theatre in New York in 1915. By the time the group moved to the Lafayette Theatre, the troupe had begun producing full-length plays. Eventually, Bush sold the company. In 1938, she costarred in *Swing It,* an all-black musical at The Adelphi Theatre in New York.

Ossie Davis, born in 1917, began to appear in theater during the late 1940s and currently has to his credit roles in theater (e.g., *Porgy and Bess*), television (e.g., *Evening Shade*), and movies—as

actor, director and writer. He is married to actress Ruby Dee.

Ruby Dee, born Ruby Ann Wallace in 1924 in Cleveland, Ohio, grew up in Harlem. She attended Hunter College to study romance languages and apprenticed with the American Negro Theatre at approximately the same time, 1941–1944. She appeared in her first Broadway production in 1946 (*Porgy and Bess*), has starred in movies, and has made guest appearances on television (e.g., on *Evening Shade*).

Reginald Fenderson's first public appearance was at four years old in his uncles' traveling show. During the 1930s and 1940s, he acted in many black films, then turned to the stage for a while before returning to Hollywood. Fenderson also worked in radio (*Amos 'n' Andy*) and television (*Ironside* and *The Bill Cosby Show*).

Lorraine Hansberry—born in 1930, wrote the play, *A Raisin in the Sun.* With this play, she was the first black playwright to win the New York Drama Critics Award, for the best play of 1959. She died in 1965.

James Earl Jones, the son of actor Robert Earl Jones, was born in 1931. He first acted on stage in New York during the 1950s, then turned to television in the 1960s and, soon after, to the movies. His return to Broadway in *The Great White Hope* was a triumphant one. He also played the lead in the movie of the same name, for which he won the Oscar for Best Actor in 1970.

Paul Robeson, born in 1898, the son of a former slave, became a singer, actor, all-American football player, and activist. In 1923, he received a law degree, but because of a lack of opportunity for blacks in that field, he became a stage performer in London. He died in Philadelphia on January 23, 1976.

PRICES FOR MOVIE, THEATER, AND TELEVISION MEMORABILIA

Comic book, *I Spy*, based on television series with Bill Cosby, 1968; excellent condition, **$25–30.**

Handbill, *Uncle Tom's Cabin*, heading reads "Little Eva's Temptation," old Tom sitting and reading to a little white girl, late 1880s; good condition (has been repaired), **$150–200.**

Lunch box

The A-Team television show costarring Mr. T, plastic, thermos bottle; very good condition, **$10–15.**

Fat Albert and the Cosby Kids, television cartoon series, lithographed tin, colorful scenes over the entire outside, rare; very good condition, **$55–65.**

Julia, television show, lithographed tin, with metal thermos bottle, rare; very good condition, **$55–65.**

Mr. T, television cartoon series, plastic, with plastic thermos bottle; very good condition, **$10–15.**

Poster, ad for *Remus on Broadway*; very good condition, $175–210. Photo by Donald Vogt.

Welcome Back Kotter, television show, lithographed tin, rare; very good condition, **$40–50.**

Magazine

Ebony, Frank Sinatra, Dean Martin, Peter Lawford, Joey Bishop, and Sammy Davis Jr. on cover, August 1960; excellent condition, **$20–35.**

Gentlemen's Quarterly, Sammy Davis Jr. on cover in plaid suit and car coat leaning against a wood fence, caption reads "Sammy Davis, Jr.: Something else!," September 1967; excellent condition, **$10–25.**

Jet, Sammy Davis Jr., closeup on cover, caption reads "Sammy Davis, Jr.: World's Greatest Entertainer 1925–1990," 1990; excellent condition, **$4–8.**

Sepia, Sammy Davis Jr. on cover embracing costumed Olga James, May 1956; excellent condition, **$10–25.**

Plaque, Amos 'n Andy radio show promotion, etched in wood, painted black, red, brown, and blue, marked "Etcht-Kraft," vary rare, 1930s; 8″ × 10″; near mint condition, **$250–325.**

Playbill

Blues for Mister Charlie, written by James Baldwin, features Al Freeman Jr. and Diana Sands, 1964; excellent condition, **$20–25.**

Carry Me Back to Morningside Heights, features Cicely Tyson, Louis Gossett, and Johnny Brown on cover, directed by Sidney Poitier, opening night, 1968; excellent condition, **$20–25.**

For Colored Girls Who Have Considered Suicide When the Rainbow Isn't Enuf, written by Ntozake Shange, opening night; excellent condition, **$10–15.**

Hello Dolly, Pearl Bailey and Cab Calloway on cover, 1967; excellent condition, **$20–25.**

Purlie Victorious, Ossie Davis and Ruby Dee on cover, 1962; excellent condition, **$25–30.**

Raisin in the Sun, Ossie Davis and Claudia McNeil on cover, 1959; excellent condition, **$25–30.**

THE MEMBER OF THE WEDDING

Playbill, *The Member of the Wedding,* Ethel Waters on cover, 1951; excellent condition, **$25–30.** Courtesy of Rose Fontanella; photo by Bob Reno.

Poster

> *Little Eva's Temptation,* stone lithograph, advertising for the minstrel show, daintily dressed Topsy, her hair in braids, holding flowers and dancing, mounted on linen for preservation, 1920s; 20″ × 28″; excellent condition, **$200–250.**
>
> "Messett's Musical Entertainers," minstrels, black dandy on stage with showgirls, linen-backed, Quigley Litho; 41″ × 13″; near mint condition, **$450–550.**
>
> "Roberts Minstrel," gloved hands extend past edge of poster, hand painted in black, white, red, blue and green, bold; 28″ × 20″; excellent condition, **$225–300.**

Poster, ad for *Black Gold,* produced by Norman Studios, all-black cast, about 18″ × 24″; excellent condition, **$175–200.** Courtesy of the Leonard Davis Collection; photo by Bob Reno.

> "Spaeth & Co., Lasses White Minstrels, The Boy from Tennessee, Billy Doss"; very good condition, **$250–300.**

Theater mask, "The Nigger Outfit," cloth and paper, black head cover, includes hat and holes for eyes, mouth and lips, fine graphic on box, very rare, Germany, 1927; 6½″ × 5½″; excellent condition, **$200–300.**

CHAPTER SIXTEEN

Sports Memorabilia

The term *sports collectibles* covers a vast range of items, from trading cards that give players' statistics to photographs, ephemera, uniforms, posters, autographs, books, bats, balls, and advertising items. Naturally, the older items are more difficult to find, thus the prices will be higher (often regardless of condition). However, condition *is* paramount when considering paper items—such as trading cards—and keeping your collection in good shape often calls for special sleeves, three-ring binders, or specially designed boxes.

In most towns, there exists a small shop that deals in sports cards. I suggest strongly that you visit your local shop and talk with the dealer about your specialized interests. That dealer will call you when and if he or she has the type of memorabilia you're interested in. A dealer can also act as teacher to help you in this vast collectibles market. There are also many books on the topic (see the "Bibliography") that will help you discern which cards to collect; who in the sports world is hot; and how to determine condition, quality, and the price to pay. One newsletter that focuses on Blacks in sports is the official newsletter of the Negro League

Baseball Museum. For subscription information contact the Negro League Baseball Museum, Lincoln Building, 1601 East Eighteenth Street, Kansas City, MO 64108.

Breaking up sets is never a good idea. You also should think of purchasing the items that are of limited quantity. For example, signed baseballs are hard to find—not made in quantity or distributed to every store that sells bubble gum, as are cards.

Naturally, most people automatically think of collecting baseball, basketball, or football cards when you mention sports memorabilia. Few realize, however, that boxing cards were around a lot earlier than baseball cards. They were often giveaways used by tobacco companies to advertise their products. However, the cards also served another purpose—to keep the paper packages stiff and the fragile cigarettes enclosed from being crushed. Goodwin & Co. was one of the first to create boxing cards, but others soon jumped on the bandwagon (e.g., Allen & Ginter, D. Buchner & Co., and P. H. Mayo & Brothers). The first cards were rough, using color over line drawings. Later, sepia photographs on black cardboard were introduced, then color lithography. Issuance of boxing cards declined throughout the 1950s to 1980s, but interest has grown lately, and these cards are once again being produced.

Of utmost importance is the knowledge you bring to this area of collecting. The history of black American athletes and what they have brought to different sports will help you decide which area to focus on. And, of course, your pocketbook decides the rest.

"Doc" Young, former sports editor for *Jet Magazine* and sports writer for a number of other periodicals, claims in his book *Negro Firsts in Sports* that the "single area of 'democratic' news coverage" in any newspaper "was the sports section." He went on to say that "Negroes were full-fledged members of integrated teams, and their presence was accepted by their teammates and by the thousands of fans who came to see them all play." Yet, it wasn't always this way. And it's still difficult for black women to be recognized and to play professionally all the sports they'd like to play.

Sports in Which Black Athletes Have Participated

AUTO RACING

Though there were many African-American racers in the nineteenth century, you seldom see black drivers today. Rojo Jack, one of America's greatest automobile racers, never had the privilege of driving in the Indianapolis 500 because of the color of his skin. Jack began racing in 1923 and was one of the premier racers of his time. He did not stop driving even after losing an eye in a 1938 accident when he was over sixty years old.

Another black racer, Joe Ray Jr., stated in 1945 that there was nothing stopping him from competing in Indianapolis except

himself. He said he hoped more Blacks would become involve in all aspects of auto racing.

BASEBALL

Blacks were playing baseball as early as during the Civil War—perhaps even earlier. The first black player to gain note played three years after the Cincinnati Red Stockings, the first American professional baseball team, was organized in 1869. Bud Fowler starred with an integrated baseball club in Newcastle, Pennsylvania, even though the National Association of Baseball Players (amateur) announced in 1867 that they "unanimously report against the admission of any club which may be composed of one or more colored persons."

Flyer, baseball game between the Springfield Brown Sox (black team) and the Hartford Giants. Courtesy of the Valerie Bertrand Collection; good condition, $75–150. Photo by Donald Vogt.

In 1884, Moses Fleetwood Walker caught barehanded for the Major League club from Toledo, the Blue Stockings. Walker graduated from Oberlin College in Ohio. Unfortunately, baseball's doors shut on Blacks in 1888. This shutout, an unwritten "law," lasted clear through to 1945.

Instead of remaining off the playing field, however, Blacks got together and formed their own teams. The first professional team was organized in 1885 by Frank Thompson. Thompson, the head waiter at the Argyle Hotel in New York, got a group of the hotel's waiters and bellmen together to play ball. During the summer of 1885, his team often played against white semipro teams in the area. When Thompson's group became a full-fledged professional team, it was called the Cuban Giants. (Black team members often "passed" as Cuban to avoid the antiblack feelings of that time.)

By 1890, most cities had black baseball teams, and the sport grew in popularity all across America. One of the most famous of the black players in the bush leagues was Andrew ("Rube") Foster. He pitched for both Major and Minor League black teams and then managed one of the big black teams, eventually becoming league president.

During the shutout period, some African-Americans still made their claim to baseball fame; however, they had to do it by passing as white. For example, Charles (Cincy) Grant played for the Baltimore Orioles in 1902. Grant was brought onto the team as an American Indian, but his loyal black fans brought banners to the games inscribed "Our Boy, Charley Grant." When people caught on to the ruse, the owner was forced to let Grant go.

Most Black Americans who played baseball during the early twentieth century played only in exhibition games (most of which, ironically, they won), or they played in the so-called Negro leagues. In 1920, Rube Foster formed the National Negro Baseball League, which was chartered in Illinois, Maryland, Michigan, New York, Ohio, and Pennsylvania. Every club in this league owned its own park. Soon after Foster's league was formed, others sprang up throughout the United States: the Eastern League (1921), with Ed Holden as president; the Negro American League (1939) in the West; and the Negro National League in the East. The first East-West black world series was played in 1924 between the eastern Hilldale team and western Kansas City team.

Some of the principal players during the 1920s to 1940s were Rube Foster, Smokey Joe Williams, Josh Gibson, and Satchel Paige. In 1962, John ("Buck") O'Neil was appointed the first black coach of the Chicago Cubs, a Major League baseball team. He also continued to scout for black players.

Branch Rickey, a white coach who became president and general manager of the Brooklyn Dodgers, was one of the people determined to get rid of the Jim Crow stands in baseball stadiums and to integrate the game itself. It took him a long time to beat down the walls of discrimination, but he finally did by threatening the Dodgers board of directors. He told them it was time to "include a Negro player or two" and went on to say that if they didn't allow Blacks on the team, they could start looking for someone to replace *him*. When he got the nod, Rickey hunted for the right person to make the break into the big leagues—and found Jackie Robinson. However, Rickey laid down the rules—no matter what happened, Robinson *couldn't fight back*. Rickey knew what Robinson was up against, and he believed the only way to fight prejudice was to turn the other cheek.

Robinson began to play for the Montreal Royals farm club, playing his first game in 1945, thus opening the doors for the many other black superstars who followed. Robinson made Rickey proud and went on to become one of the most highly

Magazine article, *Life,* Jackie Robinson and his family, August 1949; very good condition, $25–35. Courtesy of Gwendolyn Goldman; photo by Donald Vogt.

respected men in baseball history. He set many firsts as well, including first Black to become most valuable player in the Major Leagues (National League), 1949; rookie of the year, 1947; and Major League batting champ, 1949 (.349 average). He led the league with stolen bases in 1947 and 1949 and in double plays for four consecutive years (1949–1952) when he played second base. In 1962, Robinson was elected to the Baseball Hall of Fame. He died in Stamford, Connecticut, on October 24, 1972.

In 1946, Roy Campanella, son of an Italian father and African-American mother, signed on as a catcher with the New England League. He became the first "unofficial Negro Manager" for that league during a game when the white manager was ousted. Campy was also the first black baseball player to win three most valuable player

awards (National League) in 1951, 1953, and 1955. A tragic automobile accident in 1958 ended Campanella's playing days.

Born in 1931, Willie (Howard) Mays was the second man in Major League history to hit six hundred career home runs. He played for the New York Giants in 1951–1952 and again in 1954–1957, for the San Francisco Giants from 1958 to 1972, and for the New York Mets from 1972 until his retirement in 1973.

Today's baseball greats include Reggie Jackson, Darryl Strawberry, and many others. Information about contemporary players is easy to find.

BASKETBALL

It is not known who the first black basketball player was, but Edwin Henderson stated he learned the game in 1904 when he attended Harvard. Black basketball leagues played the game as early as 1906, and black colleges, such as Hampton Institute and Howard University, had courts as early as 1909. The first black high school athletic association was organized around 1905, partially through the efforts of Henderson, a black Harvard grad. In 1906, Henderson and five other black high school and college teachers formed the Interscholastic Athletic Association of the Middle States and put together a sports handbook. In 1939, Henderson wrote *The Negro in Sports,* the first book about Blacks in sports.

As in other sports, the first basketball teams to admit black players were located in the north. For example, Fenwich Williams was the captain of Vermont's team in 1908 and Charles Drew played for Amherst in 1923.

Among the earliest black basketball players, a familiar name pops up: Paul Robeson, football player, actor, singer, and dignified Renaissance man. He stood six foot, 2 inches and weighed 190 pounds and played center for Harlem's St. Christopher Club and for

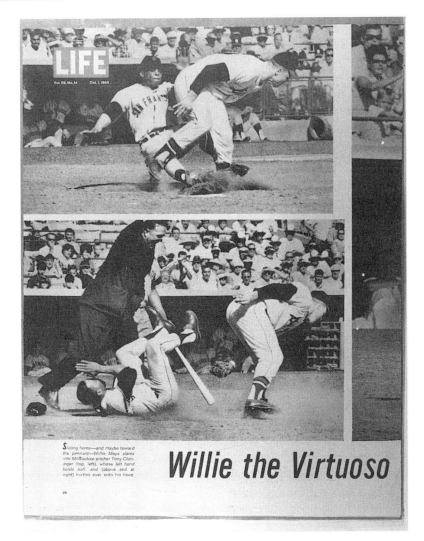

Magazine article, *Life,* **Willie Mays, October 1, 1965; very good condition, $25–35. Courtesy of Gwendolyn Goldman; photo by Donald Vogt.**

Rutgers College (1917–1919). Robeson's fellow teammates in Harlem included Harold "Legs" Jenkins and his brother Clarence "Little Fat" (or "Fats") Jenkins.

The first all-black team to win any recognition on the courts was the Rens, founded in 1923 by Robert J. Douglas; this was also the first team to challenge the Celtics for "the right to be called the greatest basketball team in the world" (see *Negro Firsts in Sports* by A. S. "Doc" Young). The Rens were purists, playing basketball as a sport, not as an act

(as did the Harlem Globetrotters later). They earned national acclaim and many youngsters dreamed of following in their glorious footsteps. Some of the first Rens stars included Eyre Saitch, Tarzan Cooper, Fats Jenkins, Pop Gates, Wee Willie Smith, Johnny Isaacs, and Pappy Ricks.

In the mid to late 1920s, the Morgan State Basketball team included Talmadge Hill, Daniel "Pinky" Clark, and Ed "Lanky" Jones. The team, undefeated in 1927, was recognized as black college basketball national champs. They continued on a winning streak (undefeated at home from 1927 to 1934). They even beat the Harlem Rens in 1929.

The diplomats of the sport, the Harlem Globetrotters, were formed in 1927, a year when the word *globetrotters* did not yet imply travel. They celebrated their twenty-fifth anniversary with a world tour—the first in the history of basketball. By 1953, there were sixty countries in the International Basketball Foundation, and the Globetrotters went on to play in each one.

The Globetrotters hired young men of exceptional basketball talent (like Wilt Chamberlain), but some of the best never joined the team. For example, Bill Russell was offered a spot on the team but turned it down, because Abe Saperstein (the Trotters' coach) talked to Russell's representative rather than directly to Russell himself.

The Trotters' way of clowning around has never been a cover for players who could not play regulation basketball—in fact, the teams have generally been able to beat any competition sent their way. Some of the most celebrated of the Globetrotters players have been Reece "Goose" Tatum, a center with a long-range looping hook shot; Meadowlark Lemon, known for his antics; and Marques Haynes, a magical dribbler who stayed with the team from 1946 to 1953.

After World War II, basketball started coming into its own as a nationally recognized sport. Some of the rules were altered as players got taller, jump shots shocked fans, and unorthodox moves became the rage. One of the first to recognize the future of pro basketball was Hal Jackson, the man who formed the Washington Bears, an all-black professional team. In 1943, the D.C.-based team went 66–0, yet they still weren't invited to participate in the pro basketball championships held in Chicago. Jackson, not one to take no for an answer, somehow got the team in, and the Bears made it to the finals. Jackson was offered a bribe to throw the game, but the players didn't want him to take it, saying the could win on their own merit. They won by two points, but had to sneak out of the arena, fearing for their lives.

World War II and the Korean War brought a different type of housing to the inner cities: projects of concrete and block, places where the only grass you saw was the kind growing up through the cracks in the sidewalk. Basketball, the only team-oriented game that favored asphalt, was the one boys and girls who lived in the projects learned. Some of the best pro basketball players—Kareem Abdul Jabbar, Julius Erving, Willis Reed, Wilt Chamberlain, Roger Brown, Walt Hazzard, and many others—learned how to slam-dunk on those concrete courts.

Bill Russell, thought to be the greatest defensive center in the history of basketball, was born William Fenton Russell in Monroe, Louisiana, in 1934. The six-foot, ten-inch star played with the Boston Celtics for thirteen seasons and later became that team's—and the NBA's—first black coach.

Wilt Chamberlain, another all-time great, smashed all existing scoring records and became the first player to score 100 points in one game in 1961–1962.

Because there are so many basketball greats, I will only mention a few here. Information is easily attainable on people like Chuck Cooper, the first black Boston Celtic; Nat "Sweetwater" Clifton, a Globetrotter who joined the New York Knickerbockers in the 1950s; Elgin Baylor; Oscar Robertson; Sam Jones of the Celtics; Julius "Dr. J" Erving, an ABA All-Star; the beloved Magic Johnson; Len Bias, a rising star struck down by drugs; the great Michael Jordan; and the up-and-coming Orlando Magic star Shaquille O'Neal.

Women have also played basketball, and their history in the sport stretches back to the early 1900s. However, finding information about which teams played and where and who the stars were is extremely difficult. It wasn't until the men's Olympic basketball team (the Dream Team of 1992) captured the interest of the American public that we discovered the women's Olympic basketball team had been winning on a regular basis. Perhaps now that we're aware of that fact, we will continue to hear something about these unsung heroes.

One of the members of the 1988 U.S. Olympic Gold Medal Women's Basketball Team, Bridgette Gordon, hails from DeLand, Florida. She now plays professional basketball in Italy.

BICYCLING

Major Taylor, one of America's great bicyclists, was born in Indianapolis in 1878. During 1898 to 1900, he won three American sprint championships and then went on to defeat European as well as Australian cyclists. Taylor battled prejudice, moving from Indianapolis to Boston because of racial problems. He maintained his status as a champion bicyclist until he retired in 1910.

BOXING AND WRESTLING

Boxing was the first sport that was fairly open to African-Americans, perhaps because Blacks themselves turned boxing into a professional sport here in the United States.

Bill Richmond, a black man, was born in 1763 in New York and became the first American to claim professional status as a fighter and also was the first American to box in another country. General Earl Percy, who commanded the British forces in New York, took Richmond to England in 1777. There Richmond fought and won several bouts with British soldiers. These were privately sponsored by Percy. While Richmond fought in England, the first "recognized" American bout was fought in America in 1816 (between Jacob Hyer and Tom Beasley, two white men). Richmond died at the age of sixty-six on December 29, 1829.

Another black American, Tom Molineaux, received fame in England in 1810. Born a slave in 1784, Molineaux fought Tom Cribb for the world heavyweight title. Although he lost, he succeeded in becoming well known as a fighter in Europe, where he was Bill Richmond's protégé. Molineaux fought Cribb again in 1811, losing badly. Molineaux became depressed, began to drink heavily, and died in Ireland at the age of thirty-four on August 4, 1818.

Other black fighters gained some fame in the 1800s, but it wasn't until the latter part of the century that George Godfrey, a Boston resident, became the first "colored heavyweight champion of America." In 1888, Godfrey was beaten by another fighter, Peter Jackson, one of the greatest heavyweight fighters in history. Godfrey's best known bout was fought against Jim Corbett at the California Athletic Club in 1891. They fought for sixty rounds before the bout was a draw. After winning the British Empire Heavyweight Title in 1892, Jackson acted for a while, touring the country with *Uncle Tom's Cabin* and other plays. Jackson still occasionally fought exhibition bouts, including a twenty-five round draw in Australia in 1899. He died in 1901 in Queensland, where his friends erected a monument in his honor.

George Dixon was born in Nova Scotia but moved to Boston when he was eight. He went on to become the first African-American to win the world bantamweight title as well as the world featherweight title. His nickname was "Little Chocolate," and even his critics stated he was the greatest pugilist of all time. He fought from 1886 to 1906, winning the bantam-weight title in London after he fought Nunc Wallace on June 27, 1890 and the featherweight title when he knocked out Jack Skelly in New Orleans on September 6, 1892. Dixon died in New York in 1909 and was elected to boxing's Hall of Fame in 1956. (Dixon wrote his autobiography in 1893—any collector who can find a copy could consider that feat equal to striking gold!)

The first black boxer to win the lightweight title, Joe Gans, was born in 1874 in Philadelphia. He started fighting in 1901, boxing three opponents in one day, winning one of the fights and receiving a no decision on the other two. In 1902, he won the world lightweight title by knocking out Frank Erne in the first round. He retained his championship until 1908; he lost his biggest battle in 1910 to tuberculosis.

Jack Johnson, the first African-American to win the world heavyweight championship, was born in Galveston, Texas, on March 31, 1878. He was known for his powerful punches as well as for his personality. Johnson was a showman, always drawing thousands of fans to his fights and often carrying on conversations with everyone in and around the ring during his fights. Enrolled in Boxing's Hall of Fame, Johnson won his title on December 26, 1908, in Sydney, Australia, and lost the title in Havana in 1915. His last recorded fight was against John Ballcort on November 27, 1945, fought when Johnson was sixty-seven years old! He died in an automobile accident the next year.

Joe Louis, the best loved black athlete of his day, was born in Lexington, Alabama, on May 13, 1914. He was the world heavyweight boxing champion from 1937 to 1949, the longest reign in the history of the heavyweight division, and the first black world heavyweight champion since Jack Johnson held that title. He was champion until his retirement in 1949. Later, he tried to make a comeback, but he was not successful in his bid to reclaim the crown.

During his long career, Louis only lost three bouts: one to Max Schmeling in 1936, one to Ezzard Charles in 1950, and the last to Rocky Marciano in 1951. In 1954, Louis was elected to the Boxing Hall of Fame.

Louis was the first black fighter to have black managers. His first was John Roxborough, then Julian Black, and later, Marshall Miles. His trainer, Jack "Chappie" Blackburn, was also black.

Sugar Ray Robinson was a six-time world champion boxer during the years 1946–1960. Many boxing authorities consider him to be one of the best boxers of all time. He won eighty-nine amateur fights and forty consecutive professional fights before being defeated by Jake LaMotta. Robinson retired in 1965 at the age of forty-five.

Born Cassius Marcellus Clay in Louisville, Kentucky, on January 17, 1942, Mohammed Ali went on to become a flamboyant and controversial boxing champion. He joined the Black Muslims in 1967 and later refused to perform military service on religious grounds, for which he was convicted of violating the Selective Service Act. The Supreme Court overturned the ruling in 1971. Ali returned to a successful career in boxing, which did not end until he captured the heavyweight boxing championship three times, becoming the first in history to do so.

In more recent years the major luminaries in boxing—including Sugar Ray Leonard, George Foreman, and Mike Tyson—have been primarily African-Americans.

FOOTBALL

The first All-American football team was created by Walter Camp in 1889. In 1892 and 1893, that team included William H. Lewis, a black center. He and William Tecumseh Sherman Jackson, a halfback, had been teammates on the Amherst College team and became the first two famous black football players in American sports history. In fact, Lewis went on to Harvard, eventually coached the line, and wrote the book *How to Play Football*. In 1900, Camp chose Lewis for his all-time All-American team. Lewis's success was not limited to sports, however. He became a successful attorney in Boston and was appointed assistant attorney general under President Taft. Jackson, meanwhile, became well known in Washington, D.C., as an innovative school administrator.

Other black players became gridiron stars before the turn of the century, but Fritz Pollard (who played college ball at Brown) became the first to play in a bowl game—the Rose Bowl in Pasadena, California, in 1916. Pollard was also the first black to play in organized pro football as a member of the Akron Indians in 1919. He eventually coached that team, becoming the first black coach of a major professional football team.

Paul Robeson, who most of us know as a great actor and orator, was regarded as one of the best all-American football players in 1917 and 1918 by a Rutgers University official.

Between 1919 and 1933, black players were recognized as part of professional football. In 1936, Homer Harris of Iowa was elected captain of a football team in Big Ten competition—no mean feat. However, black players disappeared from the game in the years before World War II until after the war. In 1946, Kenny Washington was signed to play for the Los Angles Rams, and the Rams added Woody Strode in May 1946. Bill Willis signed with the Cleveland Browns in August 1946, and only three days later, Marion Motley also signed with that team. It is said that Motley was the greatest fullback of all time (besides Jim Brown), with 826 attempts at rushing, 4,712 yards gained, and 31 touchdowns during the period from 1946 to 1953.

Joe Perry was born in 1927 and became a fullback for the San Francisco 49ers and the Baltimore Colts. He is said to be the greatest ground-gainer in the history of the National Football League. He signed as a free agent in 1948, after playing fullback for Compton Junior College.

The 1950s saw quite a few black football firsts:

November 1952: First black team to play a white team in a homecoming game (Negro Kentucky State College vs. Taylor University of Indiana)

September 1953: Ben Kelley, first black member of a predominantly white Texas college football team (San Angelo Junior College)

Leo Lewis was named to the Associated Press's Little All-American team, the first player from an all-black school to achieve that honor

1954: *Jet* magazine chose the first interracial All-American football team ever named by a black publication.

Jim Brown, born in St. Simons, Georgia, on February 17, 1936, became one of the National Football League's top all-time players, leading the league in rushing for eight of his nine seasons. A great all-around athlete, he played for the Cleveland Browns and has since gone on to star in motion pictures.

There are too many black football players of note to list here. Interested readers will find more information in books devoted to sports collectibles.

GOLF

Barriers were higher against Blacks in golf than in any other sport, possibly because golfers must be members of a club—usually an exclusive white-only club—to play on a decent course. This battle is still being fought. For example, Michael Jordan, the great basketball star, was accused of betting on his golf game in the 1990s, a tactic that did not work.

Charlie Sifford was the first important black golfer to win a pro tournament (1957). He won $1,200 after upsetting Eric Monti in a sudden-death playoff in the Long Beach Open. Before Sifford's day, there were a few black professional golfers, though most were players in college tournaments. Some of those players included Pat Ball, John Dendy, A. D. V. Crosby, George Roddy, Alfred Holmes, and Zeke Hartsfield.

Black tournaments were popular as early as 1926, and a handful of black-owned country clubs have existed since that time. However, the game has still not been totally integrated, and many court cases have been brought by golfers and organizations to change this discrimination (see *Negro Firsts in Sports* for more detailed information).

In 1959, Bill Wright became the first Black to win a major gold tournament when he was awarded the Standish Cup. At the time he was a twenty-three-year-old physical education major at Western Washington College. Wright's father was his greatest competitor—and the person Bill needed to beat to gain space in the qualifying tournament.

Ann Gregory of Indianapolis was the first black woman to play in an integrated women's amateur gold championship in 1956. Three years earlier, Lorraine Williams from Chicago became the first Black to win a national golf title when she won the Junior Girls Title.

HORSE RACING

In the early days of horse racing, from the first Kentucky Derby in 1874 and continuing through 1911, black jockeys dominated that end of the sport. Black trainers also held prominent positions, and the regard for black participants in the sport was generally high. One of the reasons for this was that when horse racing was introduced to America in 1665, slaves were given the dirtiest, and most dangerous, jobs (e.g., grooming, training, exercising, and helping at births). Few records have been kept of early black Americans who held any responsible positions in the racing world, though we do know that out of the fifteen jockeys at the first Kentucky Derby, *fourteen* were ex-slaves. Fifteen of the first twenty-eight Kentucky Derbys were won by men of color (note: the names of the Jockeys were never listed in the programs).

The first black jockey to achieve fame was named simply Abe. In 1866, he won the first Jerome Handicap at Belmont with a horse named Watson. He also won aboard another horse (Merrill) in the Travers Stakes at Belmont in the same year.

During the first Kentucky Derby in 1875, Oliver Lewis won aboard Aristides with a time of 2:37.45 (in seconds). In 1877, black jockey Bill Walker and black trainer Ed Brown teamed to win that year's Kentucky Derby. Walker became the most important jockey of his time, winning races at Churchill Downs as well as at other tracks.

Isaac Murphy, a jockey who rode his best races from 1884 to 1890, won his first Kentucky Derby in 1884 and became the first jockey to win three Derbys (1884, 1890 and 1891). His three-time record was not broken until 1930. Murphy became a race horse owner in 1886 (perhaps the first African-American to achieve that status). He died at age forty on February 12, 1896, leaving a $50,000 estate to his heirs.

After the Derby distance was shortened to one and a quarter miles from its original one and a half, black jockey Willie Simms won the first race on the new course. He went on to win many of America's classic races: the Preakness (1898), the Belmont (1893 and 1894), and the Champagne States (1895). Simms was also the first American jockey to win a race in England. He went to France and became successful there, both as jockey and trainer.

By the 1920s, however, no black jockeys rode in the Kentucky Derby. Jim Crow laws had replaced the bonds of slavery.

SAILING

Peter Jackson, known best as a boxer, was also a sailor and became a champion sailor in Australia in 1886. The boat with which he won, the *West Indian Negro,* was where he whiled away the hours, perfecting a skill that most people born in the West Indies seem to come by naturally.

TENNIS

Before Althea Gibson came on the scene, black tennis players had played in both public and collegiate tournaments. Lucy D. Stowe, who eventually became dean of women at Howard University, won the women's singles championship during the 1917 First American Tennis Association tournament.

Ora Washington began her career in tennis in 1924 and won a national black tournament, then went on to play for twelve *undefeated* years, accumulating 201 trophies—a truly impressive career. Washington was also a basketball star for eighteen years, playing for the *Philadelphia Tribune* Girls Team.

Althea Gibson, born in Silver, South Carolina, on August 25, 1927, became the first black player to win a tennis championship; she was also a moderately successful golfer after 1963. She first played for the American Tennis Association with the support of two sponsors: Dr. Hubert A. Eaton and Dr. Robert W. Johnson. With their assistance, as well as that of the American Tennis Association, Gibson rose through the ranks. But it was not a fast rise. Though she had help, Gibson still battled discrimination, breaking through barrier after barrier (e.g., finally being allowed to play in the Eastern Grass Court Championships and fighting for acceptance to play in the United States Lawn Tennis Association). At one point, she gave up and turned to teaching for a couple of years, but she returned to her first love—tennis—in the mid 1950s, becoming the first Black to win any world-class tennis singles tournament. Gibson won many tournaments, including Wimbledon,

in her illustrious career and was named Athlete of the Year in 1957, the first black woman to be awarded that prestigious title. She was elected to the National Lawn Tennis Hall of Fame in 1971.

Arthur Ashe, born in Richmond, Virginia, on July 10, 1943, was the first black man to win a major men's singles tennis championship. He won a great number of tennis championships between 1963 and 1970, then retired from amateur tennis and signed a professional contract. He then became a spokesman for sports equipment and a wealthy businessman. Unfortunately, Ashe contracted AIDS and died in 1993. His book on sports is among the best available.

TRACK AND FIELD

Though a group of black athletes competed in this field around the turn of the century, the number increased after World War I, and they also began winning more events.

Jesse Owens may have been the first to win an Olympic event, but George Poage was the first African-American to compete when he ran the 400-meter run and 400-meter hurdles in 1904. An intercollegiate champion quarter-miler in 1904, 1907, and 1908, John B. Taylor competed in the 1908 Olympics, but did not win. Howard Drew became the first black man ranked among the "world's fastest humans" when he tied the hundred yard dash record of 9.6 seconds in 1914.

In 1920, Sol Butler became the first black broad jump champion with his twenty-four-foot, eight-inch jump, but Jesse Owens, the master of the jump, established a record in the 1936 Olympics that lasted more than twenty-five years. In 1924, R. Earl Johnson won the national ten-mile run. He had won the national five-mile run in 1921, 1922, and 1923.

An especially important Olympic year was 1932, because Eddie Tolan won the

100-meter dash for the United States. It was the first time America had won that event in twelve years. Three of the six finalists in the 100-meter were American and two were black (Tolan and Ralph Metcalfe).

Jesse Owens was born in Danville, Alabama, on September 12, 1913, the seventh of eleven children in a poor cotton-farming family. He began winning track and field events while in high school and continued his winning streak throughout his college years at Ohio State. On May 25, 1935, Owens broke the world broad jump record during the Big Ten track and field championships, then became one of the world's greatest track and field athletes, winning four gold medals at the 1936 Olympic Games in Berlin, despite being ignored by Adolf Hitler. After Owens retired from competition, he held many jobs, including acting as a goodwill ambassador for the United States.

Women's sports started demanding worldwide attention after World War I when Wilma Rudolph, Ora Washington, and Althea Gibson led the way in their respective sports.

The first black American woman to win an Olympic event was Alice Coachman, who set a high jump record of five feet, six and one-eighth inches. She also did well in the 100-meter and 50-meter runs in the 1948 Olympics.

Wilma (Glodean) Rudolph was born in 1940, became a high school track and field star, and played all-star basketball (in 1956). She won three gold medals during the 1960 Olympic Games for track and field events, and a total of so many awards that Americans bowled her over with their praise. She became the second black woman to receive the Associated Press's annual Woman Athlete of the Year Award (Althea Gibson, for tennis, was first).

Poster, by Sears Roebuck & Co. in cooperation with the U.S. Olympic Committee, dated and copyrighted by *Saturday Evening Post,* **Wilma Rudolph, Olympic medals and women's team that she coached, history is on back, signed by Wes Kendall (illustrator), 1975, about 16″ × 20″; mint condition, $8– 12. Courtesy of Jay K. Hammerman; photo by Bob Reno.**

PRICES FOR SPORTS MEMORABILIA

Baseball

Baseball, signed

Roy Campanella; excellent condition, **$1,100–1,500.**

Roberto Clemente; excellent condition, **$775–850.**

Bob Gibson; excellent condition, **$25–30.**

Ferguson Jenkins; excellent condition, **$20–30.**

Fred McGriff; excellent condition, **$25–35.**

Satchel Paige; excellent condition, **$300–350.**

Darryl Strawberry, excellent condition, **$25–30.**

Bat, Hank Aaron; excellent condition, **$1400–1600.**

Bobbin' head (nodder)

Roberto Clemente, "Pirates" on shirt, rarest of the four 1961–1962 caricature dolls, possibly less than two hundred made; excellent condition, **$1,000–1,200.**

Reggie Jackson, recent issue; excellent condition, **$35–45.**

Willie Mays, "Giants" on shirt, most common of the four 1961–1962 caricature dolls, produced in two variations; **lighter-skinned version: $150–200, dark-skinned version: $275–325.**

Satchell Paige, recent issue; excellent condition, **$35–45.**

Card

Hank Aaron

1954, Topps, rookie; excellent condition, **$1,500–2,300.**

1955, Topps, second year; excellent condition, **$300–400.**

1961, Topps, most valuable player; excellent condition, **$30–60.**

1973, Topps; excellent condition, **$18–30.**

Bobbin' head (nodder), plastic, Hank Aaron, 1974; excellent condition, **$125–150.** Courtesy of Rose Fontanella; photo by Bob Reno.

Roy Campanella

1951, Bowman; excellent condition, **$175–275.**

1952, Topps; excellent condition, **$1,200–2,200.**

1953, Bowman (considered best set by collectors); excellent condition, **$165–300.**

1961, Topps, most valuable player; excellent condition, **$20–40.**

signed, Perez-Steele; excellent condition, **$300–350.**

Rod Carew

1976, Topps; excellent condition, **$5–10.**

1978, Topps; excellent condition, **$4–6.**

Roberto Clemente

1955, Topps, rookie; excellent condition, **$1,000–2,000.**

1956, Topps, second year; excellent condition, **$275–475.**

1960, Topps, last year Topps made horizontal cards; excellent condition, **$90–140.**

Bob Gibson, 1970, Topps; excellent condition, **$8–15.**

Reggie Jackson

1972, Topps, Jackson in action; excellent condition, **$15–30.**

1975, Topps, World Series; excellent condition, **$2–4.**

Ferguson Jenkins, signed, Perez-Steele; excellent condition, **$100–150.**

Willie Mays

1952, Bowman, second year; excellent condition, **$1,000–1,500.**

1953, Topps; excellent condition, **$1,700–2,700.**

1961, Topps, most valuable player; excellent condition, **$30–60.**

Willie McCovey, 1981, Fleer; excellent condition, **$1–2.**

Satchel Paige, signed, Perez-Steele; excellent condition, **$1,750–2,000.**

Jim Rice, 1976, Topps; excellent condition, **$3–6.**

Jackie Robinson

1947, Homogenized Bond; excellent condition, **$60–120.**

1955, Topps; excellent condition, **$150–250.**

Reggie Smith, 1981, Fleer; excellent condition, **$1–2.**

Willie Stargell, 1975, Topps; excellent condition, **$2–4.**

Darryl Strawberry, 1983, Topps Traded, rookie; excellent condition, **$40–80.**

Dave Winfield, 1977, Topps; excellent condition, **$15–25.**

Card Set

Rickey Henderson, Hall of Fame player combo pack including 1981 Topps, 1981 Donruss, 1981 Fleer; excellent condition, **$100–125.**

Reggie Jackson, made in limited quantity (a few thousand), 30 cards, rare, 1984; excellent condition, **$10–15.**

Cereal box

Frosted Mini Wheats (Kellogg's), Reggie Jackson; excellent condition, **$25–35.**

Kellogg's Corn Flakes, Willie Mays on back, signed, 1972; excellent condition, **$250–350.**

Wheaties (General Mills)

Roy Campanella, "The Breakfast of Champions," 1952; very good condition, **$35–45.**

Jackie Robinson; very good condition, **$110–140.**

Coin

Hank Aaron at bat, 1964, Topps; very good condition, **$18–22.**

Roberto Clemente at bat, 1964, Topps; very good condition, **$18–22.**

Willie Mays at bat, "1964 All-Stars," Topps; very good condition, **$15–19.**

Comic Book, *Negro Heroes,* "Jackie Robinson," National Urban League, spring 1947; excellent condition, **$475–525.**

Hat, Hank Aaron; excellent condition, **$900–1,000.**

Personal document, signed

Roy Campanella; excellent condition, **$550–650.**

Roberto Clemente; excellent condition, **$200–250.**

Bob Gibson; excellent condition, **$10–15.**

Cereal boxes, *left to right:* Frosted Mini-Wheats (Kellogg's) with David Robinson, basketball player; excellent condition, **$25–35**; Frosted Mini-Wheats (Kellogg's) with Karl Malone, basketball player; excellent condition, **$25–35**; Wheaties (General Mills) with Willie Mays, baseball player, autographed; excellent condition, **$50–75**; Kellogg's Corn Flakes with Willie Mays, baseball player, autographed, 1972; excellent condition, **$250–350**; Courtesy of the Leonard Davis Collection; photo by Bob Reno.

Ferguson Jenkins; excellent condition, **$65–85.**

Satchel Paige; excellent condition, **$75–90.**

Photograph

Colgate baseball team, one black player in last row, written on back "from Oriskany Falls, New York" 1918; 11½″ × 13½″ framed; excellent condition, **$100–125.**

Signed

Roy Campanella; 8″ × 10″; excellent condition, **$400–450.**

Roberto Clemente; 8″ × 10″; excellent condition, **$250–300.**

Bob Gibson; 8″ × 10″; excellent condition, **$18–22.**

Rickey Henderson; 8″ × 10″; excellent condition, **$35–45.**

Ferguson Jenkins; 8″ × 10″; excellent condition, **$12–17.**

Fred McGriff; 8″ × 10″; excellent condition, **$20–25.**

Satchel Paige, 8″ × 10″; excellent condition, **$100–130.**

Darryl Strawberry; 8″ × 10″; excellent condition, **$12–17.**

Bernie Williams; 8″ × 10″; excellent condition, **$5–10.**

Pin

Jackie Robinson, Brooklyn Eagle, unknown manufacturer; 1½″; very good condition, **$90–110.**

Dave Winfield, New York Yankees, Fun Foods, 1984; very good condition, **$0.30 each.**

Plaque, Hall of Fame, signed

Roy Campanella; excellent condition, **$575–650.**

Bob Gibson; excellent condition, **$13–18.**

Ferguson Jenkins; excellent condition, **$20–30.**

Satchel Paige; excellent condition, **$85–105.**

Poster

Hank Aaron, 1968; very good condition, **$35–45.**

Reggie Jackson, 1969; very good condition, **$100–120.**

Poster, Willie Mays, one of the original poster series of baseball greats printed by Coca-Cola, full color, history included, about 16″ × 20″; mint condition, **$8–12.** Courtesy of Aram H. Azadian Sr. of Nostalgic Americana; photo by Bob Reno.

Negro American League, pictures advertising event in Nashville, Tennessee, unusual, early 1950s; 12″ × 22″; new reprint, **$10 each.**

Stamp

Hank Aaron, Milwaukee Braves, 1961, Topps; very good condition, **$3–5.**

Chet Lemon, Chicago White Sox, 1982, Fleer; very good condition, **$0.10–0.12.**

Willie Mays, San Francisco Giants, 1962, Topps; very good condition, **$3–5.**

George Scott, Boston Red Sox, 1969, Topps; very good condition, **$0.30–0.40.**

Reggie Smith, Boston Red Sox, 1969, Topps; very good condition, **$0.45–0.55.**

Luis Tiant, Cleveland Indians, 1969, Topps; very good condition, **$0.30–0.40.**

Statue, Hank Aaron, Hartland, 150 made, 1960–1963; very good condition, **$275–325.**

Sticker

Reggie Jackson, New York Yankees, 1981 Topps; very good condition, **$0.25–0.35.**

Willie Stargell, Pittsburgh Pirates, 1981 Topps; very good condition, **$0.15–0.25.**

Basketball

Basketball, signed

Charles Barkley; excellent condition, **$35–45.**

Wilt Chamberlain; excellent condition, **$115–135.**

Patrick Ewing; excellent condition, **$65–80.**

Michael Jordan; excellent condition, **$40–50.**

Karl Malone; excellent condition, **$40–50.**

Earl Monroe; excellent condition, **$30–35.**

Hakeem Olajuwon; excellent condition, **$45–55.**

Shaquille O'Neal; excellent condition, **$40–50.**

David Robinson; excellent condition, **$38–48.**

Card

Lew Alcindor, 1969–1970, Topps, rookie; excellent condition, **$375–700.**

Nate Archibald, 1974–1975, Topps; excellent condition, **$3–6.**

Charles Barkley

1984–1985, Star NBA Reg., rookie; excellent condition, **$650–1,000.**

1989–1990, Fleer; excellent condition, **$3–6.**

Larry Bird, Patrick Ewing, and Magic Johnson, 1980–1981, Topps, rookies; excellent condition, **$400–600.**

Wilt Chamberlain

1969–1970, Topps; excellent condition, **$150–250.**

1972–1973, Topps, All-Star; excellent condition, **$20–40.**

Julius Erving

1972–1973, Topps, All-Star; excellent condition, **$50–100.**

1979–1980, Topps, All-Star; excellent condition, **$10–15.**

Patrick Ewing

1985–1986, Star NBA Reg., rookie; excellent condition, **$325–600.**

1989–1990, Hoops, All-Star; excellent condition, **$0.50–1.**

Kareem A. Jabbar

1977–1978, Topps; excellent condition, **$15–25.**

1981–1982, Topps; excellent condition, **$6–10.**

Magic Johnson, 1983–1984, Star NBA Reg.; excellent condition, **$4–8.**

Magic Johnson, 1985–1986, Star NBA Reg.; excellent condition, **$150–300.**

Magic's All Rookie Team, 1992–1993, Hoops, set of ten; excellent condition, **$400–600.**

Michael Jordan

1984–1985, Star NBA Reg., rookie; excellent condition, **$3,000–5,000.**

1988–1989, Fleer; excellent condition, **$35–60.**

Moses Malone

1975–1976, Topps, rookie; excellent condition, **$60–100.**

1976–1977, Topps, second year; excellent condition, **$15–25.**

Hakeem Olajuwon, 1984–1985, Star NBA Reg., rookie; excellent condition, **$300–500.**

Shaquille O'Neal

1992–1993, Fleer Ultra Reflectors; excellent condition, **$20–50.**

1992–1993, Hoops, draft redemption; excellent condition, **$15–25.**

1992–1993, Stadium Club, rookie; excellent condition, **$12–25.**

Scottie Pippen, 1988–1989, Fleer, rookie; excellent condition, **$40–70.**

Bill Russell, 1961–1962, Fleer; excellent condition, **$300–500.**

Isaiah Thomas

1984–1985, Star NBA Reg.; excellent condition, **$15–25.**

1989–1990, Fleer; excellent condition, **$1–2.**

Cereal box

Kellogg's Corn Flakes, 1992 Olympics' Basketball "Dream Team"; excellent condition, **$40–60.**

Frosted Mini Wheats (Kellogg's)

Karl Malone; excellent condition, **$25–35.**

"Karl Malone, Team USA," 1992; very good condition, **$18–22.**

Wheaties (General Mills)

Patrick Ewing, 1992; very good condition, **$18–22.**

Michael Jordan, his third time on box; excellent condition, **$50–60.**

Scottie Pippen, 1992; very good condition, **$18–22.**

Comic Book

Harlem Globetrotters Gold Key, April 1972; very good condition, **$9–12.**

Personality Comics, Magic Johnson, limited edition, 1992; excellent condition, **$5.75–6.25.**

Figurine, Isiah Thomas, earthenware, Garlan USA, 10,000 issued; very good condition, **$65–85.**

Jersey

Nate Archibald; very good condition, **$1,150–1,350.**

Wilt Chamberlain; very good condition, **$5,750–6,250.**

Magic Johnson; very good condition, **$4,500–5,500.**

Jo Jo White; very good condition, **$300–400.**

Lunch box, Harlem Globetrotters, various scenes of the team all the way around the box, metal, 1971; excellent condition, **$65–75.**

Photograph, signed

Charles Barkley; 8″ × 10″; excellent condition, **$18–22.**

Michael Jordan; 8″ × 10″; excellent condition, **$25–35.**

Moses Malone; 8″ × 10″; excellent condition, **$18–22.**

Hakeem Olajuwon; 8″ × 10″; excellent condition, **$20–30.**

Shaquille O'Neal; 8″ × 10″; excellent condition, **$25–35.**

David Robinson; 8″ × 10″; excellent condition, **$15–25.**

Plate, Patrick Ewing, 1,991 issued, 10¼″; very good condition, **$125–175.**

Sneakers

Wilt Chamberlain; very good condition, **$2,750–3,250.**

Magic Johnson; very good condition, **$2,000–3,000.**

Jo Jo White; very good condition, **$150–200.**

Boxing

Card, Joe Louis, 1947, Homogenized Bond; excellent condition, **$10–20.**

Card set, Joe Louis, 1951, Knock-Out bubble gum cards produced by Leaf Gum Cards of Canada; very good to excellent condition, **$20–30 each.**

Comic book, *Boxing's Best Comics,* "George Foreman"; very good condition, **$1.95.**

Figurine, Muhammed Ali, earthenware, Salvino Sport Legends, hand signed, 3,500 issued; very good condition, **$200–350.**

Gloves, signed

Cassius Clay (later known as Muhammed Ali); excellent condition, **$300–400.**

George Foreman; excellent condition, **$135–155.**

Joe Frazier; excellent condition, **$100–150.**

Jack Johnson; excellent condition, **$3,000–4,000.**

Sugar Ray Leonard; excellent condition, **$100–150.**

Joe Louis; excellent condition, **$900–1,100.**

Sugar Ray Robinson; excellent condition, **$400–500.**

Leon Spinks; excellent condition, **$90–125.**

Michael Spinks; excellent condition, **$115–140.**

Mike Tyson; excellent condition, **$220–275.**

Magazine, *Life,* "Look out—he's back," Muhammed Ali on cover, October 23, 1970; excellent condition, **$20–25.**

Personal document, signed

Cassius Clay (later known as Muhammed Ali); excellent condition, **$275–325.**

George Foreman; excellent condition, **$65–85.**

Joe Frazier; excellent condition, **$45–55.**

Jack Johnson; excellent condition, **$600–700.**

Joe Louis; excellent condition, **$450–550.**

Sugar Ray Leonard; excellent condition, **$45–55.**

Sandy Saddler; excellent condition, **$80–120.**

Leon Spinks; excellent condition, **$40–60.**

Photograph, signed

Cassius Clay (later known as Muhammed Ali); 8″ × 10″; excellent condition, **$100–150.**

George Foreman; 8″ × 10″; excellent condition, **$30–40.**

Joe Frazier; 8″ × 10″; excellent condition, **$20–30.**

Jack Johnson; 8″ × 10″; excellent condition, **$1,300–1,700.**

Sugar Ray Leonard; 8″ × 10″; excellent condition, **$15–20.**

Joe Louis; 8″ × 10″; excellent condition, **$300–400.**

Leon Spinks; 8″ × 10″; excellent condition, **$20–30.**

Michael Spinks; 8″ × 10″; excellent condition, **$20–30.**

Mike Tyson; 8″ × 10″; excellent condition, **$85–115.**

Pin

Muhammed Ali, "Sting Like a Bee," unknown manufacturer; 3¹⁄₂″; very good condition, **$18–22.**

Joe Louis, "WWII—We'll Win"; 1¹⁄₂″; very good condition, **$28–32.**

Poster advertising fight

Cassius Clay (later known as Muhammed Ali) versus Sunny Liston, May 25, 1965 (Clay won); very good condition, **$85–115.**

Joe Louis versus B. Conn, June 19, 1946, (Louis won); very good condition, **$75–125.**

Rocky Marciano versus Joe Louis, October 26, 1951 (Marciano won); very good condition, **$200–300.**

Program

Cassius Clay (later known as Muhammed Ali) versus Sonny Liston, February 25, 1964 (Clay won); very good condition, **$185–225.**

L. Holmes versus T. Witherspoon, May 20, 1983 (Holmes won); very good condition, **$20–30.**

Mike Tyson versus F. Bruno, February 25, 1989 (Tyson won); very good condition, **$35–45.**

Football

Card

Jim Brown

1959, Topps; excellent condition, **$100–200.**

1966, Philadelphia NFL; excellent condition, **$35–65.**

Tony Dorsett, 1981, Topps; excellent condition, **$2–4.**

Rosie Grier, 1961, Fleer NFL & AFL; excellent condition, **$3–5.**

Franco Harris, 1977, Topps; excellent condition, **$2–4.**

Bo Jackson, 1989, Pro-Set Series; excellent condition, **$1–2.**

Walter Payton, 1978, Topps; excellent condition, **$10–20.**

Gale Sayers, 1966, Philadelphia NFL, rookie; excellent condition, **$150–250.**

O.J. Simpson

1970, Topps; excellent condition, **$100–150.**

1973, Topps; excellent condition, **$12–25.**

Bubba Smith

1986, Topps, rookie; excellent condition, **$5–10.**

1987, Topps, second year; excellent condition, **$1–2.**

Emmitt Smith, 1991, Pinnacle; excellent condition, **$5–10.**

Lynn Swann, 1975, Topps, rookie; excellent condition, **$25–35.**

Lawrence Taylor, 1982, Topps, rookie; excellent condition, **$20–40.**

Herschel Walker, 1984, Topps USFL; excellent condition, **$45–75.**

Cereal box, Wheaties (General Mills), Walter Payton; excellent condition, **$50–70.**

Football, signed

Earl Campbell; excellent condition, **$30–40.**

Bo Jackson; excellent condition, **$30–40.**

James Lofton; excellent condition, **$28–35.**

Barry Sanders; excellent condition, **$18–23.**

Gale Sayers; excellent condition, **$35–45.**

Herschel Walker; excellent condition, **$23–30.**

Helmet

Jim Brown; very good condition, **$4,700–5,200.**

O.J. Simpson; very good condition, **$5,000–6,000.**

Jersey

Jim Brown; very good condition, **$4,000–4,500.**

Emmitt Smith; very good condition, **$1,800–2,200.**

Personal document, signed

Herb Adderley; excellent condition, **$10–15.**

Jim Brown; excellent condition, **$55–75.**

Earl Campbell; excellent condition, **$18–22.**

Gale Sayers; excellent condition, **$28–35.**

Photograph, signed

Bo Jackson; 8″ × 10″; excellent condition, **$25–30.**

James Lofton; 8″ × 10″; excellent condition, **$12–16.**

Gale Sayers; 8″ × 10″; excellent condition, **$20–30.**

Herschel Walker; 8″ × 10″; excellent condition, **$10–12.**

Spikes, Jim Brown; very good condition, **$175–225.**

Sticker

Walter Payton, 1981, Topps red border; very good condition, **$3.50–4.00.**

Gale Sayers, 1972, NFLPA; very good condition, **$5.50–6.50.**

Herschel Walker, 1987, Topps; very good condition, **$0.50–0.60.**

Paul Warfield, 1972, NFLPA; very good condition, **$2.50–3.00.**

Tennis

Personal document, signed by Arthur Ashe; excellent condition, **$12–18.**

Photograph, signed by Arthur Ashe; 8″ × 10″; excellent condition, **$20–25.**

Track and Field

Personal document, signed

Florence Griffith Joyner; excellent condition, **$15–20.**

Jackie Joyner-Kersee; excellent condition, **$15–18.**

Carl Lewis; excellent condition, **$15–18.**

Jesse Owens; excellent condition, **$50–60.**

Wilma Rudolph; excellent condition, **$7–10.**

Photograph, signed

Florence Griffith Joyner; 8″ × 10″; excellent condition, **$18–22.**

Jackie Joyner-Kersee; excellent condition, **$18–22.**

Carl Lewis; 8″ × 10″; excellent condition, **$18–22.**

Jesse Owens; 8″ × 10″; excellent condition, **$70–80.**

Wilma Rudolph; 8″ × 10″; excellent condition, **$8–12.**

Poster, full color, printed by "Sears, Roebuck & Co. in cooperation with U.S. Olympic Committee," dated and copyrighted *Saturday Evening Post,* 1975, Jesse Owens, Olympic games in 1938 Germany, illustration is signed "Robert Gunn" in lower right corner, about 16″ × 20″; mint condition; **$8–12.**

Reproductions

For the most part, reproductions are made when there is high demand for an item that is in limited supply. In a way, reproductions meet a need, for they give the collector who doesn't have a lot of cash the ability to add items to his or her collection and not break the bank. However, collectors really need to know they are purchasing a reproduction and need to be comfortable with that fact if they are going to add such items to their collection.

Among the reproductions of black collectibles being made presently are copies of iron banks, Luzianne Coffee items, souvenir objects, and advertising pieces, such as Coca-Cola and Aunt Jemima items. The best and only way to know the reproductions is to find someone who sells them, then visit that store or person and study the wares.

Compare the paint on the items you have seen at antiques shows and flea markets with the new ones. Remind yourself of the differences between old and new versions of the same thing. Is the new iron bank as heavy as the old? Are the screws that hold the bank together the same kind? Remember that old screws sometimes have a middle line that's a little off center. Check the paint. Are the colors the same? Has the paint started to wear and flake on the old metal? Old colors tend to be darker and duller. Train your eye to pick out defects. Roll the object over and over in your hand and study it. Educate yourself, and you will never again have to ask, "Is this a repro?"

The February 1993 issue of *Collectors News* stated that a current argument is whether or not the person selling reproductions should advertise that they are such. The editor of the magazine suggested that collectors clip and file such ads, if they find them, so that they can more easily spot reproductions in the future. As I'm sure you've heard many times, knowledge is power. If you can spot a reproduction because you've seen an ad featuring one, you are one step ahead of the game.

Reproduction Versus New Items

A reproduction is a copy of an item that was on the market in the past. A new item is a creation of the maker, not a copy of an old piece. New items that appear in this chapter are those that look vintage (in style or wear) but do not imitate an actual period piece. Having made that clear, I must add that I am all for collecting new items made by folk artists, craftspeople, potters, and artisans. However, if you do buy something new, it is a good idea to check for the maker's signature and a date. Someday that item will be an antique and collectible by future aficionadoes.

Some of the new items being made include figurines (such as Sarah's Attic Collectibles from the Heart), prints of paintings (I own one by Willie Nash—and intend to try to find more, as I appreciate his colorful, homey scenes), cookie jars (such as those made by Carol Gifford), dolls, and many other items.

Some Items That Have Been Reproduced

BANKS

From about 1870 until World War I, banks were made of heavy cast metal with bright enamel painting and came in hundreds of styles. Most of the popular ones, mechanical as well as still, have been reproduced and the buyer should beware. Because of the popularity and rarity of the Black-oriented models, the price range may vary from state to state.

One of the best ways to spot a repro bank is by being familiar with old banks first. Look at the old banks, feel the smoothness of the paint, note the places where wear is usually most evident. Note how the pieces of the bank fit together—old banks fit together well; repos are often loose. Check the screws. On old screws, the line in the middle is often slightly off center. New screws are obviously shiny. The color of the paint on new banks is bright. Old paint has a definite "look" to it.

Take the time to study what banks are available and the prices of the items you are attracted to. Take the time, also, to study the reproduced banks. Before buying, know your market.

Bank, mechanical, "Jolly Nigger," with hat 8″, without hat 6¾″; excellent condition, **$40–60 each.** Courtesy of the Leonard Davis Collection; photo by Bob Reno.

Banks that have been repaired and re-painted are often put up for sale. Though one cannot always buy banks in excellent condition, it is wise to be able to tell whether parts are missing, replacement parts have been made, or the old paint has been redone.

Other defects to watch for include fakes, variations, or pattern banks. Fakes were never banks to begin with. Variations may have the body of one bank with the parts of another. And pattern banks, which are extremely rare, are new, but have been made with original pieces from the old foundries.

The best defense against any and all of these incongruities is to know what you are buying *before* you buy. Most dealers are eager to share their knowledge with beginning collectors and there are many informative books as well as collector's clubs that can educate a dedicated collector.

CLOCKS

In the February 1993 edition of *Collectors News,* an alarm clock that depicts a black boy spinning dice was featured in the reproduction column written by Bill Mergenthal. This particular clock sold for $300 and is reported to be showing up on a regular basis at East Coast shows. It is definitely a new clock and should be sold as such.

IRON ITEMS

Iron toys are being reproduced (and new ones are being made). An article about iron toys was published in a special edition of *The Antique Trader Weekly* in 1994. It pointed out that "old castings made from original master patterns . . . look much sharper and crisper than modern reproductions." This is a point that is very easy to spot once you have set new and old versions of the same bank side by side. Another point is that new molds use coarse sand, making new cast iron much rougher than the old. Iron pieces that were painted were often hand done originally—today the work is done by machine,

making for quite a few mistakes (eyes that are not exactly painted where they should be, seams that don't match, etc.). Also look at the seams on your cast iron pieces—new seams are looser than old ones.

For more in-depth information, contact Mark Chervenka, editor of *The Antique and Collectors Reproduction News,* Box 71174, Des Moines, IA 50325.

KITCHEN COLLECTIBLES

The Aunt Jemima and Uncle Mose collectibles have been reproduced ad infinitum, as have most of the other kitchen collectibles (e.g., cookie jars, salt and pepper sets, wall plaques, and condiment sets). Some are marked as such. For example, the items made by Miss Martha Originals, Inc. are marked "Antique Repro." These items are also dated 1985; they are no longer being reproduced.

String holder, pottery, young man, string comes out of mouth, marked as reproduction on hat, 12"; excellent condition, $500–700. Courtesy of the Leonard Davis Collection; photo by Bob Reno.

Some of the Japanese reproductions, however, are simply marked "Japan" and some of the other reproductions on the market are not marked at all. Beware of anything with bright paint or no wear at all. Most kitchen items were used on a daily basis and should show some signs of that use.

TOYS

In the December 1992 issue of *Kovels on Antiques and Collectibles,* collectors were warned to watch out for a reproduction of the "Sambo" dart board game. The repro (12 by 20 inches) is smaller than the original version (which was 14 by 23 inches). The original came with rubber-suctioned darts that were thrown at a black boy who is wearing a straw hat and leaning over the target. It was a flat lithographed tin with a cardboard backing. The words "Wyandotte Toys" can be found in the lower right hand corner.

The repro does not have the mark and is marked instead with "AAA Sign Co., Coitsville Ohio" in black letters in the lower right corner. It is embossed, making it easy to recognize if someone has tried to tamper with the marking.

PRICES FOR REPRODUCTIONS

Art (Chapter 1)

Print, *Done Got Caught,* boy peeing through fence and goose grabbing him from other side, full color; 11″ × 14″; new, **$2–4.**

Prints, T. H. Gomillion, limited editions of 100–500, signed and numbered; 17″ × 21³/₄″; new, **$25 each.**

Photographica (Chapter 3)

Photograph, "Blacks in the Military," sets, Civil War and World War I, The Picture Bank Archives, 20 cards per set; each card 4″ × 6″; new, **$25 per set.**

Advertising (Chapter 5)

Button

Aunt Jemima Breakfast Club, bright red and yellow; 3″ diameter; new, **$1–4.**

Caroga Cane Syrup, chef; new, **$1–5.**

Uncle Remus; approximately 2″ diameter; new, **$2–4.**

Poster, Bull Durham, mammy sitting on porch smoking corncob pipe, child on ground with watermelon, caption reads "My it sure am sweet tastin'," framed; approximately 20″ × 24″; very good condition, **$28–35.**

Dolls (Chapter 6)

Girl, porcelain hands, feet and face, holding basket, looks old; 15″ high; new, **$15–25.**

"Pickaninny," porcelain, jointed arms and legs, braided hair, polka-dotted dress; 4″ tall; new, **$5–8.**

Kitchen Collectibles (Chapter 7)

Cookie jar

Aunt Jemima, made from the original mold, handmade and hand glazed in antique crackle, food-safe and non-toxic glaze, six antique colors available, inscribed "McCoy 93" on bottom, distributed by McCoy Pottery; 10¹/₂″ high × 7¹/₂″ at bottom; new, **$42.**

Baker, very colorful, 11″ tall; new, **$7.50–15.**

Chef, hand made, hand glazed, food-safe glaze; distributed by McCoy Pottery; new, **$850–900.**

Chef or baker, earthenware, 11″ high; new, **$8–12.**

Luzianne Coffee lady, green dress, yellow top, red and turquoise, inscribed "McCoy 93" on bottom, distributed by McCoy Pottery, 12″ × 7″; new, **$35.**

Mammy

> Mosaic, hand made, hand glazed in food-safe glaze, inscribed "McCoy 93" on bottom, distributed by McCoy Pottery, $12^{1}/_{2}'' \times 7''$; new, **$100.**
>
> Pearl, handmade, hand glazed in food-safe glaze, antique crackle, available in white, yellow, blue, green and pink, inscribed "McCoy 93" on bottom, distributed by McCoy Pottery; $9^{1}/_{4}'' \times 6^{1}/_{2}''$
>
> > Red top and white shirt, blue apron, squatty body; excellent condition, **$95–115.**
> >
> > Washing clothes in washtub, blue; excellent condition, **$25–35.**

Memo pad holder

Mammy

> Cast iron, complete with paper and pencil; 10″ high; new, **$12–15.**
>
> Earthenware, marked "Miss Martha," Miss Martha Originals, Inc., Antique Repro" stamped on bottom, 10″ tall, white dress trimmed in red, complete with paper and pencil, 1985; mint condition in original package, **$40–50.**
>
> Plastic, colorful, complete with paper and pencil; 10″ high; new, **$12–15.**

Aunt Jemima, handmade, hand glazed, inscribed "McCoy 93" on bottom, distributed by McCoy Pottery; new, **$20.**

Recipe box, Aunt Jemima, distributed by McCoy Pottery; new, **$185–250.**

Salt and pepper shakers

> Aunt Jemima and Uncle Moses, hard plastic, original colors, marked "Miss Martha," "Miss Martha Originals, Inc., Antique Repro" stamped on bottom, 1985;
>
> > $3^{1}/_{2}''$; good condition, **$18–28 for the set.**
> >
> > 5″; good condition, **$45–55 for the set.**
>
> Luzianne, handmade, hand glazed, inscribed "McCoy 93" on bottom, distributed by McCoy Pottery; new, **$110 for the set.**
>
> Mammy and butler, plastic, yellow, red, black and white, discontinued in 1985
>
> > 3″ high; **$8–12 for the set.**

5″ high; **$12–15 for the set.**

Mammy, IAC International, #7135, porcelain, hands on hips, 4″; new, **$5.**

Sugar and creamer, Aunt Jemima and Uncle Mose, lids, yellow, marked "Miss Martha," "Miss Martha Originals, Inc., Antique Repro" stamped on bottom, in original package, 1985; good condition, **$85–95.**

Toothpick holder, mammy; 3″ high; new, **$2–4.**

Paper Ephemera (Chapter 8)

Postcard, "Run Along Sonny, I Didn't Order No Coal," full color; 11″ × 14″; very good condition, **$2–5.**

Pottery, Porcelain, and Glass (Chapter 9)

Bell, bisque

> Mammy, colorful, 3″ high; new, **$2–4.**
>
> Mammy, white dress; 5″ high; new, **$3–6.**

Figurine

Bisque

> > Boy holding watermelon, colorful; $2^{1}/_{2}''$ long; new, **$2–4.**
> >
> > Jazz band, old New Orleans jazz band, four different musicians; 3″ tall; new, **$10–15.**
> >
> > Nodder, boy with watermelon and hat; 7″ tall; new, **$6–12.**

Earthenware

> > Boy on potty, marked "Occupied Japan"; 3″ tall; very good condition, **$12–15.**
> >
> > Child with watermelon on potty, yellow clothes and red cap; 5″; new, **$4–8.**
> >
> > I'm Not Showin' Off, Miss Martha's Collection, Childhood Games Series, second issue, open edition, first available spring 1993; $4^{1}/_{2}''$ high; new, **$40.**
> >
> > Nodder, boy with watermelon; new, **$7–10.**
> >
> > Terra-cotta, Pierrot-type clown, painted, marked "Goldshire Reproduction"; $14^{1}/_{2}''$ tall; mint condition, **$500–700.**

Toys (Chapter 10)

Bank

  Bisque

    Chef, colorful; 5½" high; new, **$5–10.**

    Mammy, blue, black and white; 5" tall; new, **$2–4.**

    Mammy, bobbing head; 8" high; new, **$7–12.**

  Cast Iron

    Aunt Jemima

      Painted in various colors, can also be used as doorstop, 5 lbs.; 7¾"; tall; new, **$6–10.**

      With spoon, black, white and red, hand painted; 6" tall; new, **$5–8.**

    Butler (Uncle Moses)

      5" tall; new, **$5–8.**

      8" tall; new, **$7–10.**

      10" tall; new, **$12–15.**

    Darktown Battery, cast iron, mechanical, pitcher, batter and shortstop at the ready; very good condition, **$27–50.**

    Jolly Nigger, coin flips into man's mouth from his hand when ear is turned; 5⅛" × 5" × 6⅛" high; very good condition, **$11–15.**

    Mammy

      Sitting on chamber pot, colorful; 6" high; new, **$5–8.**

      With hands on hips; 6" high; new, **$2–5.**

    Mammy-type, IAC International, #1582, hands on hips, 8"; new, **$12.**

Miscellaneous Everyday Items (Chapter 11)

Ashtray, earthenware, boy standing next to commode, colorful, 5" long; new, **$4–8.**

Clock

  Blackface, child on knees with right hand up, alarm; very good condition, **$275–325.**

  Joe Louis World Champion, hand-painted metallic bronze finish, bisque, reproduction of 1930s clock; 11" high × 8" wide; mint condition, **$125–145.**

Doorstop, Aunt Jemima, iron, colorful, red and white, 11" high; new, **$10–15.**

Bank, mechanical, iron, "Dinah," 6¼"; excellent condition, **$40–60.** Courtesy of the Leonard Davis Collection; photo by Bob Reno.

BIBLIOGRAPHY

Adler, Mortimer J., Charles Van Doren, and George Ducas, eds. "The Negro in American History III. Slaves and Masters 1567–1854" in *Encyclopaedia Britannica*. Chicago: Encyclopaedia Britannica/William Benton, 1972.

Alexander, Lamar. "Find the Good and Praise It." Article on Alex Haley. *Parade Magazine* (January 24, 1993): 4.

American Heritage, ed. *American Heritage: Three Centuries of American Antiques*. New York: Bonanza Books, 1967.

Ames, Alex. *Collecting Cast Iron*. Derbyshire, UK: Moorland Publishing, 1980.

Amos, Wally. "Sweet Nostalgia." *Art & Antiques* (summer 1988): 78.

Art and Antiques, ed. *Americana: Folk and Decorative Art*. New York: Billboard Publications, 1982.

Axe, John. *Collectible Black Dolls*. Riverdale, Md.: Hobby House Press, 1978.

———. *Effanbee: A Collector's Encyclopedia*. Riverdale, Md.: Hobby House Press, 1983.

Balliett, Whitney. "First Lady of Song (Ella Fitzgerald)." *The New Yorker* 69 (April 26, 1993): 105.

Barenholtz, Bernard, and Irene McClintock. *American Antique Toys 1830–1900*. New York: Harry N. Abrams, 1980.

Baskin, Wade, D.Ed., and Richmond N. Runes, J.D. *Dictionary of Black Culture*. New York: Philosophical Library, 1973.

Bennett, Lerone Jr. *Before the Mayflower: A History of Black America*. Chicago: Johnson Publishing Company, Inc., 1969.

Berghahn, Marion. *Images of Africa in Black American Literature*. Totowa, N.J.: Rowman and Littlefield, 1977.

Berry, Mary Frances. *Military Necessity and Civil Rights Policy: Black Citizenship and the Constitution, 1861–1868*. Port Washington, N.Y.: Kennikat Press, 1977.

"Black Americana 1630–1984." *Antiques and the Arts Weekly.* (February 22, 1985).

The Black Americana Collector 1, no. 2 (December 1982–February 1983).

The Black Americana Collector 1, no. 3 (March–April 1983).

The Black Americana Collector 1, no. 5 (July–August 1983).

The Black Americana Collector 2, no. 2 (September–October 1984).

Bloom, Cathie. "Ethnic Items Are Increasing In Collectibles Field." *Collectors News* (February 1993): 20.

Boggan, Jacqueline. "Tomorrow's Collectibles Today." *Black Ethnic Collectibles Magazine* 5, no. 4 (winter 1992): 10.

Bogle, Donald. *Blacks in American Films and Television*. New York: Garland Publishing, 1988.

Bogle, Donald, ed. *Black Arts Annual 1988–1989*. New York: Garland Publishing, 1990.

Book review of *Higher Ground, A Novel in Three Parts* by Caryl Phillips. *The New York Times Book Review* (September 24, 1989): 27.

Brennan, Shawn, and Julie Winklepleck. *Resourceful Woman*. Detroit: Visible Ink Press, 1994.

Buckley, Stephen. "Smaller Voice for the Major Minority?" *The Orlando Sentinel* (August 1, 1993): G-6.

Campbell, Mary. "Black Pianist Wants Career to Show Hope, Possibilities." *The Orlando Sentinel* (April 18, 1993): D-3.

Carroll, John M. *The Black Military Experience in the American West.* New York: Liveright, 1971.

Cederholm, Theresa Dickason, ed. *Afro-American Artists.* Boston: Trustees of the Boston Public Library, 1973.

Chervenka, Mark, ed. "New and Reproduced Toys In Cast Iron." *Toy Trader—Supplement to the Antique Trader Weekly* (June 1993): 56B–57B.

Christopher, Catherine. *The Complete Book of Doll Making and Collecting.* New York: Dover Publications, 1971.

Collector Books, ed. *The Standard Value Guide to Old Books,* 2nd edition. Paducah, Ky.: Collector Books, 1979.

Collector's Showcase 2, no. 1 (September 1982–October 1982).

Colt, Charles C. Jr., ed. *Official Sotheby Park Bernet Price Guide to Antiques and Decorative Arts.* New York: Simon and Schuster, 1980.

Congdon-Martin, Douglas. *Images in Black: Three Hundred Years of Black Collectibles.* West Chester, Pa.: Schiffer Publishing, 1990.

Copelon, Dianne. "New Museum Dedicated to Showing Photographs." *The Orlando Sentinel* (April 9, 1992): I-12.

Crane, Elaine and Jay David, eds. *The Black Soldier: From the American Revolution to Vietnam.* New York: William Morrow and Company, 1971.

Curtis, Tony. comp. *Antiques and Their Values, Dolls and Toys, 1980.* Galashiels, Scotland: Lyle Publications, 1980.

"CW's Folk Art Center Wins Grant to Research Works of Joshua Johnson." *Antiques and the Arts Weekly* (May 10, 1985).

Davis, John P. *The American Negro Reference Book,* vols. I and II. Englewood Cliffs, N.J.: Prentice-Hall/Educational Heritage, 1966.

Dennis, Denise, and Susan Willmarth. *Black History for Beginners.* New York: Writers and Readers Publishing, 1984.

Dixon, Paul, with Patrick J. Hannigan. *The Negro Baseball Leagues: 1867–1955.* Mattituck, N.Y.: New Amereon House, 1992.

Douglas, Diandra. "Do I have the Collecting Bug? I *Am* a Collecting Bug." *Art & Antiques* (Fall 1993): 90–92.

Dover, Cedric. *American Negro Art.* Greenwich, Conn.: The New York Graphic Society, 1960.

Dowd, Jerome, M.A. *The Negro in American Life.* New York: Negro Universities Press, 1926.

Driskell, David. *Two Centuries of Black American Art.* New York: Knopf, 1956.

Dubin, Steven C. "Symbolic Slavery: Black Representations in Popular Culture." *Social Problems* 34, no. 2 (April 1987): 122–140.

Eagles, Charles W., ed. *The Civil Rights Movement in America.* Jackson, Miss.: University Press of Mississippi, 1986.

Ebony, ed. *The Negro Handbook.* Chicago: Johnson Publishing, 1966.

Edwards, Paul K. *The Southern Urban Negro as a Consumer.* College Park, Md.: Prentice-Hall, 1932.

"Exhibited Black Artists Sharing Traditions in D.C." *Sater's Antiques and Auction News* 16, no. 7. (March 22, 1985).

Failing, Patricia. "Black Artists Today: A Case of Exclusion." *ARTnews* (March 1989): 124–131.

Ferris, William. *Afro-American Folk Art and Crafts.* Boston: G. K. Hall & Co., 1983.

Fleming, Lee. "1492 and All That: Political Correctness and Multiculturalism Meet the National Gallery of Art." *Museum & the Arts Monthly* (October 1991): 93–96.

Fogel, William, and Stanley L. Engerman. *Time On The Cross.* Lanham, Md.: University Press of America, 1984.

Foner, Eric. *Reconstruction: America's Unfinished Revolution 1863–1877.* New York: Harper & Row, 1988.

Franklin, John Hope, and August Meier. *Black Leaders of the Twentieth Century.* Urbana, Ill.: University of Illinois Press, 1982.

Frazier, E. Franklin, Ph.D. *The Negro in the United States.* New York: MacMillan, 1957.

Garrett, Daniel. "Behind a Veil: Henry Ossawa Tanner's Triumph—and the Price of His Exile." *Art & Antiques* (February 1991): 78–96.

———. "Changing Traditions: Painters Add to What They've Learned." *Art & Antiques* (summer 1992): 23.

Garrett, Romeo B. *Famous Facts about Negroes.* New York: Arno Press, 1972.

Gatewood, Willard B., Jr. *Smoked Yankees and the Struggle for Empire: Letters from Negro Soldiers 1898–1902.* Urbana, Ill.: University of Illinois Press, 1971.

Gayle, Addison J., ed. *The Black Aesthetic.* New York: Doubleday, 1971.

George, Nelson. *Elevating the Game: Black Men and Basketball.* New York: Harper Collins, 1992.

Ginzberg, Eli, ed. *The Negro Challenge to the Business Community.* New York: Columbia University Press, 1964.

Greene, Lorenzo Johnston. *The Negro in Colonial New England 1620–1776.* New York: Atheneum Publishers, 1968.

Greene, Veryl C. "The 'Jocko' Statue." *Black Ethnic Collectibles* (spring 1991): 12–13.

Harbison, Robert. "Plain Folk: Itinerant Portrait Painters Immortalized America's Soul by Accident." *Art & Antiques.* (October 1988): 108–113.

Haskins, James. *Black Theater in America.* New York: Thomas Y. Crowell, 1982.

Healey, Barth. "Stamps: The Black Heritage Series Has Been Recognizing Distinguished Citizens Since It Began in 1978." *The New York Times* (February 7, 1993).

Heilbut, Anthony. "Postscript Marian Anderson." *The New Yorker* 69 (April 26, 1993): 82–83.

Hewett, David. "Canada Reclaims a Black Sculpture." *Maine Antique Digest* (November 1993): 12-A.

Hicks, Jonathan. "Ideas & Trends: More New Magazines and These Beckon to Black Readers." *The New York Times* (August 5, 1990): 20-E.

Holway, John. *Voices from the Great Black Baseball Leagues.* New York: Dodd, Mead & Co., 1975.

Hornung, Clarence P. *Treasury of American Design,* vols. I and II. New York: Harry N. Abrams, 1950.

Hubbard Burns, Diane. "Why Blacks Are Scarce in Ballet." *The Orlando Sentinel* (June 13, 1993): D-8.

Hudgeons, Thomas E. III, ed. *The Official 1983 Price Guide to Antiques by the House of Collectibles.* Orlando, Fla.: House of Collectibles, 1982.

Hughes, Langston. *A Pictorial History of Black Americans.* New York: Crown, 1956.

"In The Galleries." Article on Romare Bearden. *Art and Antiques* (July 1992): 87.

Jacobsen, Anita, ed. *Jacobsen's Painting and Bronze Price Guide,* vol. VI. Dallas: Anita Jacobsen, 1983.

Jordan, Casper LeRoy. "Stamp Collecting: A Form of Black Collectibles." *Black Ethnic Collectibles* (spring/summer 1992): 4.

Kaduck, John M. *Advertising Trade Cards.* Des Moines, Ia.: Wallace-Homestead, 1976.

Katz, William Loren. *The Black West.* Garden City, N.Y.: Anchor Press, 1973.

Kenner, Hugh. "Cut and Paste: Romare Bearden's Collages Reflect His Life in Many Worlds." *Art & Antiques* (July 1992): 96.

King, John T. and Marcet H. King. *Stories of Twenty-three Famous Negro Americans.* Austin, Tx.: Steck-Vaughn Company, 1967.

Kovel, Ralph and Terry Kovel. *Kovels' Antiques Price List, 13th edition.* New York: Crown, 1980.

———. *Kovels' Antiques Price List,* 14th edition. New York: Crown, 1981.

———. *Kovels' Antiques Price List,* 15th edition. New York: Crown, 1983.

———. *Kovels' Know Your Antiques.* New York: Crown, 1981.

———. *Kovels' Know Your Collectibles.* New York: Crown, 1981.

Lavitt, Wendy. *American Folk Dolls.* New York: Knopf, 1982.

Lindenberger, Jan. *Black Memorabilia for the Kitchen.* West Chester, Pa.: Schiffer Publishing, 1992.

———. "Collector is Captivated by Black Memorabilia." *Collectors News* (February 1993): 18.

Lipman, Jean. *American Folk Art: Wood, Metal and Stone.* New York: Dover, 1972.

Livingston, Jane, and John Beardsley. *Black Folk Art in America: 1930–1980.* Jackson, Miss.: University Press of Mississippi, 1980.

Logan, Rayford W., and Michael R. Winston. *Dictionary of American Negro Biography.* New York: Logan and Winston, 1982.

Mackay, James. *An Encyclopaedia of Small Antiques.* New York: Harper & Row, 1975.

Major, Charles. "Collector Plates: Coming of Age for African American Collectors." *Black Ethnic Collectibles Magazine 5,* no. 4 (winter 1992): 16–17.

"Market Trends, Reproductions & Advertising." *Collectors News* (February, 1993): 9.

"Masonic Mystery." *Maine Antique Digest* (June 1993 and July 1993): 3-A.

McClinton, Katherine M. *The Complete Book of Small Antiques Collecting.* New York: Bramhall House, 1953.

Mergenthal, Bill. "Fool Me Once ...." *Collectors News* (February 1993): 7.

Metcalf, George R. *Black Profiles.* New York: McGraw-Hill, 1968.

Meyer, George H. "Personal Sculpture—Folk Art Walking Sticks." *Antique Review* (August 1992): 39–42.

Miller, Elizabeth W. *The Negro in America: A Bibliography.* Cambridge, Mass.: Harvard University Press, 1966.

Miller, Robert W. *Price Guide to Dolls 1982–1983.* Des Moines, Ia.: Wallace-Homestead, 1982.

Moore, Deedee. "Shooting Straight: The Many Worlds of Gordon Parks." *Art & Antiques* (1992).

Morrow, Lynn. *Black Collectibles.* Langeley Park, Md.: Karen Brigance, 1982.

———. *Black Collectibles.* 2nd ed. Langeley Park, Md.: Karen Brigance, 1983.

Muller, Charles. "Elijah Pierce, Woodcarver." *Antique Review Preview* (February 1993): 1–19.

"News Digest Million-Dollar Deal." *Antique Monthly* (January 1992): 6.

Parsons, Talcott, and Kenneth Clark, eds. *The Negro American.* Boston: Houghton Mifflin, 1965.

Patterson, Lindsay. *The Afro-American in Music and Art.* New York: Association for Study of Afro-American Life and History, 1978.

———. *Introduction to Black Literature in America—From 1746 to Present.* New York: Association for Study of Afro-American Life and History, 1978.

Peiser, Judy. "Down-Home Learning." *The New York Times* 142, issue 49291, sec. 4A (April 4, 1993): 42.

Ploski, Harry A., and James Williams. *The Negro Almanac—A Reference Book on the Afro-American,* 4th edition. New York: John Wiley, 1983.

Porter, Dorothy B. *The Negro in the United States: A Selected Bibliography.* Washington, D.C.: Library of Congress, 1970.

Pratt, John Lowell. *Currier and Ives, Chronicles of America.* Maplewood, N.J.: Promontory Press, 1968.

Pugh, Elaine. "Center Publishes Roland L. Freeman Portfolio." *The Southern Register* (winter 1993): 12.

Reed, Robert. "Past Boxing Cards Have Punch." *The Antique Shoppe* (December 1992): 18-A.

———. "Treasured Slave Quilts." *Antiques & Collecting* (May 1991): 39.

Reno, Dawn E. *Advertising Identification and Price Guide.* New York: Avon Books, 1993.

"Restlessness Fuels Career of Gordon Parks." *The Orlando Sentinel* (April 9, 1992): I-12.

Richards, David. "'Cry, the Beloved Country' Teaches a Tragic Lesson." *The New York Times* (July 25, 1993): H-5.

Robinson, Wilhelmina S. *Historical Afro-American Biographies.* New York: Association for Study of Afro-American Life and History, New York, 1978.

Rodger, William, ed. *The Official 1982 Price Guide to Old Books and Autographs.* Orlando, Fla.: House of Collectibles, 1982.

Rodgers, Carole G. *Penny Banks, a History and a Handbook.* New York: Dutton, 1977.

Rosenblum, Naomi. *A World History of Photography.* New York: Abbeville Press, 1984.

Roucek, Joseph S. and Thomas Kiernan, eds. *The Negro Impact on Western Civilization.* New York: Philosophical Library, 1970.

Rutherford, Margaret, and Anthony Curtis, eds. *The Lyle Official Antiques Review 1982.* Toronto: Voor Haede Publications, 1981.

Sampson, Henry R. *Blacks in Black and White: A Source Book on Black Films.* Metuchen, N.J.: The Scarecrow Press, 1977.

Savage, George. *Dictionary of 19th Century Antiques and Later Objets d'Art.* New York, Putnam, 1978.

Schwartz, Marvin D., and Betsy Wade. *The New York Times Book of Antiques.* New York: Quadrangle Books, 1972.

"Sharing Traditions: Five Black Artists in 19th Century America." *Antiques and the Arts Weekly* (May 10, 1985).

Sieber, Roy. *African Textiles and Decorative Arts.* New York: The Museum of Modern Art, 1972.

Singleton, Esther. *Dolls.* New York: Payson & Clarke, 1927.

Sinor, Paul. "Made in Occupied Japan." *Antiques & Collecting* (July 1992): 33.

Sloan, Irving J. *The Blacks in America 1492–1977,* 4th edition. New York: Oceana Publications, 1977.

Smith, Barbara. "The Past Has Fled." Book review of *Higher Ground,* a novel by Caryl Phillips. *The New York Times Book Review* (September 24, 1989): 27.

Smith, Jessie Carney. *Epic Lives.* Detroit: Visible Ink Press, 1993.

Smith, Patricia R. *Modern Collector's Dolls.* Paducah, Ky.: Collector Books, 1975.

Smythe, Mabel M. *The Black American Reference Book.* New York: Prentice-Hall, 1976.

"Society Formed for Tobacco Jar Collectors." *The Antique Trader Weekly* (January 27, 1993).

Solis-Cohen, Lita. "Strutting to a Different Drummer." *Maine Antique Digest* (September 1992): 6-D.

———. "Pook Sells Stoneware Grotesque Jug for $41,800." *Maine Antique Digest* (July 1993): 28-A.

"Sotheby's/Phillips' New York American Paintings and Prints." *Maine Antique Digest* (April 1985).

"Sports Memorabilia Strong at Leland's 'Souvenirs' Auction." *The Antique Trader Weekly* (May 19, 1993).

Szabo, Andrew. *Afro-American Bibliography.* San Diego, Calif.: San Diego State College, 1970.

Szwed, John F., ed. *Black America.* New York: Basic Books, 1970.

"Those Black Kitchen Collectibles." *The Antique Shoppe* (December 1992): 8A–12A.

Time-Life Books, ed. *The Encyclopedia of Collectibles*. Alexandria, Va.: Time-Life Books, 1978.

"Toledo's Newest Trio." *Antique Monthly* (December 1992): 12.

Toppin, Edgar A. *A Biographical History of Blacks in America Since 1528*. New York: David McKay Company, 1969.

Turner, Darwin T., ed. *Black American Literature/Poetry*. Columbia, Ohio: Charles E. Merrill Publishing, 1969.

———. *Afro-American Writers*. New York: Appleton Century Crofts, 1970.

Tyree, Omar. "I'm a Young Black Male Who's *Not* in Trouble." *The Orlando Sentinel* (August 1, 1993): G-4.

Vincent, Steven. "Tour de Force." *Arts & Auction* (April 1993): 79–85.

Vogel, Carol. "I.B.M. to Close Its Midtown Gallery." *The New York Times* (March 23, 1993): C section.

Wagner, Jean. *Black Poets of the United States*. Urbana, Ill.: University of Illinois Press, 1974.

Weisbrot, Robert. *Freedom Bound: A History of America's Civil Rights Movement*. New York: W. W. Norton, 1990.

Wentworth Higginson, Thomas. *Army Life in a Black Regiment*. Boston: Fields, Osgood & Co., 1870.

Wesley, Charles H., Ph.D. *Negro Labor in the United States 1850–1925, A Study in American Economic History*. New York: Vanguard Press, 1927.

West, Cornel. "In Search of Black Leaders." *The Orlando Sentinel* (August 1, 1993): G-6.

Willis-Thomas, Deborah. *Black Photographers, 1840–1940, An Illustrated Bio-bibliography*. New York: Garland Publishing, 1985.

———. *An Illustrated Bio-bibliography of Black Photographers 1940–1988*. New York: Garland Publishing, 1989.

Winchester, Alice, ed. *The Antiques Book*. New York: Bonanza Books, 1970.

Wirt, John. "Parks' Films Are Still 'n' Motion." *Sunday News-Journal* (Daytona Beach, Fla.; April 26, 1992): 1-H.

Witkin, Lee D., and Barbara London. *The Photograph Collector's Guide*. Boston: Little Brown, 1979.

Wood, Joe. "John Singleton and the Impossible Greenback of the Assimilated Black Artist." *Esquire* 120 (August, 1993): 59.

Young, A. S. "Doc." *Negro Firsts in Sports*. Chicago: Johnson Publishing Company, 1963.

Young, Jackie. *Black Collectibles: Mammy and her Friends*. West Chester, Pa.: Schiffer Publishing, 1988.

Zeller, Leslie. *Book Collecting*. New York: Cornerstone Library, 1978.

Zonay, Jeanne. "A Collecting Dream of Black Heritage," *Collectors News* (February 1993): 18.

LIST OF CONTRIBUTORS

AUCTIONEERS

Bertoia & Brady Auctions
2413 Madison Avenue
Vineland, NJ 08360

Collection Liquidators
341 Lafayette Street
New York, NY 10012

Garth's Auctions, Inc.
2690 Stratford Road
P.O. Box 369
Delaware, OH 43015

C. E. Guarino
Box 49
Berry Road
Denmark, ME 04022

The Gene Harris Antique Auction
    Center
203 South 18th Avenue
Marshalltown, IA 50158

James D. Julia
P.O. Box P-830
Fairfield, ME 04937

Kent Michelson Auction Service
Freeman, Missouri

AUTHORS

Evelyn Ackerman
P.O. Box 2117
Culver City, CA 90230

COLLECTORS

Evelyn Ackerman
P.O. Box 2117
Culver City, CA 90230

American Eye
Washington, D.C.

Mary Cantrell
505 Pratt Avenue NE
Huntsville, AL 35801

James Christopher
Bold Soul—Black Memorabilia
    Museum
2029 South Campbell Avenue
Tucson, AZ 85713

Leonard Davis
New York

Rose Fontanella
324 Avenue F
Brooklyn, NY 11218

James Holloway
2131 Rheem Avenue
Richmond, CA 94801

Steven D. Lewis
Lewis and Blalock Collection
P.O. Box 88679
Indianapolis, IN 46208

Al Marzorini
1405 North Carolina Avenue NE
Washington, DC 20002-6437

Robert and Dawn Reno
Florida

Diane Stary
1007-F South Oak Park
Oak Park, IL 60304

DEALERS

Aram H. Azadian Sr.
3067 El Monte Way
Fresno, CA 93721

Bill Butts
Main Street Fine Books and
    Manuscripts
301 South Main Street
Galena, IL 61036

Bill Ferguson
Ferguson's Antiques
80 Park Drive
Morgan Hill, CA 95037

Rose Fontanella
324 Avenue F
Brooklyn, NY 11218

Jay K. Hammerman
3515 Cedarlawn Drive
Colorado Springs, CO 80918

Timothy Hughes
P.O. Box 3636
Williamsport, PA 17701

George Theofiles
Box 1776
New Freedom, PA 17349

Ken Owings Jr.
Antiques Americana
Box No. 19
North Abington, MA 02351

Frank and Barbara Pollack
1214 Green Bay Road
Highland Park, IL 60035

ASSOCIATIONS AND
NEWSLETTERS

The Song Sheet
National Sheet Music Society
310 Tahiti Way #214
Marina del Rey, CA 90292
Linda G. Siegel, ed.

Cookie Jarrin'
The Cookie Jar Newsletter
RR #2
Box 504
Walterboro, SC 29488

INDEX

Abbott, Robert, 145
Abda (slave), 229
Abrams, Dick, 259
Abramson, Charles, 9
Acts of Art Gallery of New
    York, 9
Adams, John Henry, Jr., 6
Adams Express Company, 244
Adam (slave), 229
Advertising, 75–100
    firms and products with
        African Americans in,
        84–86
    prices of, 87–100
    reproduction prices, 292
    types of collectible, 78–84
African-American art
    artists in, 10–14
    history of, 3–10
    price guidelines, 16–22
    reproduction prices, 15–16
    printmakers in, 15–16
    prints in, 14–15
African-American folk art,
    23–45
    baskets, 26–28
    biographies of artists, 35–39
    boats, 28
    carvings, 28–30
    gravestones, 31–32
    ironwork, 32–35
    musical instruments, 35
    prices of, 40–45
Ailey, Alvin, 251
Albumen prints, 48
Alexander, Sadie T. M., 234
Alex Haley Remembers figure
    series, 164
Aliened American, 145
Allen, Debbie, 257
Allen, James Latimer, 49
Ambrotypes, 47
American Indians, African-
    Americans as, 223
Amos, John, 264
Amos 'n Andy, 263, 265
Anderson, Eddie (Rochester),
    264
Anderson, Marian, 248
Andirons, 195
Andrews, Benny, 9
Angelou, Maya, 59
Anti-Slavery Standard, 150
Apple and nut dolls, 106

Aristotype, 48
Armstrong, Louis, 248–249,
    260
Art. See African-American art;
    African-American folk art
Asante, Kwasi, 218–219
Ashby, Steve, 35
Ashe, Arthur, 279
Atlanta World, 146
Audubon, John J., 15
Automata, 176
Auto racing, 270
Avon collectibles, 193

Bachus, Bertha, 203
Bailey, Pearl, 265
Baker, Josephine, 247, 265–266
Baldwin, James, 58, 61
Ball, James Presley, 49
Ball, Pat, 277
Banks, 176–180, 290–291
    reproductions of, 290–291
Banks, Julia, 200
Bannarn, Henry, 8
Bannister, Edward Mitchell, 5,
    9, 10, 16, 17
Baraka, Amiri (LeRoi Jones),
    61–62
Barnett, Marguerite Ross, 232
Barry, Marion, 234
Barthe, Richard, 8, 10
Baseball, 270–272, 281–284
Basie, Count, 249
Basketball, 272–275, 284–286
Baskets, 26–28
Bates, Peg Leg, 251
Battery, Cornelius M., 49
Baylor, Elgin, 274
Bearden, Romare, 35
Beasley, Tom, 275
Beavers, Louise, 260
Beckwourth, Jim, 223
Belafonte, Harry, 260–261
Bernstein, Theresa, 13
Bethune, Mary McLeod, 232,
    234
Bethune, Thomas Greene,
    264–265
Bias, Len, 274
Bicyling, 275
Bill, Cherokee, 222
Black, Julian, 276
Blackberry Bonnet Collection,
    164

Blackburn, Jack (Chappie), 276
Blackburn, Robert, 8
Black Heritage Collection, 164
Black Laws, 5
Blackman, Rosa, Wildes, dolls,
    106
Black Muslims, 232
Black Panthers, 232, 233
Blake, Eubie, 247
Blues, 247
Board games, 180
Boats, 28
Bolden, Charles (Buddy), 249
Boles, Elvira, 199
Bolling, Leslie, 8
Books, 56–71
    biographies of authors,
        61–67
    children's, 56–58
    prices of, 68–71
    slave writings as, 58–59
    twentieth century, 59–60
Boston Guardian, 145
Bottle dolls, 106
Bottles, advertising on, 79
Boxes, advertising on, 79
Boxing, 275–276, 286–287
Bradford Exchange, 166
Bradley, Thomas, 234
Bradley, Will, 215
Brady, Mathew B., 49
Braugher, Andre, 264
Brochures, 142
Brooks, Clarence, 261
Brooks, Gwendolyn, 59, 62
Brotherhood of Sleeping Car
    Porters, 231
Brown, Ed, 278
Brown, Elmer, 6
Brown, Frederick, 9
Brown, Grafton T., 15
Brown, H. Rap, 233
Brown, Jim, 277
Brown, Roger, 274
Brown, Sterling, 62
Brown, William Wells, 59, 62
Bruno, Ben, 223
Bryan, John, 30
Bryon, Archie, 26
Buffalo Soldiers, 218
Burleigh, Harry Thacker, 249
Burnett, Joseph, 229
Burnside, Archie, 26
Bush, Anita, 266

Butler, David, 35
Butler, Sol, 279

Cabinet cards, 48
Caesar of Griswold, 229
Calendars, 142
Calloway, Cab, 251
Cameo Doll Products/Strom-
    becker Doll Corp., 110
Camp, Walter, 276
Campanella, Roy, 272
Card games, 180
Carmichael, Stokely, 233, 234
Carroll, Diahann, 257, 261, 263
Carvings, 28-30
    prices of, 41-43
Catlett, Elizabeth, 9
Ceramic figurines, 164
Cereal boxes, advertising on,
    79-81, 283
Chamberlain, Wilt, 274
Charles, Ezzard, 276
Chauvin, Louis, 247
Chein Industries, Inc., 183
Chenault, Lawrence, 259
Chestnutt, Charles Waddell, 62
Chicago Defender, 145
Child, Lydia M., 62
Children's books, 56-58
Chisholm, Shirley, 233
Christy, Howard Chandler, 215
Cigar store figures, advertising
    on, 83-84
Cinque Gallery, 9
Civil rights movement,
    232-233
Claiborne, William C., 216
Clarion of Freedom, 145
Clark, Daniel (Pinky), 273
Clark, Ed, 9
Clark, Peter H., 145
Clay, Cassius Marcellus, 276
Cleaver, Eldridge, 59, 234
Clifton, Nat (Sweetwater), 274
Clocks, 193-194, 291
    reproductions of, 291
Cole, Johnnetta Betsch, 232
Colescott, Robert, 9
Collins, Cardiff, 233
Collins, Marva, 232
Colored American, 144
Combs, Luzia, 203
Commemorative items, 194
Condiment sets, 121
Constance Collection, 164
Cookbooks, 121-122
Cookie jars, 122-124
Cooper, Annie J., 233
Cooper, Chuck, 274

Cooper, Ralph, 261
Cooper, Tarzan, 273
Corbett, Jim, 275
Cosby, Bill, 257, 263, 264
Cowboys, African-American,
    221-222
Cribb, Tom, 275
Crosby, A. D. V., 278
Crump, Edward (Boss), 249
Cuffee, Paul, 229-230
Cullen, Countee, 62
Currier, Nathaniel, 15
Currier and Ives, 15, 244

Daguerreotypes, 47
Daily Defender, 146
Daily World, 146
Dance. *See* Music and dance
    memorabilia
Dance Theatre of Harlem, 251
Dandridge, Dorothy, 260, 261
Dart, Isom, 222
Dave the Potter, 165
Davidson, Bruce, 49, 144
Davis, Angela, 233, 234-235
Davis, Ossie, 260, 266
Davis, Sammy, Jr., 251, 261
Davis, Ulysses, 35
Dawson, William, 35-36
Day, Thomas, 30
Day, William H., 145
DeBulger, L., 259
DeCarava, Roy, 49-50
Dee, Ruby, 260, 266
Deluxe Topper Toys, 110
Dendy, John, 277
Denmark, James, 9
Dexter, Samuel, 216
Dish towels, 126
Dixon, George, 275-276
Dodson, Owen, 59
Dolls, 101-120
    history of, 102
    manufacturers of, 110-112
    prices of, 113-120
    reproduction prices, 113-
        120
    types of, 102-110
Doorstops, 195-196
Douglas, Robert J., 273
Douglass, Frederick, 59, 62-63,
    144
Dove, Rita, 59
Doyle, Sam, 26
Du Bois, W. E. B., 63-64, 231
Dunbar, Paul Laurence, 64
Duncan Royale, 164
Duncanson, Robert Scott, 4-5,
    9, 10-11, 50

Eaton, Hubert A., 279
Ebony, 144
Edmondson, William, 31-32, 36
Edwards, Melvin, 9
Effanbee Doll Corp., 110-111
Eldridge, Eleanor, 58
Elevator, 144
Ellington, Edward Kennedy
    (Duke), 247, 249
Ellis, Joel, dolls, 107
Ellison, Ralph Waldo, 58, 59,
    64
Erving, Julius (Dr. J), 274
Essence, 144
Etcetera Collections, 164
Evers, Medgar Wiley, 235

Fagan, Garth, 251
FairChildren New England rag
    dolls, 107-108
Farley, James Conway, 50-51
Federal Art Project of the WPA,
    8
Fenderson, Reginald, 266
F&F Tool and Die Company,
    127
Fisher Price Toys, 111
Fitzgerald, Ella, 249
Flagg, James Montgomery, 244
Flipper, Henry O., 218-219
Folk art. *See* African-American
    folk art
Folk music, 244-245
Foner, Eric, 150
Football, 276-277, 287-288
Forever Friends Collector's Club,
    164
Fortune, Thomas, 146
Foster, Andrew (Rube), 271
Foster, William, 258
Fowler, Bud, 270
Frederick Goldscheider
    Company, 166
Freedom's Journal, 144
Freelon, Alan, 6
Freeman, Roland, 51
Fuller, Meta Warwick, 5, 11

Ganaway, King Daniel, 51
Gans, Joe, 276
Gardner, Newport, 249
Garnet, Henry Highland, 217
Garth Fagan Bucket Dance
    Company, 251
Gates, Pop, 273
Gatlan U.S.A., 164
Genius of Freedom, 144
Gibbs, Mifflin W., 145
Gibson, Althea, 279, 280

Gibson, Charles Dana, 215
Gibson, Josh, 271
Giles, William, 216
Gilpin, Charles, 247
Glass. See Pottery, porcelain, and glass
Globe, The, 146
Glover, Danny, 260
Godfrey, George, 275
Goldberg, Whoopi, 260, 261
Golden Shred Company, 194
Golf, 277-278
Golliwogs, 194
Goodridge, Glenalvin, 51
Goodridge, Wallace, 51
Goodridge, William, 51
Goodridge Brothers, 51
Gordon, Bridgette, 275
Gospel music, 247
Gossett, Louis, Jr., 260, 261
Gotz, 111
Grant, Charles (Cincy), 271
Graupner, Johann Christian Gotlieb, 249
Graves, Tom, 197
Gravestones, 31-32
Greenfield, Elizabeth Taylor, 249
Greenleaf, Richard, 229
Greeting cards, 142
Gregory, Ann, 278
Gregory, Dick, 235
Grierson, Benjamin, 219
Grocery list and memo pad holders, 124
Gudgell, Henry, 29, 30
Gunn, Archie, 244
Gunzel, Hildegard, 111-112

Haley, Alex, 64
Hall, Prince, 198, 230
Hamilton Mint, 166
Hammon, Jupiter, 59, 64
Hammons, David, 8, 9
Handy, William Christopher, 249
Hansberry, Lorraine, 266
Harlem Globetrotters, 257
Harlem Renaissance, 6, 59, 247
Harleston, Edwin A., 6
Harper, Frances Ellen Watkins, 64-65
Harper, William A., 5, 6, 11
Harper's Weekly, 143
Harris, Homer, 277
Hartsfield, Zeke, 278
Hasbro Toys, 111
Hassinger, Maren, 9
Hatch, Edward, 219

Hayden, Palmer, 6, 8
Haynes, Lloyd, 263
Haynes, Marques, 274
Hazzard, Walt, 274
Henderson, Edwin, 272
Herald of Freedom, 145
Hernandez, Aileen Clark, 233
Hertle, James, Sr., 36
Hill, Candace, 9
Hill, Talmadge, 273
Himstedt, Annette, 111-112
Hines, Gregory, 260
Hitching posts, 196-197
Hodges, Ben, 222
Holden, Ed, 271
Holiday, Billie, 249-250
Holly, Lonnie, 26
Holmes, Alfred, 278
Homer, Winslow, 244
Hoover, Herbert, 232
Horne, Lena, 250
Horse racing, 278
Horsman Dolls, 112
Houston, Charles Hamilton, 232
Howard, Bob, 263
Hughes, Langston, 65
Hulsinger, George, 6
Humidors (tobacco jars), 167
Hummel, 164
Hunster, T. E., 6
Hunt, Richard, 9
Hyatt, Isaiah, 104
Hyer, Jacob, 275
Hyer sisters, 265

Ideal Toy Corp., 112
Ingraham, Joseph H., 65
Ingrams, Bell, 6
Iron collectibles, 195-199, 291
    reproductions of, 291
Ironwork, 32-35
Irving, Julius, 274
Isaacs, Johnny, 273
Ives, Edward, 183
Ives, James Merritt, 15

Jabbar, Kareem Abdul, 274
Jackson, Andrew, 217
Jackson, George, 59
Jackson, Hal, 274
Jackson, Jesse, 233, 235
Jackson, Mahalia, 250
Jackson, Nigel, 9
Jackson, Peter, 275, 278-279
Jackson, Reggie, 272
Jackson, William Tecumseh Sherman, 276-277
Jackson-Jarvas, Martha, 9

Jamison, Judith, 251
Jazz, 247
Jenkins, Clarence (Fats), 273
Jenkins, Harold (Legs), 273
Jerome, Clauncey, 193
Jet, 144
Jewelry, 197
Johnny Griffin Collectibles, 197-198
Johnson, Bill, 221
Johnson, Britton, 223
Johnson, Henry, 220
Johnson, Jack, 259, 276
Johnson, James Weldon, 65, 231, 250
Johnson, Joshua, 36-37
Johnson, Malvin Gray, 6, 8
Johnson, Noble M., 259, 261
Johnson, R. Earl, 279
Johnson, Robert W., 279
Johnson, William Henry, 8, 11
Jones, Caesar, 229
Jones, Ed (Lanky), 273
Jones, James Earl, 260, 264, 266
Jones, John, 235
Jones, Lois Mailou, 9
Jones, Sam, 274
Joplin, Scott, 247
Jordan, Michael, 274, 277
Journal of Negro Education, 143
Jubilee Singers, 250
Just above Midtown Gallery, 9

Karamu House, 6
Kelley, Ben, 277
Kennedy, Flo, 233
King, Martin Luther, Jr., 221, 233, 235
Kitchen collectibles, 121-140
    prices of, 128-140
    reproductions of, 291-293
    types of, 121-127
Kitt, Sandra, 65

LaMotta, Jake, 276
Lange, Katherine (Kate), 26
Langston, Charles H., 145
Langston, John Mercer, 230, 236
Lawn items, 198
Lawrence, Jacob, 9
Lee, Spike, 260
Lee-Smith, Hughie, 6
Lemon, Meadowlark, 274
Leonard, Leon Lank, Sr., 11
Leslie's Weekly, 143
Lewis, Edmonia, 4, 5, 9, 11-12, 230

Lewis, Leo, 277
Lewis, Oliver, 278
Lewis, William H., 276–277
Liberator, The, 150
Life, 144
Lincoln, Abraham, 217
Lincoln Motion Picture
    Company, 220, 258–259
Lladro, 164
Lobby cards, 257
Locke, Alain, 59
Louis, Joe, 276
Love, Nat, 221–222
Lovejoy, Alec, 260
Lovejoy, Elijah, 59
Loving, Al, 9
Luca family, 265
Lucas, Charles, 26
Lyles, Carrie, dolls, 108
Lynch, John Roy, 236
Lyon, Danny, 51–52, 144
Lyon, Jules, 52

Mackenzie, Ronald S., 219
Madame Alexander Dolls, 112
Madison, James, 216
Madison, Reginald, 37
Magazines, 142–144
Maggie Head dolls, 108
Majolica, 166
Malcolm X, 59, 233, 236
Manning, Frederick S., 244
Marciano, Rocky, 276
Marshall, Thurgood, 234
Marx Brothers, 183
Maryland Institute, 9
Masonic collectibles, 198–
    199
Mattel, Inc., 112
Matthews, Artie, 247
Matthews, Charles, 264
Maurer, Louis, 230
Mays, Willie (Howard), 272
McCoy Pottery, 127
McDaniel, Hattie, 262
McGreath, Marriet, 201
McKissick, Floyd, 233
McMillan, Terry, 59
McQueen, Thelma (Butterfly),
    262
Mechanical toys, 180
Mergenthal, Bill, 291
Metcalfe, Ralph, 280
Metcalfe, Tolan, 280
Metropolitan Life Gallery, 9
Meyer, George, 30
Micheaux, Oscar, 259–260
Miles, Marshall, 276
Miley, Bubber, 249

Militaria and related collectibles,
    215–227
  history, 216–221
  prices of, 224–227
Miller, Eleazer Hutchinson, 13
Miller, Howard, 30
Mills, Florence, 247
Minton, Herbert, 166
Mirror of the Times, 145
Miss Martha Originals, 164, 291
Mitchell, Arthur, 251
Molineaux, Tom, 275
Moore, Audley, 233
Moore, Bernard, 32
Morehead, Scipio, 12
Moreland, Mantan, 262
Morgan, Garrett A., 220
Morgan, Sister Gertrude, 37–
    38
Morgenthaler, Sasha, dolls, 109
Morris, Lenwood, 6
Morrison, Toni, 59
Moses, Ethel, 260
Moss, Leo, dolls, 109
Motley, Archibald, 6, 7, 8
Motley, Marion, 277
Motley, Willard, 59
Mount, William Sidney, 13
Movie, television, and theater
    memorabilia, 257–268
  collectibles, 257–258
  movies, 258–262
  prices of, 267–268
  television, 263–264
  theater, 264–265
Murphy, Eddie, 258, 260, 262
Murphy, Isaac, 278
Murrow, Edward R., 263
Muse, Clarence, 262
Music and dance memorabilia,
    243–256
  collectibles, 243–244
  dance, 251
  musical entertainers,
    248–251
  musical instruments, 35
  prices of, 252–256
  types of, 244–247

Nanton, Tricky Sam, 249
Nash, Willie, 290
Nast, Thomas, 230
National Association for the
    Advancement of Colored
    People (NAACP), 231
National Conference of Artists
    (NCA), 8
National Museum of American
    Art, 9

National Negro Business League,
    146
National Organization for
    Women (NOW), 233
Negro Digest, 144
Negro Masonry, 230
Nengudi, Senga, 9
Newsom, Carmen, 260
Newspapers, 144–146
Niagara Movement, 231
Nicholas, Denise, 263
Nichols, Charles H., 58
North Star, 144

Occupied Japan items, 124
O'Grady, Lorraine, 9
O'Neal, Shaquille, 274
O'Neil, John (Buck), 271
Outerbridge, John, 8
Outsider Art, 26
Owens, Jesse, 279, 280
Owusu, Asanti, 30

Paige, Satchel, 271
Paintings. *See* African-American
    art; African-American folk
    art
Paper ephemera, 141–162
  method of collecting, 141
  prices of, 151–162
  reproduction prices, 293
  slavery-related, 148–150
  types of, 142–150
Parks, David, 221
Parks, Gordon, 52, 221
Parrish, Maxfield, 215
Parsons, Albert, 145
Pennington, James, W. C., 65
Penny woodens, 109
People's Voice, 146
Percy, Earl, 275
Perry, Joe, 277
Perry, Lincoln, 251
Pershing, John J., 218
Pfeiffer, 244
Phillips, Caryl, 65–66
Phillips, Ulrich B., 149
Photographica, 46–55, 244, 257
  biographies, 49–53
  prices of, 53–55
  reproduction prices, 53–55
  types of, 47–48
Phylon, 143
Pierce, Elijah, 38
Pindell, Howardena, 9
Piper, Adrian, 9
Pippin, Horace, 8
Plaques, 125
Platinum prints, 48

Playbills, 257
Poitier, Sidney, 260, 262
Political memorabilia
    biographies of activists and
        politicians, 234
    history of, 228–239
    prices of, 237–239
Pollard, Fritz, 277
Porcelain. *See* Pottery, porce-
    lain, and glass
Porcelain collector plates, 166
Posey, Pearlie, 199
Postage stamps, 146–147
Postcards, 48, 147–148
Posters, 148, 257–258
Pot hangers, 125
Pottery, porcelain, and glass,
    163–173
    handmade pieces, 164–165
    prices of, 167–173
    reproduction prices, 293
    types of items collected,
        163–167
Potthast, Edward H., 13
Powell, Adam Clayton, 146,
    236
Powell, Colin, 221
Powers, Harriet, 199, 201, 203
Prang, Louis, 15–16, 244
Preer, Evelyn, 259
Prescott, Caesar, 229
Price, Florence B., 250
Price, Leslie, 8
Print collecting, 14–16
Prints. *See* African-American
    art; African-American folk
    art
Prior, William Matthew, 38
Prosser, Gabriel, 216
Pryor, Richard, 260, 262
Public Works of Art Project, 8
Pull toys, 180
Punderson, Prudence, 204
Purviance, Florence, 8
Puzzles, 180–181

*Quarterly Review of Higher
    Education among Negroes,*
    143
Quilts, 199–203

Rag dolls, 102–104
Ragtime music, 247
Ram's Horn, 144
Randolph, Philip, 231, 236
Rashad, Phylicia (Ayers–Allen),
    264
Ray, Joe, Jr., 270
Reader's Digest, 144

Reason, Patrick H., 16
Red Wing Potteries, Inc., 127
Reed, Willis, 274
Remco Industries, 112
Remington, Frederic, 13
Reproductions, 289–294
    versus new items, 289–290
    prices of, 292–294
Rice, Thomas D., 264
Richards, Thomas, 229
Richardson, Uncle Toby, 33–34
Richmond, Agnes M., 7, 13–14
Richmond, Bill, 275
Rickey, Branch, 271
Ricks, Pappy, 273
Rimmer, William, 10
Ringgold, Faith, 9
Roberts, Needham, 220
Robertson, Oscar, 274
Robeson, Paul, 247, 266,
    272–273, 277
Robinson, Bojangles, 251
Robinson, Jackie, 271–272
Robinson, Sugar Ray, 276
Rock, John, 236
Rockwell, Norman, 244
Roddy, George, 278
Rogers, William, 30
Roosevelt, Eleanor, 248
Roosevelt, Teddy, 220
Roosevelt, Theodore, 231
Roseland, Harry, 14, 17
Roxborough, John, 276
Rubber dolls, 104
Rucker, Leon, 30
Rudolph, Wilma (Glodean), 280
Russell, Bill, 274
Russwumn, John B., 144

Saar, Betye, 9
Saffen, Judge, 229
Sailing, 278–279
Saitch, Eyre, 273
Salki, Charles, 6
Salt and pepper shakers,
    125–126
Salted paper print, 48
Samplers and needlework,
    203–204
Saperstein, Abe, 274
Sarah's Attic Collectibles, 164,
    290
Sarony, 244
Schmeling, Max, 276
Schoenhut, A., Company, 183
Scott, Emmett J., 145
Scott, James, 247
Scott, Joyce, 9
Scott, W. E., 6

Scott, William, 6
Sculpture. *See* African-American
    art; African-American folk
    art
Scurlock, Addison N., 52–53
Sears, 112
Sewing items, 204
Shaw, Artie, 249–250
Shawnee Pottery, 127
Sheet music, 243–244
Shepherd, Harry (Henry), 52
Sifford, Charlie, 277
Simmons, Peter, 34–35
Simms, Willie, 278
Sims, Bernise, 26
Sissle, Noble, 247, 262
Slavery–related ephemera,
    148–150
Slave writings, 58–59
Smith, Bessie, 250–251
Smith, George Washington, 264
Smith, James, 259
Smith, Wee Willie, 273
Smith, William E., 6
Smithsonian Institution's
    National Museum of
    American Art, 9
Southern Christian Leadership
    Conference (SCLC), 232
Spirituals, 245–246
Sports memorabilia, 269–288
    prices of, 281–288
Staples, Marcus, 26
Starling, Marion Wilson, 58
Stephens and Brown Manufac-
    turing Company, 183
Stereograph, 48
Stowe, Harriet Beech, 264
Stowe, Lucy D., 279
Strauss Company, 183
Strawberry, Darryl, 272
Strode, Woody, 277
Studio Museum, 9
Styron, William, 229
Sudduth, Jimmy Lee, 26
Sullivan, Kaylynn, 9
Sullivan, Louis, 234
Sun Rubber, 112
Sweeney, J. W., 264

Tablecloths, 126
Table games and toys, 181
Taft, William Howard, 231
Tanner, Henry Ossawa, 5–6, 7,
    9, 12–13, 17
Tatum, Reece (Goose), 274
Taylor, John B., 279
Taylor, Major, 275
Taylor, Sara Mary, 199

Television. *See* Movie, television, and theater memorabilia
Tennis, 279, 288
Terra-cotta, 166–167
Terry, Lucy, 66
Texas Freeman, 145
Textiles and sewing collectibles, 199–204
Theater memorabilia. *See* Movie, television, and theater memorabilia
Thomas, James Henry, 38
Thompson, Robert Farris, 165
Thompson, W. O., 6
Threadgill, Robert, 9
Time, 144
Tin and cast-iron toys, 181–183
Tins, advertising on, 81–82
Tintypes, 47
Toaster cover dolls, 126–127
Tobacco jars (humidors), 167
Tolan, Eddie, 279–280
Topsy Turvy dolls, 105, 110
Tourist trade items, 204
Toys, 174–192, 181, 258
    prices of, 184–192
    reproductions of, 292, 294
    types of, 176–183
Track and field, 279–280, 288
Trade cards, 82–83, 150
Trade signs, advertising on, 83–84
Trash, Dox, 8
Traylor, Bill, 38–39
Treasured Customs, 112

Trotter, W. M., 145
Truman, Harry, 221
Tubman, Harriet Rose, 58, 229, 245
Turner, Nat, 58, 216, 229
Turrell, Mary Church, 236
Tyson, Cicely, 262

Uneeda Doll Co., 112

Van Der Zee, James, 53
Van Peebles, Melvin, 262
Vassa, Gustavus, 67
Vesey, Denmark, 216
Vinyl dolls, 106
Vogue Doll Co., 112
Voting Rights Act (1965), 232–233

Waco Spectator, 145
Wadsworth, Captain, 229
Walker, Alice, 59
Walker, Bill, 278
Walker, Inez Nathaniel, 26
Walker, Margaret, 59
Walker, Moses Fleetwood, 271
Walker, William Aiken, 14, 18
Wallace, George, 233
Waring, Laura Wheeler, 6
Warner, Pecolia, 199
Washington, Augustus, 53
Washington, Booker T., 59, 145, 146, 231, 236
Washington, George, 216
Washington, Kenny, 277
Washington, Ora, 280

Waters, Ethel, 263
Weaver, Robert, 233–234
Welch, Marcella, dolls, 110
Wesley, John, 104
Weston, Horace, 265
Weusi Ya Nambe Yasana Gallery, 9
Wheatley, Phyllis, 59, 67
White, George, 39
Whittier, John Greenleaf, 58–59
Wholman, 244
Wilder, Douglas, 234
Wilkins, Roy, 146
Williams, Billy Dee, 260
Williams, Fenwich, 272
Williams, George Washington, 67
Williams, James, 58
Williams, Joe, 271
Williams, Lorraine, 278
Williams, Moses, 220
Willis, Bill, 277
Willis, Lester, 30
Winfrey, Oprah, 264
Woodruff, Hale, 8
Work songs, 246
Works Progress Administration (WPA), 8
Wrestling, 275–276
Wright, Bill, 278
Wright, Richard, 58, 59, 67

Yerby, Frank, 59
Young, Andrew, 234, 236
Young, Coleman, 234, 237
Young, Lester, 250

ABOUT THE AUTHOR

For the past decade, Dawn Reno has educated herself and others about black collectibles by delving into the history surrounding the items collected. Internationally recognized as one of the experts in the field, she has written other books about antiques and collectibles as well (*American Country Collectibles, American Indian Collectibles, Advertising Collectibles,* and *Native American Collectibles*). She is also the author of *All That Glitters,* a novel nominated for *Romantic Times'* Best Contemporary Glitz Novel of 1993.

Currently, Reno is also awaiting publication of her children's book, *The Good Lion. A* new novel entitled *The Silver Dolphin,* and a book about contemporary Native American artists were published in the fall of 1995. She lives in central Florida with her photographer husband and three cats, where she is working on a new novel, a book about Marilyn Monroe collectibles, and several children's books.